The Business of Keyboarding

SECOND EDITION

The Business of Keyboarding

SECOND EDITION

Sheila Culliford
Sir Oliver Mowat Collegiate Institute
Scarborough, Ontario

Susan MacLennan
Sir Oliver Mowat Collegiate Institute
Scarborough, Ontario

Shirley Wong
University of British Columbia
Vancouver, British Columbia

John Wiley & Sons

Toronto   New York   Chichester   Brisbane   Singapore

Care has been taken to trace ownership of copyright material contained in this text. The publishers will gladly receive any information that will enable them to rectify any reference or credit line in subsequent editions.
The publisher has made every attempt to ensure the accuracy of postal codes used in this text. In any case where a fictitious address has been used, the postal code will reflect the address's postal region only.

Design: Marc Mireault

Canadian Cataloguing in Publication Data

Culliford, Sheila Geller, 1948-
    The business of keyboarding

2nd ed.
First ed. published under title: The business of typing.
For use in grade 10.
Includes index.
ISBN 0-471-79645-X

1. Electronic data processing—Keyboarding.
2. Typewriting. I. McLennan, Susan. II. Title.
III. Title: The business of typing.

Z49.C82 1989   652.3'025   C89-093472-X

Dedication
To Mary, Michael, and Adam

PROOFREADER'S MARKS

Mark and Meaning	Example	Edited Version
∧ insert a word	the ‸blue purse	the blue purse
# insert a space	the happy‸boy	the happy boy
⊙ insert a period	I know⊙	I know.
⌄ insert a comma	John‸Jane, and Joe	John, Jane, and Joe
¶ begin a paragraph	¶ The new . . .	The new . . .
≡ capitalize	sandra agreed	Sandra agreed
lc lower case	Going home	going home
ℓ delete a word	the ~~big~~ old house	the old house
⌒ close up a space	awk ward	awkward
⑤⌐ indent to the right	⑤⌐ The cost of fuel	The cost of fuel
⌐⑤ indent to the left	⌐⑤ The cost of fuel	The cost of fuel
∿ transpose	the chair yellow	the yellow chair
⠿ stet (let it stand)	where ~~are~~ you going STET	where are you going
◯ write it out in full	②computers	two computers
— underscore	The Wizard of Oz	The Wizard of Oz
ss single space	single ss space	single space
ds double space	double ds space	double space
ts triple space	triple ts space	triple space

CONTENTS

Index vii

Preface x

Acknowledgements xii

MODULE 1. Getting Ready 1

MODULE 2. Skill Development 42

MODULE 3. Timed Writings 77

MODULE 4. Proofreading, Editing, and Composing 120

MODULE 5. Language Usage 143

MODULE 6. Centering 199

MODULE 7. Tables and Business Forms 231

MODULE 8. Correspondence and Memos 288

MODULE 9. Making Copies 365

MODULE 10. Outlines, Notes, and Reports 375

MODULE 11. Career Search 429

MODULE 12. On the Job 451

MODULE 13. Desktop Publishing 472

INDEX

A

Abbreviations 32, 312
Account, statement of 275–276
Accuracy assignments 46–76
Addresses
  Envelopes 311
  Letters 293
Advertisements,
  formatting 497–500
Agenda 424
Air Mail notation
  Envelopes 311
  Letters 307–308
Aligning scale 5
Alignment
  Numbers in columns 241
  Pivoting 218–219
  Ruled line 267
Ampersand 33
Application, letter of 436–437
Application form 441–443
Apostrophe 156
Applying for a job 435–447
Articles 419–420, 486–494
"At" sign 33
Attention line 303

B

Backspace key 4, 5
Balance sheet 278
Bank reconciliation statement 279
Bell allowance 18
Bibliography 398
Block centering 214
Block style 298, 302
Bold print 206
Boot 13
Business forms 266–287
  Balance sheet 278
  Bank reconciliation
    statement 279
  Card files 283–285
  Cheques 281–282
  Designing of 286–287
  File labels 285–286
  Financial statement 277–280
  Invoice 273–274
  Preprinted 269
  Profit and loss statement 280
  Purchase order 270–272
  Statement of account 275–276

C

Capitalization 147–148
Canada, geographic
  names 196–198
Card files 283–285
Career search 429–450
  Assessing yourself 432
  Information resources 433
  Interview 444–446
  Job application 441–443
  Resumé 438–439
Carrier return 31
Cellular telephone 417–418
Cent sign 53
Centering 199–230
  Assignments 207–213,
    215–218, 220–222, 224–230
  Block 214
  Centre point, finding the 16
  Extended 206
  Display techniques 206–207
  Horizontal 202
  Paper and spacing facts 203
  Pivoting 218–219
  Vertical 204–205
Centering key 5
Cheques 281–282
Closed punctuation 298
Code key 5
Colon 153
Column headings 240–241, 246,
  251
Comma 150–152
Complimentary closing 294
Composing at the
  keyboard 133–139
Confidential notation 207
Contents, table of 395
Copies, making 365–375
  Electronically-controlled
    printing 372
  Facsimile 373–374
  Photocopying 368–371
Correction key 4, 5
Corrections 22–26
  Correction fluid 23
  Correction tape 20
  Crowding 24
  Erasable bond 25
  Eraser tape 23
  Erasing 22
  Reinserting pages 24–25

Self-correcting typewriters 25
  Spreading 24
Correspondence and
  memos 288 364
Crowding 24
Cylinder 4
Cylinder knobs 4

D

Daisy-wheel printer 372, 477
Dash 33
Date line 293
Decimal tab set key 5
Degree sign 40
Desktop publishing 472–500
Dictionary 139–140
Digital fascimile receivers
  (Fax) 373
Division of words 36–39
Division sign 41
Display guidelines and
  techniques 205–207
Dollar sign 33
Dot matrix printer 372, 477
Duplicating processes, *see* Copies,
  making

E

Editing 129
  Assignments 130–132
Elite spacing 14
Enumerations 378
Envelopes 310–311
  Folding and inserting letters
    into 313
  Window 313
Equals sign 40
Erasing 22
Ergonomics 9–10
Exclamation point 159

F

Fascimile receivers (Fax) 7,
  373–374
File labels 285–286
Financial statements 277–280
Fitness, on the job 11
Floppy disk 8

Folding of letters   313
Footnotes   408
Format line   17
Forms, *see* Business forms
Fractions   32, 34
Frequently misspelled
 words   175–181
Full block style   298, 300

G

Graphic design   480
Gross Words Per Minute
 (GWPM)   81

H

Half-space key   5
Hardware   8, 12, 477
Home row   30
Homonyms   192–193
Horizontal centering   202
Hyphen   33, 160–161

I

Impression control   5
Initials line   294
Interoffice
 memorandums   352–361
 Composition   363–364
Interview, job   406–407, 444–446
Invoices   273–274
Itinerary   425

J

Job interview   406–407, 444–446
Justification   8, 12, 207

L

Labels   285–286
Language usage   143–198
Laser printer   372, 477
Leaders   219–222
Letterhead   292
Letters   291–351
 Application letter   436–437
 Attention line   303
 Blind courtesy copy
  notation   307
 Block style   298
 Company name   305
 Complimentary closing   294

(Letters   *continues*)
 Composition   362
 Confidential notation   307
 Copy notation   306, 307
 Date line   293
 Displayed material   309
 Enclosure notation   306
 Enumerations   334
 Envelopes   310–311
 Essential letter parts   292–294
 Folding and inserting into
  envelopes   313
 Form letters   347
 French   295–296
 Full block   298, 300
 Initials line   294
 Inside address   293
 Mailing notations   307, 337
 Memorandums   352
 Placement   296–297
 Postal code   311
 Postscript   308
 Punctuation styles   298
 Reference initials   294
 Registered notation   307
 Return address   310
 Salutation   293
 Semi-block style   298, 301
 Signature   294
 Special Delivery notation   307
 Subject line   304
 Two-page letters   309–310, 340
 Writer's identification   294
Line endings   36
Line scale   4
Line space regulator   4, 5, 18–19

M

Mailing notations   307
Manual, keyboarding   26–28
Margin, setting the   17–18
Margin release   4, 5
Margin scale   5
Margin sets   4
Margin stops   5
Memorandums, *see* Interoffice
 memorandums
Memory   8, 13
Microcomputers
 Functions and terms   7–9
 Main parts of   6
Minus sign   40
Minutes of a meeting   421
Misspelled words, *see* Frequently
 misspelled words

N

Net Words Per Minute
 (NWPM)   81
Newspaper articles   419–420,
 486–494
Notes and outlines   375–385
Number keypad   75
 Assignments   75–76
Number sign   34
Numbers, rules for   164–166

O

On the job (office
 simulation)   451–471
On-off switch   4, 5
Open punctuation   298
Ornamental keyboarding   206
Outlines   375–385

P

Paper
 Centre point   16
 Inserting   16
 Removing   16
 Sizes   15, 203
 Spacing facts   18–19, 203
Paper bail   4, 5
Paper guide   4
Paper injector/ejector   5
Paper release lever   4, 5
Paper support   5
Parentheses   157–158
Percent sign   33, 166
Period   150
Personal inventory   432–433
Personal notation   307
Photocopies   368–371
Pica spacing   14
Pitch selector   5
Pivoting   218–219
Plus sign   40
Postal code   311
Posture, typing   29
Print point indicator   4
Printer return   5
Profit and loss statement   280
Proofreader's marks   128
Proofreading   120–142
 Assignments   124–127
 How to proofread   123
Program, *see* Software
Program, two-page   223–229
Proportional spacing   15
Publications   479–482

Punctuation styles 298
Purchase order 270–272

Q
Question mark 159
Quotation marks 161–162

R
Ratchet release lever 4
Reference materials 139–140
    Assignments 140–142
Registered notation 307
Relocate key 5
Repeat key 5
Reports 386–419
    Bibliography 398
    Contents page 395
    Endnotes 412
    Footnotes 408
    Multipage 400–401
    One-page 386
    Title page 393
Resumé 438–439
Return address 310
Return key 4
Reverse print 207
Ribbon cassettes, changing 20–21
Ruled lines, typing on 267

S
Salutation 293
Save 9
Semi-block style 298, 301
Semicolon 154–155
Serif 481
Shift key and lock 5
Simulation, office (on the
    job) 451–471
Software 9, 12, 477
Space bar 4, 5
    Assignment 34–35
    Rules 32–34
Spacing after
    Abbreviations 32
    Fractions 32, 34
    Punctuation 32–34
Spacing, variable 18–19, 203, 206
Special characters, construction
    of 40–41
    Addition sign 40
    Cent sign 53
    Dash 33
    Degree 40

(Special characters   *continues*)
    Division sign 41
    Equals sign 40
    Exclamation mark 40
    Minus sign 40
    Multiplication sign 41
    Subscript 40
    Superscript 40
Special Delivery notation 307
Specialized vocabularies 182–192
Speed and accuracy,
    developing 45
    Assignments 46–76
Speed chart 81
Spelling
    Assignments 169–174
    Commonly confused
        words 194–195
    Frequently misspelled
        words 175–181
    Homonyms 192–193
    Rules 168–169, 170–171, 172,
        173
    Specialized
        vocabularies 182–192
Spreadsheet 494
Squeezing 24
Statement of account 275–276
Subject line 304
Syllabic intensity (SI) 81

T
Tab stops
    Clearing 19
    Setting 20
Table of contents 395
Tables 231–266
    Boxed 262–265
    Formatting 235–240
    Long column headings 240–245
    Mixed column
        headings 251–256
    Ruled tables 259–262
    Short column headings 246–251
    Two-line column
        headings 257–259
Tabulator key 4, 5, 19
Technique 29
Telephone information 416–417
Timed writings 77–119
    Assignments 83–119
    Calculation of speed 82
    Formatting 82
Title page 393

Two-point punctuation 298
Typewheel/ribbon 5
Typewriters
    Main parts of 4, 5
    Self-correcting 25

U
Underscoring 206

V
Vertical centering 204–205
Vertical spacing 18–19, 203
Videoconferencing 417
Voice mail 418

W
Window envelopes 313
Word division 36–39
Word processors, main parts of 6
Words
    Commonly confused 194–195
    Frequently misspelled 175–181
Work station routine 28–29
Wraparound 31

Z
Zip code 311

The Business of Keyboarding has been developed to meet the needs of keyboarding students who wish to increase their skills beyond the level of basic keyboard facility. The second edition of *The Business of Keyboarding* offers students materials that stress a realistic, coherent approach to the mastery of modern communication skills.

The 13 modules that make up *The Business of Keyboarding* provide an abundance of assignments that reinforce the skills needed in today's business world. Within each module, new concepts are illustrated with a formatted model for students to copy. The model is followed by numerous assignments offering a variety of arranged, unarranged, handwritten, and rough-draft materials. These assignments give the practice needed for proficiency in formatting a wide variety of business documents. Composing assignments, which are included at the end of each module, afford students the opportunity to improve their keyboarding and communication skills. All the assignments can be keyed on any kind of machine, from standard typewriters to microcomputers. In short, *The Business of Keyboarding* will enable students to:

1. Increase their mastery of the alphanumeric and symbolic keyboard.

2. Produce standard business communications that meet the quality expectations established by the business community.

3. Increase their facility at composing business communications at the keyboard.

4. Enhance their self-image, and practise efficient work habits and businesslike attitudes.

5. Explore keyboard-related career paths.

6. Practise the work habits necessary to maintain success on the job.

ORGANIZATION

The Business of Keyboarding consists of 13 modules, each dealing with a specific aspect of keyboarding mastery and format. When introducing new concepts to their students, teachers will not have to search through the entire text to find appropriate concept reinforcement assignments. All the material needed to teach a concept thoroughly is contained in the relevant module.

The business world is using line counts to measure employee productivity. In this text, line counts based on a 60-stroke line have been used for designated production assignments.

MAJOR FEATURES

Emphasis on the Automated Office   Assignments in *The Business of Keyboarding* use the terminology and concepts of today's automated office to provide students with on-the-job realism. All assignments can be integrated with any kind of keyboarding machine.

Flexibility   The numerous skill-building and formatting assignments in *The Business of Keyboarding* allow teachers flexibility in emphasizing instructional objectives.

Modular Approach   The organization of the material in *The Business of Keyboarding* into modules allows teachers to match the number of assignments and the level of difficulty to the needs of individual students.

Progression of Difficulty   Production materials in *The Business of Keyboarding* are sequenced from the simple to the complex.

Emphasis on English Usage and Composing Skills   The importance of acceptable grammar, punctuation, and word usage is stressed throughout *The Business of Keyboarding*. The text also provides students with abundant composing opportunities.

Period Format   *The Business of Keyboarding* is structured for use in long or short periods, and semestered classes.

ACKNOWLEDGEMENTS

A textbook is the product of many minds. The authors would like to thank the following people, without whom *The Business of Keyboarding* would not have been published.

Reviewers:
June Bourdon
Sir John A. Macdonald Collegiate
Agincourt, ON

Nellie Burke
St. John's, Newfoundland

Hilda Dymott
Malvern Collegiate
Toronto, Ontario

H. Mel Fisher
University of Lethbridge
Lethbridge, Alberta

Janet Russell
Maples Collegiate
Winnipeg, Manitoba

Editors:
Grace Deutch
Robert Kirk
Rena Leibovitch
Elizabeth McCurdy
Jane McNulty

MODULE 1

GETTING READY

Courtesy of Biltrite Nightingale Inc.

CLASSIFIED
Lost and Found

LOST

My passing mark in Math. Finder please telephone 633-0000 and ask for Tim.

FOUND

Physics textbook with wrong answers to questions in chapter 3. Will return to owner in exchange for right answers to chapters 4-9. 677-0000.

Personals

Are you at home alone in the evenings? Want fun and popularity? It's as close to hand as your lips are to your teeth . . . with a TAMMY!

A TAMMY TAMBOURINE with quadraphonic sound can spring you onto the centre of any stage. Don't be a fan. Be the **STAR**. On sale now for ONLY $75. Tel: 644-0000 evenings. Ask for Robbie.

Miscellaneous

**ART AUCTION OF ORIGINAL oils, water colours, charcoal sketches, and sculpture on Saturday, June 12. All pieces signed by the artist, a famous Canadian impressionist. No reserve prices!! This selection produced by artist during her most creative period (Art 9, 10).

Sale starts 10:00 a.m., 4733 Laurel Street (lane), Rexdale.

Help Wanted

Mother with twins, age 5, desperately needs babysitter who is available 5 days a week from 5 to 9 for damage control. Must be strong and able to run fast while minding two fun-loving, active, but lovable boys. $20 per hour and meals provided. Knowledge of furniture and general household repair would be useful. Telephone 681-0000 as soon as possible.

INTRODUCTION

Module 1 gives you the basic information you need to operate any type of keyboarding equipment, be it an electric or electronic typewriter, a word processor, or a microcomputer. The module explains the terminology involved in word processing and keyboarding concepts, and gives the essentials of machine manipulation, for example, setting the paper guide, inserting and removing paper, establishing margins, line spacing and tabulations. Information on type and paper sizes is also included. The module also discusses ergonomics, the study of the relationship between humans and their working environment.

The information in this module will serve as a useful reference for all aspects of your keyboarding course.

OBJECTIVES

1. To identify the main parts of electric and electronic typewriters, microcomputers, and word processors.

2. To define common word processing functions and terms.

3. To define the term "ergonomics."

4. To operate computers, word processors, electronic typewriters and memory typewriters.

5. To calculate and set margins.

6. To set the line space regulator and set and clear tab stops.

7. To change a ribbon or ribbon cassette on a typewriter or printer.

8. To make corrections using an eraser, correction fluid, erasable bond paper, self-correcting typewriters, word processors, and microcomputers.

9. To apply the procedures for spreading and squeezing when making corrections.

10. To know correct keyboarding technique, including space bar rules.

11. To divide words correctly at the end of a line.

12. To construct special characters that are not on the machine.

ASSIGNMENT
13:17

TWO-COLUMN CLASSIFIED ADS

Typist:

1. Use a 30-character line and single spacing.

2. Start the text on line 7.

Micro operator:

1. Use a 30-character line and single spacing.

2. Start the text on line 7.

3. Use 16-pt. Helvetica bold for the headings and 10-pt. Helvetica light for the text.

4. Print the page and store it in file "13:17."

CLASSIFIED
Lost and Found

LOST
My passing mark in Math. Finder
please telephone 633-0000 and ask for
Tim.

FOUND
Physics textbook with wrong answers
to questions in chapter 3. Will
return to owner in exchange for right
answers to chapters 4-9. 677-0000.

Personals

Are you at home alone in the
evenings? Want fun and popularity?
It's as close to hand as your lips
are to your teeth . . . . . .with a
TAMMY!

A TAMMY TAMBOURINE with quadraphonic
sound can spring you onto the centre
of any stage. Don't be a fan. Be
the **STAR**. On sale now for ONLY
$75. Tel: 644-0000 evenings. Ask for
Robbie.

Miscellaneous

**ART AUCTION OF ORIGINAL oils, water
colours, charcoal sketches, and
sculpture on Saturday, June 12. All
pieces signed by the artist, a famous
Canadian impressionist. No reserve
prices!! This selection produced by
artist during her most creative
period (Art 9, 10).

Sale starts 10:00 a.m., 4733 Laurel
Street (lane), Rexdale.

Help Wanted

Mother with twins, age 5, desperately
needs babysitter who is available 5
days a week from 5 to 9 for damage
control. Must be strong and able to
run fast while minding two fun-
loving, active, but lovable boys.
$20 per hour and meals provided.
Knowledge of furniture and general
household repair would be useful.
Telephone 681-0000 as soon as
possible.

CONTENTS

Main Parts of an Electric Typewriter 4

Main Parts of an Electronic Typewriter 5

Main Parts of a Microcomputer or Word Processor 6

Common Microcomputer and Word Processing
Functions and Terms 7

Ergonomics 9

Keeping Fit on the Job 11

Capabilities of Different Equipment 12

Keyboarding on a Microcomputer or Word Processor .. 13

Type Sizes and Styles 14

Proportional Spacing 15

Paper Size 15

Inserting and Removing Paper 16

Text Formatting 17

Clearing and Setting Tabs 19

Changing Ribbon Cassettes 20

Making Corrections 22

Your Keyboarding Manual 26

Work Station Routine 28

Preparing to Keyboard 29

Finger Placement on the Home Row 30

Striking the Keys 30

The Space Bar and Carrier Return 31

Space Bar Rules 32

Space Bar Assignments 34

Line Endings — Word Division 36

Word Division Assignments 38

Constructing Special Characters 40

CLASSIFIED SECTION

UUUUUUUUUUUUUUUUUUUUUUUUUUUUUUUUU

U-drive RENTALS
a complete line of . . .

SKATEBOARDS

SCOOTERS

SKATES

GO-CARTS

Special rates for students!
Rent by the second, minute or hour.

!!!FREE INSURANCE!!!

88 Pacific Street, Oakville

688-1111

UUUUUUUUUUUUUUUUUUUUUUUUUUUUUUUUU

+ +

NEW ARRIVALS FOR SUMMER

ACID WASH WEAR
Guaranteed to
shred before
FALL!

. . . JEANS, SHORTS, SHIRTS . . .
JACKETS, COATS, AND MORE!!!!

Tcentoppers
993 Marks Street, Rexdale
699-1234

+ +

MAIN PARTS OF AN ELECTRIC TYPEWRITER

(parts may vary from machine to machine)

1. Cylinder knob
2. Line scale
3. Left margin set
4. Margin release
5. Tabulator
6. Tab set and clear
7. Space bar

8. Return key
9. Correcting key
10. On-off switch
11. Backspace key
12. Right margin set
13. Ratchet release lever
14. Paper release lever

15. Line space regulator
16. Cylinder
17. Print point indicator
18. Paper bail
19. Paper guide

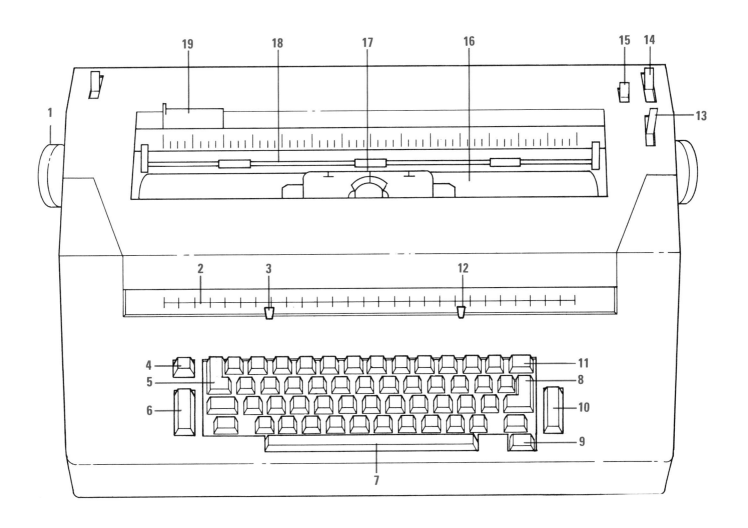

ASSIGNMENT
13:16
QUARTER-PAGE CLASSIFIED ADS

Typist:

1. Use a 30-character line and single spacing.

2. Start the text on line 7.

Micro operator:

1. Use a 30-character line and single spacing.

2. Start the text on line 7.

3. Use 16-pt. Helvetica bold for the heading and 10-pt. Helvetica light for the text.

4. Print the page and store it in file "13:16."

```
          CLASSIFIED SECTION

UUUUUUUUUUUUUUUUUUUUUUUUUUUUUUUUUUUUUUU

        ***U-drive RENTALS***

a complete line of . . .

    SKATEBOARDS

    SCOOTERS

    SKATES

    GO-CARTS




Special rates for students!  Rent by
the second, minute or hour.

        !!!FREE INSURANCE!!!

    88 Pacific Street, Oakville


            688-1111

UUUUUUUUUUUUUUUUUUUUUUUUUUUUUUUUUUUUUUU
```

```
+ + + + + + + + + + + + + + + + + + + +

       NEW ARRIVALS FOR SUMMER


           ACID WASH WEAR
           Guaranteed to
           shred before
             FALL!

  . . . JEANS, SHORTS, SHIRTS . . .
    JACKETS, COATS, AND MORE!!!!
           Teentoppers
       993 Marks Street, Rexdale
             699-1234


+ + + + + + + + + + + + + + + + + + + +
```

MAIN PARTS OF AN ELECTRONIC TYPEWRITER

(parts may vary from machine to machine)

1. Hinged paper support with scale
2. Automatic paper injector/ejector
3. Variable line space
4. Paper bail
5. Typewheel/ribbon
6. Centering key
7. Margin stops and scale
8. Margin release
9. On-off switch
10. Automatic line spacing/ margin adjust
11. Code key (depress to use functions)
12. Repeat key
13. Tab key/automatic paragraph indention
14. Left shift key and shift lock
15. Half-space key and left-hand margin stop selector
16. Space bar
17. Paper release lever
18. Aligning scale
19. Backspacing key
20. Correction key
21. Relocate key (printer returns to the correct point after carrying out corrections)
22. Impression control
23. Line space regulator
24. Pitch selector
25. Half-line space down (for subscripts)
26. Half-line space up (for superscripts)
27. Tab set/tab clear key
28. Decimal tab set key
29. Printer return
30. Right-hand shift key
31. Printer return without line spacing and right-hand margin stop

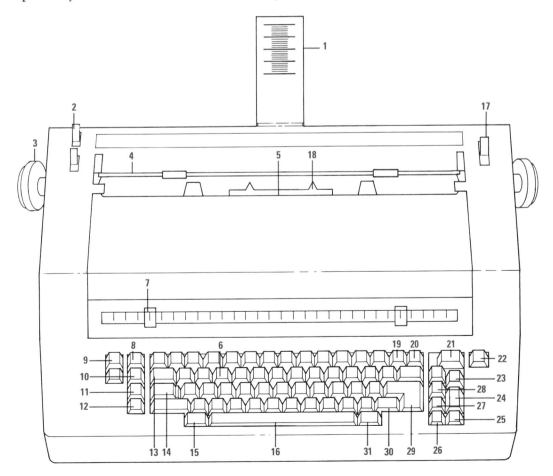

STRATH'S MONEY IN GOOD HANDS

By Denise Taylor

Now that we are coming to the end of the year, it is my pleasant duty to tell you how your money was spent. When I ran for the position of Secretary-Treasurer last year, I told you that our finances were sick and that I was the doctor with the remedy to restore their health.

In past years, the Student Council funds were spent as requests for money came in and were approved by the executive. This meant that those who asked early got money and those who were slow sometimes did not. Even though funds had been allocated, the money may not have been available.

As soon as I was elected, I threw my spreadsheet onto the screen and entered the budget for the year. This showed the amount each club, team and project was to get, so I could advise the executive what each request should be. In addition, my spreadsheet showed the balance that was available at any time, so we were never short.   No complaints were received, and our finances are now in good health.

Statement of Receipts and Payments
For the year ended June 30, 19--

	Budgeted	Actual
Receipts:		
Fees	$2000	$1950
Dances	400	150
Fund-raisers	1000	1400
Total Receipts	$3400	$3500
Payments:		
Clubs:		
Camera Sharpshooters	$200	$200
Chess Knights and Daze	50	50
Micro Madhackers	300	300
Strathcona Reports	550	675
Total Clubs	$1100	$1225
Intramural Sports:		
Baseball Blues	$ 700	$ 675
Basketball Babes	800	800
Ping Pong Aces	75	69
Track and Fielders	650	600
Total Intramural Sports	$2225	$2144
Balance on hand	$ 75	$ 131

MAIN PARTS OF A MICROCOMPUTER OR WORD PROCESSOR

1. Keyboard
2. Screen—video display terminal (VDT)
3. Dual disk drive
4. Program diskette

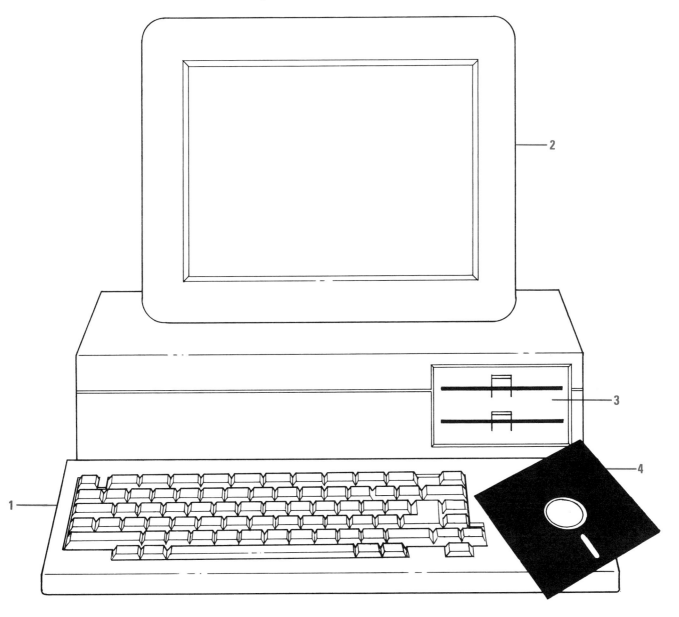

STRATH'S MONEY IN GOOD HANDS
By Denise Taylor

Now that we are coming to the end of the year, it is my pleasant duty to tell you how your money was spent. When I ran for the position of Secretary-Treasurer last year, I told you that our finances were sick and that I was the doctor with the remedy to restore their health.

In past years, the Student Council funds were spent as requests for money came in and were approved by the executive. This meant that those who asked early got money and those who were slow sometimes did not. Even though funds had been allocated, the money may not have been available.

As soon as I was elected, I threw my spreadsheet onto the screen and entered the budget for the year. This showed the amount each club, team and project was to get, so I could advise the executive what each request should be. In addition, my spreadsheet showed the balance that was available at any time, so we were never short. No complaints were received, and our finances are now in good health.

Statement of Receipts and Payments
For the year ended June 30, 19--

Receipts:	Budgeted	Actual
Fees	$2000	$1950
Dances	400	150
Fund-raisers	1000	1400
Total Receipts	$3400	$3500
Payments:		
Clubs:		
Camera Sharpshooters	$200	$200
Chess Knights and Daze	50	50
Micro Madhackers	300	300
Strathcona Reports	550	675
Total Clubs	$1100	$1225
Intramural Sports:		
Baseball Blues	$ 700	$ 675
Basketball Babes	800	800
Ping Pong Aces	75	69
Track and Fielders	650	600
Total Intramural Sports	$2225	$2144
Balance on hand	$ 75	$ 131

COMMON MICROCOMPUTER AND WORD PROCESSING FUNCTIONS AND TERMS

The following functions and terms are fast becoming part of everyday business language. Become familiar with them, because they are used throughout this text.

Accessing   Obtaining connection to a centralized system.

Automatic Decimal Tab   Automatically aligns columns of decimal numbers, with the decimal points positioned one under the other.

Automatic Hyphenation   Places a special temporary hyphen in a word. This hyphen is removed automatically should the operator edit or change the line endings later. Automatically divides the word at the end of a line and inserts a hyphen.

Automatic Underscore   Permits the operator to underscore words, phrases, lines, and paragraphs as they are being keyed.

Backspace Strikeover   Text-editing procedure whereby the operator positions the cursor or backspace key under an incorrect character and strikes the correct key over it. System automatically removes the previous character by storing a new one in its position.

Centre   Allows the operator to key in text, which is then automatically placed in the centre of the line.

CPU (Central Processing Unit)   Part of the computer that performs arithmetic and logic operations.

CRT (Cathode Ray Tube)   Video display terminal similar to a television screen.

Cursor   Lighted square or hyphen on a video display screen that indicates your position on the screen. It is the size of one character.

Daisy Wheel   Printing tool for a word processor; wheel-shaped, with characters placed at the ends of spokes.

Delete   Removes text from a document. The text may be a character, word, line, paragraph, or page. After removal, the document is automatically adjusted without the operator having to re-key the document.

Document   Portion of a text that the system treats as a single unit; ranges from a short paragraph to the maximum capacity of the storage medium.

Editing   Act of revising and correcting text or a manuscript prior to its production as a final document.

ASSIGNMENT 13:15   *HALF-PAGE ARTICLE AND SPREADSHEET*

Typist:

1. Use a 63-character line and single spacing.
2. Start the text on line 7.

Micro operator:

1. Use a 63-character line and single spacing.
2. Start the text on line 7.
3. Key the titles in 16-pt. Helvetica medium, the text in 10-pt. Helvetica light, and the by-line in 10-pt. italic light.
4. Use a spreadsheet for the statement and enter the formulas for the totals and balances.
5. Print the page and store it in file "13:15."

FAX (Facsimile Telephone)   Transmission of graphic information over telephone lines by optical scanning.

File   A collection of one or more records.

File Index   List of documents currently on storage medium (disk).

Filing   Storing documents electronically in a word processing system.

Floppy Disk   Flexible disk for recording information; may be mini, regular, or two-sided.

Format   Set-up of a document on a page; also, to plan the set-up of a document on a page.

Hard Copy   Paper print-out from a computer or word processor.

Hardware   Physical components of a computer or word processing equipment.

Indent   Allows the operator to indent automatically an entire block of text. Can be used to alter an existing document, or to create an indented block during text input.

Input/Output Devices   Physical devices for communication to and from the computer.

Insert   Allows the operator to enter a new word, words, lines, etc., in a particular position in the text. After insertion, the document is automatically adjusted without the operator having to re-key it.

Interface   Connector between two pieces of equipment, such as a computer and a telephone.

Justification   System's ability to make right-hand margins even. Eliminating the ragged right-hand margin makes the document look more professional.

Keyboarding   Act of operating a typewriter or other type of keyboard to produce a printed document.

Media   Recording supplies commonly used with word processing equipment, e.g., floppy disks.

Memory (Storage)   Section of the computer or word processor where information is stored.

Merge   Function that combines text from two independent documents during printing.

Mode   System function or operating state selected by an operator to achieve a specific result, such as insertion, deletion, or merge.

Move Text   Allows the operator to select a particular text in a document, which is then moved automatically to another part of the same document, or another document, without having to be deleted and then re-keyed.

THIS MONTH'S "SPIRIT OF STRATHCONA" WINNERS

All winners receive complimentary dinners for two at Mountain Mystique restaurant with limousine service.

MARCEL WOLFF

Leading the list is Mangy Marcel. This Capricorn's secret was silently discovered by our private detective.   Mangy's secret? Organizing the fitness program at the Lions' Seniors' Home every Thursday for the past two years.

FRANCINE HUYNH

Another secret volunteer whose work was uncovered by one of our spies.   This brain bank of chemistry formulas allows others to access her data base.   She is the voice that answers when you call the Dial-for-Chemistry hot line. Bouquets of roses for Francine.

Page Amount of text designated by the operator to occupy a single sheet of paper.

Page Break Establishes the end of one page and the beginning of the next.

Program A set of instructions that causes the computer to perform certain tasks.

Save Instruction given to the word processing system to store a document for future use.

Software Programs that make a computer operate in the required manner.

ERGONOMICS

Ergonomics is the term used to describe how the human body and office furniture or equipment interface. Successful office equipment systems are designed with the users in mind. Manufacturers of all kinds of office furniture and equipment pay a great deal of attention to the ergonomic design of their products. They are careful to include comfort factors that allow specific users to adjust the equipment to meet their particular needs, instead of having to adjust the body to suit the equipment. A system that is ergonomically designed is comfortable for the operator, and thus increases productivity. The operator should not suffer from eyestrain, hand fatigue, backache, and similar discomforts. An ergonomically designed system should also be quiet and not produce glare.

Check now to see if the equipment and furniture you are using has been ergonomically designed.

1. Is your chair adjustable in height and swivel?
2. Does the backrest of your chair fit the small of the back comfortably, and provide good support?
3. Do you have a footrest to help avoid fatigue?
4. Do you have a copy holder to cut down on eyestrain?
5. Is your work area well ventilated so that the heat generated by the machines may escape quickly?

ASSIGNMENT 13:14   *QUARTER-PAGE ARTICLES*

Typist:

1. Use 60- and 30-character lines with single spacing.

2. Start the headline on line 5 and the two paragraphs on the left side of the page.

3. Write the size of the pictures (40 × 40 mm) opposite each paragraph.

Micro operator:

1. Use 60- and 30-character lines with single spacing.

2. Use 16-pt. Helvetica bold for the headline and 10-pt. Helvetica light for the text.

3. Key the headline on line 5 and the two paragraphs on the left side of the page.

4. Print the page and store it in file "13:14."

5. Write the size of the pictures (40 × 40 mm) opposite each paragraph.

THIS MONTH'S "SPIRIT OF STRATHCONA" WINNERS

All winners receive complimentary dinners for two at Mountain Mystique restaurant with limousine service.

MARCEL WOLFF

   Leading the list is Mangy Marcel. This Capricorn's secret was silently discovered by our private detective. Mangy's secret? Organizing the fitness program at the Lions' Seniors' Home every Thursday for the past two years.

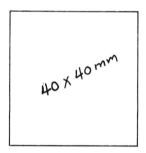

FRANCINE HUYNH

   Another secret volunteer whose work was uncovered by one of our spies. This brain bank of chemistry formulas allows others to access her data base. She is the voice that answers when you call the Dial-for-Chemistry hot line. Bouquets of roses for Francine.

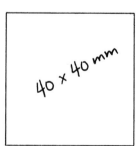

6. What is the noise level in your work area? Is the floor carpeted? Is there rubber matting beneath your printer? Does your printer have an acoustic cover?

7. Is the lighting adequate to prevent glare or eyestrain?

How did your work area rate? If you answered "yes" to most of the above questions, your work area has been ergonomically designed.

Courtesy of Biltrite Nightingale Inc.

MY STAY AT STRATHCONA

By James Chung

I came to Strathcona because my father is a friend of Jimmy Hartmann's father.

I was glad to leave Hong Kong in July because it is one of our hottest months. To my surprise, instead of snow and mountains, the picture I had of Canada, it was as muggy and hot in Toronto as in Hong Kong.

I already knew Mr. Hartmann when he stayed with us, and I met Jimmy at the airport.

Later, we drove to the Hartmann's summer home. It was here my name changed. At home I am called "Yeewah," which means "strong country," and only my teachers at school call me "James." But the neighbours I met at the lake called Jimmy "Big Jim" and me "Small Jim." Then Mr. and Mrs. Hartmann did the same. Actually, I am older than Jimmy by eight months, so I should be the one called "Big Jim" even though he has grown faster since we were born.

My first day at school made me nervous. So many new faces that all looked alike. I felt I would never remember them. But I was happy because Jimmy's friends made me feel very welcome.

Now it is time for me to leave. I enjoyed my stay in Toronto. In Hong Kong, we don't say "good-by," we say "Joy geen, or until we meet again."

KEEPING FIT ON THE JOB

Occasionally, you may experience a sore back, neck, or shoulders after you have been keying for a while. To relieve this discomfort, try the following "Five-Minute Office Workout" exercises. Do as many of these quick at-the-desk exercises as you can. You'll find they not only relieve muscle soreness, they also help you keep in shape.

Try each of these exercises 5 times!
Inhale slowly during each separate exercise motion.
All movements should be slow and controlled.

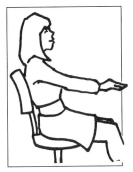

1. Place hands flat on desk and push back. Inhale and contract stomach muscles - exhale and release. Slowly stretch arm, shoulders, and neck. Hold for a count of 3 - exhale and relax.

6. Sitting in a chair, relax abdominal and back muscles. Inhale, and tuck pelvis under by pressing abdominal muscles tight to spine, which pushes lower back flat against chair back. Hold for a count of 3 - exhale and relax.

2. Slowly stretch arms overhead. Pull in abdomen and hold for a slow count of 3. Exhale slowly as you lower arms and release abdominal muscles.

7. Standing, reach hand towards ceiling. Stretch fingers; make a fist twice. Bring arms straight down to shoulder level, repeat fist.

3. Remove shoes, sit with with feet flat. Slowly press right foot up so your weight rests on the balls of the foot. Repeat motion with left foot. Release right foot, while controlling the movement as the foot returns to its flat position. Repeat using left foot.

8. Standing - knees bent - reach up with right hand. Push hand over left side twice. Repeat with left hand. Repeat at shoulder, waist, knees, toes. Always bend knees. Work your way back up.

4. Place hands under legs for balance. Straighten legs completely. Flex both feet, then point toes. Next, cross right foot over left. Repeat, alternating left and right feet.

9. Sitting or standing, lift left shoulder; lower. Lift right shoulder; lower. Lift both shoulders; lower.

5. Arms out to sides. Bend at the elbows and touch fingers to shoulders. Stretch arms out and twist like you are opening and closing a door.

10. DO THESE LAST. Standing or sitting, look left, middle, right, middle. Repeat procedure, looking up to ceiling, to left and right. Roll head FORWARD ONLY, from side to side.

Courtesy of PINC Performance Inc. and The Cohen Group

Typist:

1. Use a 30-character line and single spacing.

2. Type the article in two columns, leaving space for a quarter-page picture in the top right corner.

3. Centre the title and the by-line over the left column.

4. Write the size of the picture (80 × 70 mm) in the blank space.

Micro operator:

1. Use a two-column format and single spacing.

2. Use 16-pt. Helvetica medium for the title and 10-pt. italic light for the by-line. Centre these lines over the left column.

3. Key the text in 10-pt. Helvetica light in two columns, leaving space for a quarter-page picture in the top right corner.

4. Print the article and store it in file "13:13."

5. Write the size of the picture (80 × 70 mm) in the blank space.

MY STAY AT STRATHCONA
By James Chung

I came to Strathcona because my father is a friend of Jimmy Hartmann's father.

I was glad to leave Hong Kong in July because it is one of our hottest months. To my surprise, instead of snow and mountains, the picture I had of Canada, it was as muggy and hot in Toronto as in Hong Kong.

I already knew Mr. Hartmann when he stayed with us, and I met Jimmy at the airport.

Later, we drove to the Hartmann's summer home. It was here my name changed. At home I am called "Yeewah," which means "strong country," and only my teachers at school call me "James." But the neighbours I met at the lake called Jimmy "Big Jim" and me "Small Jim." Then Mr. and Mrs. Hartmann did the same. Actually, I am older than Jimmy by eight months, so I should be the one called "Big Jim" even though he has grown faster since we were born.

My first day at school made me nervous. So many new faces that all looked alike. I felt I would never remember them. But I was happy because Jimmy's friends made me feel very welcome.

Now it is time for me to leave. I enjoyed my stay in Toronto. In Hong Kong, we don't say "good-by," we say "Joy geen, or until we meet again."

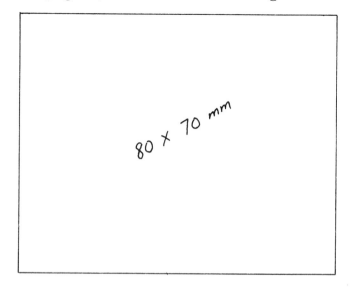

80 × 70 mm

CAPABILITIES OF DIFFERENT EQUIPMENT

COMPUTERS

Computers are excellent for processing information, and can be used for a variety of applications. A computer's electronic and mechanical parts, referred to as **hardware**, work in conjunction with a series of **software programs**. These programs cause the computer to perform specific operations.

Every digital computer system contains at least four standard components: input, output, processing, and storage. Computers are capable of performing calculations, data manipulation, and simple decision making. With a word processing program, a microcomputer can do everything a word processing machine can do. Word processing software is included as standard equipment with most computers.

WORD PROCESSORS

A word processing system has three basic components: input, processing, and output. The system allows the operator to key in information (input), change or edit the information (processing), and print the information (output).

Word processors have many automatic features that could soon make conventional typewriters obsolete. A word processor allows the operator to key in information and then manipulate this data in several different ways, for example, the margins can be altered to fit either more or less text on a page; the text can be automatically **right-justified** so that all the material lines up on the right-hand side of the page. (The text you are reading now is right-justified.) Correcting errors, inserting new information, moving paragraphs, and storing the final output are some additional features of word processors.

ELECTRONIC TYPEWRITERS

Electronic typewriters do not have as many capabilities as microcomputers or word processors but they do have many functions that make for efficient keyboarding.

Most electronic typewriters have automatic paper injection and removal. These machines can centre automatically, relocate positions, correct errors, and align decimals. Other features include repeat keys and pitch change.

Some electronic typewriters may have additional functions to those listed above. If you are using an electronic typewriter, check the operating manual that comes with your machine to find out your typewriter's capabilities.

A CHRISTMAS DREAM

By Trudy McPherson

My real name is Trudy, but everyone calls me "BTS." This stands for "Born To Shop," because that's what I love best. I love going into the stores and the biggest thrill I can think of is to buy something at 80% off.

Imagine my surprise when my aunt called me inviting me to go to Seoul.

Our first stop was in Toyko. The stores in Ginza were awesome. Girls wearing long dresses with beautiful obi sashes bowed to greet us at the door. I couldn't get over the supermarkets where you would push a button if there was a TV on the shelf and a program came on explaining the product below.

Then on to Seoul, a short hop by plane. Next day, we asked the hotel clerk where the stores were and we didn't understand what he was saying, because the answer he kept repeating was "downstairs, down."

When we went down the stairs, we were STUNNED! Instead of being in a tunnel leading to the other side of a street, we were in an underground shopping mall! Blocks and blocks of shops and restaurants! A fantastic maze of boutiques and stalls!

Our stay in Seoul was too short. Our shopping kept us busy, but we squeezed in some sightseeing. We saw two fabulous palaces — Kyongbok Kung and Ch'angdok Kung — and Chingwan temple. But the main thing I remember is the number of churches in the city. Whenever you look at the skyline, you can see steeples and crosses. My aunt said I was the perfect shopping companion and there isn't anybody else that she would rather shop with.

MEMORY TYPEWRITERS

Memory typewriters have greater capabilities than electronic machines, but fewer than word processors or microcomputers. These typewriters let you store text in memory. Page formats can be stored, permitting quick and easy completion of forms and tables. How much data you can store depends on the model of machine you are using.

If you are using a memory typewriter, your text is shown on a small display above the keys. You can make corrections on the display before you print your final copy.

Memory typewriters can centre automatically, align decimals, and perform most of the functions of electronic typewriters. They also have repeat keys.

KEYBOARDING ON A MICROCOMPUTER OR WORD PROCESSOR

Every major piece of keyboarding equipment is different. Aside from the basic QWERTY keyboard, there are no true universal standards. Machines differ in operation, and use different words and abbreviations for similar functions. As a result, it is important that you become familiar with the operating manual provided by the manufacturer of your machine. This familiarity is a critical step in learning how to use your equipment. The operating manual should provide the following essential data:

1. The capabilities of this particular machine.

2. An explanation of the different function keys, their labels, and how they work.

3. Examples of work requiring special functions.

4. Service hints, and a guide for trouble-shooting error conditions.

Most manuals are straightforward, and have clear illustrations and practice exercises that can help you perform unfamiliar tasks and use the advanced features of your machine.

Before you begin to keyboard, make sure the components of your equipment are properly connected. Turn on your equipment, and **boot**, or load, the text editing or word processing program.

Typist:

1. Centre the title and the by-lines.

2. Use a 30-character line with single spacing and type the article in two columns.

Micro operator:

1. Centre the title in 16-pt. Helvetica medium and the by-line in 10-pt. light italic.

2. Key the text in 10-pt. Helvetica light in a two-column format.

3. Print and store the article in file "13:12."

A CHRISTMAS DREAM
By Trudy McPherson

My real name is Trudy, but everyone calls me "BTS." This stands for "Born To Shop," because that's what I love best. I love going into the stores and the biggest thrill I can think of is to buy something at 80% off.

Imagine my surprise when my aunt called me inviting me to go to Seoul.

Our first stop was in Toyko. The stores in Ginza were awesome. Girls wearing long dresses with beautiful obi sashes bowed to greet us at the door. I couldn't get over the supermarkets where you would push a button if there was a TV on the shelf and a program came on explaining the product below.

Then on to Seoul, a short hop by plane. Next day, we asked the hotel clerk where the stores were and we didn't understand what he was saying, because the answer he kept repeating was "downstairs, down."

When we went down the stairs, we were STUNNED! Instead of being in a tunnel leading to the other side of a street, we were in an underground shopping mall! Blocks and blocks of shops and restaurants! A fantastic maze of boutiques and stalls!

Our stay in Seoul was too short. Our shopping kept us busy, but we squeezed in some sightseeing. We saw two fabulous palaces — Kyongbok Kung and Ch'angdok Kung — and Chingwan temple. But the main thing I remember is the number of churches in the city. Whenever you look at the skyline, you can see steeples and crosses. My aunt said I was the perfect shopping companion and there isn't anybody else that she would rather shop with.

TYPE SIZES AND STYLES

Many machines now allow you to vary the size and style of type to use for a document. The standard type sizes are **10-pitch (pica type)**, **12-pitch (elite type)**, and **15 pitch**, which is available for many electronic typewriters. There are many varieties of pitches for word processors. They range from 6.6 to 60.

```
If your machine has 10-pitch, 10 characters
and/or spaces can be keyed in each 2.5 cm.

If your machine has 12-pitch, 12 characters and/or spaces
can be keyed in each 2.5 cm.

If your machine has 15-pitch, 15 characters and/or spaces can be
keyed in each 2.5 cm.

If you are using a microcomputer, and your printer has 18-
or 24-pitch, 18 or 24 characters and/or spaces can be
printed out in each 2.5 cm.
```

What type size and style is your machine set for?

Here are some samples of commonly used typestyles:

If you are using SCRIPT, 12-pitch, the upper- and lower-case alphabets and numbers will look like this:

ABCDEFGHIJKLMNOPQRSTUVWXYZ
abcdefghijklmnopqrstuvwxyz   1234567890

If you are using CLASSIC GOTHIC, 12-pitch, the upper- and lower-case alphabets and numbers will look like this:

ABCDEFGHIJKLMNOPQRSTUVWXYZ
abcdefghijklmnopqrstuvwxyz   1234567890

If you are using MODERN PICA, 10-pitch, the upper- and lower-case alphabets and numbers will look like this:

ABCDEFGHIJKLMNOPQRSTUVWXYZ
abcdefghijklmnopqrstuvwxyz   1234567890

If you are using SENATORIAL, 10-pitch, the upper- and lower-case alphabets and numbers will look like this:

ABCDEFGHIJKLMNOPQRSTUVWXYZ
abcdefghijklmnopqrstuvwxyz   1234567890

EDITORIAL

By Rachael Miyasakai

Strathcona students now have a once-in-a-lifetime opportunity to participate in an experience in international living.

Our agreement with Robson School was signed in an exciting and heartwarming ceremony. As we waited for the second hand to get to the top of the clock, we somehow felt the presence of the Robson group. It was a strange feeling knowing that they were waiting, exactly as we were, even though they were halfway around the world. Strathcona is proud to be the first school in the province to establish ties with a school in Hong Kong.

Eleven students have already applied to go to Robson, and the Selection Committee will find it difficult to choose the lucky six, who will be the first participants. Those chosen bear the heavy responsibility of being the "model students" representing the others who wish to follow them. All of us at Strathcona stand ready to help in any and every way.

PROPORTIONAL SPACING

Work printed in proportional spacing looks very professional and attractive. Proportionally spaced characters take up different amounts of space according to their width. For example, the letter **m** is wider than the letter **i** and, therefore, takes up more space. Capital letters also take up more space than lower case letters.

Proportional **This is a sample of proportional type.**

PAPER SIZE

Letter-size Paper (Metric)

Letter-size Paper (Imperial) also known as P4

Six lines of typing occupy 2.5 cm.

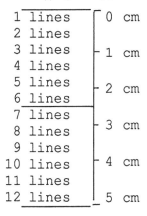

1 lines		0 cm
2 lines		
3 lines		1 cm
4 lines		
5 lines		2 cm
6 lines		
7 lines		3 cm
8 lines		
9 lines		
10 lines		4 cm
11 lines		
12 lines		5 cm

Wide Edge Inserted First P5

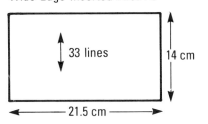

33 lines — 14 cm — 21.5 cm

Narrow Edge Inserted First P5

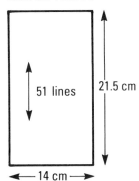

51 lines — 21.5 cm — 14 cm

ASSIGNMENT
13:11
HALF-PAGE ARTICLES

Typist:

1. Use a 60-character line, single spacing, and a 5-character tab.

2. Centre the titles, starting on line 9.

Micro operator:

1. Use a 60-character line, single spacing, and a 5-character tab.

2. Key the titles in 16-pt. Helvetica medium, the by-lines in 10-pt. Script light, and the text in 10 pt. Helvetica light. Start on line 9.

3. Print the articles and store them in file "13:11."

```
                        EDITORIAL
                   By Rachael Miyasakai
     Strathcona students now have a once-in-a-lifetime opportunity to
participate in an experience in international living.
     Our agreement with Robson School was signed in an exciting and heart-
warming ceremony. As we waited for the second hand to get to the top of the
clock, we somehow felt the presence of the Robson group.  It was a strange
feeling knowing that they were waiting, exactly as we were, even though they
were halfway around the world.  Strathcona is proud to be the first school in
the province to establish ties with a school in Hong Kong.
     Eleven students have already applied to go to Robson, and the Selection
Committee will find it difficult to choose the lucky six, who will be the
first participants. Those chosen bear the heavy responsibility of being the
"model students" representing the others who wish to follow them.  All of us
at Strathcona stand ready to help in any and every way.
```

INSERTING AND REMOVING PAPER

INSERTING

1. Move the paper guide to the extreme left.

2. Pull the paper bail forward.

3. Find the centre of the paper by folding it from left to right, and slightly creasing it at the midpoint.

4. Holding the paper in your left hand, place it behind the cylinder. Turn the right cylinder knob with your right hand. Some machines may have an index key, which automatically "feeds" the paper into the machine, and a reverse index key, which rolls the paper down.

5. Line up the crease on the paper with the midpoint on the paper bail scale, or the scale on the front of the machine.

6. If the paper is not straight, pull the paper release lever forward, and adjust the top part of the paper until it is even with the bottom part. Or pull the paper release lever forward and adjust the paper so that it is aligned with the aligning scale, making sure your crease is still at the midpoint. Push back the paper release lever.

7. Roll the paper up. Place the paper bail over the paper so that the rubber rollers are resting on it equal distances apart.

8. Move the paper guide so that it is *flush* against the paper.

9. Note the number on the scale where you have placed the paper guide. If the paper guide is always at this number, you will not have to fold the paper each time you insert it, unless you use a paper of a different width.

10. Before you start to keyboard, always check to see if the paper guide is in the correct position.

REMOVING

1. Before removing the paper from the machine, proofread your work carefully. It is much easier to make corrections while the paper is still in place than it is to reinsert the paper accurately so that the corrections are aligned with the material already printed.

2. Pull the paper release lever forward with your right hand. Remove the paper from the machine with your left hand.

3. Push the paper release lever back into place.

4. Some machines have a reverse index key that automatically rolls the paper out of the machine.

STRATHCONA REPORTS
A Publication of Strathcona School Student Council

RECORD NUMBER SEEK STUDENT COUNCIL POSITIONS

The following candidates are nominated:

President: Arlene Wong, Alice Dang, Simon de Courcy, Eva Hara

Vice-president: David Varoglu, Wendy McLean

Secretary-Treasurer: Eric Alsina, Kathleen Bengtsson

Boys' Athletics: Bill Woo, Bjorn Berggren

Girls' Athletics: Helen Gudbrandsen, Jacquie Lanen

At the close of nominations, properly completed applications had been received from the candidates shown above. The next issue of STRATHCONA REPORTS will be an election special, featuring the candidates and their platforms

Once again, the Nominating Committee had to deal with late and improperly completed applications. This seems to be a problem that never goes away, even though the rules are written on the application.

NOMINATIONS MIXUP

Even though there are more candidates seeking office than in any other year, the number should have been higher.

Seven applications had to be rejected. Two were not signed by the candidates, and three did not have the required ten signatures of students. The last two were submitted after the deadline.

The Nominating Committee held a meeting to discuss the seven rejections. It decided it had no choice but to refuse all the applications that were not filed properly.

TEXT FORMATTING

On a word processor or microcomputer, the information on how a document is to be formatted is set up on the **format line**. The operator creates the format line, which allows for the positioning of tabs, and indicates line length, and line spacing. The information in this line may be modified at any point, which means that format changes are possible within the same document.

ESTABLISHING THE MARGINS

1. Line up the centre point of the paper with the machine midpoint.

2. Determine the length of line needed for the assignment. Although the line can be any length, the most common lengths are 40, 50, 60, and 70 characters.

3. To display your work to best advantage, the margins must be of equal width. You must have an equal number of spaces and strokes to the left and right of the centre point of the paper. Here's how to calculate the number of strokes for the left and right margins:

   - Note the number on the carrier position scale that you have chosen as your centre point.

   - Note the length of the line, for example, 50 or 60 characters.

   - Divide the number of strokes in the line by 2.

   - Set the left margin stop at the centre point, *minus* half the number of characters in the line.

   - Set the right margin stop at the centre point, *plus* half the number of strokes in the line.

   Example
   - Centre point is 50
   - Line length is 50 strokes
   - Number of strokes in line divided by 2 = 25
   - Left margin stop should be set at 50 − 25 = 25
   - Right margin stop should be set at 50 + 25 = 75

4. Add five spaces to the right margin stop for the bell allowance. The **bell allowance** is the number of strokes that can be keyboarded *after* the bell has rung. (On some machines the carrier will lock on the sixth stroke after the bell allowance, and you will not be able to keyboard any more characters on that line.)

STRATHCONA REPORTS
A Publication of Strathcona School Student Council

RECORD NUMBER SEEK STUDENT COUNCIL POSITIONS

The following candidates are nominated:

President: Arlene Wong, Alice Dang, Simon de Courcy, Eva Hara

Vice-president: David Varoglu, Wendy McLean

Secretary-Treasurer: Eric Alsina, Kathleen Bengtsson

Boys' Athletics: Bill Woo, Bjorn Berggren

Girls' Athletics: Helen Gudbrandsen, Jacquie Lanen

At the close of nominations, properly completed applications had been received from the candidates shown above. The next issue of STRATHCONA REPORTS will be an election special, featuring the candidates and their platforms.

Once again, the Nominating Committee had to deal with late and improperly completed applications. This seems to be a problem that never goes away, even though the rules are written on the application.

NOMINATIONS MIXUP

Even though there are more candidates seeking office than in any other year, the number should have been higher.

Seven applications had to be rejected. Two were not signed by the candidates, and three did not have the required ten signatures of students. The last two were submitted after the deadline.

The Nominating Committee held a meeting to discuss the seven rejections. It decided it had no choice but to refuse all the applications that were not filed properly.

There is no bell on machines that have word wraparound, so you do not need to add the bell allowance to the right margin stop.

5. Margins may also be established by **counting in** an equal number of spaces from each side of the paper, and setting the margins accordingly.

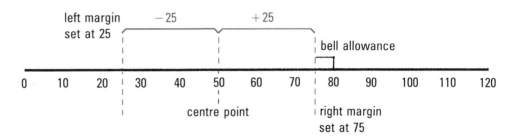

THE LINE SPACE REGULATOR

The setting of the **line space regulator** determines the number of blank lines left between keyed lines. The choice of spacing used determines the attractiveness and readability of the document.

How vertical spacing is set depends on the machine you are using. Refer to the illustrations of electric and electronic machines (pages 4 and 5) for the position of the line space regulator. On personal computers and word processors, the spacing can be established on the format line before the document is begun; when the document is printed, it will be spaced according to your instructions.

1. If the line space regulator is set on 1, there will be no blank lines between the printed lines.

```
This is single spacing.
This is single spacing.
This is single spacing.
```

ASSIGNMENT 13:10   THE FRONT PAGE

Typist:

1. Obtain two sheets of dry transfer lettering in the same type style (e.g., Helvetica); one of 36-pt. bold letters and the other of 16-pt. medium letters.

2. Using the 36-pt. sheet, prepare the newspaper's title by rubbing the letters flush with the left margin on line 7.

3. Use the 16-pt. size for the subtitle.

4. Use the 36-pt. bold dry transfer letters for the newspaper's title on line 6 and 16-pt. medium letters for the subtitle on line 9. Draw a 60-character line across the page.

5. Use 16-pt. medium letters for the headline.

6. Use a 60-character line and single spacing for the first article. Start on line 7.

7. Use a 30-character line and single spacing for the second article.

Micro operator:

1. Look at the type styles in your program and select one without serifs.

2. Enter the title in 36-pt. bold letters and the subtitle in 16-pt. medium letters.

3. Print the name and the subtitle.

4. Repeat the process with a serif type style.

5. Store the titles in file "13:10."

6. Use 36-pt. Helvetica bold for the newspaper's title on line 6 and 16-pt. Helvetica bold for the subtitle on line 9. Use 6-pt. type to draw a 60-character line across the page.

7. Use 16-pt. Helvetica bold for the headline.

8. Use a 60-character line and single spacing for the first article. Use a 30-character line for the second article.

9. Use 16-pt. Helvetica medium for article titles and 10-pt. Helvetica light for the text.

10. Print the page and store it in file "13:10."

2. If the line space regulator is placed on 2, there will be one blank line between the printed lines.

```
This is double spacing.
           X
This is double spacing.
           X
This is double spacing.
```

3. If the line space regulator is set on 3, there will be two blank lines between the printed lines.

```
This is triple spacing.
           X
           X
This is triple spacing.
           X
           X
This is triple spacing.
```

The following line-spacing abbreviations are used in the assignment instructions throughout this text:

↓1—single spacing (*No* blank lines between the printed lines of text.)

↓2—double spacing (*One* blank line between the printed lines of text.)

↓3—triple spacing (*Two* blank lines between the printed lines of text.)

CLEARING AND SETTING TABS

The **tabulator key** or **bar** is used to move quickly to designated points on the carrier. Some machines have preset tab stops every five or ten spaces. On other typewriters, the tab stops must be set.

TO CLEAR TABS

1. Locate the tab key or bar on your machine. Depress it to move to the tab stop you want to clear.

2. Press the tab clear key to clear the stop.

3. Continue to tab and clear until all unnecessary stops are removed.

4. Return to the left margin.

ASSIGNMENT

13:9

Key this report and place it in your handbook.

FORMAT DECISIONS FOR A NEW PUBLICATION

You must now make some important decisions about the publication's format. Remember, you need to make the newspaper look interesting to attract as many readers as possible. After considering the various sizes of paper, you picked P4 sulphite bond. Now you are ready to select the style and size of type.

How many type styles should be used? Even though there are many available, you decide to use only two styles. One style will be used for the authors' bylines and the other style will be used for all other text. This consistency provides a sense of harmony because it will unite all the parts of the newspaper. If additional styles were used, a reader might find it confusing.

What styles should be used? Bradley is rejected because it looks old-fashioned and your readers are primarily teenagers. Outline is too difficult to read. Helvetica is chosen because its sharp, clean outlines appear modern and it is one of the easiest type styles to read. Italic is chosen for the by-lines.

What sizes of type should be used? Because the decision was made to use only one type style, Helvetica, for all text material except the by-lines, your selection of varying sizes of type will be the only way a reader can identify the various parts of the newspaper. The following are selected:

Part of Newspaper	Type Style	Type Size	Weight
Title	Helvetica	36 pt.	Bold
Headlines (Titles of Articles)	Helvetica	16	Medium
Text of Articles	Helvetica	10	Light
By-lines	Italic	10	Light

TO SET TABS

1. Space forward using the space bar to the desired tab stop point.

2. Press the tab set key.

3. Whenever an indention is required, press the tab key or bar to move to the desired position.

Word processors and microcomputers have commands for formatting and clearing tab stops. Check with your teacher or your operating manual if you are using one of these machines.

CHANGING RIBBON CASSETTES

All electronic typewriters and printers for computers and word processors use cassette ribbons. The cassettes snap into place in the machine. No threading is required, except to place the ribbon between the ribbon guides located on either side of the print element.

The highest quality (and most expensive) ribbons are **single-strike ribbons**. As the name suggests each section of the ribbon is used only once.

TO CHANGE A RIBBON CASSETTE

1. Insert a piece of paper into the machine. Turn off the machine.

2. Lift the cover off the machine.

3. Observe how the old ribbon is threaded through the ribbon guides.

4. Pull the ribbon load lever forward, and remove the old ribbon cassette using both hands and lifting straight up.

5. Position the replacement cassette over the appropriate posts and push down.

6. Thread the ribbon through the guideposts, tighten it, and push back the ribbon load lever.

7. Replace the cover, turn the machine on, and key a few letters to make sure that the ribbon is inserted correctly.

ASSIGNMENT
13:8   Key this report and place it in your handbook.

TYPE

When an editor talks about "type," he or she is referring to the letters, numbers, and symbols -- the characters -- that a reader sees on a printed page. The sizes and styles of type selected for a publication are important in determining whether or not a reader finds the publication attractive.

A type style describes the way a letter looks. The letter "A" may occur in a very fancy form -- "A" in a style called Roman, for example, or it may be in a plain, stark style "A" in a style called Futura. A fancy or elaborate type style leaves the reader with a feeling of formality and elegance. That is why styles such as Roman or Olde English are popular choices for wedding invitations. On the other hand, bare, simple styles, such as Helvetica or OCR, provide the reader with a sense of being up-to-date and modern because these styles are used in many computer printers.

The major difference between a plain or fancy type style is whether there are serifs on the letters. Serifs are the thin, small lines used to finish off a main stroke of a letter, such as at the top and bottom of M. A plain, or "non-serif" type style has no serifs.

There are so many different type styles available that it is impossible to list them. You may have used some of them already if you have a typewriter with an element or a printwheel. If you look at either of these, you will be able to see the name of the type style, such as Courier or Prestige. Desktop publishing software usually provides many type style options, but whether you can use them depends on your printer.

The size of type is measured by the height and the width of the letters. The height is described in a unit called a "point" (abbreviated "pt."). One point equals 0.0351 cm, which is so small you can't read it. Most of the typewriters and printers you use have letters of 11-point height.

The width of a letter is measured in a unit called "pitch." There is a wide range of pitch sizes available and if you had a microcomputer and a laser printer, you could pick whatever size you want. Desktop publishing programs also provide "letterspacing," which means you can adjust the spaces between letters and words to fit a line of text. In offices, the most commonly used pitch sizes are 10, 12, and 15 pitch.

The last important factor that affects the appearance of type is the thickness of the line that forms the letters. This is called the "weight" of the type. For example, the letter "W" can be formed with a thin or thick line. A very thin outline can make the "W" appear delicate and dainty, while a thick outline makes it look heavy and important. If you use desktop publishing software, you may choose a certain weight of type to create a certain impression. Weight can be stated in different ways, but three terms commonly used are "light," "medium," and "bold."

Changing Correction Tapes   The procedure for changing correction tapes is similar to that used for changing ribbons. However, installation and removal of ribbons and correction tapes varies from machine to machine. Always check your operating manual for the proper method for your equipment.

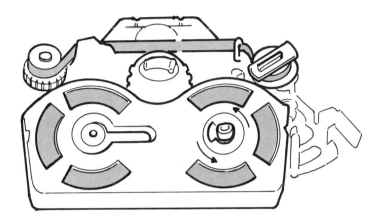

Changing a Ribbon Cassette for a Typewriter

For clean, sharp, easy-to-read letters, keep your ribbon in good condition.

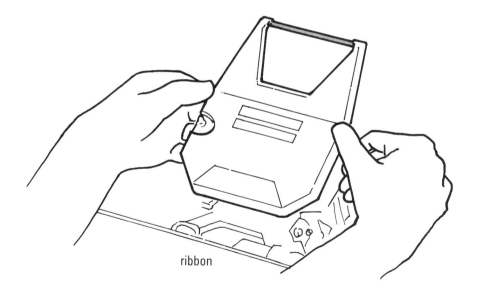

ribbon

Changing a Ribbon Cassette on a Printer

Key this report and place it in your handbook.

GRAPHIC DESIGN

An editor follows the rules of graphic design to make each page attractive or appealing to the reader. As a reader turns the pages, he or she will scan the contents, making a decision to either stop and read a page, or go on to the next one. What can an editor do to entice the reader to stop and read?

One of the most effective ways to catch a reader's eye is to use graphics. A graphic is an illustration, such as a photograph or a cartoon. The graphics must match the purpose of the publication and each graphic must blend with the text, unless it is meant to stand alone. For example, a scholarly journal often features diagrams and graphs, but not pictures. A TV guide features pictures, but not graphs. Most readers are likely to skip over a page that has only text on it. But most readers pause to look at a graphic, especially if there is a person in the illustration.

A well-arranged page has the following characteristics:

1. <u>Simplicity</u>. Each article in a publication is about a specific topic or idea. An editor must decide how many and which articles to fit on a page. Simplicity means that there should be only a few topics or ideas on a single page, helping the reader to decide whether or not he or she wants to stop and read the page.

The topic of each article is shown in its title. A title should be short and accurate.

2. <u>Balance</u>. The articles and graphics should be arranged so that they balance or offset each other. As a reader looks at a page, he or she should feel that everything is in the right position. A reader feels uneasy if there are two columns of text on a page, and one of them looks very wide, while the other one looks too narrow. Such a page appears "heavy," or out of balance.

3. <u>Unity</u>. This means that all of the material on a page is related by the same theme or idea. For example, an editor decides that a page will display the names of the service and sports award winners. An article about the new swimming pool should not appear on this page because the result will be disunity. The reader would expect to find the information about the swimming pool in another section of the newspaper.

4. <u>Emphasis</u>. The most important item on a page should be obvious to the reader. For example, the lead article or graphic could be placed in the centre of the page with a heavy line around it.

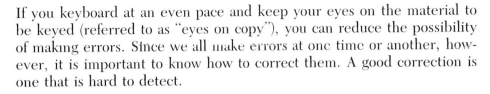

MAKING CORRECTIONS

If you keyboard at an even pace and keep your eyes on the material to be keyed (referred to as "eyes on copy"), you can reduce the possibility of making errors. Since we all make errors at one time or another, however, it is important to know how to correct them. A good correction is one that is hard to detect.

Correct errors as they are made. Proofread carefully *before* removing work from your machine or printing it.

ERASING

With the popularity of self-correcting machines, word processors, and microcomputers, **erasing** is becoming less common. There may be times, however, when you will be required to erase.

Erasing takes time, patience, and practice. Your eraser should be clean, and sharp enough to erase one letter at a time without smudging adjacent letters.

Technique

1. If you have a movable carrier, decide whether your error is to the right or left side of the centre point; then press the margin release key, and move the carrier to the extreme right or left. If the carrier cannot be moved, use the space bar to move the print point to the extreme left or right.

2. Roll the paper up so that the error is just above the paper bail. Lift up the paper bail. If the error is near the bottom of the page, roll the paper down to bring it over the cylinder.

3. Erase the error with a *light, circular* motion.

4. Brush or blow away any erasure crumbs remaining on the paper. Do *not* blow the crumbs into the machine.

5. If you have a piece of white chalk, use it to fill in lightly the space where the error was.

6. Roll the paper back to its original location. Position the print point so that the spot where the error was made is aligned with the print point indicator. Keyboard the correct letter.

ASSIGNMENT

13:6

Key this report and place it in your handbook.

PLANNING A NEW PUBLICATION

A publication is seldom the only one of its kind. It must compete with other publications for the attention of readers. How well it competes will depend on the artistic and organizational ability of the editor. The right kind of material must be collected and laid out in order to attract the reader's eye. Just fitting words and pictures onto a page and hoping for the best is not good enough.

These are some basic questions that must be answered before a publication is started:

1. <u>What is the publication's purpose?</u> Why do we need a new publication? What similar publications are available? Let's assume that the Student Council of your school receives numerous requests for a school newspaper. The answers to these questions could be: "To inform students about current events," and "There is no other publication available."

2. <u>What content should be published?</u> The answer: school events, such as field trips; sports events; and letters to the editor.

3. <u>Who will do the work?</u> Who is qualified to collect articles from authors? Who knows what responsibilities an editor must assume to produce a good school newspaper?

To your surprise, you receive an invitation to be the editor of your school's newspaper. The letter states that you are the first choice for the position because you are creative and responsible, and you possess strong human relations skills. You accept the offer and you are ready to start.

To make a publication attractive and interesting to the readers, an editor follows the principles of page composition and graphic design. As editor of your school's newspaper, these are some basic questions that you must answer about page composition.

1. <u>What paper size should be used?</u> Paper of an odd size is more expensive and may be difficult to buy in the future. A commonly used size, such as P4, is cheaper than an odd size even though both are of the same quality. A standard size is easy to buy because many stores stock it. You choose size P4 for the school newspaper.

2. <u>What kind of paper should be used?</u> Newsprint paper is very cheap, but it will also make your newspaper look cheap. One way of finding the answer to this question is to estimate how long the publication is likely to be kept after it is read. Most students throw a school newspaper away after they finish reading it, so a lightweight, sulphite bond paper, which is quite inexpensive, can be used.

3. <u>How big is the working area of the page?</u> Recall that the working area is the part of the page that is covered with words and/or pictures. What is left is called "white space." The amount of white space must be generous because readers find it difficult to follow the text on a page on which everything is jammed together. But there should not be too much white space because it leaves the reader with the impression that the contents are very skimpy.

CORRECTION FLUID

Do *not* use painting or brushing strokes when applying correction fluid. Both methods result in a messy error.

Technique
1. Make sure the lid is on securely; then shake the bottle of correction fluid well.

2. Roll the paper up so that the error is just above the paper bail. Lift up the paper bail. If the error is near the bottom of the page, roll the paper down to bring it over the cylinder. Move the carrier to the extreme right or left to prevent the fluid from dripping into the machine.

3. Remove the brush from the bottle, and determine whether the liquid is the right consistency. If it is too thick, add thinner, or it will make a blot on the paper. If the fluid is too thin, it will not cover the error effectively. Remove any excess fluid before applying it to the paper.

4. Apply the fluid by touching or dotting it to the error, one character at a time. Follow the outline of the letter being corrected; too much fluid above or below the printed line attracts attention to the error.

5. Replace the cap tightly on the bottle.

6. Let the fluid dry thoroughly.

7. Reposition the paper, and keyboard the correction.

ERASER TAPE

With this method, errors are easily corrected, but they are also easily detected when the paper is held up to the light. The substance that coats the error on some poorer qualities of eraser tape eventually wears off, making corrections seem like strikeovers.

Technique
1. Line up the error with the print point indicator.

2. Insert the tape behind the ribbon and over the incorrect letter, with the treated, white side facing the error.

3. Holding the tape over the letter, strike the incorrect letter again.

4. Remove the tape. Backspace to the beginning of the copy to be corrected, and keyboard the correction.

Key this report and place it in your handbook.

DESKTOP PUBLISHING SOFTWARE

Many desktop publishing programs can be purchased. The first ones were aimed at business users and were therefore very expensive. These programs still found a market because they allowed companies to produce high-quality publications "in-house" at a lower price than sending the material to a commercial typesetter or printer.

It is possible to buy "typesetting" software packages that produce characters in different type styles and sizes at very low cost. At a slightly higher price, "simplified" desktop publishing programs can be bought; the basic procedures are provided in these programs. They cost approximately 20% of the sophisticated, high-level programs.

Regardless of the level of sophistication, all desktop publishing programs provide the basic procedures in composing the pages of a publication.

1. Page definition: determining the size of the "working area" of a page and the top, bottom and side margins. (The working area is the part of the page on which text and/or pictures appear.)

2. Layout: determining the locations and sizes of the material that is to appear on the page. If a graphic is used, the operator can reproduce it in different sizes and place it in several locations to determine the best dimensions and positions. The text can be arranged and rearranged in seconds, for example, by changing a single column into two or three columns. All these changes can be seen on the screen in "WYSIWYG" (what you see is what you get) desktop publishing programs.

3. Type styles and sizes: selecting the best styles and sizes is easy because different fonts can be brought onto the screen, allowing the operator to see what the page will look like before making design decisions.

4. Graphics file: most programs have a file of high-quality illustrations of objects such as a typewriter, a monitor, an automobile, etc. These pictures can be drawn onto the screen in seconds and included in the publication.

5. Scanned images: any type of picture or graphic can be copied into a publication, using a supplementary device called a scanner.

Using a desktop publishing program allows an editor to produce an attractive publication with great efficiency.

SQUEEZING

```
They said they  wold  go.
They said they would  go.
```

NOTE

Different machines use different methods for squeezing. To find out what method to use with your machine, check with your teacher or consult your operating manual. If you are using a word processor or electronic typewriter, check the instructions for "inserting."

If the correction you are keyboarding contains one letter *more* than the erased word, then **squeezing** (also called **crowding**) is used to insert the extra letter. Use the half-space lever for this procedure. In squeezing, one-half space is left before and after the corrected word.

Technique

1. Erase the entire word that contains the error.

2. Position the print point indicator to the beginning of the word that has been erased.

3. Holding the half-space lever forward, insert the correct word.

SPREADING

```
She was dicttating a memo.
She was  dictating  a memo.
```

NOTE

Different machines use different methods for spreading. To find out what method to use with your machine, check with your teacher or consult your operating manual. If you are using a word processor or electronic typewriter, check the instructions for "deleting."

If the correction you are keying contains one letter *less* than the erased word, then **spreading** is used to stretch out the word. Again, use the half-space lever for this procedure. In spreading, one and one-half spaces are left before and after the corrected word.

Technique

1. Erase the entire word that contains the error.

2. Position the print point indicator one space to the right of the word to be corrected.

3. Holding the half-space lever forward, insert the correction.

REINSERTING PAGES

It is easier to make corrections while the paper is still in the machine. However, if you do have to reinsert a page to make a correction, these procedures should be followed.

Technique

1. Erase the error.

2. Reinsert the paper.

3. Reposition the paper accurately with the help of the paper release lever and the print point indicator.

Key this report and place it in your handbook.

DESKTOP PUBLISHING HARDWARE

The equipment used for desktop publishing consists of a microcomputer and a printer. These machines — called hardware — are not specialized in that they can be used for any other microcomputer application as well, such as word processing, spreadsheets, data bases, and accounting.

The most important factor is the quality of the printer. Printers are classified into two categories: impact and nonimpact. Impact printers form characters by having the print head (which holds the characters) strike the ribbon against the paper. Nonimpact printers use heat, laser beams, or photography to form the characters, and no contact is made with the paper. The three most common kinds of printers are:

1. Dot-matrix (Impact). The characters are formed by tiny dots. The readability of the text is determined by the number of dots used to form a character; the more dots used, the darker the character and, therefore, the easier it is to read. A dot-matrix printer is the cheapest kind of printer and it can produce graphics or illustrations. The quality of the images is so poor, though, that this type of printer is generally considered unsuitable for desktop publishing.

2. Daisy-wheel (Impact). These printers are similar to typewriters. The letters, numbers, and symbols are located at the end of the spokes of a wheel that resembles a flower, hence its name. These printers are also called "letter quality" printers because the text they produce is of much higher quality compared to dot-matrix printers. However, daisy-wheel printers will not produce graphics, limiting their usefulness for desktop publishing.

3. Laser (Nonimpact). A laser light or beam forms the image of the characters, producing output of very high quality. The characters are almost identical to those provided by commercial typesetting companies. Laser printers can produce both graphics and text, making them ideal for desktop publishing.

The use of a computer can save an editor a great deal of time in the preparation of high-quality publications. Good publications can still be produced using a typewriter with a carbon ribbon. Characters of different styles and sizes can be produced with dry transfer fonts: the letters are rubbed onto a sheet of paper. The text and graphics can be pasted onto a page layout sheet, which is ready to be copied or printed. The resulting publication can be so pleasing that the average reader could not tell whether a computer was used or not. The equipment used is less important than the skill and creativity used to collect the material and to lay out the pages.

4. Test the paper alignment by placing the ribbon in the stencil position, or use the correcting key to strike over a period. If necessary, make further adjustments.

5. Return the ribbon to normal position, and keyboard the correction.

ERASABLE BOND PAPER

Erasable bond paper has been coated with a special chemical to prevent the ribbon ink from being absorbed into the paper. As a result, you can make clean corrections quickly and easily using a pencil eraser. However, there are some drawbacks to using this type of paper. Erasable bond is more expensive than regular bond paper. Printed characters smudge easily because the ink is not completely absorbed into the paper, and they fade after a period of time.

Technique
1. Erase the error, and brush or blow away any eraser crumbs remaining on the paper.

2. Keyboard the correct character(s).

SELF-CORRECTING TYPEWRITERS

Many typewriters are equipped with this feature, which allows the operator to make excellent corrections quickly and easily using lift-off or chalk tape. The key that activates the lift-off tape is sometimes marked with an **X**, and is often situated on the lower right portion of the keyboard.

Technique
1. Backspace to the error by depressing the correction key.

2. Strike the incorrect letter again. This lifts the error off the page and onto the spool of correction tape. (This step is not necessary on some machines. Check your operating manual.)

3. Without backspacing, insert the correct letter, and continue keyboarding.

ASSIGNMENT

13:3

Key the following report and place it in your handbook.

PARTS OF A PUBLICATION

A publication is anything that is printed, usually in large amounts. A publication may be sold, such as a detective pocketbook, or it may be free, such as an advertising flyer stuffed into your mailbox.

A publication can be very complicated, such as a volume of the encyclopedia, or very simple, such as a page announcing a garage sale. The parts of a publication are determined by its objective. For example, an encyclopedia contains articles on every known subject. The flyer for the garage sale provides information about the date, time, and place of the sale.

A school newspaper usually has some or all of the following parts.

1. The title should be short and easy to remember. It should also indicate the target audience and the contents of the publication. For example, if the school's name is Strathcona, the newspaper could be Strathnews, Strath Update, or Strath Reports.

2. The masthead lists the editor and others who helped with the publication, as well as when the issue was published (for example, Winter 19--).

3. News events: special happenings such as a visit to the school by the Prime Minister, or how a student rescued two friends after their canoe tipped in the middle of the lake.

4. Sports: intramural scores, inter-school league games, and tournaments.

5. Social events: student get-togethers such as a Halloween or Valentine dance; meals such as "Dinner in Montreal" featuring French Canadian cuisine; or field trips to community organizations.

6. Special columns: advice to parents and others who live with students, and "how to" columns on car repair, for example, or finding part-time work.

7. Student Council and club events: information about upcoming activities and meeting dates.

8. Advertisements: full-, half-, or quarter-page ads sold to merchants provide an important source of income for the newspaper.

WORD PROCESSORS AND MICROCOMPUTERS

In general, corrections can be made quickly and simply on word processors and microcomputers. However, a large number of corrections on a page may take longer to correct automatically than rekeying the page.

One method of making corrections is to move the cursor to the error, and keyboard the correct characters. There are several commands that can be used to insert or delete characters or entire words. Ask your teacher, or refer to your operating manual.

YOUR KEYBOARDING MANUAL

To develop good organizational skills, you should maintain a keyboarding manual. These are some guidelines for setting up a keyboarding manual:

1. Use a separate three-ring binder for all your keyboarding work. A loose leaf format enables you to insert and remove material easily.

2. Use dividers for each section of your manual. Use the headings given in the following sample "Keyboarding Manual Format," or use a format that your teacher suggests.

3. Design a title page for each section. Be creative. Include appropriate cartoons, articles, photos, and drawings.

4. Keep all the material on each topic, including tests, in the appropriate section.

5. Label each new formatting concept within a section with an appropriate title; for example, Business Letter Styles, Semi-Block Style, Open Punctuation. (Use the headings in your text as a guide.)

6. Keep your manual neat. Make sure there are no ripped or messy pages—and no doodles!

ASSIGNMENT

13:2

Key these terms and definitions.

DESKTOP PUBLISHING GLOSSARY

Alignment or justification. How the text lines appear on a page; for example, centered, which means the left and right margin widths are equal.

Font. A word used by printers and typesetters to stand for one set of characters identified by size and style, such as 18-point Courier bold or 36-point Helvetica italic. A font of characters includes letters, numbers, and symbols. There are many type fonts available.

Graphics. The pictures or illustrations in a publication.

Icon. A symbol or picture that represents a command in a software program, such as a picture of a tiny paintbrush to show the option for graphics.

Kerning. Adjusting the amount of white space between the letters of a word, usually by moving the letters closer together. This can be done if desktop publishing software is used, but it cannot be done on a typewriter because the character size is fixed.

Leading. The amount of white space between the lines of text. Leading cannot be adjusted on a typewriter where the line spacing is fixed at single, line-and-a-half, double, or triple spacing.

Mouse. A device used in place of a keyboard to operate a microcomputer. The operator uses a mouse to move an arrow (cursor) on the screen and makes a choice by pressing a button.

Non-printing characters. Letters and symbols that can be seen on a computer monitor, but are not printed on paper. An example is "¶," which shows the end of a line.

Publication. Anything that is printed, such as a newspaper, handbill, or magazine, usually in large amounts.

Text. The words in a publication. A page in a publication may be composed of text, graphics, or text and graphics.

Text block. A section or portion of a page containing words. It may begin or end in the middle of a sentence.

Window. A section or part of a computer screen. The number of windows that can be seen is controlled by the software. A window and its contents usually appear on top of the previous image displayed, so that both are visible. A window that contains commands or options is often called a "dialog box."

KEYBOARDING MANUAL FORMAT

1. **RULES AND PROCEDURES**
   a) Title Page
   b) Responsibility Sheets
   c) Machine Parts
   d) Space Bar Rules
   e) Word Division Rules

2. **PROOFREADING, EDITING, AND COMPOSING**
   a) Title Page
   b) How to Proofread
   c) Proofreading Assignments
   d) How to Edit
   e) Proofreader's Marks
   f) Editing Assignments
   g) Composing Assignments

3. **TIMED WRITINGS**
   a) Title Page
   b) How to Format a Timed Writing
   c) Personal Timed-writing Record
   d) Timed Writings

4. **USING LANGUAGE**
   a) Title Page
   b) Assignments

5. **CENTERING**
   a) Title Page
   b) How to Centre Horizontally
   c) How to Centre Vertically
   d) Display Techniques
   e) Centering Assignments
   f) How to Block Centre
   g) Block-centering Assignments
   h) Pivoting and Leaders
   i) Pivoting and Leader Assignments

6. **TABLES AND BUSINESS FORMS**
   a) Title Page
   b) How to Format Tables
   c) Table Assignments
   d) How to Format Long Column Headings
   e) Long Column Heading Table Assignments
   f) How to Format Short Column Headings
   g) Short Column Heading Table Assignments
   h) How to Format Mixed Column Headings
   i) Mixed Column Heading Table Assignments
   j) Keyboarding on Lines
   k) Business Forms

7. **LETTERS, ENVELOPES, AND MEMOS**
   a) Title Page
   b) Basic Letter Parts
   c) Letter Placement Chart
   d) Business Letter Styles
   e) Letter Punctuation Styles
   f) Letter Assignments
   g) How to Format Envelopes
   h) Envelope Assignments
   i) How to Format a Subject Line
   j) Subject Line Assignments
   k) How to Format an Attention Line
   l) Attention Line Assignments
   m) How to Format a Form Letter
   n) Form Letter Assignments
   o) Additional Letter Parts
   p) How to Format a Memo
   q) Memo Assignments

8. **OUTLINES, NOTES, AND MANUSCRIPTS**
   a) Title Page
   b) Outlines and Notes
   c) One-page Reports
   d) The Title Page
   e) The Table of Contents
   f) The Bibliography
   g) Multi-page Reports
   h) Footnotes
   i) Endnotes
   j) Newspaper Articles
   k) Minutes of Meetings
   l) Itineraries

9. **MAKING COPIES**
   a) Title Page
   b) Assignments

CONTENTS

Desktop Publishing Glossary 475

Parts of a Publication 476

Desktop Publishing Hardware 477

Desktop Publishing Software 478

Planning a Publication 479

Graphic Design 480

Type 481

Format Decisions for a New Publication 482

NUMBER KEYPAD ASSIGNMENT

ASSIGNMENT

2:30

Keyboard each line twice.

1. 555 545 444 454 555 545 444 454 4 5

2. 555 565 666 656 555 565 666 656 6 5

3. 555 525 222 252 555 525 222 252 2 5

4. 444 414 111 141 444 414 111 141 1 4

5. 666 636 666 656 666 636 666 656 3 6

6. 555 585 888 858 555 585 888 858 8 5

7. 444 474 777 747 444 474 777 747 7 4

8. 666 696 666 696 666 696 666 696 9 6

HOW TO FORMAT AN ITINERARY

An itinerary is a step-by-step plan outlining a trip. It specifies all the details as to when, where, and how an executive travels, along with the appointments and meetings to be attended.

An itinerary should be formatted in such a way that all information is clear and easily understood. Display the dates prominently if the trip spans several days.

1. Use a 60-character pica line or a 70-character elite line.

2. The starting line can vary, depending on the length of the itinerary. In general, start on line seven.

3. Centre headings (i.e., name of traveller and dates).

4. Set a tab stop 15 spaces in from the left margin.

5. Single space each item but leave a blank line between each one.

6. Leave a triple space before each new day's schedule.

MODULE
3

TIMED
WRITINGS

Courtesy of Ontario Hydro

Format this agenda using the spacing and style indicated.
Use a 60-character pica or a 70-character elite line.

↓ 13
MEETING OF THE EXECUTIVE COMMITTEE
↓ 2
Boardroom
↓ 2
April 28, 19--
↓ 2
10:00

↓ 3

AGENDA
↓ 3

1. ²∧∧ Approval of the agenda   10:00
         ↓ 2
2.   Reading/approval of minutes of meeting held on
         March 25, 19--   10:05
         ↓ 2
3.   Business arising out of the minutes   10:10
             ↓ 2
1 →   a) Report by Collingwood Project Committee
                ↓ 2
             b) Report on proposed bond issue by
                Vice-President of Finance   10:25
                ↓ 2
             c) Report on job sharing project by Manager
                of Personnel.   10:45
                ↓ 2
4.   New business   11:00
             ↓ 2
5.   Date of next meeting   11:00
             ↓ 2
6.   Adjournment   11:05

INTRODUCTION

Timed writings let you check on your keyboarding progress. They tell you how many words per minute you can key.

As you work through the timed writings in this module, your chief goal is to increase your keyboarding speed. To help you achieve this goal, always aim to key a few more words on each successive timing.

Accuracy development is another important function of timed writings. Be sure to analyze each timing carefully to determine whether you should spend more time on developing accuracy.

You will not improve your speed (or accuracy) merely by doing one timed writing after another, however. Practising good keyboarding techniques, striking the keys with a steady rhythm, and keeping your eyes on the copy will help you improve both your speed *and* your accuracy.

OBJECTIVES

1. To format pages correctly for taking timed writings.
2. To calculate gross words per minute (GWPM) and net words per minute (NWPM).
3. To record personal progress on a keyboarding speed chart.
4. To analyze individual timings to determine the need to improve speed or accuracy in specific keyboarding skills.
5. To gain awareness of the purpose and importance of timed writings.

SPECTRUM RECORDS LIMITED
Minutes of Executive Committee Meeting
April 28, 19—

The regular bi-monthly Executive Committee meeting was held at 14:00 in the Boardroom. The meeting was called to order by Roberta Czimbalmos, Chairperson.

PRESENT & ABSENT	Roberta Czimbalmos, President, Adam W. Culliford, Vice-President, Marketing Michael A. P. MacLennan, Vice-President, Finance Catherine Paglialunga, Vice-President, Personnel Ginette L. Duke, Vice-President, Operations Laurie N. Dukovski, Manager of Personnel, was a guest of the meeting.
AGENDA	After discussion and UPON MOTION by Michael MacLennan, the Agenda was adopted as presented.
MINUTES	UPON MOTION by Ms Duke, the Minutes of the previous meeting were approved as presented.
COLLINGWOOD PROJECT	Adam Culliford reported on behalf of the Collingwood Project Committee. Two proposals to promote the Collingwood Project were presented. A small motel could be converted into a sales training centre at a cost of $270 000, or a new centre could be built at a cost of $1 million. The reason for considering a new site is the difficulty in accessing the motel. The Executive Committee will review both proposals before the next meeting.
BOND ISSUE	Michael MacLennan stated that the latest increase in interest rates has made the bond issue impossible at this time. This was discussed at some length, and the Committee decided to shelve the proposal for the time being.
JOB SHARING PROJECT	Laurie Dukovski reported that the pilot project begun in February appears to be very successful. There are now 38 staff members participating in this project and initial reports show that they are happy with the scheme. A formal report will be submitted after the six-month trial period.
NEW BUSINESS	There was no new business to discuss.
NEXT MEETING	The date and time of the next meeting was set for May 28, 19— at 10:00. It will be held in the Boardroom
ADJOURNMENT	The meeting was adjourned at 11:05.

_____
Chairperson

_____
Secretary

CONTENTS

Taking Timed Writings 81

Your Keyboarding Speed Chart 81

Formatting a Timed Writing 82

Calculating Your Speed 82

Timed Writings Assignments 83

    Time Management (SI 1.3) 84

    The Canadian Office Today (SI 1.4) 85

    Office Skills (SI 1.4) 86

    Computing Systems (SI 1.4) 87

    Mainframes (SI 1.4) 88

    Hardware and Software (SI 1.4) 89

    Assessing Advertising (SI 1.4) 90

    Getting Along (SI 1.4) 91

    Speaking and Listening Skills (SI 1.4) 92

    Your Work Station (SI 1.4) 93

    Initiative (SI 1.4) 94

    Proofreading Counts! (SI 1.4) 95

    Cost Benefit (SI 1.4) 96

    Good Consumerism (SI 1.4) 97

    Quantity vs. Quality (SI 1.4) 98

    Letter Writing (SI 1.4) 99

    Credit (SI 1.4) 101

    Computer Skills (SI 1.5) 103

ASSIGNMENT   Format these minutes using the spacing indicated.

10:35

↓ 13
J. & S. HOLDINGS LIMITED
Regular Monthly Meeting
February 20, 19--

↓ 3

The regular monthly meeting of J. & S. Holdings Limited was called to order at 14:30 by the President, Andrew Boychuk. J. Courtice was the recording secretary.

↓ 2

Present & Absent   Forty-three members of the Board were present and comprised a quorum.

↓ 2

Agenda   After discussion and UPON MOTION by Andrea Chronas, the Agenda was adopted as presented.

↓ 2

Minutes Approved   The minutes of the last regular meeting, held on January 24, 19— were read. Catherine Ruddell called attention to the fact that the name of the speaker was Amelia Howe, not Amelia Howell. Minutes were approved as corrected.

↓ 2

Treasurer's Report   The Treasurer reported that the present balance to be placed on the file is $12 340.

↓ 2

Special Committee Report   Eric McKenzie, Chair of the Grounds Improvement Committee, reported that a plan for landscaping the grounds had been submitted on February 6, by J. P. Cousteau Landscaping Co., and that planting ten trees and eight shrubs would cost $1950.

↓ 2

Eric asked for appropriation to cover the cost.

↓ 2

Alexandra Lawson moved that the SUM of $1950 BE APPROPRIATED. The motion was seconded by Vito Crisalli and was then passed.

↓ 2

Adjournment   The meeting was adjourned at 16:00.

↓ 4

_____
Secretary

The Business Letter (SI 1.5) 104

Computers and Job Loss (SI 1.5) 105

Planning Your Career (SI 1.5) 107

Computer Use Among Employees (SI 1.5) 108

Advertising (SI 1.5) 109

Microcomputers (SI 1.5) 110

Money (SI 1.5) 112

Electronic Filing and Retrieval (SI 1.5) 114

Electronic Mail/Messaging (SI 1.5) 115

Word Processing (SI 1.5) 117

Electronic Meetings and
Teleconferencing (SI 1.5) 118

Desktop Publishing (SI 1.5) 119

ASSIGNMENT 10:34 Compose an article for your school newspaper.

HOW TO FORMAT MINUTES OF A MEETING

Minutes of a business meeting are transcribed as a record of what was discussed during the meeting. Here are some guidelines for setting up minutes of a meeting:

1. Minutes are usually single spaced and paragraphs may be indented five or ten spaces (indents are optional).

2. Centre the date.

3. Centre and key the name of the company or the group in all caps.

4. Side headings (also called "marginal subject headings") are used to identify important aspects of the meeting.

5. A wide left margin should be set to allow for marginal subject headings (this also makes the minutes more readable and makes it easier to locate specific information).

6. Marginal subject headings have major words capitalized and are underscored.

7. Use a 60-character pica or a 70-character elite line.

8. Motions are typed in all capital letters.

9. Space is provided for the signature of the presiding officer or secretary (or both) at the bottom of the final page.

TAKING TIMED WRITINGS

Timed writings measure how many words per minute you keyboard. The total number of words you keyboard in a minute, not counting any errors, is called **Gross Words Per Minute (GWPM)**. When you subtract any errors you have made, you will have your speed in **Net Words Per Minute (NWPM)**. A timing may be one minute, three minutes, or five minutes in length. Begin with timings of one minute, and slowly work up to five-minute timings. (The syllabic intensity (SI) at the end of each Timed Writing is the number of syllables in each word divided by the number of five-stroke words in the Timed Writing.)

Timed writings do more than just help you increase your keyboarding speed. By analyzing each timing, you can determine whether you should spend more time on improving your accuracy. If you have more than one error per minute, you should concentrate on accuracy development; if your error rate is less than one error per minute, you should work on improving your speed. To improve your accuracy score, key at a slower rate. To increase your speed score, key at a slightly faster rate.

Setting personal goals is one of the keys to getting the most benefit from taking timed writings. Aim to do a few more words on each timing. When you reach your goal, set yourself a new one. Keep a record of your progress, noting both your GWPM and your NWPM.

YOUR KEYBOARDING SPEED CHART

To record your progress, prepare a keyboarding speed chart to keep in your keyboarding manual. File your chart at the beginning of the "Timed Writings" section in your manual. Here is a sample keyboarding speed chart. If you wish, use these headings in your chart.

MY KEYBOARDING SPEED CHART   NAME: _Jackie Saad_

DATE	LENGTH OF TIMING	GWPM	ERRORS	NWPM
Sept. 14	5 min	30	3	24

To make articles look more professional, however, use the following format:

1. Key the article using the same line length as in the publication (usually, 50-character pica/60-character elite).

2. Use double spacing.

3. Page 1 headings should include the number of lines and the number of characters per line.

4. Page 2 headings consist of the author's name, followed by a dash pivoted from the right margin on line seven.

APPLYING YOUR SKILLS—ARTICLES

ASSIGNMENT

10:33

Key a copy of this article, following the instructions given. If you are using a word processor or a computer, justify the right margin.

↓ 13

FOOD FOR THOUGHT
↓ 2
Eileen Roth
↓ 2
(16 lines, 60-character line)
↓ 3

5→ This year's nutrition campaign, "Food for Thought"

focussed on increasing students' awareness of nutritional foods.

Many activities were held during early November. Some

of these included Celebrity Cooks, Veg-O-Grams, and prizes

for nutritious lunches. A nutrition assembly was also held--

who can forget "Chuck the Chicken"? Daily specials were also

featured in the cafeteria, emphasizing health foods.

All in all, the campaign resulted in more "food

awareness" among students.

FORMATTING A TIMED WRITING

1. Set margins for a 70-character line.

2. Set the line space regulator on 2 for double spacing.

3. Set a tab stop five spaces in from the left margin, and indent the first line of each paragraph.

4. On line 6 from the top of the paper, key the following heading. Leave enough space after each item to insert the information when you have finished the timing. Triple space after the heading.

WORDS: GWPM: ERRORS: NWPM: NAME:

CALCULATING YOUR SPEED

1. Use the word count at the right of each timing to determine how many words you have keyed.

2. If you finish in the middle of a line, use the scale at the bottom of each timing to calculate how many extra words you have keyed. Add this count to the total number of words in the last completed line. The result will tell you the total number of words you have keyed in the time allowed. Enter this total to the right of Words in your heading.

3. To calculate Gross Words Per Minute, divide the total number of words you have keyed by the number of minutes allotted for the timing. Now record your GWPM score.

4. Proofread your timing carefully, and circle *all* errors. Record the total number of errors.

5. To calculate Net Words Per Minute, multiply the total number of errors by two, and subtract the result from your gross speed. Record your NWPM score.

Format these footnotes *correctly* on the appropriate pages.

FOOTNOTES

[1]Kathy Eisner: Telephone Tips (St. John's, Atlantic Press Ltd., 1981), p. 126.
[2]Steven S. Willoughby. Handling the Telephone. (Red Deer, Thorndike Printers Ltd., 1978), p. 79.
[3]Ibid., p. 85.
[4]Jeanet Hilburn. The Office Telephone (St. John's: Atlantic Press Ltd., 1980) p. 89.
[5]Dorothy McClean. The Wrong Number: (Windsor. Robertson Printing Co. Ltd. 1981) p. 107.

Format the report's Bibliography *correctly*.

BIBLIOGRAPHY

Eisner, Kathy, Telephone Tips, St. John's, Atlantic Press Ltd., 1981.

Hilburn, Jeanet, The Office Telephone, St. John's, Atlantic Press Ltd., 1980.

McClean, Dorothy, The Wrong Number, Windsor, Robertson Printing Co. Ltd., 1981.

Yarrow, Christinna, Office Procedures—The Right Way? Sackville, New Brunswick: Cameron Press, 1979.

Willoughby, Steven S. Handling the Telephone, Red Deer, Thorndike Printers Ltd., 1978.

Atkinson, Paul, Telecommunications, Toronto, Barry Printers, 1981.

HOW TO FORMAT ARTICLES

You may be asked to key an article for your school newspaper or for an organizations's newsletter or magazine. You can use the following format:

1. Key a 60-character pica line or a 70-character elite line.

2. Use double spacing.

3. Centre headings.

NOTE

In keyboarding, all words are considered to be an average of five strokes.

Sample Calculation

Suppose you keyed a total of 200 words in a five-minute timing:

· Total number of words in 5 minutes = 200

· GWPM = 200 ÷ 5 = 40

· Number of errors = 3

· NWPM = 40 − (3 × 2) = 34

WORDS:	GWPM:	ERRORS:	NWPM:	NAME:
100	20	3	14	*Grant Pastuk*

TIMED WRITINGS CHECKLIST

1. Check your posture. Good posture helps you to key with greater accuracy and speed.

2. Relax! You aren't running a race.

3. Keep your eyes on the copy. You lose time by looking up. You are also likely to leave out words, start again at the wrong place, and make many errors.

4. Strike the keys with sharp, clean strokes.

5. Key at a smooth, comfortable pace. Develop and maintain an even rhythm. *Don't* strike the keys very rapidly when you come to an easy combination of letters and then slow down on more difficult passages.

6. Never stop keying during a timed writing, even if you make many mistakes. Keep keying for practice and to develop endurance.

TIMED WRITINGS ASSIGNMENTS

PREVIEW WORDS

At the beginning of each timed writing you will find a number of preview words. Before you take a timed writing, key each preview word several times until you are comfortable with it.

These phones are becoming more and more popular
and are us easy to use as an ordinary phone --
simply dial.

Voice Mail

Voice mail is the computerized processing of a
speaker's voice to transmit a message. It involves
a special device obtained through your telephone
company. By pushing certain buttons, you can program
the transmission of a message to a particular
phone number, including special commands (e.g.,
time of call). The message is digitalized and
stored in the computer. If the person is not in,
the voice mail system will keep calling at regular
intervals.

Courtesy of Panasonic OA

ASSIGNMENT
3:1

TIME MANAGEMENT

PREVIEW WORDS
beneficial possible management approximately complete
handicrafts perhaps novel indicate don't preparatory laboratory
inclusive requires columns   words

Learning how to manage your time can be easy and beneficial. It 13
is possible to get everything that must be done finished and still 26
have time for things that you want to do. All it takes is a little 39
planning. 41

The first step in time management is to know what must be done 53
and approximately how long it will take to complete. The easiest way 66
to keep up with these items is to make a list. Begin the list with 79
the items which have to be done that you don't really like to do, such 93
as laundry, grocery shopping, house cleaning, and studying. 104

After listing these dreaded chores, add to the list the things 116
you want to do. Maybe you like to play tennis twice a week, or paint 129
every day, or work on handicrafts. Perhaps there is a new novel that 143
you want to read, or a movie you must see. Put everything you can 156
think of on the list. 160

Now, start at the top of the list and indicate how often (once a 172
week, etc.) each item must be done and approximately how long it will 185
take. Don't forget items such as school classes, keying practice, and 199
term papers that include preparatory work and library or laboratory 212
time. The more inclusive the list, the better you can manage your 225
time. 226

Once you have completed the "how often" and "how long" columns 238
for every item, make a "must do" list for each day of the week. Then, 251
put the lists in a place where you see them first thing each day, and 266
check off each item as you finish it. Do not forget to update your 279
master list and daily lists each week. Don't forget to include items 292
such as studying. In a matter of a few weeks, you should find that 304
you can do everything you must do and things you want to do, too. 317
Good time management requires planning. 325

. . . . 1 . . . . 2 . . . . 3 . . . . 4 . . . . 5 . . . . 6 . . . . 7 . . . . 8 . . . . 9 . . . .10 . . . .11 . . . .12 . . . .13 14

SI 1.4

<u>Person-to-Person</u> calls are made with the assistance of an operator, who connects the caller to a specific person, department, or extension.

<u>Conference calls</u> are arranged through the operator so that several people in different places can speak and be heard during the same call.

¶ <u>Credit Card calls</u> can be made by dialing the operator and giving your telephone credit card number. ¶ With a <u>Collect call</u>, the person or firm you are calling agrees to pay for the call.

ADVANCED BUSINESS TELECOMMUNICATIONS

Videoconferencing

Videoconferencing enables televised communication between groups of people in rooms equipped with special apparatus. One-way videoconferencing allows a group to see the person speaking. Questions can be addressed to the person through a special telephone hookup. Two-way videoconferencing allows both groups to see each other. This method of communicating saves travel time and expenses.

Cellular Phones

Cellular phones have replaced mobile car radiotelephones. A cellular phone tunes itself to the closest and strongest transmitter. If you are in Hamilton, for example, the cellular phone will tune itself in to Hamilton. However, if you are driving from Hamilton to Toronto, the phone will tune itself in to Toronto as you approach that city.

ASSIGNMENT   THE CANADIAN OFFICE TODAY

3:2

PREVIEW WORDS
clerical automated electronic equipment traditional monitors
similar appearances deceiving processing integrated operator words

During the last hundred years, when people talked about the	12
office, everyone knew that it was the place where the clerical work of	26
a firm was performed. No matter what kind of business——whether a car	40
wash or a bank——the office was still the site where the clerical work	54
was done. This was the place where the paperwork, such as the pay	67
cheques for the staff or statements for customers, was prepared.	80
Today a new word is added before the term "office." We now talk	94
about the "automated," "electronic," or "high tech" office. All of	108
these words describe an office where the most advanced equipment is	122
used. Does it look different from the old or traditional office?	135
The answer is based on the extent to which an office is using	148
computers. When you walk through the door, you will see video	161
displays on the desks. These are also called monitors or screens	174
because they look similar to what you have at home as part of your	187
television set. But these monitors will not reveal the amount of	200
computing power an office has. What you see is not what you get;	213
appearances can be deceiving.	219
An office can use the most advanced equipment, regardless of	231
the furniture. The question you must ask is what kind of central	244
processing unit, called the CPU, is being used. This is where you	257
will find the computing power of any system.	266
There are three major kinds of computing systems that a firm can	279
use. A quick look around the office will not reveal what type is	292
used. You must look carefully at the equipment, not the furniture.	305
A special desk used for computer equipment is called an integrated	319
work station. It is designed for operator comfort and does not show	333
the kind of system in use.	338

. . . . 1 . . . . 2 . . . . 3 . . . . 4 . . . . 5 . . . 6 . . . . 7 . . . . 8 . . . . 9 . . . .10 . . . .11 . . . .12 . . . .13 14

SI 1.4

ASSIGNMENT

10:32

Format the following multipage report complete with footnotes, Contents page, and Bibliography. The footnote and Bibliography information is found at the end of the report.

Telephone Information

Every one can use the telephone, or so they think—but using the phone properly is another matter altogether. The telephone is an important tool for communication. Here is some telephone information that might help you use the phone more efficiently.

OUTGOING and INCOMING CALLS

Placing a Call

When placing a call, speak clearly in a normal pleasant tone. Pronounce words distinctly. Speak directly into the mouthpiece of the phone and always be polite and helpful—you are representing your company! Get out any files you may need during the conversation, and write down in advance the key points you want to discuss. Make certain you have the correct number and dial it carefully. The number for directory assistance is 411. Let the telephone ring eight to ten times before hanging up. When some one answers the phone, state your name and the name of your company and ask for the department or person to whom you wish to speak. If the person is unavailable, leave a message with your name, your company's name, and your phone number.[1]

If you do not know a long distance number, you can still dial direct by dialing 1, then the area code, then 555-1212.[2] That area's operator will come on the line, and following your request, a recording will provide the number you want.

If a number has an INWATS (Incoming Wide Area Telecommunications Service) it means a caller can dial a business or company long distance without being charged.[3] To call an INWATS number, dial 1-800, then the number of the customer who has the INWATS service. A Zenith number is similar to an INWATS number, but this number requires the assistance of an operator.[4] To dial Direct for overseas calls, dial 011, then the country code, then the routing code plus the local number.[5]

Types of Calls

[5] A station-to-station call is made from one telephone number to another, with charges beginning as soon as someone answers.

ASSIGNMENT OFFICE SKILLS

3:3

PREVIEW WORDS
ceases improvement secretaries marketplace concise
understand dictionary investment mathematical budgets
bookkeeping management interruptions

words

Learning never ceases. Although you may have good office skills, 12
there is always room for improvement. Here are some office skills 25
that secretaries should have in today's marketplace. 35

Let us first look at business writing skills. What you write may 49
be read by many people, so the content must be concise and easy to 62
understand. Skilled writers answer the basic "who, what, when, and 75
where" questions when they write. A dictionary and style manual are 88
also a sound investment to aid you in writing. If you still find it 101
difficult to put your thoughts on paper, perhaps a writing course 114
would help. 116

How are your mathematical skills? It is important to know basic 129
mathematical skills if you work in an office. You may be required to 142
prepare budgets, perform bookkeeping jobs, and calculate percentages. 155
Knowledge of accounting is also very helpful. 164

A major office skill is time management. Do you complete the 177
most important job first? Make a list of things to do and set the 190
order of importance for each item on the list. Block your time so 203
each job is done at a certain time of day. You will not get much done 216
if you allow constant interruptions. If help is offered, use it. 229
Learning these time management skills will help you produce work you 243
can be proud of. 246

. . . . 1 . . . . 2 . . . . 3 . . . . 4 . . . . 5 . . . . 6 . . . . 7 . . . . 8 . . . . 9 . . . .10 . . . .11 . . . .12 . . . .13 14

SI 1.4

Know Yourself

Before you can plan a career, you must understand yourself. What activities do you like to do best? What do you least like to do? Do you enjoy being with others as part of a team, or do you prefer to work alone? Do you enjoy leadership roles? Do you enjoy travel and meeting new people? Do you enjoy the outdoors? Which gives you the most pleasure—working with your head or working with your hands?

Part of understanding yourself involves identifying your interests. For example, which of the following interests you most—cars, computers, or clothes? Matching your interests with a career often results in greater job satisfaction.[2]

The next step in career planning is to attempt to match your interests with existing occupations. All occupations in Canada have been divided among twenty-three groups by Employment and Immigration Canada. There are hundreds of separate occupations within each group, but all occupations within a group require roughly the same interests and abilities. These occupations are listed in booklets published by Employment and Immigration Canada.

Understanding yourself also involves recognizing your abilities and aptitudes. What are you good at? You might be interested in keyboarding, but unless you have the skill acquired in a keyboarding course, you will not be very fast at manipulating the keyboard. To be useful in a chosen career, aptitudes must be developed into skills.

---

[2]Margaret Berry, The Real You (Edmonton: Arnold Publishing Ltd., 1988), p. 43.

Courtesy of Panasonic OA

ASSIGNMENT
3:4
COMPUTING SYSTEMS

PREVIEW WORDS
microcomputers   minicomputers   microprocessor   standalone
diskette   technician   calculate   financial   chequebooks   exciting
efficient   words

There are three major kinds of computing systems that a firm can	13
use: microcomputers, minicomputers or a mainframe.	23
The smallest system is the micro, where the CPU is located on a	34
small chip called a microprocessor. This system is also called a	47
"standalone" because it is a complete system within itself. When you	61
look at a standalone, you will see a monitor or screen, the system	74
unit, and a keyboard. The system unit is a flat box and the screen	87
is placed on top of it. As you look at the system unit, you will see	101
the slots or openings, called the diskette drives. This is where the	115
operator inserts the program and the data diskettes.	125
You cannot see the microcomputer chip, but you do not need to.	138
You never have to use it, and if it has to be repaired, you must	151
call a technician.	155
The micro is also called the personal or home computer. Many	167
people find they can save a lot of time when they use it to calculate	181
their financial records, such as chequebooks and income tax. Children	195
love it because they can play exciting games that they can share with	209
their friends.	211
The computing power of a micro is based on the amount of memory	224
it has and the operating speed of the microprocessor. The computing	238
power will also determine the price you pay. The larger the memory	251
and the faster the speed, the higher the price. Standalones can be	264
joined together into a network so that many users can share the CPU.	278
Minicomputers are in the middle range of computing power. They	291
are larger than micros and smaller than mainframes. Many firms are	304
finding it more efficient to have a mini for each department, instead	318
of using a single mainframe.	324

. . . . 1 . . . . 2 . . . . 3 . . . . 4 . . . . 5 . . . . 6 . . . . 7 . . . . 8 . . . . 9 . . . .10 . . . .11 . . . .12 . . . .13 14

SI 1.4

APPLYING YOUR SKILLS—MULTIPAGE REPORTS WITH FOOTNOTES (OR ENDNOTES)

ASSIGNMENT

10:31

Format the following multipage report with footnotes. (You may use endnotes if you prefer.) Prepare a contents page and a bibliography as well.

CAREER PLANS

[Adapted from The World of Business: A Canadian Profile, 2d ed. Terry Murphy et al. Toronto: John Wiley & Sons Canada Limited, 1987, pp. 533-535.]

Now is the time to start thinking and planning for the future. Some high school students have a clear idea of the job or career that appeals to them from among the thousands of jobs available. Most students, however, have not yet made any career decisions.

Before you choose a career, examine your interests, abilities, and aptitudes, and decide what you want from a career.[1] Using these factors as guidelines, research the types of jobs that are available in your chosen field and the educational attainments required to obtain these jobs. And, finally, find out how to go about getting a job in the field you have selected.

Planning a Career

Activities and tasks that are planned are almost always more successful than those that are not planned! One of the most important tasks you face is deciding on a career. Effective planning involves gathering information both about yourself and about possible careers. A careful study of this information will help you to develop one or more career objectives. Once you understand your career objectives, you can then devise a plan for achieving your goals.

---

[1]Sarah Teillet, Career Choice (Montreal: Lifetime Press Ltd., 1988), p. 134.

ASSIGNMENT 3:5   MAINFRAMES

PREVIEW WORDS
mainframe organizations Seoul received government pension imagine millions developed supercomputers enormous access terminal identity

words

A mainframe is the biggest computer and is used by the largest	12
organizations.	15
A firm with its head office in Toronto uses one to maintain	27
contact with its branch offices in Hong Kong, Kobe and Seoul, through	40
a computer network. A message sent will be received within seconds.	53
The government uses a mainframe for storing and checking income tax	66
returns, and issuing all the pension cheques that are sent out each	79
month. Can you imagine how much computer memory is needed to keep	92
the records for the millions of Canadians receiving these benefits?	105
Mainframes were the first computers developed and all have huge	117
memories with very fast operating speeds. The biggest and fastest	130
mainframes are called supercomputers and their prime use is in	142
science. They can hold enormous amounts of data, such as the weather	156
in all the airports in the world at a given time, and they can process	170
more than a billion commands in one second. During the first flight	183
to the moon, television showed the operator using a supercomputer at	197
the launch station. He read the speed rates of the wind on the ground	211
and in the air from the monitor when he directed the liftoff.	222
Hundreds of people can access or use a mainframe at the same	234
time. They sit at a work station called a terminal. These terminals	248
can be located far from the building holding the CPU, and contact is	262
made through telephone lines.	267
The cost of using a mainframe is very high. To control access,	280
every user is given a name, called the computer identity or i.d.,	293
and a budget. The user then makes up a secret password to use with	307
the i.d. The computer system checks both the i.d. and the password	321
before the user is allowed to enter.	328

. . . . 1 . . . . 2 . . . . 3 . . . . 4 . . . . 5 . . . . 6 . . . . 7 . . . . 8 . . . . 9 . . . .10 . . . .11 . . . .12 . . . .13 14

SI 1.4

APPLYING YOUR SKILLS—ENDNOTES

On separate pieces of paper, format and key the following endnote assignments using correct endnote format.

ASSIGNMENT

10:29

ENDNOTES

[1]Auren Uris, 101 Of The Greatest Ideas In Management (Toronto: John Wiley & Sons Canada Limited, 1987), p. 45.

[2]Spencer R. Weart, Nuclear Fear (Cambridge: Harvard University Press, 1988), p. 92.

[3]Jim Wilkie, Metagama: A Journey From Lewis To The New World (Toronto: Doubleday Canada, 1988), p. 194.

ASSIGNMENT

10:30

ENDNOTES

[1]Richard Ellman, Oscar Wilde (New York: Viking, 1988), p. 500.

[2]Ibid., p. 545.

[3]Don Dickinson, Fighting the Upstream (Toronto: Oberon Press, 1988), p. 77.

ASSIGNMENT 3:6   *HARDWARE AND SOFTWARE*

PREVIEW WORDS
hardware software jargon options tractor whether whistles
different interchangeably application packages data base
spreadsheet graphics easy-to-read

words

	words
Does hardware last longer than software? Do we buy hardware in	14
a lumber yard? Can you squash software?	19
In the jargon of computer science, the term "hardware" refers to	33
the machines and parts that make up a system. The term "software"	46
refers to the program or set of commands to run the machines.	58
If you are thinking of buying a system, you are likely to ask	70
about the machines you need; that is, what kind of system unit,	83
monitor, and printer you should buy. These are the major parts of a	97
micro system, but there are other options, such as a mouse to use in	111
place of your keyboard, or a tractor feed for your printer.	123
But whether you buy a plain, basic system or one with "bells and	136
whistles," the hardware alone is totally useless. To operate the	149
hardware, you need software. The hardware is like an empty car	162
waiting for a driver to start the motor, shift gears, and step on the	176
gas before it can move. The driver in a computer system is the	189
software.	191
There are two major types of software. System software, called	204
the Disk Operating System, is a set of commands to control the	217
equipment. Most people shorten this to DOS. Different DOS commands	231
are written for different kinds of machines, and cannot be used	244
interchangeably. For this reason, computer equipment can be	256
classified by the kind of DOS required.	261
The other type of software is "application" programs. These are	275
packages you use to produce the product or output that you want from	289
your computer system. For example, if you want to write a book, use	303
word processing software. Use a data base to create forms or lists of	317
names. Spreadsheet programs are used for financial statements, while	331
graphics will produce easy-to-read charts.	339

`. . . .1 . . . .2 . . . .3 . . . .4 . . . .5 . . . 6 . . . .7 . . . .8 . . . .9 . . . .10 . . . .11 . . . .12 . . . .13 . . . .14`

SI 1.4

ENDNOTES

Endnotes provide the same information as footnotes, but all the information is printed on a separate page at the end of the report instead of on the pages containing the references.

1. Centre the title, "ENDNOTES," on line 13 in all capitals. A page number is not required.
2. Triple space after the title.
3. Use the same margins as were used for the report.
4. Indent five spaces for the first line of each entry.
5. Single space each endnote, and double space between each.
6. Use the same sequence and the same punctuation as used in footnotes.
7. Key each entry in the numerical order of the references in the text of the report.

↓ 13
ENDNOTES
↓ 3

5 → [1]Edith Fowke, <u>Red Rover, Red Rover: Children's Games Played in Canada</u> (Toronto: Doubleday Canada, 1988), p.100.
↓ 2
[2]Robin Skelton, <u>The Memoirs of a Literary Blockhead</u> (Toronto: Macmillan, 1988), p.267.

[3]<u>Ibid.</u>, p.301.

ASSIGNMENT 3:7   ASSESSING ADVERTISING

PREVIEW WORDS

messages combined personal commercial magazine factors
performance salespeople chief contribution responses lotion   words

While ads offer the feature of sending selling messages to future 12
buyers at a very low cost, there are some problems to be faced. Ads 26
should be combined with heavy doses of personal selling. First, there 39
is a time limit on the length of message that can be conveyed in a TV 53
commercial or magazine page. Even if it were possible to increase the 66
length of a commercial to half an hour, or to expand an ad to fill a 80
number of pages, it does not seem likely that future customers would 93
be that much more likely to buy. 99

Advertising is only one of a number of factors in the marketing 111
mix. For this reason, it is very hard to decide on its contribution 124
to the sales performance of a firm. Suppose a firm were to increase 137
its advertising costs, reduce the price of its products, and at the 150
same time hire five new salespeople. And suppose as well that this 163
firm then had an increase in sales. How much of this increase would 177
be due to advertising? to price? to sales effort? It is quite 189
possible that advertising was the chief factor, but it is also 201
possible that price or personal selling also were major reasons. 214
There is no way of knowing exactly the contribution made by any of 227
these items. 229

A further reason for problems in finding the effect of ads on 242
sales is that the responses of people to ads vary with their 254
changing wants and needs. For instance, the public responds more to 267
ads for suntan lotion in the summer than in the cold days of winter. 280

. . . . .1 . . . .2 . . . .3 . . . .4 . . . .5 . . . .6 . . . .7 . . . .8 . . . .9 . . . .10 . . . .11 . . . .12 . . . .13 14

SI 1.4

3 Timed Writings **90**

APPLYING YOUR SKILLS—FOOTNOTES

1. The two assignments below show the last line of text on a page, the divider line, and footnote information.

2. Format and key each assignment on a separate piece of paper.

3. If you are using a typewriter, estimate where to place the warning stop line, mark it in pencil, and roll the paper back two lines from this point to enter the last line of text, then the footnotes.

ASSIGNMENT

10:26

> **NOTE**
>
> A page of text does not have to end with a complete sentence.

It draws attention to the fact that we are more alike than

—————————

[1]Wilfred Cude, The Ph.D. Trap (West Bay: Medicine Label Press, 1988), p. 50.
[2]Ibid., p. 81.
[3]Neil K. Besner, The Light of Imagination: Mavis Gallant's Fiction (Vancouver: The University of British Columbia Press, 1988), p. 10.

ASSIGNMENT

10:27

and she finally realized that she could only count on herself.

—————————

[1]Ishmael Baksh, Black Light (St. John's: Jesperson Press Ltd., 1988), p. 22.
[2]Ibid., p. 69.

ASSIGNMENT

10:28

The information in the following footnotes is out of order. Arrange the information appropriately, and key the assignment using the correct footnote format.

[1]A Basket Of Apples (Toronto: McClelland & Stewart, 1988), p. 44. Shirley Faessier.
[2]p. 59., Ibid.
[3]p. 84. R. C. Grogin, The Bergsonian Controversy in France (Calgary: The University of Calgary Press, 1988).

PREVIEW WORDS
vital   element   reflected   enormous   criticism   understanding
businesslike   qualities   evaluated   assigned   organized   convictions
responsibility   words

Getting along is a vital element of your job. It is not   12

necessary to "like" someone in order to get along with the people with 25

whom you work. The golden rule "Do unto others as you would   36

have them do unto you" applies no matter what they are like.   48

How others "see" you will be reflected in your ability to get   60

ahead. Learn to control your temper if you are given to outbursts, or 73

are under an enormous amount of stress. Can you accept criticism and 87

still do your job? Even though it may be easier said than done--stop 100

and think before you react.   105

Are you aware of how you get along with others? Don't place   117

people in "categories," no matter what walk of life they are from. 130

Are you understanding? Be pleasant and businesslike, and keep in mind 143

you reflect your company on all occasions.   151

If your objective at work is to stand out from the crowd, you   163

should get ahead quickly. What qualities will you need to develop in 177

order to "stand out"?   180

Every day you will be evaluated on how well you accept your   193

assignments or new work assigned to you. If you are an organized 206

person, you should have no trouble in performing them. By all means 219

keep calm and stick up for your convictions; but taking on added   232

responsibility will be looked upon as an asset by your supervisors. 245

. . . . 1 . . . . 2 . . . . 3 . . . . 4 . . . . 5 . . . . 6 . . . . 7 . . . . 8 . . . . 9 . . . .10 . . . .11 . . . .12 . . . .13 14

SI 1.4

10. If two or more consecutive footnotes refer to different works by the same author, do not repeat the author's name in the second and subsequent footnotes. Instead, key ten hyphens, followed by a period; then skip two spaces and key the title. (See the sample footnotes in the following section.)

REPORTS WITH SAMPLE FOOTNOTES

↓13

FACSIMILE TRANSMISSION

↓ 3

5 → Electronic facsimile systems play an important role in office environments, yielding substantial cost savings to users. Facsimile systems enable users to send duplicates of important documents and information around the world. Using the latest technology, pages can be transmitted vast distances in under one minute.[1]

Facsimile utilizes scanning for hard-copy communication, in which dark areas on the page are translated into electronic impulses of various amplitudes or frequencies.[2]

Office workers and business people use facsimile transmission to help expedite their documents. Many people find it easier and quicker than conventional business communications. Users find that electronic facsimile transmission has several advantages over the postal system, telephone message services, and even teleprinters.

Faxpack service enables users to communicate between a variety of previously incompatible machines.[3]

_____

↓ 1

↓ 2

5 → [1]Robert L. Schweiger, "Electronic Facsimile Users Find it Quick, Affordable," The Office, January 1988, p.159.

↓ 2

[2]"Facsimile Equipment Services: The Real Communication Link," The Office, July 1979, p.94.

↓ 2

[3]"Facsimile Transmission at a Stamp's Cost," The Office, May, 1988, p.58.

SPEAKING AND LISTENING SKILLS

PREVIEW WORDS
Jessica salient hesitant communicate language requisite
detrimental listening concentrate questions   words

Jessica had some salient comments to contribute to her staff   12

meeting; however, she was too hesitant to make any contribution. Many   25

people are too shy to speak in front of a group.   35

How can you communicate good ideas if you do not speak well?   47

Speaking well involves a good command of language, good diction, and   60

the requisite self-confidence to actually make a contribution.   72

Your body language—your posture and gestures—also conveys your   84

thoughts. Look directly into the eyes of the person to whom you are   97

speaking. Smile and nod. Become aware of any detrimental traits you   111

possess and attempt to correct them.   118

Do you have good listening skills? If you answered "no," you   130

should attempt to improve them. The key here is to concentrate on   143

what is being said. Take notes if it helps, and don't interrupt until 157

the speaker is finished. Wait for the complete message, then ask   169

questions if anything remains unclear.   176

If you still have problems with communications, perhaps a course   188

in public speaking would be wise. The others in the class will be   201

there for the same reason. It is likely that in your job you will   214

have to speak in front of one or more persons, and to groups. The   227

more you do it, the easier it gets.   234

. . . . 1 . . . . 2 . . . . 3 . . . . 4 . . . . 5 . . . . 6 . . . . 7 . . . . 8 . . . . 9 . . . .10 . . . .11 . . . .12 . . . .13 14

SI 1.4

b) Place a light pencil line at the right side of the paper as the warning stop line.

[1] Freelance Editors' Association of Canada, *Editing Canadian English* (Vancouver: Douglas & McIntyre Ltd., 1987), p. 140.

You may also prepare a Report Guidesheet with lines ruled at three-line intervals. By placing this sheet behind the paper on which you are keying, you can see exactly how much space you have for the footnotes. Note: If you are using a word processor or microcomputer, estimate mathematically on which line to end the text. For example, if there are two footnotes, allow three lines for each, for a total of six lines. Add the six lines to the top and bottom margin allowances (6 + 6 + 6 = 18), and subtract from 66, the number of lines on the page (66 − 18 = 48). Stop keying the text when you reach line 48. Some word processing equipment will position the text automatically.

3. When you come to the warning stop line, *single space*, and at the left margin, separate the text from the footnote information by keying a 20-character line of underscores. This is called the *divider line*. Erase the stop line when you are finished.

4. Double space following the divider line.

5. Indent the first line of each footnote *five* spaces.

6. Enter each footnote in the following order:

   • Footnote number (superscript or raised number);

   • Author's first name or initials and author's surname, followed by a comma;

   • Name of publication, underscored;

   • Opening parenthesis, followed by place of publication, a colon, name of publisher, a comma, year of publication, and closing parenthesis, followed by a comma;

   • The page reference, followed by a period.

7. Single space each footnote; leave a double space between footnotes.

8. The expression *ibid.* followed by a page number may be used to indicate that the material is taken from the source cited in the preceding footnote.

9. The expression *op. cit.* following the author's last name and followed by a page number, may be used to refer to material by that author noted in a previous footnote.

ASSIGNMENT YOUR WORK STATION

3:10

PREVIEW WORDS

practical material regularly misplaced finished doubly friction
equipment collected difficult quality surroundings accident   words

Here are some practical hints about what you should do to keep a   12

neat and tidy work station.   17

There should be a specific place for the material or equipment   29

that you use regularly. You should not have to spend a lot of time   42

looking for misplaced supplies or equipment, or borrowing supplies   55

from other workers because you can't find yours.   64

When you have finished using something, get into the habit of   76

putting it back in its place. This will make it easier to find things   89

when you need them, and it only takes a second to do. This habit is   103

doubly important when several people share the same materials and   116

supplies. Not returning borrowed items wastes time and may lead to   129

friction between you and co-workers.   136

Before you leave each night, get into the habit of cleaning up   148

your work area. Put your equipment back where it belongs, file your   161

papers, and throw away any junk that has collected throughout the day.   175

Junk includes things such as scraps of materials, paper, or coffee   188

cups.   189

It is difficult to produce good quality work in dirty or untidy   201

surroundings. When your work station is messy, you may not notice   214

hidden pens, glue, or half-empty coffee cups until they blot your   227

neatly finished work. You will find that in the end it saves more   240

time to take a few minutes to tidy up than to spend time later to   253

clean up after an accident.   258

`. . . .1. . . .2. . . .3. . . .4. . . .5. . . .6. . . .7. . . .8. . . .9. . . .10. . . .11. . . .12. . . .13. . . .14`

SI 1.4

6. Remember to wrap each article separately. When required, "FRAGILE" stickers should be placed above the address and below the postage on the outside of the parcel (parcels can only be insured for loss, not damage).

7. Place the article in the insert and cover with packing material.

Addressing

The address should be bold, legible, and complete, with Postal Code included. Place the forwarding address and the return address on two sides of the parcel. Note that both addresses and a list of contents should be placed inside the parcel. For correct postage, customs declaration forms, or information concerning parcels destined for other countries, take the parcel to your local post office.

FOOTNOTES

Footnotes identify the sources of quoted material in a report. There are many different styles of footnotes, but the following format is widely used.[1]

1. Footnotes are numbered consecutively and are indicated in the text of a report by superscripts, or raised numbers.

2. Space must be left at the bottom of a page to accommodate the footnotes on that page. As a guide to indicate the last line to be keyed on a page, use a warning stop line. To determine where the warning stop line should be:

   a) Roll your paper up from the bottom margin (which is 2.5 cm or six lines from the bottom of the paper) three lines for each footnote on the page.

ASSIGNMENT INITIATIVE

3:11

PREVIEW WORDS
initiative something direction valuable workforce organizations
potential demonstrate educational attempting additional

words

Initiative means doing what should be done without being told to	12
do it. When you initiate something, it means that you start it. If	26
you are a person who comes up with a new idea, who solves small	38
problems on the job with no prompting or help or direction, or who can	52
be trusted to work on your own, then you are showing initiative.	65
Initiative is a very valuable trait for anyone in the workforce,	77
both on the job and outside the job, i.e., at home, at school, or in	86
social or church organizations. The person who shows initiative does	94
better work and finds the job or task at hand more enjoyable than the	107
individual who must be led and directed at all times. The person who	121
shows initiative is the one most likely to have the potential to be	134
able to advance in the company or organization.	143
Here are some other ways that you can demonstrate initiative in	155
work or educational settings. Show a willingness to work. Don't just	169
put in your time. You should do extra work when needed, or put in	182
extra time if it will get the work done. Offer to help others in	195
their work if you have the time, and help is needed. Maybe you can	208
come up with new and better ways of getting the job done.	219
Initiative starts with knowing what your job is and what you are	233
supposed to do. There is no point in attempting additional work until	246
you are doing your regular tasks well.	254

`. . . .1 . . . .2 . . . .3 . . . .4 . . . .5 . . . .6 . . . .7 . . . .8 . . . .9 . . . .10 . . . .11 . . . .12 . . . .13 . . . .14`

SI 1.4

Closing an Interview

The interviewer will usually signal that the interview has come to an end. This signal can be a quick look at the clock, or a question such as, "Is there anything more you would like to know about the job?" Be prepared to ask any final questions you may have. Then make a polite departure (shake hands) and be sure to take all your belongings with you.

ASSIGNMENT

10:25

Format the following multipage report. If you wish, prepare a Contents page.

THE PROPER PACKAGING OF ITEMS FOR MAILING

Whether you are mailing a birthday gift or sending out printed forms and pamphlets to a business firm, it is helpful to know the basic techniques of sending packages or printed matter through the mail.

Printed Matter and Fragile Objects

1. Items packed together in one container should be individually wrapped.
2. Cards, brochures, and other printed materials should be mailed in sturdy envelopes.
3. Printed forms, manuscripts, booklets, and other paper items should be bundled before being placed in a shipping package or container.
4. Bundles of paper should be tied securely before being packed for shipping.
5. Fragile articles require a strong container and adequate interior cushioning (an insert should be set inside the carton).

3:12

PREVIEW WORDS
computer   processing   garbage   abbreviated   microbiologist
lecture wonderful preformed avoided carefully entirely   words

Most people feel that the computer and word processing machines	12
used in the office today are the answer to any quality problems that	25
they may have in their office. But this is wrong because, as the	38
saying goes, "where ever garbage goes in, garbage comes out." (You	51
have most likely heard this saying in the abbreviated phrase, "garbage	64
in, garbage out.")	68
Here is an example of how quality problems are not solved with	80
the use of the new machines. This is the case of a microbiologist who	93
wrote a note in which she discussed her lecture on how a meat product	105
could be "pre-formed" before it was baked. She wrote out the text by	122
hand for a WP operator. In her long hand notes she wrote "pre-formed"	135
as "preformed" (without the hyphen). After the notes had been	148
prepared, she noticed that the word "pre-formed" had been spelled as	162
"performed." When she went back to the WP operator to see how this	175
could happen on their wonderful new word processing system, she found	189
that by not placing a hyphen between "pre-" and "formed," the system's	202
spelling-checking software package corrected her spelling of "pre-	215
formed" to "performed," since there was no such word as "preformed" in	229
the system. This type of error can easily be avoided if humans take	241
the time to proofread and check work carefully, and don't rely	253
entirely on machines to do the perfect job.	261

. . . . 1 . . . . 2 . . . . 3 . . . . 4 . . . . 5 . . . . 6 . . . . 7 . . . 8 . . . 9 . . . .10 . . . .11 . . . .12 . . . .13 14

SI 1.4

ASSIGNMENT 10:24

Format this multipage report. If you wish, prepare a Contents page and a Bibliography. (Reference used: *Business Etiquette Today*, by Jacqueline Dunckel. Vancouver: Self Counsel Press, 1987.)

THE JOB INTERVIEW

The job interview is a discussion between the employer and the applicant. Its purpose is to determine if the applicant is the right person for the job, and if the job is the right one for the applicant. Usually, the employer phones the applicant to arrange a suitable time and place for the interview.

Creating a Good Impression

It is essential that you be on time for the interview. Promptness indicates reliability. Because the interview is your first meeting with the employer, it is important to create a favourable first impression. You should be courteous, neat, and well-groomed, and you should exhibit good posture.

What to Bring With You

It is a good idea to bring along an extra copy of your resumé, although you should be thoroughly familiar with the information it contains. You can be sure the interviewer will ask detailed questions about it. It is also useful to bring samples of your work or projects, if they relate to the particular job you are applying for. Also, bring along any reference letters that you did not include in your original application.

The Interview

During the interview, you will be asked many questions. The interviewer's first questions usually pertain to the information in your resumé. Questions then shift to information about you and why you would like the job. Be prepared for questions such as, "Tell me about yourself" or "Why do you want this job?"

Page 2

Before your interview, try to find out some basic information about the company. What does it sell? What services does it offer? Who are its customers? You should also know the name and title of the interviewer. Use his or her name during the interview. The best rule to follow is "Be positive — and be prepared."

ASSIGNMENT   COST BENEFIT

3:13

PREVIEW WORDS
electric answer question technology can't employee either
efficiency especially repetitive deviates probably   words

When will a company replace its electric machines with computers?	14
Before we answer this question, we need to understand that a firm	27
will not buy new machines just because they can provide a higher level	41
of technology. Unless it is replacing a machine that can't be fixed,	55
the "cost benefit" must be proven.	62
The cost benefit is the amount of money that can be saved when	74
the purchase of a new machine allows an employee to work more	86
efficiently. In other words, when a worker uses a computer, the work	100
will be done better — either faster or more accurately. The savings	114
in time means that this worker can produce more at the same cost to a	128
firm.	129
Computers can be used to raise the efficiency of office employees	142
for certain types of work. They cannot be used for all the tasks that	156
are carried out each day on the job, especially those that require	169
decision–making and reasoning. A computer is excellent for repetitive	183
work, that is, work that is done over and over again. The same	196
applies to tasks where the same process, which should not be changed	210
in any way, is used. This process can be stored into computer memory.	224
The computer does this kind of work more efficiently than a human	238
worker for two reasons. It can operate at a higher speed than a	251
human. It never deviates or strays from the process written in the	264
program. For example, if you ask a human to add two numbers ten	277
times, you are likely to get ten correct answers. But if you ask the	291
person to add the number ten thousand times, you will probably get	304
some wrong answers because a human is likely to get tired or stop	317
paying attention to the task. Computers never get tired and will	330
continue to operate at very high speed without errors.	341

. . . . 1 . . . . 2 . . . . 3 . . . . 4 . . . . 5 . . . . 6 . . . . 7 . . . . 8 . . . . 9 . . . .10 . . . .11 . . . .12 . . . .13 14

SI 1.4

Format this multipage report attractively.

EFFECTIVE WORK HABITS

Leigh was depressed. She had been assigned a presentation on the topic "Effective Work Habits and Businesslike Attitudes," but she had not planned her research and preparatory time properly. As a result, her presentation was boring and disorganized.

Evaluation

Upon reading her classmates' unfavourable evaluation of her presentation, Leigh realized she could improve her performance in future by changing her attitudes about homework and by learning how to manage her time better.

Two weeks later, Leigh was given an assignment in her Information Processing course. The topic was "How to Improve One's Self-image." This time, Leigh was determined not to let things slide beyond her control. She started working on this assignment as soon as she received it.

Implementation

First, Leigh made a list of the tasks comprising the assignment. She listed a trip to the library, a talk with a guidance counsellor, and a survey of some of her friends. These tasks represented the starting point of what would become a well-organized and interesting report.

Next, Leigh drew up a work schedule to help her plan her time efficiently. When it was time to start writing her report, Leigh felt confident. She had effectively focussed her resources, time, and energy in preparing her presentation. When she received a mark of 85 per cent on her project, Leigh's attempt to maintain a positive attitude and practise good work habits was reinforced.

ASSIGNMENT   GOOD CONSUMERISM

3:14

words

No matter what your age, sex, or colour, you are a consumer 12
because you purchase products and use services. What have you bought 26
or used today? Bus tickets to get to school? A snack or lunch? Some 40
new clothes? When you spend your money, you like to get value. To do 54
this you must plan and spend wisely. You need to develop specific 67
attributes to become a competent consumer, for example, be aware of 80
your inherent values and goals; make sound decisions; scrupulously 92
plan your purchases before making them; and use excellent shopping 104
skills. 105

Whatever you decide you desire from life guides you in setting 117
your goals. Goals are something you work to achieve. They may be 130
short-term and easy to meet in a short period of time; or long-term, 143
to be met later in time. As you grow older, your goals change. 153

Youngsters have few choices to make in life, and they have very 167
little or no money to spend upon these choices. Teenagers have many 180
more choices to make, and often have sums of money to buy things. 193
Because teens have not established buying patterns yet and are free to 206
spend most of their money as they want, advertisements are usually 219
designed with the ideal goal of attracting the teenage market. 231

Many people need to know more about buying wisely. First, you 243
decide exactly what you want to purchase before you shop. If you have 257
no plan, you are susceptible to buying useless products. This is 270
called impulse buying. Only if you persevere in using lists will you 283
be successful in avoiding your natural tendency to follow your 295
impulses. Do not window shop, and only carry as much money as you 308
need to buy the items on your list. It is also wise to leave your 321
credit cards at home. Be firm and resist buying goods just because 334
you think you would like to have them. 341

. . . . 1 . . . . 2 . . . . 3 . . . . 4 . . . . 5 . . . . 6 . . . . 7 . . . . 8 . . . . 9 . . . .10. . . .11. . . .12. . . .13. . . .14

SI 1.4

Page Numbers   38

↓ 2

5 → The first page of a multipage report is not numbered. Page 2, and   39

all subsequent pages, begin seven lines from the top of the page. The   40

page number is centred, or pivoted from the right margin. Triple space   41

after the page number.

5 → On a personal computer or word processor, it is easy to continue   42

keyboarding screen after screen (page after page) of material. This   43

is called repagination. As the cursor moves to the end of the page on   44

the screen, it merely flips over into a new page. Repagination fills   45

out pages that are too short, and shortens pages that are too long.   46

If you are using a computer or word processor, consult your operator's   47

manual.

↓ 3

Quoted Material   48

↓ 2

5 → For quoted material of less than four lines, use quotation marks,   49

and include the quoted material in the body of the paragraph. Quotations 50

of four lines or more are single spaced and indented five spaces from   51

both the right and left margins. Quotation marks are not used.   52

ASSIGNMENT
3:15
QUANTITY VS. QUALITY

PREVIEW WORDS
occupation complete documents employee society deleterious
fallacies quantities quality despite essential inevitably eliminate words

One of the worst ways of determining the effectiveness of a   12
person in an occupation is to look at how much that person has done,   25
for example, many people can complete "X" number of pages of documents 38
in a day. Many times, this is the only method an employer uses to   51
determine the value of an employee to the firm. As this is such a   64
widespread way of finding out the value of the work of an employee,   77
the employee often feels that this is the only way of determining   90
his/her worth to the employer and to the whole society.   100

But the idea of getting work done in volume is one of the more   112
deleterious fallacies that crop up every day in each of our lives.   125
Often, a large quantity of work that is done is not of such great   138
benefit to the employer as is generally supposed by both the person   151
doing the work, and the person for whom the work is done. This is due 164
to the fact that in our great rush to do huge quantities of work, the 177
quality of the work often suffers to the extent that the work itself 190
is of no use to the employer, despite the fact that it was done at a 203
very fast rate.   206

This is the essential element of the debate concerning quantity   218
versus quality: where do you draw the line in trying to eliminate the 232
errors that each of us imperfect humans is inevitably going to commit? 245

If you use the quantity side of the debate and get vast amounts   259
of work done that is of no use to anyone, you know that you will   272
eventually have to change your ways of doing things. So why not   285
examine each task you perform to try to eliminate as many errors as   298
possible so that the work you do is really finished and ready for use 311
instead of being just done?   316

. . . . .1. . . . .2. . . . .3. . . . .4. . . . .5. . . . .6. . . .7. . . . .8. . . . .9. . . . .10. . . . .11. . . . .12. . . . .13. 14

SI 1.4

5 → Leave at least six blank lines at the bottom of each page   19
(again, in order to give the page a balanced look). So you will   20
know when to stop keying, place a light pencil mark approximately   21
six lines from the bottom right-hand side of the page. Use this as   22
your "warning line". Erase this line when the report is completed.   23

5 → A Report Guidesheet outlining the 66 lines on a page, and where   24
the main title, margins, warning line, and second page heading occur   25
can be drawn up and used as a backing sheet. On electronic machines   26
or word processors, set the automatic page end for six lines from the   27
bottom.

5 → Leave at least two lines of a paragraph at the bottom of a page   28
and two lines at the top of the next page. Do not divide the last   29
word on a page.

↓ 3

The Title and Subtitles   30

↓ 2

5 → Centre and key the title on line 13. Triple space after the title.₃₁
If there is a subtitle, however, double space after the title. Centre   32
the subtitle horizontally, and capitalize the first and main words.   33
Subtitles of more than one line are single spaced. Triple space after   34
the subtitle, before the body.   35

↓ 3

5 → Triple space before a side heading, and double space after it.   36
Side headings begin at the left margin and are underscored.   37

ASSIGNMENT   LETTER WRITING

3:16

PREVIEW WORDS
attempted acquired organized outline communicate concepts
dictionary personal informal attempt salutation paragraphs
complimentary question signature   words

Have you ever attempted to compose a letter? To write letters   12

well requires special skills--skills that can be acquired by educating 25

yourself.   27

Letters must be well organized. Why are you writing this letter? 39

What is your purpose? What point do you want to make? What factual   52

content will be required to prepare the letter? Have these facts with 66

you when you write.   69

Prepare a rough outline of what you want to communicate. Put   81

down key words and concepts that you want to make obvious. Use easy-   94

to-understand words. Have a dictionary or word finder near you to   107

check the spelling of unfamiliar words. Once a rough draft of a   120

letter is completed, it is time to key it properly.   130

A personal letter is one written from one friend to another.   143

Because a personal letter is informal, it can be written as if you   156

were talking to a friend.   161

When typing a personal letter, first attempt to determine how   173

much you want to say. If you have a lot to talk about, maybe the   186

letter will take up more than one page. If you don't have a lot to   199

say, perhaps you will want to double space the body so the letter   212

will look good on the page. The usual line length for letters is a   225

60-character line.   228

(continued on next page)

APPLYING YOUR SKILLS—MULTIPAGE REPORTS

ASSIGNMENT 10:22

Format the following multipage report using the spacing indicated. If you wish, include a Contents page and use this text as a Bibliography entry.

↓ 13

MULTIPAGE BUSINESS REPORTS 1

↓ 3

5 → In business, a report can be either formal or informal in tone. 2

The purpose of a report is to present factual information on a particular 3

subject or subjects. Usually, one or more rough copies (drafts) will 4

be keyed before a report is presented in its final form. 5

5 → An informal report might consist of a letter, a memorandum, or 6

an outline. Formal reports, however, are keyed according to the 7

following guidelines.

↓ 3

HOW TO FORMAT A FORMAL BUSINESS REPORT 8

↓ 3

Spacing and Tab Stops 9

↓ 2

5 → The body of the report is usually double spaced. One tab stop is 10

set for the standard paragraph indentation of five spaces, and one tab 11

is set at the centre point, for centering lines and page numbers, where 12

appropriate. If you wish to pivot the page number on succeeding pages, 13

you may set a tab stop seven spaces from the right margin. 14

↓ 3

Margins

↓ 2

Warning line: Approx. 2.5 cm; erase when paper is removed

5 → Unbound and topbound reports are keyed on a 60-character pica line 15

and a 70-character elite line. 16

5 → If the report is bound at the left side, set the left margin in 17

an extra five spaces. The right remains the same. 18

Begin keying your address on line 12, single spacing between your 240
street address, your city, province, your postal code, and the current 254
date. Do not use an inside address in a personal letter. Depending 267
on the length of the letter, drop about six lines after the date to 280
key the salutation. If the letter is short, drop more; if long, less. 294

Always double space before and after the salutation, between 306
paragraphs, and between the body and the complimentary closing. Never 319
key your name in a personal letter; always sign it. 329

A personal—business letter is one that you may also use often. 341
It is the form to use when writing to a company or firm with a 353
question or complaint. 357

A personal—business letter contains an inside address, that is, 369
the name and address of the person or company to whom the letter is 382
being sent. This is keyed at the left margin, below the return 395
address. In this kind of letter, your name is keyed below the 407
signature. Other parts of the letter are keyed in the same form as a 420
personal letter. 423

. . . . 1 . . . . 2 . . . . 3 . . . . 4 . . . . 5 . . . . 6 . . . . 7 . . . . 8 . . . . 9 . . . .10 . . . .11 . . . .12 . . . .13 14

SI 1.4

9. Leave at least six blank lines at the bottom of each page (in order to give the page a balanced look, like a picture in a frame). So you will know when to stop keying, place a light pencil mark approximately six lines from the bottom right-hand side of the page. Use this as your "warning line." Erase this line when the report is completed. (You can also draw up a Report Guidesheet, outlining the 66 lines on a page, and where the main title, margins, warning line, and second page heading occur; you can use this as a backing sheet. On electronic machines or word processors, set the automatic page end for six lines from the bottom.

10. On a personal computer or word processor, it is easy to continue keying screen after screen (page after page) of material. As the cursor moves to the end of the screen page, it simply flips over into a new page. Check your operator's manual.

11. Leave at least two lines of paragraph at the bottom of a page and two lines at the top of the next page. Do not divide the last word on a page.

12. The first page of a multipage report is not numbered.

13. Page 2, and all subsequent pages, begin seven lines from the top of the page. The page number is centered or placed at the right margin. Triple space after the page number.

ASSIGNMENT CREDIT

3:17

PREVIEW WORDS
recognize pressure materialistic displays majority circumstances payments receive inflation bankrupt destroyed spendthrift unemployment desperate financial emergencies reminder pressing

words

Nobody seems to recognize fully the huge pressure placed on the   12
consumer by our materialistic society to go into debt.   23

Ads in all media and store displays urge us to buy. Ads for easy   36
credit urge us to borrow in order to buy. When people do use credit-- 50
charge accounts or cash loans--most never think that it will be hard 63
to meet the credit payments.   68

No doubt there are a few who know they will be unable to pay.   80
The large majority, however, pay their debts. But there are times   93
when through circumstances beyond her control, a person cannot meet 106
payments. Perhaps she has lost her job. Perhaps she is ill and   119
doesn't receive sick pay because she is not in a unionized job.   131
Perhaps inflation is eating away more of her income than before.   143

A report on the causes of wage earners going bankrupt in Canada   155
has destroyed the myth that the debtor is a lazy, careless,   167
spendthrift who drinks to excess. In 71 per cent of the cases, the 180
causes were found to be problems beyond a debtor's control--poor   193
health, medical bills of dependents, and unemployment. In 26 per cent 206
of the cases, the causes were money mismanagement, and in the rest, 219
marriage problems.   222

(continued on next page)

Format this Bibliography attractively.
Note: The list is not in alphabetical order.

BIBLIOGRAPHY

Murphy, Terry et al. *The World of Business: A Canadian Profile*. 2d ed. Toronto: John Wiley & Sons Canada Limited, 1987.

Misener, Judi and Sandra Steele. *The Business of English*. Toronto: Oxford University Press, 1986.

Culliford, Sheila Geller and Susan MacLennan. *The Business of Keyboarding*. 2d ed. Toronto: John Wiley & Sons Canada Limited, 1989.

MULTIPAGE REPORTS

1. Centre and key the title on line 13. Triple space after the title.

2. Double space the body of the report.

3. Use a 60-character pica line or a 70-character elite line, if the report is unbound. If it is bound at the left side, set the left margin in an extra five spaces. The right margin remains the same.

4. Indent five spaces at the beginning of each paragraph except the first.

5. Main headings are centered and keyed in all caps. Triple space before and after main headings.

6. Triple space before a side heading and double space after it. Side headings begin at the left margin and are underscored.

7. For quoted material of less than four lines, use quotation marks, and include the quote in the body of the paragraph.

8. Quotations of four lines or more are single spaced and indented five spaces from both the right and left margins. Quotation marks are not used.

Credit is so easy to get from so many sources that its supply   235

sometimes seems endless--but when we are really in need and at the   248

desperate stage, it may not be so endless. In fact, it may be very   261

hard to get. So it is necessary to have a plan for financial   273

emergencies--such as when we may have to borrow money to make payments 286

on money we borrowed earlier.   292

What happens when people don't pay their bills? After a month, a   305

reminder notice, which often begins, "A friendly reminder," is sent. 318

If the customer still does not pay, he receives a second notice which 331

may suggest that he get in touch with the creditors and let them know 343

if he is having problems. Then, new plans may be worked out. If   356

payment still is not made, further notices are sent until a final   369

demand for payment is made. Each notice will be a little more   381

pressing and a little less friendly. After a six-month period without 394

payment, such debts are called "bad debts." Finally, the account may 408

be referred to a collection agency, and the customer may be taken to 421

court to force him to pay.   426

. . . .1 . . . .2 . . . .3 . . . .4 . . . .5 . . . 6 . . . .7 . . . .8 . . . .9 . . . .10 . . . .11 . . . .12 . . . .13 14

SI 1.4

APPLYING YOUR SKILLS—THE BIBLIOGRAPHY

ASSIGNMENT
10:19

Format this Bibliography using the spacing indicated.

↓ 13
BIBLIOGRAPHY
↓ 3

5 →   Dohaney, M. T. The Corrigan Women. Toronto: Ragweed Press, 1988.
↓ 2
Rees, Ronald. New and Naked Land. Saskatoon: Western Producer Prairie Books, 1988.
↓ 2
Skvorecky, Josef. Talkin' Moscow Blues. Toronto: Lester & Orpen Dennys, 1988.

ASSIGNMENT
10:20

Format this Bibliography attractively.

> **NOTE**
>
> The expression *et al.* following the name of an author means "and others." It is keyed in lower case and is underscored.

BIBLIOGRAPHY

Anderson, Ruth T. et al. The Administrative Secretary: Resource. New York: McGraw-Hill Book Co., 1970.

Culliford, Sheila Geller. The Keyboarding Book. 2d ed. Toronto: John Wiley & Sons Canada Limited, 1986.

Menning, J. H. and C. W. Wilkinson. Communicating Through Letters and Reports. 5th ed. Albany, N.Y.: Richard D. Irwin Inc., 1972.

ASSIGNMENT   COMPUTER SKILLS

3:18

PREVIEW WORDS

invaded interview position personnel secretarial surprised underneath administrative assistant payable receivable requirements verbal applicant's cooperatively specified abilities accurately

	words
How much do you need to know about computers to get a job in an	13
office? Have computers invaded the world of business to the point	26
where you won't even get an interview unless you know word processing	40
and spreadsheets? What kinds of skills do you need to get a position	54
in an automated office?	59

One way of getting this information is to read the Help Wanted ads in the newspaper. As you scan the Office Personnel and Secretarial columns, you may be surprised to find very few ads have the word "computer" in the job titles. Only two positions—word processor operator and computer information processor—indicate that some form of computer will be used on the job.

Does that mean that all the talk about the need to know how to use computers is pointless? Were all those hours spent staring at the monitor until you were cross-eyed wasted?

Not at all. If you read the fine print underneath the job titles of administrative clerk, administrative assistant, legal secretary, and accounts payable and receivable clerks, you will get a good idea of the importance of possessing computer skills.

The major requirements employers want for all of the positions seem to be good verbal and written communication skills, with a typing or keying speed of 50 to 60 words per minute. These are followed by an applicant's ability to accept responsibility, display a good attitude and work cooperatively with the other employees. Finally, the types of computer system and software that are used on the job are specified.

So, you can see that computer skills are less important on the job than the abilities to write a letter, answer the telephone, and take messages accurately. These are followed by doing your work well and on time, and getting along with others.

words
72
84
97
110
123
132
144
157
166
178
191
204
213
225
239
253
266
279
292
295
308
322
336
345

. . . . 1 . . . . 2 . . . . 3 . . . . 4 . . . . 5 . . . . 6 . . . . 7 . . . . 8 . . . . 9 . . . .10 . . . .11 . . . .12 . . . .13 14

SI 1.4

THE BIBLIOGRAPHY

The Bibliography is the final section of a report. It is a list of the articles or books used as references. Several different formats are used for Bibliographies. Here are guidelines for one common style:

1. Begin by centering the title in all capitals on line 13, or centre the entire Bibliography vertically on a full page.

2. Use the same margins as for the report.

3. Key the first line flush with the left margin, and indent the second line five spaces.

4. Single space each entry, but double space between entries.

5. Arrange the entries in alphabetical order by author, with the author's surname first, followed by first name or initials. If there is more than one author of a text, only the first author's name is inverted. A period follows the author's name.

6. After keying the name, key and underscore the title of the text or article. Then key a period.

7. Key the place of publication, followed by a colon.

8. Next, key the name of the publisher, followed by a comma.

9. Finally, key the year of publication, followed by a period.

Author's name. Title of Publication. Place of publication: Name of publisher, year of publication.

Anderson, Marie and Tyler Vichert. How to Get Along with Others. Winnipeg: New West Press Ltd., 1987.

ASSIGNMENT 3:19   THE BUSINESS LETTER

PREVIEW WORDS
business communication traditional disadvantage preparing
keyboarding language concise accurate courteous natural
organization individuality introduction conclusion impression
extremely envelopes   words

The business letter is a popular form of written communication in   13

business because it is traditional and, therefore, comfortable to the   26

reader. It offers time to write and read and provides a record that   39

can be kept on file. A disadvantage of the business letter is the   42

cost of preparing, writing, keyboarding, and sending it.   53

The language of letters should be concise, direct, accurate, and   67

precise. A courteous, natural, positive tone is best. Planning and   80

organization are required for writing effective letters. Writing with   94

the reader in mind, while expressing individuality, creates interest.   107

A model letter begins with a positive introduction, leads the reader   120

logically from point to point, and ends with a dynamic conclusion.   133

Because the format and keying provide the first impression for   145

the reader, they are extremely important. Several styles and formats   158

are popular, and the writer should select one that complements the   172

writing style and the printed letterhead. Business envelopes should   185

be keyed in correct format to help the post office speed the mails.   198

. . . . 1 . . . . 2 . . . . 3 . . . . 4 . . . . 5 . . . . 6 . . . . 7 . . . . 8 . . . . 9 . . . .10 . . . .11 . . . .12 . . . .13 14

SI 1.4

ASSIGNMENT
10:17

Format this Contents page attractively.

CONTENTS

	Page
1. MANAGEMENT	1
A Brief History of Business Management	3
Management Awareness	6
Participatory Management	17
Summary	20
2. HISTORY OF CANADIAN BUSINESS	24
External Policies	27
Internal Policies	32
Summary	38
3. BUSINESS AND GOVERNMENT	44
Forms of Government Involvement	48
Competition and the Government	55
Summary	61

ASSIGNMENT
10:18

Format this Contents page attractively.

CONTENTS

	Page
I. COPIERS	
Kinds of Copiers	1
Colour Copying	3
Colour Conversion	6
Digital Zoom	17
Words and Pictures	21
Copying from Slides	24
Copying Costs	27
II. THE SECRETARY'S ROLE	
What is a Secretary?	30
The Secretary's Education	33
The Secretary's Responsibilities	35
The Secretary of the Future	38

3
∧

3
∧

ASSIGNMENT 3:20   COMPUTERS AND JOB LOSS

PREVIEW WORDS
procedures threatened magnified creative applications artificial
intelligence imagination expert understandable extreme predicted
apparently precisely experienced

words

During the past decade, developments in computer technology have   13

resulted in many changes in office procedures. More changes have   26

taken place during this time than in the past one hundred years.   39

People who don't use computers often stand in awe or feel threatened   52

by them.   54

Their fear is magnified if their own jobs consist of tasks that   67

can be performed by a computer. Even those whose work requires   79

decision-making and creative skills are concerned, because they read   92

about the current research being done in new applications for   104

computers.   106

The development of artificial intelligence will produce software   120

that can solve problems requiring reasoning and imagination--something   134

that computers cannot do now. One type of artificial intelligence,   147

called "expert systems," provides a set of commands that follow the   160

process used by the best experts in the field in solving a problem.   173

The day that voice input can replace the keyboard has been promised   186

for a long time. What will happen to data entry operators?   198

(continued on next page)

APPLYING YOUR SKILLS—THE CONTENTS PAGE

ASSIGNMENT

10:16

Key this sample Contents page using the spacing indicated.

CONTENTS ↓ 2
Page
↓ 2

1. ₂^^ STANDARD OFFICE PROCEDURES 1
↓ 2

7 Mail Handling 6
^ Photocopying and Duplicating 10
Telecommunications 19
Word Processing Terminology 23
↓ 3

2. ₂^^ HUMAN RELATIONS 42
↓ 2

7 Working with Others 46
^ Adaptability 49
Taking Criticism....................................... 54
Team Work 63

While concern about job loss is understandable, extreme worry is 211
not warranted. While there has been some job loss, the number is far 225
lower than first predicted. Instead, the use of computers has 237
resulted in much more information being produced and used. Those who 251
pay for the computers hope that the added information will result in 265
better efficiency and decision—making. But apparently no one can 278
calculate precisely what the cost savings are. 287

In addition, experienced computer users know how often "down 299
time" can take place, even in the most expensive systems. This is the 313
time when the system breaks down and everything stops. Perhaps you 326
have been in the bank when you could not get your passbook up—dated 340
because the system was down. Down time occurs more often than experts 354
care to admit. 357

. . . . 1 . . . . 2 . . . . 3 . . . . 4 . . . . 5 . . . . 6 . . . . 7 . . . . 8 . . . . 9 . . . .10 . . . .11 . . . .12 . . . .13 14

SI 1.4

THE CONTENTS PAGE

A Contents page is placed at the beginning of reports that contain many divisions and subdivisions, so that the reader can see at a glance what the various sections are and how to locate them in the report. Section headings and subheadings are listed in sequence, along with corresponding page numbers.

Here are some guidelines for preparing a Contents page:

1. Key the heading "Contents" on line 13, or centre it vertically on the page.

2. Centre the heading horizontally and key it in all caps, then triple space.

3. Use the same line length as that used in the report.

4. Section headings are numbered and keyed in all caps.

5. Subheadings within each section are indented at least three spaces to the right of the starting point of the section heading and are single spaced.

6. Triple space before each section heading.

7. Pivot the page number for each subheading from the right margin or centre the page number under a column titled "Page."

8. Leaders may be used between the headings and subheadings and the page numbers. Leave one or two spaces before and after each leader.

9. Follow the same pattern for all headings and subheadings.

ASSIGNMENT 3:21   PLANNING YOUR CAREER

PREVIEW WORDS
Activities successful Effective planning possible information
objectives understand leadership outdoors pleasure identifying
satisfaction scientific technical creative   words

An old saying goes like this, "If you fail to plan, then you plan   12
to fail." Activities and tasks that are planned are almost always   25
more successful than those that are not planned. One of the most   38
important tasks you face is deciding upon a career. Effective   50
planning involves gathering information about yourself and about   63
possible careers. A careful study of this information will help you   76
to develop one or more career objectives for yourself. Once you   89
understand your career objectives, you can then decide how to achieve   102
your goals.   104

Before you can plan a career, you must understand yourself. What   117
activity do you like to do best? What do you least like to do? Do   130
you enjoy being with others as part of a team, or do you prefer to   143
work alone? Do you enjoy leadership roles? Do you enjoy travel and   157
meeting new people? Do you enjoy the outdoors? Which gives you the   170
most pleasure--working with your head or working with your hands?   183

Part of understanding yourself involves identifying your   195
interests. For example, which of the following interests you most--   208
cars, computers, or clothes? An interest that you can match with a   221
career often results in greater job satisfaction. Another interest   234
factor that is involved relates to how you like to work. Do you like   247
working with things or objects, or do you prefer communicating ideas   260
about or to people? Do you like business contact with people, or   273
working in scientific and technical areas? Is routine work for you,   286
or do you like working in abstract or creative ways?   296

. . . . 1 . . . . 2 . . . . 3 . . . . 4 . . . . 5 . . . . 6 . . . . 7 . . . . 8 . . . . 9 . . . .10 . . . .11 . . . .12 . . . .13 14

SI 1.4

APPLYING YOUR SKILLS—THE TITLE PAGE

ASSIGNMENT

10:15

Using the format for keying a title page, create and key three attractive title pages on topics of your choice.

```
                         SAMPLE TITLE PAGE




                         FOR: YOUR INSTRUCTOR

                         BY: YOUR NAME

                         DATE: CURRENT DATE




                         KEY THE NAME OF YOUR SCHOOL IN ALL CAPS
```

ASSIGNMENT 3:22 COMPUTER USE AMONG EMPLOYEES

PREVIEW WORDS
impossible generation categories executive management
automation supervisors responsible throughout   words

As you prepare for a career in business, you must understand the	13
role of computers because it will be impossible to avoid using them	26
during your working life. But what about the older generation? What	40
is happening to the workers who started their careers before computers	54
became standard in an office?	60
One way of describing a business firm is to classify all the	73
employees into three categories. At the top is senior management, led	87
by the president or the chief executive officer. At the bottom is the	101
largest group, the line and support workers, including the office	114
staff. In between is middle management, those who supervise the line	128
and support workers.	132
It is reported that senior management seldom use computers	144
themselves, although they use the resulting information in their	157
decision-making. The most important role of managers is to support	170
automation in the office, even though they never touch a keyboard.	183
Firms that have tried to automate without the full support of senior	197
management have often failed.	203
Supervisors and those in middle management are far more at ease	216
with technology and many of them prefer to do their own keying. This	230
is not strange because they are younger than senior management and	243
they probably learned to use computers in school. They are	255
responsible for planning and checking the accuracy of the reports they	269
pass on to senior management, so they need to use the keyboard to	282
correct errors. They are also keying throughout the day, sending	295
messages to those they supervise.	302
We live and work in a period called the Information Age, in which	315
the use of automation is increasing. As time passes, we will reach	329
the point where even the president and chief executive officer will	342
want a keyboard and screen nearby as the day's work begins.	354

. . . . 1 . . . . 2 . . . . 3 . . . . 4 . . . . 5 . . . . 6 . . . . 7 . . . . 8 . . . . 9 . . . .10 . . . .11 . . . .12 . . . .13 14

SI 1.4

THE TITLE PAGE OF A REPORT

The first page of a report, called the title page, specifies the topic of the report, the name of the person for whom the report is prepared, the author of the report, and the date the report is due. Some title pages also indicate the name of the school, business, or organization with which the author is associated.

Here are some guidelines for preparing a title page:

1. Insert the paper, and space down to line 13. Set the left margin ten spaces to the left of the midpoint.

2. Depress the shift lock, and key the title and all other information in capitals.

3. After keying the title, space down 18 lines and key the word "FOR:" followed by the name of the person to whom the report is be submitted.

4. Double or triple space, and key "BY:" followed by your name.

5. Double or triple space, and key "DATE:" followed by the current date.

6. Space down another 18 lines, and key the name of your school or company.

7. If a border is desired, reinsert your page, *longer edge first*, after you have carried out steps 1 to 6 above and space down six lines. From the left edge to the right edge of the paper, key a solid line of any letter, number, or special character on the keyboard. Single or double space, and key a second or third line of this character.

ASSIGNMENT 3:23 ADVERTISING

PREVIEW WORDS

Advertising business potential television commercials billboards newspapers strategies testimonial repetitive identify techniques attract athletic promotions operation

	words
Advertising is used by all types of business to help keep	11
consumers on top of all the new goods and services being offered.	24
Most firms make use of a mix of types of advertising media to reach	37
their potential customers; for example, television and radio	49
commercials, billboards, newspapers, magazines, posters, and direct	62
mail flyers and letters.	66
Ads use precise strategies, such as testimonial ads, emotional	78
ads, and repetitive ads to get customers to buy. Informative ads,	91
which provide useful product information to aid the consumer in making	104
a wise decision, are an obvious way to get people to buy.	115
The makers of products make use of many techniques in addition to	127
ads to try to help the consumer in the selection of each product, for	141
example, trademarks, slogans, or jingles.	149
But the most important thing that is used to identify the product	162
is the label that is on the product. If the maker of the product puts	175
its own label on the product, it is called a brand name label. If the	188
maker of the product makes the product for some other firm to sell	201
under its own mark, it is called a private label. Stores sometimes	214
sell products that are called no-name brands with no acknowledgement	227
to any producer.	230
Companies use sales promotion techniques as well as ads to	241
attract buyers. These techniques might include free gifts, coupons,	254
sale days, and the funding of athletic teams.	263
Ads and sale promotions do well for the economy by increasing the	275
demand for products and services. This increased demand keeps	287
factories in operation and workers employed.	295
All consumers should think of their budgets, and their real	306
needs, before giving in to the great promises of these ads and	318
techniques.	320

. . . . 1 . . . . 2 . . . . 3 . . . . 4 . . . . 5 . . . . 6 . . . . 7 . . . . 8 . . . . 9 . . . .10 . . . .11 . . . .12 . . . .13 14

SI 1.4

ASSIGNMENT

10:14

Format this one-page report attractively.

Partialnership

The partnership form of ownership is similar, in some respects, to individual proprietorship. Partners may hire staff to run the business, but liability with regard to the customers and creditors of the business rests with the partners. In a partnership, 2 or more persons must be involved, and their association must be registered in accordance with the laws of the province in which the business is to be carried on.

Frequently, a partnership is formed by relatives or friends who have confidence in one another and who are able to work together. In other situations, business colleagues may form a partnership. In either case, an agreement should be drawn up in order to clarify matters that might otherwise cause conflict. These matters usually included are

1. the amount of each partner's investment;
2. commencement date of the partnership;
3. duration of the business;
4. division of any profits or losses;
5. procedures to be followed when a partner withdraws cash from the business;
6. payment of interest on invested capital;
7. procedures to be followed to terminate the partnership.

ASSIGNMENT MICROCOMPUTERS

3:24

PREVIEW WORDS

multi-task documents electronic whereas calculator attractive
invoices modem telecommunications instantaneously ledger
Osaka Singapore Canberra

words

The microcomputer can be said to be a multi-task machine because   13

it can be used for many kinds of work. Let's look at five   25

applications.   27

One is word processing, where the output is documents containing   40

primarily words (as opposed to numbers). A micro is much better than   54

an electronic typewriter if the document is very long. This is   67

especially true when it is known that the first draft will require   80

many changes. An electronic typewriter can still produce short,   93

routine documents, such as memos, faster than a micro because the   106

output is produced at the same time as the input. That is, when you   120

finish keying, the memo is ready, whereas with a micro, you need to   133

use the commands to print.   138

Another important use is spreadsheets, where the micro replaces   152

the electronic calculator. In a spreadsheet program, the micro   165

calculates so quickly that the answers seem to appear on the screen at   179

the same time as the numbers are keyed. The program can also be very   193

long, so that thousands of answers can be produced without errors.   206

Attractive graphs can also be produced from the numbers entered in a   219

file, which saves a lot of time.   225

(continued on next page)

ASSIGNMENT

10:13

Format this one-page report attractively.

THE POSTAL CODE

¶ Millions of dollars have been spent ~~in~~ on automating the Canadian mail delivery system in an effort to provide the most efficient mail service possible. mail can be handled mechanically only if the Address can be read by machines. This means that the address must be positioned properly, and the Postal Code must be included on the envelopes.

the appropriate Postal code can be found on letterheads, on the return address of envelopes, or in Postal Code directories. Once you have found a ~~a~~ Postal Code, allways note it in your address files for convenient future reference.

¶ When keying the Postal Code, insert a single character space between the first ③ digits and the last three digits, e.g. K3B 5P6. No other characters (hyphens, commas, periods, etc.) should appear in the Postal Code. The Postal Code ~~is preferred~~ should be keyed as the last line of the address. If this not possible because of space ~~all~~ limitations, the Postal Code may be shown on the same line the as city and province, providing it is sepreted from these by at least ② character spaces.

A data base program will produce lists of information, such as   238

names and addresses. These lists can be sorted in any order and are   252

often used to prepare mailing labels. It will also produce business   266

forms, such as invoices.   271

If you buy a modem and a telecommunications program, you can send   284

electronic mail to other computer networks anywhere in the world.   297

Messages can be sent and received instantaneously from, say, Osaka,   310

Singapore or Canberra.   314

An accounting program will produce ledger accounts and financial   327

statements at the same time as a journal entry is keyed. There are   340

packages for large and small firms.   347

. . . . 1 . . . . 2 . . . . 3 . . . . 4 . . . . 5 . . . . 6 . . . . 7 . . . . 8 . . . . 9 . . . .10 . . . .11 . . . .12 . . . .13 14

SI 1.4

Format this one-page report attractively.

CAREER ADVANCEMENT

In order to advance in the secretarial field, an employee must specialize and show initiative. Some areas of specialization include computer graphics, systems analysis, and database management. Although these areas may sound very technical, they are really just an extension of more familiar secretarial duties.

If you have good organizational skills, you may perhaps advance within the information and administration sectors. If you have an eye for layout and design, you may advance in the field of information formatting and packaging. Those who enjoy research may find opportunities with companies that buy and sell databases.

In high school, you will develop your reading, writing, listening, reasoning, and oral skills. Education does not stop, however, with the attainment of your high school diploma. In order to advance in your career, you must strive constantly to learn. This involves taking courses and attending workshops in the area you have targeted: computers, management, graphics, etc. Professional development should be a life-long career goal.

ASSIGNMENT   *MONEY*

3:25

PREVIEW WORDS
nineteenth countries precious acceptable currency cheques
commerce financial institution functions important medium
exchange standard

words

By the nineteenth century, paper money was being used in most   12

countries, and as time passed, people began to accept paper money   25

instead of precious metal coins. As people gained faith in paper   38

money, it became more widely used. Today, paper money is wholly   51

acceptable. We all have confidence in its value and that allows us to   64

buy the goods and services we need and want.   72

Today, the major forms of money used in Canada are coins, paper   84

money, and cheques. These are the common forms of money used in most   97

other parts of the world. The coins and paper money we use are our   110

currency. All currency is issued under the control of the federal   123

government. Coins are produced––minted––at the Royal Canadian Mint.   136

The Bank of Canada issues the paper money.   144

Cheques make up a large part of day-to-day commerce. A cheque is   157

an order telling a financial institution to pay a certain amount of   170

money to another person or business. Anyone who writes a cheque   183

should have enough money to cover it. If money is not available, that   197

person is guilty of a crime. Cheques are used as money because most   210

people and businesses are prepared to accept them in return for goods   224

and services. Employers often pay their staff by cheque. Governments   237

pay for nearly everything by cheque. It is much easier and safer to   250

pay by cheque than to carry around large amounts of money.   261

(*continued on next page*)

Format this one-page report attractively.

EFFECTIVENESS ON THE JOB
by
Beth MacDonald

How can you maximize your effectiveness on the job? One way is to really know your company. What products and services does it offer? What are its image and reputation? Do you know who your company's customers are?

Do you really know your job? What does your job description specify in terms of duties and responsibilities? Once you know exactly what is required of you, you can perform your job more efficiently.

Effectiveness results not only from knowing your job, but also from knowing the main duties and responsibilities of your boss and co-workers. Another important aspect of job effectiveness is knowing the company's customers. Ask yourself how you can maintain good relationships with them and perhaps help acquire more clients for your company.

It is important to fulfill your job description well, but it is also important to "go that extra step" to demonstrate your commitment and initiative. In this way you will stand out as an effective employee.

Our money has several functions, each of which is important. For 274

many of us, money is often just the thing we use to get the goods we 287

need to buy. But money is much more than a medium of exchange. It is 300

a standard of value, a store of value, and a standard of future 313

payment. 314

Money allows you to obtain the goods and services you want 326

without having to trade or barter for them. Suppose that you want to 339

buy a compact disc, and the only thing you have to trade is your time 352

and services as a babysitter. This will be fine if the owner of the 364

record store has children to put into your care. If this is not the 377

case, you will have to look around to find a store owner who needs 390

your services in exchange for the disc you want. Without money, it 403

could take you a long time to get the disc you want. With money, you 416

can buy the disc at any store that sells it, and the store owner can 429

use the money you provide to buy goods from other people. Money is 442

the medium through which most day-to-day business exchanges occur--it 456

is the medium of exchange. 461

. . . . 1 . . . . 2 . . . . 3 . . . . 4 . . . . 5 . . . . 6 . . . . 7 . . . . 8 . . . . 9 . . . .10 . . . .11 . . . .12 . . . .13 14

SI 1.4

ASSIGNMENT

10:10

Format this one-page report using the spacing indicated.

↓ 13
THE ULTIMATE GOAL
↓ 2
by
↓ 3
Meghan Bird
↓ 3

5 → The ultimate goal in pursuing a career is to find one that is both psychologically and financially rewarding. Even with careful planning, however, it may be necessary to explore several fields before achieving this goal.

5 → There are many sources of information about jobs, including school guidance departments, newspapers, employment centres and agencies, friends, and relatives.

5 → Applying for a job usually involves filling in an application form and submitting it to a potential employer, along with a covering letter, a resumé, and letters of reference. The next step is a personal interview with the potential employer, for which the applicant should be well prepared. These preparations inlude a neat, well-groomed appearance; some research leading to knowledge of the goals and operations of the company; and extra copies of your covering letter, resumé, and any other relevant material.

5 → Whether or not you are offered the job, a follow-up letter or telephone call is advised, to express your appreciation for having been granted an interview.

ASSIGNMENT 3:26   ELECTRONIC FILING AND RETRIEVAL

PREVIEW WORDS

electronic retrieval information documents contributed
computerized terminals communications prospects legislation   words

The electronic filing and retrieval system permits the user to   12

store and access information, using the electronic work station. Text   25

documents and text and voice messages are examples of the type of   38

information that can be manipulated. Instead of having a four-drawer   52

filing cabinet full of papers in labelled file folders, the user has a   65

few disks that contain the same amount of information.   75

Data that are stored for future reference are referred to as a   87

"data base." A data base gets larger and larger as the volume of data   101

contributed increases. A library that has been computerized is a good   114

example of a very large data base, which can be accessed by the use of   128

computer terminals. The course notes of a student, which could be   141

stored on one disk, represent a much smaller data base.   152

External and internal communications can form different data   164

bases for business. For example, a salesperson might build a local   177

data base about prospects and contacts, whereas an accountant might   190

create a data base about income tax legislation for farmers.   201

Electronic filing and retrieval is another data-handling tool   214

that helps to get the right data to the right place and to the right   227

people at the right time and in the most cost-effective way.   239

. . . . .1 . . . .2 . . . .3 . . . .4 . . . .5 . . . .6 . . . .7 . . . .8 . . . .9 . . . .10 . . . .11 . . . .12 . . . .13 14

SI 1.4

APPLYING YOUR SKILLS—ONE-PAGE REPORTS

ASSIGNMENT 10:9   Format this one-page report using the spacing indicated.

↓ 13
THE HISTORY OF THE TYPEWRITER   1
↓ 3

5 → An English engineer, Henry Mill, is credited with the invention of   2

the typewriter. Records show that on January 7, 1714 he was granted a   3

patent by Queen Anne for a "writing machine."   4

5 → Nothing much is known about this machine, however, and it wasn't   5

until 1829 that actual diagrams of a typewriter were patented in   6

America. Called "typographer," this machine operated by rotating   7

to the appropriate spot on the paper when a lever was depressed.   8

5 → Later models featured a cylinder designed to hold paper. Most   9

typewriters were too large to be practical (some were as large as   10

pianos) and they were much slower that handwriting!   11

5 → The first practical and complete typewriter was marketed in   12

1874 by a gun manufacturing company called E. Remington and Sons.   13

Although the Remington typewriter could produce scripts neatly and   14

quickly, it did not sell well.   15

5 → Further technical developments followed until, today, the   16

market is flooded with many makes and varieties of typewriters.   17

Henry Mill could not have imagined the great economic and time-   18

saving advantages resulting from his invention of a writing machine.   19

PREVIEW WORDS
device distributes permanent administrator department indicate
required messaging automatic addressing distribution recognize
automatically productive communicate

words

The electronic mail device distributes documents at the speed of 13

light rather than at the speed of hand-delivered mail. It also makes 26

a permanent record of these documents which can be found at a later 39

date by a search of subject, author, keyword, or date. If you, as an 52

office administrator, wanted to send a note to your department 64

members, you could do so by using a work station. You would simply 77

key in the message, indicate to whom it should be sent and who is 90

sending it, and then strike the enter or return key. When your 102

employees signed on at their work stations, your message would be in 116

their personal mail file, and they could read their mail on the screen 129

and respond if required. 134

An electronic messaging system permits both the sending and the 146

receipt of messages through the use of both text- and voice-messaging 159

tools. With the help of a good text-messaging system, a person can 172

compose and send messages quickly, using simple commands such as 185

compose, reply, forward, file, send, and delete. The system provides 198

for automatic addressing, use of distribution lists, and creation of 212

various folders for filing mail. It can even recognize nicknames. A 225

person can sit at an electronic work station and, by pushing a few 238

special-function keys or by using a hand-held "pen," make a document 251

that is placed in an electronic file, labelled, and mailed 263

automatically.   *(continued on next page)* 265

ONE-PAGE REPORTS

A report of up to 200 words can be keyed on one page. To format a one-page report using a typewriter, word processor, or microcomputer, follow these guidelines:

1. Centre the title on line 13 in all capitals.

2. Triple space after the title, unless a by-line is included. If a by-line is featured, double space after the title and key the word "by," then double space and key the writer's name. Triple space following the name.

3. Use a 60-character pica line or a 70-character elite line, if the report is unbound. If the report is bound on the left, set the left margin in an extra five spaces. The right margin remains the same.

4. Double space the text of the report.

5. Indent five spaces at the beginning of each paragraph except the first, which should be flush left.

6. Do not number the page.

Voice-messaging systems have most of the same features as text- 277
messaging systems, except that the medium used is voice, rather than 290
text. With the help of a good electronic messaging system, a person 304
can compose and send messages very quickly. 312

Electronic messaging allows workers in an office to be more 324
productive because they can communicate faster. If it is true that 337
"time is money," then this electronic tool could save a business many 350
dollars. 351

. . . . 1 . . . . 2 . . . . 3 . . . . 4 . . . . 5 . . . . 6 . . . . 7 . . . . 8 . . . . 9 . . . .10 . . . .11 . . . .12 . . . .13 14

SI 1.4

Format this note attractively.

ORGANIZING EFFECTIVE MEETINGS

Many people do not like to attend meetings. Often meetings are viewed as boring and a waste of time. To organize effective meetings, here are a few suggestions:

1. Distribute or post a notice of the meeting well in advance and make copies of an agenda for all participants.
2. Specify when the meeting will start and when it will end.
3. START THE MEETING PROMPTLY.
4. Keep the meeting on time and on track.
5. Use visual aids to make key points.
6. Write down all suggestions offered by those attending the meeting.
7. Speak clearly and succinctly, and encourage others to do the same.
8. Prepare the minutes of the meeting soon afterwards and distribute them to all participants.

ASSIGNMENT
3:28

WORD PROCESSING

PREVIEW WORDS
processing input output operator automatic typewriters
museums diverse margins justified textbook Correcting
inserting standard efficient

words

A word processing system has three basic parts: input, 11

processing, and output. The system allows the operator to key in data 24

(input), to change or to edit the data (processing), and to print the 38

data (output). Word processors have so many automatic features that 51

they could soon make the old style of typewriters a relic of the past, 64

found only in museums. 68

A word processor allows the operator to key in data and then use 80

this data in diverse ways. As an example, the margins can be changed 93

to get more or less on a page, and the text can be automatically 106

right-justified so that all of the text lines up on the right-hand 119

side of the page, just as you find in a textbook. Correcting errors, 132

inserting new information, moving parts of a text, and storing the 145

input are some of the tasks that word processors can now do. 157

Of all the electronic tools listed here, the word processor was 170

the first to be used in offices. Most computers now come with word 183

processing software as standard equipment. For efficient production 197

of required material, operators of word processing equipment must have 210

good keyboarding skills. 214

. . . . 1 . . . . 2 . . . . 3 . . . . 4 . . . . 5 . . . 6 . . . . 7 . . . . 8 . . . . 9 . . . .10 . . . .11 . . . .12 . . . .13 14

SI 1.4

Format this note attractively.

COMMUNICATION SKILLS

Do you sometimes have problems communicating your ideas and instructions? Here are a few suggestions to help you communicate more effectively:

1. Be specific! Say, "I need the document by Friday", not "Get the document to me by next week."

2. Establish eye contact with the person to whom you are speaking.

3. Discuss the most important points at the beginning of a discussion.

4. Written instructions should be expressed simply, in point form.

5. Ask the person to whom you are speaking to repeat the instructions back to you after your discussion.

PREVIEW WORDS
meeting Computers business province instance electronic discussed integrated technologies together produces teleconferencing and/or participants involved

words

When we think of a meeting, we think of a few people in the same   12
room, talking. Computers have changed this view by giving people in   25
business the chance to talk to each other without being in the same   38
room, or even in the same province.   45

One instance of this new type of meeting can be called an   56
"electronic" meeting. People sit at their own desks and call up the   69
list of things that are to be discussed at the meeting that they are   82
attending. Then, after reading those lists, they key in their   94
comments on the things that were discussed at the meetings and send   108
these comments to all the people who were "at" the meeting. The   121
integrated office system, using computer and office technologies,   133
gathers together all of these comments by all of the people who were 146
"at" the meeting and produces a set of minutes for distribution--   159
electronically, of course.   164

The other type of computer conference is known as   173
teleconferencing. This is basically a "telephone" meeting. The   186
teleconference can be audio and/or video, so that all participants can 199
hear and/or see all of the other meeting participants. Access to a   212
telephone is all that is required to take part in this type of   224
meeting, so participants can be almost anywhere in the world.   236
Electronic meetings and teleconferencing save the time and money   249
normally involved when participants have to travel to attend a   261
meeting.   263

. . . . 1 . . . . 2 . . . . 3 . . . . 4 . . . . 5 . . . . 6 . . . . 7 . . . . 8 . . . . 9 . . . . 10 . . . . 11 . . . . 12 . . . . 13 14

SI 1.4

ASSIGNMENT 10:6

Format this note attractively.

MACHINE EDITING FUNCTIONS

Many electronic typewriters, computers, and word processors have editing functions that make the task of keying correspondence and reports much easier. Some of these features are:

1. Search and Replace: This function searches through a document and stops at any operator-defined entry, such as a specific name or number. The replace feature allows the operator to substitute one word, phrase, name, or number for another.

2. Hyphenation: When a word must break at the end of a line, this feature automatically divides the word correctly.

3. Pagination: The process of splitting multipage documents into pages of standard length by inserting page breaks.

4. Block Move: A block of text is deleted from one position within the document, and moved elsewhere.

5. Merge: A feature that combines text from two separate documents.

ASSIGNMENT DESKTOP PUBLISHING

3:30

PREVIEW WORDS
desktop magazines accommodate publication deletion
automatically adjust quality arrangement proportional
innumerable appropriate selection

words

A desktop publishing program, or DTP, helps an editor lay out 12
the pages of anything that will be printed in great numbers, such as 25
flyers, newspapers, magazines, or newsletters. An editor saves a 38
lot of time by using a microcomputer because changes can be made 51
instantaneously. In the past, if an article had been typed and filled 65
a page, adding a picture meant that the text had to be cut to 77
accommodate the picture. The remainder of the article then had to be 91
pasted onto the next page. If this change were made in the middle of 105
a publication, many pages would have to be changed. 115

By using desktop publishing software, any addition or deletion 128
could be made, and the program would automatically adjust the rest of 142
the material. The entire publication could be seen, page by page, and 156
nothing would be printed until all the work was finished. 167

But producing a quality publication that attracts readers 179
requires more than desktop publishing software. 188

If you were the editor of the school's yearbook, these are the 201
things you would have to consider. 208

A major factor is the arrangement of the material on a page, 220
which is called the layout. You must apply the rules of good graphic 234
design. The top, bottom, and side margins, as well as the other blank 248
parts of a page, are called the white space. The amount of white 261
space has to be proportional, neither too little nor too much. 273

Every picture or graphic should be related to the text. Most 285
readers are far more likely to look at a picture than read words. 298

Lastly, you must consider the size and style of the type, which 311
are the letters of the words. There are innumerable sizes and styles 325
available. An appropriate selection will determine the quality of 338
your publication. 341

. . . . 1 . . . . 2 . . . . 3 . . . . 4 . . . . 5 . . . . 6 . . . . 7 . . . . 8 . . . . 9 . . . .10 . . . .11 . . . .12 . . . .13 14

SI 1.4

Format this note attractively.

PARCEL MAILING CHECKLIST

Before you mail a parcel, check the following:

1. Did you use a sturdy container of appropriate size and strength?

2. Did you use enough cushioning material of appropriate density?

3. Are individual items separated from each other by wrapping or dividing material?

4. Are liquids carefully packed in absorbent material in case of spillage?

5. Was heavy printed matter tied securely before wrapping to prevent shifting?

6. Are heavy contents secured within the container?

7. Were "Fragile" or "Perishable" stickers attached, if required?

MODULE
4

PROOFREADING, EDITING, AND COMPOSING

Courtesy of Xerox Canada Inc.

**ASSIGNMENT
10:3**

Format this outline attractively.

SECRETARIAL PROFESSIONAL DEVELOPMENT PROGRAM

I. SETTING YOUR GOALS
   A. Developing a personal goal-achievement strategy
   B. Monitoring your progress

II. UNDERSTANDING BEHAVIOUR
   A. Behavioural styles
   B. Tension and stress management
   C. Motivation

III. PRODUCTIVITY
   A. Time management techniques
   B. How to delegate
   C. Using central services

**ASSIGNMENT
10:4**

Format this outline and add appropriate comments under each topic.

QUALITIES OF A GOOD SECRETARY

1. Responsibility
2. Flexibility
3. Patience
4. Assertiveness
5. Good Communication Skills
6. Courtesy

INTRODUCTION

Proofreading is an essential keyboarding skill. Learn to take a few minutes to look over your work carefully while it is still in the machine or on the screen. This module contains many assignments to help you develop your proofreading skills.

Special symbols, called Proofreader's Marks, are used to edit documents and indicate necessary corrections. In this module you will learn these symbols, and how to use them to show changes that have been made on rough-draft material.

Whether you are planning to use your keyboarding skills in your career or in your personal life, knowing how to compose at the keyboard will save you much time and effort. In this module, and throughout this text, you'll find many opportunities to develop your composing skills.

To be able to proofread, edit, and compose effectively, you need to be familiar with standard reference materials such as a dictionary, thesaurus, or word finder. Practice in consulting these materials is also included in this module.

OBJECTIVES

1. To proofread effectively.

2. To recognize and use standard proofreader's marks.

3. To edit on a typewriter, word processor, and microcomputer.

4. To compose directly at the keyboard.

5. To use standard reference materials, such as a dictionary, word finder, thesaurus, or dictionary of synonyms.

8. GENERAL REFERENCE BOOKS: Specialized books providing detailed information on specific subjects. These include:

↓ 2

    a) grammar references
    b) hotel, trade, and geographic references;
    c) legal references;
    d) postal and shipping references;
    e) quotations;
    f) yearbooks.

ASSIGNMENT 10:2

Format this outline attractively.

KEYBOARDING II
STUDENT RESPONSIBILITY SHEET

1. <u>Performance Expectations</u>

  a) Courtesy
  b) Punctuality
  c) Productivity

2. <u>Supplies</u>

  a) Paper
  b) Pen or pencil
  c) Keyboarding binder
  d) Keyboarding text

3. <u>Class Routine</u>

  a) Place only typing paper, a pen or pencil, and a keyboarding text on your desk. Store all other supplies in the desk.
  b) When you arrive in class, begin your warm-up immediately. The page number of the warm-up will be written on the board.
  c) Before leaving the classroom, please check that
    i) all scrap paper is in the garbage;
    ii) your machine is turned off;
    iii) your chair is pushed in.
  d) If your machine is not working, inform your instructor <u>immediately</u>.

4. <u>Absenteeism</u>

  a) Notify your instructor beforehand of any absences due to other school activities.
  b) Upon returning to class following an absence, each student is responsible for finding out what was covered during the classes missed.

CONTENTS

Proofreading 123

Proofreading Assignments 124

    Names and Numbers 124

    Sentences 126

Standard Proofreader's Marks 128

Editing 129

Editing and Proofreading Assignments 130

Composing at the Keyboard 133

Composing Assignments 134

Using Standard Reference Materials 139

Reference Materials Assignments 140

APPLYING YOUR SKILLS—OUTLINES AND NOTES

ASSIGNMENT 10:1

Format this outline using the spacing indicated.

↓ 13

BASIC REFERENCES

↓ 2

Indispensable Office Tools

↓ 3

1. ALMANACS: A published collection of facts on many subjects, including Canada and other countries; includes federal and provincial governments, government officials, populations, geography, etc.

↓ 2

2. BIBLIOGRAPHICAL WORKS (for example, *Who's Who*): Books containing information about prominent people, including their ages, accomplishments, occupations, and backgrounds.

↓ 2

3. DICTIONARIES: Books containing spellings, definitions, and derivations of words.

↓ 2

4. DIRECTORIES: Books listing names and addresses of people within a community, profession, industry, or business.

↓ 2

5. ENCYCLOPEDIAS: Books in several volumes containing short articles on almost every subject, arranged in alphabetical order.

↓ 2

6. INDEX: A list appearing in the final pages of a book or periodical, citing in alphabetical order the specific subjects covered in the book or periodical.

↓ 2

7. SECRETARIAL HANDBOOKS: Reference books containing information on secretarial skills, such as letter set-up, filing, office procedures, etc.

↓ 2

PROOFREADING

Developing proofreading skills is an essential part of keyboarding. Proofreading a document carefully takes time; however, it is time well spent. A quick glance is not sufficient to spot that one error that will turn an otherwise first-rate piece of work into a second-rate effort.

Always look over your work *before* you remove it from your machine or screen. You'll find corrections are much easier to make at this stage.

HOW TO PROOFREAD

1. Look at the text, while it is still in the machine. Is it attractively placed on the page?

2. Look the text over for obvious errors, for example, typographical errors, word division errors, or spacing errors.

3. Read the text for meaning. Does it make sense? Is the grammar correct?

4. Double check names, addresses, postal codes, amounts, and numbers. Have names been spelled correctly? Are numbers in the correct order?

5. Double check for errors by reading the material from *right to left*.

6. If a page must be re-done, read from the *original* document.

7. Consult a dictionary when in doubt about the spelling or meaning of a word.

OUTLINES AND NOTES

An outline is a brief, orderly presentation of the major topics and subtopics of a report. Outlines help the writer of a report to organize ideas. Outlines also communicate at a glance the intent of the report. An outline is not part of a report; it is a separate document that precedes the report. Notes are similar to outlines, but are more detailed.

Here are some guidelines for keying outlines and notes:

1. The title should be keyed in all capital letters and centered on line seven for a one-page outline or note, or on line 13 if there is more than one page.

2. Use a 60-character pica line or a 70-character elite line if the note is unbound. If it is bound on the left side, set the margin in an extra five spaces. The right margin remains the same.

3. For enumerated items, key the number at the left margin and indent the text two spaces. If there are more than nine items in the enumerated material, move the left margin one space to the left in order to align the numbers. Remember to return the left margin to the original position when the enumeratioin is completed.

4. Triple space before major headings, and double space after these headings.

5. Single space the body of each section. If the outline or note is short, however, it may be double-spaced.

6. Leave a bottom margin of 2.5 cm (approximately six lines) on each page.

7. Do not number the first page. On all subsequent pages key a page number on line seven (centered or pivotted from the right margin), followed by a triple space.

PROOFREADING ASSIGNMENTS

ASSIGNMENT

4:1

Most proofreading errors occur because we don't see them.

NAMES

On a sheet of paper, key the numbers 1 to 20.
Set a 40-character line.
Double space.
Compare each of the pairs of names shown in columns **A** and **B** below.
Beside the appropriate number, key IDENTICAL, if the pair of names is the same; or DIFFERENT, if they are spelled differently.
Proofread line by line using a ruler.
After completing the assignment, exchange papers and have another student proofread your work.

	A	B
1.	Mr. Clarence Osborn	Mr. Clarence Osborn
2.	Ms Toni Vassiliou	Mrs. Toni Vassiliou
3.	Alexandra Chronopolous	Alexander Chronopolous
4.	Katherine Stevenson	Katharine Stevenson
5.	Joanne Awalt	Joanne Awalt
6.	Nick J. Brooks	Nick J. Brook
7.	Dr. Peter Gunter	Mr. Peter Gunter
8.	Prof. Gary Cameron	Prof. Gerry Cameron
9.	Dean Laurence Smith	Dean Lawrence Smith
10.	Miss Margery Downing	Miss Margery Downing
11.	Mr. Joshua Schutte	Mr. Joshua Schutte
12.	Mr. Bradford Gilchrist	Dr. Bradford Gilchrist
13.	K. W. Webster	W. K. Webster
14.	Prof. Harry Taylor	Prof. Harry Taylor
15.	Mr. Russell Mueller	Prof. Rusell Muellar
16.	Mrs. Sydney Mayo	Mrs. Sydney Mayo
17.	Dr. Lysle Adams	Dr. Lysel Adams
18.	Mrs. Marie Jones	Ms Marie Jones
19.	Anna Rita Guido	Anna Rita Guindon
20.	Mr. Marcello Pasquini	Mr. Marcelo Pasquini

CONTENTS

Outlines and Notes 378

Applying Your Skills—Outlines and Notes 379

One-Page Reports 386

Applying Your Skills—One-Page Reports 387

The Title Page of a Report 393

Applying Your Skills—The Title Page 394

The Contents Page 395

Applying Your Skills—The Contents Page 396

The Bibliography 398

Applying Your Skills—The Bibliography 399

Multipage Reports 400

Applying Your Skills—Multipage Reports 402

Footnotes 408

Applying Your Skills—Footnotes 411

Endnotes 412

Applying Your Skills—Endnotes 413

Applying Your Skills—Multipage Reports with
Footnotes (or Endnotes) 414

How to Format Articles 419

Applying Your Skills—Articles 420

How to Format Minutes of a Meeting 421

Applying Your Skills—Minutes 422

How to Format an Itinerary 425

Applying Your Skills—Itineraries 426

Composing Outlines, Notes, and Reports 427

ASSIGNMENT 4:2

NUMBERS

On a sheet of paper, key the numbers 1 to 10.
Use the same format and instructions as in Assignment 4:1 to compare the two columns of figures below.
Beside the appropriate number, key IDENTICAL, if the pair of numbers is the same; or DIFFERENT, if they are different.

	A	B
1.	$345.96	$345.96
2.	$268.00	$258.01
3.	$739.89	$379.98
4.	$234.78	$234.78
5.	$367.59	$357.95
6.	$205.05	$502.05
7.	$132.29	$132.29
8.	$347.98	$374.98
9.	$907.90	$709.90
10.	$345.65	$345.56

ASSIGNMENT 4:3

Use the same format and instructions as in Assignment 4:1 to compare the two columns below.

	A	B
1.	9 Chipper Crescent	9 Chiper Crescent
2.	1208 Yonge Street E.	1208 Yonge Street W.
3.	1286 Midland Avenue	1826 Midlande Avenue
4.	2A Chrystal Court	200A Crystal Court
5.	301 Don Mills Road Apt.609	301 Don Mills Road Apt. 906
6.	7878 Dundas Street East	7878 Dundase St. E.
7.	85 Glenview Road	85 Glen View Road
8.	21 Commonwealth Avenue	12 CommonWealth Ave.
9.	3749 Lakeshore Rd. East	3747 Lakeshore Blvd. East
10.	3856 Avenue Road	3865 Avenue Road
11.	49 Marcus Street	49 Marcos Street
12.	2368 Shepherd Avenue	2363 Shepard Avenue
13.	287 King Street West	827 King Street East
14.	83 Ridgeway Cres.	83 Ridgway Cres.
15.	647 Hannover Street	647 Hanover Street
16.	983 Bradford Blvd.	893 Brantford Blvd.
17.	47 Penfield Court	74 Pennfield Court
18.	893 Peppertree Avenue	983 Pepper Tree Avenue
19.	87 Lansdowne Ave.	87 Landsdown Avenue
20.	988 Glen Watford Ct.	988 Glen Waterford Ct.

INTRODUCTION

In business environments, notes and outlines are constantly composed and circulated. Most people draft a report and then revise it, sometimes several times. You may receive many handwritten rough drafts of notes and reports. You will then use your own judgment and the skills you learn in this module to format them attractively. You can apply these skills immediately as you format your own course assignments, and also perhaps those of students who have not taken keyboarding courses (if you decide to do some freelance work).

OBJECTIVES

1. To prepare notes and outlines from examples, rough-draft copy, and your own composition.

2. To set up one-page reports and multipage reports, with and without footnotes.

3. To create an attractive title page for a report.

4. To format a Contents page and a Bibliography.

5. To format newspaper articles correctly.

6. To key footnotes in a manuscript.

7. To format itineraries and minutes of meetings.

ASSIGNMENT **4:4**

SENTENCES

Set a 60-character line.
Proofread the following sentences, noticing all the spelling errors.
Key the sentences, correcting the errors.
Single space each sentence; double space between sentences.
Underscore all corrected words.

> **Example**
> Your going too be late for work if you don't hurry.
> <u>You're</u> going <u>to</u> be late for work if you don't
> hurry.

1. If you are forteen years old, you arn't aloud to drive an autobille.

2. A good dresmaker can altar that outfitt for you so that it fits properlly.

3. People looking for work should consult the adds in the newspapers.

4. Its to bad that there not coming to you're house tonite.

5. In the darkness, the enemy attackted.

6. The saying is that lightening does not strike the same place twice.

7. When it is rainning, the sail of umberellas increases tremendiously.

8. Lee is a candidate for presdent of the Students Counsell.

9. Why do so many people mispell Febuary?

10. The comercial for the camera says that its so simple any one can operate it.

11. They instaled a new gass furnace this year.

12. You have an excelent chance of sucess if you work hard at your studys.

13. The parsel was delivered in a cardboard box that was sealed with gummed tape.

14. Thankyou for your letter in referrence to our equiptment.

15. Your orders will be shipped promply.

MODULE

10

OUTLINES, NOTES, AND REPORTS

Courtesy of Panasonic OA

ASSIGNMENT

4:5

Set a 60-character line.
Proofread the following sentences, noticing all the spelling errors.
Key the sentences, correcting the errors.
Single space each sentence; double space between sentences.
Underscore all corrected words.

1. Shortages occurring at the heighth of the season can be a disaster to a department store.

2. Some factory workers where shields to protect there eyes.

3. The winer of the photography contest one a camra as a prize.

4. Alot of light industry is moveing to suburban areas.

5. Goods shiped by frieght are less expansive than by air.

6. The casheir, at the end of the day, found her registar tottalled $355.

7. Jay walking is ilegal in Edmonton.

8. The auditor could not read the bookeper's illegible handwriting.

9. Most employes are paid once a weak.

10. All applicants for the secraterial position were required to fill out the questionaire.

11. All stationery is orderred by Ms. Petrovsky.

12. The personal manager was reluctent to recommend him for a promotion.

13. Many offices are changeing from regular electric typewriters to the more advanced word processing machines.

14. Our school will be celebratint it's tenth anniversary next year.

15. When imature personnel are hired, unecessary chances are taken.

16. A competent secretary should always be concerned with accurate transcription.

17. I'll agree with you on that point.

18. If I havent herd from you by noon I'll continue to work on the project.

19. He was hopping to get a gold watch for his birthday.

20. The students were very eager to learn how to type thier esays.

appropriate intervals when the phone lines are busy. Some machines have an automatic document feeder that can send up to five pages, with no need for a worker to oversee the transmission. Now, computer-generated documents can be distributed and printed on facsimile units.

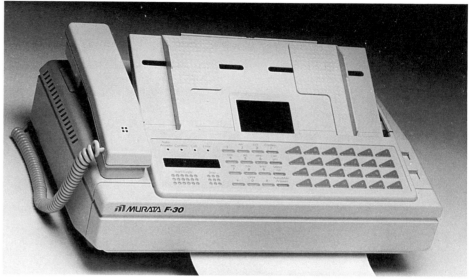

Courtesy of Murata Business Systems Inc.

ASSIGNMENT

9:1

Research one of the following topics related to copying, and prepare a detailed report on your findings:

1. The history of office copying.

2. Some features of various brands of photocopiers.

3. Methods of copying, other than photocopying.

For information on equipment brands, contact some manufacturers and request copies of promotional brochures, and any other relevant print materials they can supply.

Make a good-quality photocopy of your report to submit to your instructor.

STANDARD PROOFREADER'S MARKS

A rough draft of an assignment or exercise may have to be changed because errors were not corrected during keyboarding, or because the originator of the document may want to make changes before the final copy is printed. A standard set of symbols, called Proofreader's Marks, is used to indicate the changes that are to be made.

Throughout this text you will be given numerous assignments that must be corrected according to the proofreader's marks indicated. Learn these marks, and use them whenever an opportunity arises.

PROOFREADER'S MARKS

MARK AND MEANING	EDITED VERSION	CORRECTED VERSION
∧ insert a word	the _blue_ purse	the blue purse
# insert a space	the happy#boy	the happy boy
⊙ insert a period	I know⊙	I know.
ˌ insert a comma	John˄Jane, and Joe	John, Jane, and Joe
¶ begin a paragraph	¶The new . . .	The new . . .
≡ capitalize	s̲a̲n̲dra agreed	Sandra agreed
lc lower case	_lc_ Going home	going home
ℒ delete a word	the ~~big~~ old house	the old house
⌒ close up a space	awk⌒ward	awkward
⑤ indent to right ⑤ or left	⑤The cost of fuel ⑤The cost of fuel	The cost of fuel The cost of fuel
∩ transpose	the ⟨chair / yellow⟩	the yellow chair
ˌˌˌˌ stet (let it stand)	(STET) where a̲r̲e̲ you going	where are you going
◯ write it out in full	②computers	two computers
___ underscore	The Wizard of Oz	The Wizard of Oz

SS single,
DS double and
TS triple space
	single double triple
	SS
	space DS
	        space TS
	           space
		single double triple
		space
		        space
		           space

You should know that luck had very little to do with their
success. All those who make it to the top, no matter what they
do, will tell you that they learned all they could about their
work, either in school or on the job, or both. They will tell

Daisy-wheel

You should know that luck had very little to do with their
success. All those who make it to the top, no matter what
they do, will tell you that they learned all they could
about their work, either in school or on the job, or both.

Dot matrix

You should know that luck had very little to do with their success. All
those who make it to the top, no matter what they do, will tell you that
they learned all they could about their work, either in school or on the
job, or both.

Laser

Sample letter-quality printouts

DIGITAL FACSIMILE RECEIVERS
(FAX MACHINES)

A Fax machine is an office copier that can transfer copies over a telephone line, within seconds, to another Fax machine anywhere in the world. Text, illustrations, charts, and graphs can be transferred. A document can be transmitted from Toronto to Vancouver in just under ten seconds— for less than a dollar.

The facsimile process is very similar to that of the office photocopier. The difference is that for a facsimile machine, the input device is in one location and the output device is in another location. The material to be copied is placed on the input device and is then transmitted electronically, by means of audio signals, when you dial the telephone number.

Fax machines are now found in almost every office. The widespread use of these machines has cut down on mail delivery costs and courier charges. Fax machines can be programmed to send messages after business hours, to take advantage of low-cost nighttime telephone rates. These machines feature auto-dialing, which repeats the telephone number at

EDITING

Once you have proofread your work, or received a marked-up original, you are ready to begin editing. Editing means revising and correcting the document. If you are using an electric or electronic typewriter, re-key the rough draft, making all the necessary changes.

If you are using a word processor or microcomputer, you may have to recall the text to the screen. Word processing programs allow you to make the following types of corrections:

1. *Insert* characters, words, lines, or paragraphs in a particular location. After the insertion, the program automatically adjusts the rest of the document.

2. *Delete* characters, words, lines, or paragraphs from a particular location. After the deletion, the program automatically adjusts the rest of the page.

3. *Search and replace*   This feature finds all or selected occurrences of a word or phrase, and replaces them with another as required. For example, you may have used the name "Ellis" throughout a report or letter, and now want it changed to "Yeung." The machine will find wherever "Ellis" appears in the text and replace it throughout with "Yeung." This feature may also be used to locate short forms or abbreviations keyed in the original, for example, medical or technical terms, and then replace them with the long form.

As you can see, it is very easy to edit work on equipment using word processing programs.

ELECTRONICALLY CONTROLLED PRINTING

Even though photocopying is widely used in today's automated offices, you may need to know about some alternative forms of duplicating. For example, **electronically controlled printers** are fairly standard in automated offices; they combine xerography with computer and laser technology. These printers produce images received in digital form from a computer, instead of producing copies of an original paper document. Some electronically controlled printers can serve as printers for word processing and data processing, and some can make xerographic copies. The three most common electronic printing devices are described below.

DAISY-WHEEL PRINTER

The daisy-wheel printer gets its name from the flower-like shape of its print element. This is a circular disk with letters and characters on spokes radiating from the centre of the wheel. Some daisy wheels print in one direction, while others are bi-directional, meaning that they print in both carriage directions. The daisy wheel is a popular form of printer because it produces documents that are of typewriter quality. A variety of daisy wheels can be used to produce different kinds and sizes of type.

DOT MATRIX PRINTERS

Dot matrix printers use tiny, moving wire rods to print out characters made up of separate, tiny dots. The quality of dot matrix printouts was once noticeably inferior to the daisy wheel. Now, however, many of these printers are equipped with a letter-quality selection feature.

LASER PRINTERS

Laser printers use laser beams—amplified and concentrated light waves—as part of the printing process, producing documents of excellent quality at high speed. Many companies are now using laser printers with desktop publishing software programs to produce high-quality annual reports, company newsletters, and other similar materials.

EDITING AND PROOFREADING ASSIGNMENTS

ASSIGNMENT

4:6

The following assignment contains many errors. Key it first as shown. Set a 60-character line.

Begin the title on line 13, then triple space after the title.

Double space the body.

After you have finished keying the assignment, remove it from the machine, or print out a hard copy.

Using proofreader's marks, correct all the errors on your copy. Show where paragraphs should begin, and indent them five spaces.

Key a correct copy, following the proofreader's marks on your original copy.

Proofread your final copy carefully before removing it from the machine, or printing it out.

KEYEING LETTERS

A keyed telter should look like a picture in a frame? As in any typed work, it should not be removed from the typewriter until it has been proofraed carefully.

In order four the letter to qualify as mailable, concentrate on the following areas when proofreading:

1. Is the letter and punctuation style correct!

2. Are the various letter parts in the proper place?

3. are the sentences complete?

4. Is the spelling spelling correct.

5. Are words divided correctly?

5. Is the letter placed attractively the on page?

If a letter is to high on a pge, room can be taken up by allowing more space for the signature and leaving extra blank lines before keying the reference initials. If a letter is too low on a apge, leave only two or three lines for the signature and key the reference initials on the same line as the keyed name at the left margin.

7. If a problem arises, such as a paper jam or toner depletion, consult the trouble-shooting guidelines in the operator's manual. The appropriate pages in the manual are often tabbed, for easy reference, by means of a symbol that matches the trouble-shooting code lit up on the machine.

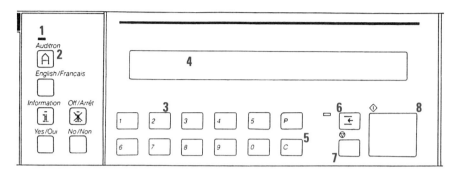

Typical photocopier key pad

1. Indicator light
2. Print or administrator mode
3. Number keys
4. Message display

5. Clear key
6. Interrupt key
7. Stop
8. Start

PHOTOCOPIER MISUSE

While photocopiers can increase office productivity and reduce costs, misuse and carelessness can offset these gains.

Some examples of copier misuse are:

1. copying material for personal or non-business use;

2. making more copies than necessary; and

3. damaging copies or wasting paper, due to careless operating techniques.

To control and reduce costs, office supervisors sometimes:

1. select an appropriate central location for the copier;

2. provide a sign-in book in which users identify themselves and indicate the number of copies made;

3. provide a full-time operator for a busy machine; and/or

4. limit access to the copier by means of a key issued to selected workers.

ASSIGNMENT 4:7

Follow the instructions given for Assignment 4:6.

KEYING A PERSONAL LETTER

Apersonal letter is a letter written from one friend to another? Since a personal letter is imformal, it canbe writetn as is you are "alking' to a friend. The most usuall line legnth for personal-letters is 50-chraacters. If your letter is very shorte, you could double space, but if you have alot too say, single space. Begin keying yuour addres on line twelve, single spacing between your street address, your city and province, your costal pode and the currant date. DO NOT use an inside address in a personal lettre. Drop down six to nine lines for the salutation, depending on the legnth of the letter. The punctuation after the salutaion in a personal letter is usually a coma! always double spce before and after the salutation, between paragrafs; and between the body and the complimentery closing. Nevery key your name in a personal letter, always sign ti.

Courtesy of Olivetti Canada Ltd.

PHOTOCOPYING AND THE FILE COPY

When business letters are keyed, a file copy is always kept as a record. If a letter has been stored on a computer disk, you do not have to make a file copy.

The most common method of producing a file copy is to photocopy the original. Photocopying provides an exact duplicate, including letterhead and corrections.

As you learned in Module 8, a Courtesy Copy (CC) or Photocopy (PC) notation is used when a person other than the addressee is receiving a copy of the same letter. A Blind Copy (BC) notation is used to indicate that the addressee is unaware that copies are being distributed. The typist or word processor keys the notation below the enclosure notation or the reference initials, whichever comes last. In the distribution of copies, a check mark is placed beside the name of each person receiving a copy. No notation is used for copies made for files.

HOW TO PHOTOCOPY EFFICIENTLY

Every copier is unique. Before operating your copier, check the instruction manual.

1. Lift the cover of the photocopier, and place the document *face down* on the platen (the glass plate). Make sure the glass is clean. If it is not, follow the instructions for cleaning as outlined in the manual.

2. Replace the cover.

3. Make sure there is enough paper in the paper feed tray. If not, add more paper according to the manufacturer's instructions. You can bend and "fan" the paper before inserting it, to help avoid paper jams.

4. Decide if the copy is to be the same size, reduced, or magnified, and adjust the setting appropriately. (Consult the operator's manual, if necessary.)

5. Decide on the number of copies required and press the number selector button(s).

6. After the correct number of copies has been "run off," remove the original and return the number selector to zero.

ASSIGNMENT 4:8

Set a 60-character line.
Double space.
Begin on line 12.
Key the following paragraphs, making the changes indicated by the proof-reader's marks.

CAREER PLANS

It is never too early to begin planning for a career. Before you can select a career, you must assesss yourself and the job market. Most experts believe that today's young people will change careers 4 to 5 times before they retire but the chance of chooosing a career and being happy with your choice is much greater you if plan carefully.

what do you like to do? What interests you?What are you good at doing--what are your aptitudes? What occupations match the interests and aptitudes that you possess? Answers to questions likethese will permit you to focus on some of the 23 different occupational groups that exist in the job Field. Future changes in the job market should also bee researched, since some types of jobs are dis appearing and newones are being created. Matching your and interests aptitudes with information on existing and future careers will allow you to set a realistic career objective.

Information on the many sources of career information is available through your school guidance counsellor. Your guidance counseller al so can help you to map out a plan to reach your career objective including advice what on courses to take in school to prepare yourself for career choice

5. Remove all staples and paper clips. Peel off any adhesive notes if pages are to be "fed" into the machine automatically.

Most new models of office photocopiers offer these special features:

1. Reduction in size to varying percentages of the original document.

2. Enlargement to varying percentages of the original document.

3. Two-sided copies (produced automatically by pressing a button).

4. Collating (each copy of a multi-page document is sorted in order).

5. Stapling of collated documents (corner stapled and/or side stapled).

6. Binding with plastic strips or tabs.

7. Colour copies (ranging from two-colour to full-colour).

8. Handling of oversized originals, e.g., drafting plans.

9. Interrupt feature (this allows you to "run" another photocopying job and then resume the first job, without losing your place).

10. Copy dark/copy light/maximum contrast (the copy can be made darker, lighter, or as sharp and crisp as possible).

11. Automatic document feeder (each page of a document that is to be photocopied can be "fed" into the machine automatically, without lifting the cover).

COMPOSING AT THE KEYBOARD

Whether you are going to use your keyboarding skills professionally or in your personal life, knowing how to compose directly at the machine will save you considerable time and effort. It is also much easier to revise and edit keyboarded material than handwritten copy. Get into the habit of keying your thoughts directly onto the paper or, if you are using a micro-computer or word processor, the screen.

COMPOSING ASSIGNMENTS

ASSIGNMENT 4:9

Create a line of drills for each of the following ten specifications:

1. words ending in "ed"
2. words ending in "ing"
3. words ending in "ly"
4. double letter words (e.g., letter)
5. words beginning with "con"
6. words keyed only with the left hand (e.g., sew)
7. words keyed only with the right hand (e.g., him)
8. alternate hand drills (e.g., was, pin)
9. three-letter word drills (e.g., hat)
10. four-letter word drills (e.g., drip)

ASSIGNMENT 4:10

For every letter of the alphabet, compose and key a sentence containing as many words with that letter as possible.

Example
Using the letter *q*:
The Queen worked quite quickly when making quantities of quilts.

PHOTOCOPYING

Modern photocopying equipment has increased productivity in the office, eliminating the hours required to re-key documents using carbon paper. Photocopiers produce high-quality copies directly from an original, at amazing speeds.

Until about 15 years ago, office workers relied on carbon paper, mimeograph duplicators, and stencils to produce multiple copies. However, the invention of **xerography** revolutionized office procedures. This technology relies on magnetic attraction. In photocopiers, tiny, negatively charged particles are spread on positively charged paper in an arrangement that exactly copies the image on the original.

Today, photocopiers offer a variety of high-tech features. Full-colour copiers, often found in advertising or art departments, can reproduce colour photographs and transparencies. Many businesses use this kind of copier to reproduce charts and graphs designed by computers.

Highlight colour copiers create single-colour copies of an original. The colour in the toner cartridge determines the colour of the document. By substituting a cartridge of another colour and running the document through again, various colours can be added. The highlight colour copier is suitable for producing posters and brochures.

Copiers can print on letter- and legal-size paper, and some can reproduce oversized originals, such as engineering blueprints and architectural plans. Many copiers feature automatic printing on both sides of the sheet, called duplexing, as well as document binding by means of corner stapling, side stapling, or plastic strips.

The person responsible for choosing a copier for an office must consider the volume and type of copying required. Some companies have a central copying centre with expensive, high-quality equipment operated by specially trained staff. Other companies have copying machines located throughout the office. The design of photocopiers varies greatly. If you are responsible for photocopying, you should always consult the operator's manual to become familiar with the unique features and capabilities of each machine in your office.

Here are some tips for making good photocopies, with minimal waste:

1. The type on the original document should be crisp.

2. The paper should be flat, with no upturned or folded corners.

3. Place the paper face-down on the glass surface. Align the edges exactly, according to the arrow(s). (Some machines cut off a small portion at the top of the page if the top edge is not aligned properly.)

4. Correction fluid should be applied thinly on originals.

ASSIGNMENT 4:11

In two columns, key the dates for the following events:

1. Christmas Day
2. New Year's Day
3. St. Patrick's Day
4. St. Valentine's Day
5. Canada Day
6. your birthday

ASSIGNMENT 4:12

In two columns, key a list of the parts of the microcomputer, word processor, or typewriter and their functions.

ASSIGNMENT 4:13

Compose and key a list of good keyboarding techniques.

ASSIGNMENT 4:14

In two columns, key a list of all the words you associate with each of the following items:

1. food
2. keyboarding
3. money
4. Saturday
5. car
6. career
7. nature
8. holidays
9. friend
10. music

ASSIGNMENT 4:15

Use the letters in each of the following words to construct and key as many different words as you can.

Example
curtain—tin, an, tic, cur, cut, nut, curt, in

1. snowman
2. delightful
3. laughter
4. refrigerator
5. hospital
6. compose
7. machine
8. calendar
9. keyboard
10. learning

CONTENTS

Photocopying 368

Photocopying and the File Copy 370

How to Photocopy Efficiently 370

Photocopier Misuse 371

Electronically Controlled Printing 372

Digital Facsimile Receivers 373

ASSIGNMENT 4:16

Using complete sentences, key your answers to the following questions:

1. What is the name of your school?
2. When is your birthday?
3. What is your address?
4. What is your telephone number?
5. Why are you taking keyboarding?
6. What is your favourite food?
7. What is the title of the book you are currently reading?
8. What day of the week is it?
9. On the 24-h clock, what time is it?
10. Who is your favourite singer?

ASSIGNMENT 4:17

Using several sentences, key a description of the following:

1. a friend
2. your room
3. a favourite holiday
4. the last movie you saw
5. your favourite outfit
6. your keyboarding classroom
7. your locker
8. your favourite meal
9. a view from a window
10. a frightening experience

ASSIGNMENT 4:18

In a short paragraph, key an explanation of "how to . . ."

1. cook a grilled cheese sandwich
2. babysit
3. study
4. make a bed
5. keyboard
6. ride a bike
7. iron a shirt
8. play your favourite sport
9. wrap a present
10. find a word in the dictionary

INTRODUCTION

If you work in an office you must often determine the most economical way of making copies. Today, offices are equipped with high-speed copying and sometimes phototypesetting machines. The development of portable or desktop copiers means that even the smallest businesses can have their own copying machines. You should know how to produce the exact quantity and quality of copies, as quickly and cheaply as possible.

Given keen competition among manufacturers of office equipment, technical improvements and innovations appear constantly. Office workers often undergo brief on-site training sessions in the use of new and increasingly sophisticated copying equipment.

OBJECTIVES

1. To know how to photocopy documents efficiently.

2. To understand the proper use of photocopiers.

3. To know ways to control and reduce photocopying costs.

4. To understand how documents are transmitted and received by means of a digital facsimile (Fax) machine.

5. To learn some basic facts about electronically controlled printing.

ASSIGNMENT 4:19

Key a description of each of the following items as if you were describing them to someone who had never seen them before:

1. a chocolate chip cookie
2. a lacrosse stick
3. a clock
4. a pair of socks
5. a typewriter
6. a trombone
7. a baby
8. a doghouse
9. a telephone
10. a radio

ASSIGNMENT 4:20

In your own words, define the following:

1. fast
2. cold
3. beauty
4. noise
5. ill
6. sad
7. perfect
8. nervous
9. crowded
10. boiling

ASSIGNMENT 4:21

Key a paragraph containing all of the following special characters, numbers, and words:

1. $
2. ship
3. ( )
4. 2000
5. unhappy
6. !
7. crowded
8. 15
9. ¢
10. 1/2

ASSIGNMENT 4:22

Compose a minimum ten-question keyboarding quiz on each of the following subjects:

1. centering
2. letters
3. tabulation
4. manuscripts
5. machine parts
6. technique
7. spacing and paper facts
8. word division
9. envelopes
10. care of the typewriter, word processor, or microcomputer

MODULE
9

MAKING COPIES

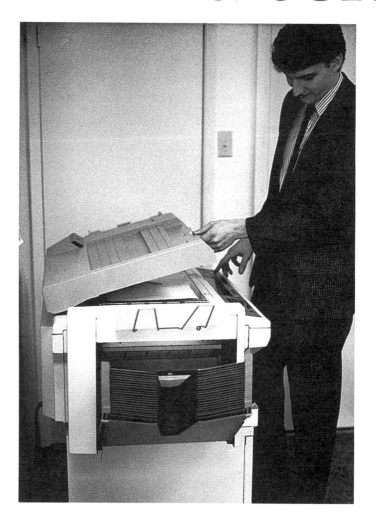

ASSIGNMENT 4:23

Key an explanation of each of the following famous proverbs and sayings:

1. "He can't see the forest for the trees."
2. "A stitch in time saves nine."
3. "Every cloud has a silver lining."
4. "A bird in the hand is worth two in the bush."
5. "An apple a day keeps the doctor away."
6. "It's always darkest before the dawn."
7. "People who live in glass houses shouldn't throw stones."
8. "A penny saved is a penny earned."
9. "Don't cry over spilt milk."
10. "That's the way the cookie crumbles."

ASSIGNMENT 4:24

Key and complete the following sentences:

1. My favourite film star is . . . because . . . .
2. My favourite book is . . . because . . . .
3. My favourite food is . . . because . . . .
4. If I could be any animal I would be a . . . because . . . .
5. If I could be an instrument I would be . . . because . . . .
6. My favourite colour is . . . because . . . .
7. If I could go anywhere I would go to . . . because . . . .
8. My favourite subject is . . . because . . . .
9. If I could be a piece of furniture I would be a . . . because . . . .
10. My favourite TV show is . . . because . . . .

ASSIGNMENT 4:25

If you were the columnist, "Dear Gabby," what response would you key to the following questions:

1. Many weddings have been made unpleasant by the presence of noisy children. Should children be invited to weddings?
2. Should a curfew that requires all students to be off city streets by 20:00 be imposed?
3. In order to promote better nutrition, should junk food be banned from high school cafeterias?
4. Should jeans be allowed as part of modern office dress?

COMPOSING MEMOS

Compose and key a rough draft of each of the following memos. Proofread your rough draft, using the appropriate proofreader's marks, and key the memo again, making all the corrections and changes you have indicated.

ASSIGNMENT

8:88

A memo to all students involved in school clubs, detailing times for yearbook photos.

ASSIGNMENT

8:89

A memo to all students, providing guidelines on how to study.

ASSIGNMENT

8:90

A memo to all employees regarding the importance of being punctual.

ASSIGNMENT

8:91

A memo to all keyboarding students explaining the details of a "Type-A-Thon" to raise money for the Foster Child Campaign.

ASSIGNMENT

8:92

A memo to all business students outlining how they should dress for an office job.

ASSIGNMENT

4:26

Key a paragraph detailing what you did yesterday from the moment you got up until the time you went to bed.

ASSIGNMENT

4:27

1. Put yourself in the position of a small child and key a description of the world as you see it.

2. Key a description of the world as a senior citizen would see it.

ASSIGNMENT

4:28

Key a paragraph describing each of the following sensations:

1. the smell of Thanksgiving dinner
2. the sight of the first snowfall
3. the sound of a keyboarding classroom
4. the taste of a piece of chocolate cake
5. the touch of a mohair blanket

ASSIGNMENT

4:29

Key a telephone conversation between you and your best friend.

ASSIGNMENT

4:30

Key a paragraph describing what you will have accomplished ten years from now.

ASSIGNMENT

4:31

Key a paragraph describing the perfect

1. job
2. date
3. meal
4. house
5. outfit

ASSIGNMENT

4:32

Key a paragraph telling the things you like best about keyboarding, the things you don't like, and how you would change the course if you had the chance.

ASSIGNMENT

8:84

A letter apologizing to an individual who is dissatisfied with one of your company's products.

ASSIGNMENT

8:85

A form letter inviting previous graduates to a Tenth Anniversary Reunion.

ASSIGNMENT

8:86

A form letter asking members of a club you belong to for donations.

ASSIGNMENT

8:87

A form letter to club members cancelling a meeting.

ASSIGNMENT 4:33	Key a summary of a newspaper article you have brought to class.
ASSIGNMENT 4:34	Key a summary of what you learned in your favourite class of the day.
ASSIGNMENT 4:35	Key a paragraph describing your best friend.

USING STANDARD REFERENCE MATERIALS

Whether you are composing your own material or keyboarding assigned text, you will want to have good reference books close by. Standard reference texts such as a dictionary, word finder, thesaurus, or dictionary of synonyms will enable you to find the right words to express your thoughts—and the right way to spell the words you need.

LOCATING WORDS QUICKLY IN THE DICTIONARY

To locate words quickly in the dictionary, you must first find the two guide words between which the entry occurs. The two guide words are usually shown at the top of each page. The word on the left-hand page is the first main vocabulary entry on that page. The word on the right-hand page is the last main entry on that page. Guide words enable you to see at a glance whether the entry you are looking for falls on a particular page.

How quickly can you locate words? Use the guide words to help you find these words:

autocracy	dictatorship
oligarchy	facism
monarchy	hegemony
constitution	totalitarian
plebiscite	

COMPOSING LETTERS

Compose and key a rough draft of each of the following business letters. Proofread your rough draft, using the appropriate proofreader's marks, and key the letter again, making all the corrections and changes you have indicated.

ASSIGNMENT 8:77

A letter to an employee congratulating her on a recent promotion.

ASSIGNMENT 8:78

A letter from a travel agency confirming a holiday.

ASSIGNMENT 8:79

A letter to a customer whose account is overdue.

ASSIGNMENT 8:80

A letter from an advertising agency to a client describing a new marketing campaign for one of the client's products.

ASSIGNMENT 8:81

A letter asking a person to be a guest speaker at your firm's Professional Development Day.

ASSIGNMENT 8:82

A letter thanking the guest speaker who spoke at your firm's Professional Development Day.

ASSIGNMENT 8:83

A letter from your company informing an individual that he or she has won a prize in your firm's contest.

SELECTING A DEFINITION

Read the explanatory notes in your dictionary concerning definitions. Notice particularly the order and designation of meanings.

1. A word may have more than one definition. Check the definitions against the context of your document.

2. In some dictionaries, the definitions are shown in historical order; in others, the most common usage is given first.

3. In some dictionaries, the definitions are numbered, unless the meaning is somewhat different from that of the main entry.

4. Some dictionaries use the word in a partial or complete sentence.

DICTIONARY SIZES

Dictionaries come in several different sizes—unabridged, abridged, and pocket-sized. **Unabridged** dictionaries are usually found only in the reference section of a library. **Abridged** dictionaries are smaller desk dictionaries used in colleges and business. A **pocket-sized** dictionary is usually published in paperback, and will fit easily into a purse, briefcase, or even a pocket. It is the one generally used for in-class reference. To save space, this type of dictionary has fewer vocabulary entries than the abridged version. The explanatory material and vocabulary information are also very concise. The most useful types of dictionaries for composing at the typewriter are the abridged and pocket-sized dictionaries.

REFERENCE MATERIALS ASSIGNMENTS

ASSIGNMENT 4:36

Locate the following words in your dictionary.
Key the definitions given for each word.
Choose one definition for each of the ten words. Using the definition you have chosen, key a sentence for each word.

1. opulence
2. apoplexy
3. essence
4. somatic
5. vista

6. open
7. opinion
8. draw
9. symmetrical
10. stifle

MEMO

TO: ALL SECRETARIES   SUBJECT: <u>Job Description of Duties</u>

FROM: <u>Sandra Zacharidis</u>   DATE: Current

¶ A problem has arisen lately regarding some key responsibilities associated with the Secretary IV position. To <u>clarify</u> matters, I have prepared a list of ~~duties~~ : these responsibilities

1. prepare answers to routine customer correspondence,

2. gather data for company reports;

3. prepare sales figures, budgetary items ⊕ statistical reports ;

4. attend meetings ⊕ take Minutes;

5. organize conferences ⊕ meetings;

6. purchase office supplies and evaluate ~~automated~~ office systems;

7. transcribe documents ;

8. make travel arrangements and prepare itineraries;

9. maintain effective records management; and

10. familiarize new employees with company procedures

AT:yi   A.T.

Key the dictionary guide words for each of the following words.
Set up your work attractively on a full sheet using three columns. In column one, key the word, in columns two and three, key the guide words.

1. tapestry
2. coronary
3. semantic
4. dolphin
5. escrow
6. quorum
7. lava

8. hackneyed
9. cough
10. bursary
11. iodine
12. obscurity
13. scallop
14. vixen

15. zombie
16. meticulous
17. ingenious
18. diplomacy
19. plausible
20. summation

There are errors in most of the words listed below. They are either misspelled, wrongly capitalized, or incorrectly hyphenated.
Key the acceptable form as shown in your dictionary.
If more than one acceptable form is shown, give the preferred form.
Centre your work attractively on a full sheet.

1. rubarb
2. bilingualizm
3. imerge
4. judgement
5. representive
6. over-look
7. Hibiscus
8. sulfur
9. woollen
10. coordination

11. leopard
12. stone deaf
13. figi
14. vaccum
15. extra-ordinary
16. sumerian
17. clean up
18. bursery
19. atlantic provinces
20. oxymoron

MEMO

TO: ALL STAFF   SUBJECT: DESKTOP PUBLISHING

FROM: ANNA TICAS   DATE: current

Since everyone will be attending training sessions over the next few months to become familiar with desktop publishing software, I thought I would provide an overview of the software in this memo.

Desktop publishing software is a tool that enables the user to combine graphics and text into documents on a WYSIWYG (what you see is what you get) display, which can then be edited appropriately. The copy and layout is similar to that appearing in books and magazines. Documents can be composed, revised and printed, without using the services of a professional typesetter.

In your sessions, you will become familiar with the many features of this software, such as proportional text features, multiple font selection features, hyphenation, justification, and graphics integration, just to name a few. The use of our desktop publishing software will enable us to produce professional-looking annual reports, presentations, and pamphlets.

AT: yi   AT

Use a dictionary to find out the part of speech to which each of the following words belongs. If a word belongs to more than one part of speech, give all parts.
Use each word correctly in a sentence.
Set up your work attractively on a full sheet.

1.	ridicule	6.	fuse
2.	duck	7.	cough
3.	function	8.	massacre
4.	power	9.	flag
5.	official	10.	poison

Use a thesaurus or a dictionary of synonyms to find *two* synonyms for each of the following words.
Set tab stops for three columns. In column one, key the words; in columns two and three, key the synonyms.

1.	confine	11.	authentic
2.	impediment	12.	disclose
3.	infuriate	13.	attractive
4.	elude	14.	injure
5.	comrade	15.	lean
6.	propaganda	16.	reprimand
7.	grandiose	17.	stingy
8.	resilient	18.	jest
9.	deceive	19.	ravage
10.	balcony	20.	rob

ASSIGNMENT

8:74

Send a clean copy of the following memo concerning Group Term Life Insurance to all staff members. It is from John Hinchley in the Payroll Department. Use the current date.

¶ Please (certain/make) that your Enrolment Card is complete correctly with regard to the following:

1. Correct Social insurance number;
2. Correct birth date;
3. beneficiary stated;
4. signed and dated by you.

¶ The following are the monthly amounts to be paid by payroll deduction for coverage under this plan, effective January 1. The company will pay 60% of the premium for the months of January, february, and March. Effective April 1, the company will pay the cost of the first $25 000 of coverage and the employee will pay the full coast of any coverage in excess of this amount.

Amount of Insurance	Employee Cost	Company Cost
$ 3 000	$ .26	$ 1.32
10 000	.88	.40
25 000	2.20	3.30
40 000	3.52	5.28
60 000	5.28	7.92
80 000	7.04	10.56

MODULE

5

LANGUAGE USAGE

Courtesy of Biltrite Nightingale Inc.

ASSIGNMENT 8:72

Send the following memorandum from Lorraine Zylmans to Business Education Heads regarding Business Education Week, April 15–19. Send a copy of the memo to Adam Gordon. The memo is keyed on March 20. Determine the appropriate paragraphing.

Our exhibit for this year's Business Education Week, April 15–19, will be on the lower floor of the Prince Rupert Shopping Centre, near the entrance to Eaton's. This area is most suitable because of its layout and the availability of electrical outlets. We intend to set up a "Model Office." Arrangements have been made through Adam Gordon, the manager of the Prince Rupert Shopping Centre, to inform the merchants in the centre that the Model Office will be prepared to do assignments for them. A copy of the memo sent to the merchants is attached. A list of the equipment and supplies to be transferred to the Model Office is provided for your information. For each time slot, there should be three students capable of operating the equipment. We will also have displays of work representing various subjects taught by business education departments. Please forward to me the names of staff and students who are interested in participating in this event. I would like this information by April 1.

ASSIGNMENT 8:73

Send the following memo to Irene Beck from Elaine Teillet, Program Director. Read the memo and decide on an appropriate subject line. The memo is dated April 15. Determine appropriate paragraphing and format.

An In-Service Program for employees involved in Data Processing is being organized for June. Please select from the topics listed below the ones that you feel would be most helpful to you. Indicate your priority by marking the most important as "1" and the second most important as "2". Other topics may be added. Please return your choices to me at the Program Department by May 1. This is only a survey, the date and formal registration information will be sent out in early May. Topics: Organizing and Servicing a Microcomputer; Structured Problem Solving; Microcomputer Technology; File Structures; File Access Methods.

INTRODUCTION

Learning correct language usage is not limited to the English classroom. The study of the English language is a basic part of your education. Being able to speak and write well is an important lifeskill.

This module discusses some of the basic rules of English usage. The many assignments provided are designed to strengthen your knowledge of these usage principles, and to increase your ability to communicate effectively. Numerous spelling rules and assignments are also provided to help you increase your spelling proficiency.

OBJECTIVES

1. To know and apply capitalization rules.
2. To use standard punctuation marks correctly.
3. To improve spelling proficiency.

ASSIGNMENT

8:71

To: All In-Class Teachers

From: Ed Preston
           Safeway Driving School Co-ordinator

DATE: 19-- 05 17

SUBJECT: Written Driving Examination

Attached please find the supervision schedule for the driver education examination. Teachers assigned to supervise must obtain examination papers, attendance sheets, and necessary supplies from the office and report to the examination room at least fifteen minutes before the exam time.

Read the front page of the examination paper to see if any special instructions, supplies, or equipment are needed. Desks should be checked before and after each examination to make sure that no paper has been left behind.

Circulate the attendance sheets for students' signatures immediately after the examination has begun. Circle the names of all students who are absent from the examination. The attendance teachers will collect the sheets fifteen minutes after the examination begins.

                              E.P.

EP:yi

Attachment

CONTENTS

Capitalization Rules 147

Capitalization Assignment 149

Period (.) Rules 150

Comma (,) Rules 150

Comma Assignment 152

Colon (:) Rules 153

Semicolon (;) Rules 154

Colon and Semicolon Assignment 155

Apostrophe (') Rules 156

Apostrophe Assignment 157

Parentheses ( ) Rules 157

Parentheses Assignment 158

Question Mark (?) Rules 159

Exclamation Point (!) Rules 159

Question Mark, Exclamation Point, and Period
Assignment 159

Hyphen (-) Rules 160

Hyphen Assignment 161

Quotation Marks (" ") Rules 162

Quotation Marks Assignment 163

Number Rules 164

Number Assignment 167

Spell It Correctly! 168

Spelling Assignments 169

ASSIGNMENT

8:70

TO: All Directors of Operations

FROM: R.J.M. Burger
        Vice-President and General Manager

DATE: 19-- 01 30

SUBJECT: Capital Expenses for 19--

Please forward to Ernie Rodrigues, no later than March 3, all proposed Capital Expenditures and District Office Expenses, including vehicles (cars, trucks, etc.) for the last quarter of the year. Please include sales and gross profit forecast for the same period.

Please take into consideration at this time any proposed new locations in your area and also the upgrading of existing buildings. For further information, please do not hesitate to call Ernie Rodrigues.

R.J.M.B.

RJMB:yi

Frequently Misspelled Words Assignments 175

Specialized Vocabularies Assignments 182

    Numbers 182

    Office Automation 183

    Law 184

    Retailing 185

    Real Estate 186

    Medicine 186

    Insurance 187

    Time 188

    Transportation 189

    Finance 190

    Politics and Government 191

    Adopted From Other Languages 191

Homonyms 192

Homonyms Assignments 192

Commonly Confused Words 194

How Well Do You Know Canada? 196

ASSIGNMENT
8:69

TO: All Office   SUBJECT: Personnel
         Managers   Development

FROM: Pierre Nadeau   DATE: 19— 04 02
         Office Co-
         ordinator

A meeting with Alice Huggins, Chairperson of the
Personnel Development Program, will be held on
Thursday, April 10 from 15:30—16:30. The meeting
will be held in Room M51—52.

                    A G E N D A

1. Opening Remarks   Pierre Nadeau

2. Personnel Development   Alice Huggins
   Program

3. Our Office Standards   Helen Tindall

4. Professional Secretaries   Sandra Mounstephen
   International

5. Advancement Opportunities   Open Discussion

                    P.N.

PN:yi

CAPITALIZATION RULES

Use a capital letter . . .

1. for the first word of a complete sentence, a quoted sentence, and a line of poetry (Some modern poets do not follow this rule.)

   ```
   This pencil is sharp.
   Jackson said, "Look at the kite in the sky."
   And it must follow, as the night the day,
   Thou canst not then be false to any man.
   ```

2. for proper nouns and adjectives derived from proper nouns

   ```
   Terry Fox, the Bumanis family, the Canadian
   people
   ```

3. for the titles of organizations and institutions

   ```
   Boy Scouts,
   St. Michael's Hospital
   ```

4. for the names of political parties

   ```
   New Democratic Party
   ```

5. for the names of religions and sects

   ```
   Hindus, Protestants, Roman Catholics
   ```

6. for nationalities

   ```
   Belgians, French, Canadians
   ```

7. for geographical names

   ```
   Okanagan Valley, Hudson Bay
   ```

8. for names of buildings

   ```
   Pacific Palisades, First Canadian Place
   ```

9. for the names of publications

   ```
   The Globe & Mail
   ```

ASSIGNMENT

8:68

TO: Division Supervisors

FROM: B. Viner, Personnel Department

DATE: 19-- 07 18

SUBJECT: Staff Appointment

I am pleased to announce the appointment of Mary Difebo to replace Jeff Hamilton in the position of Supervisor: Accounts, effective July 20, 19--.

In this position, Mary will be reporting to me and will be responsible for all new accounts.

Mary has a B.A. in Economics and Marketing from McMaster University and has recently been employed with O.R. Marketing Services Ltd.

I am sure you will all join me in welcoming Mary to our company and wishing her success in her new assignments.

                              B.V.

BV:yi

10. for the names of government bodies and agencies

    `the Senate, Transport Canada`

11. for the days of the week, months of the year, and holidays

    `Monday, August, Easter`

12. for the words "north," "south," "east," "west," etc., when they refer to regions *not* directions

    `They want to take a holiday in the Far East.`

    (Region)
    but

    `You must turn east at the next intersection.`
    (Direction)

13. for titles before proper names, and titles of high government officials without proper names

    `Aunt Adrienne, Captain Cook, the Governor`
    `General, the Prime Minister`

14. for historical events, documents, and periods

    `the Korean War, the Charter of Rights &`
    `Freedoms, the Education Act, the Roaring`
    `Twenties, the Renaissance`

15. for trade names

    `Apple computers`

16. for the first word and all names in the salutation of a letter, and for the first word *only* of the complimentary closing

    `Dear Joseph and Rosie`
    `Yours sincerely`

17. for words indicating an important division in parts of a book or play

    `Vol. II, Act I, Chapter 8`

18. for academic degrees

    `B.Sc., M.A., Ph.D., LL.B.`

APPLYING YOUR SKILLS

MEMOS

Format the following either on forms provided by your teacher, or according to your own design.

ASSIGNMENT

8:67

```
                    INTEROFFICE MEMORANDUM

TO:        All Office Staff

FROM:      J. B. McBride

DATE:      19-- 12 01

SUBJECT:   Staff Christmas Party

Plans for the annual Christmas Party are underway.
The proposed date is Friday, December 20.

On Monday, December 4 at 17:00, there will a
meeting in the staff lounge for people interested
in helping with the planning.

Please call or speak to Sally Medland (extension
415) if you are able to attend. Come and give us
some new and refreshing ideas.

                         J.B.M.

JBM:yi
```

CAPITALIZATION ASSIGNMENT

ASSIGNMENT

5:1

Set a 60-character line.
Key the following sentences, capitalizing words as necessary.
Single space each sentence; double space between sentences.

1. when do you expect your grandmother to arrive?

2. duncan replied, "the train will be two hours late."

3. the industrial revolution had profound effects in england.

4. jason's birthday fell on tuesday, february 14, which is valentine's day.

5. their cottage was located near lake louise.

6. angela couldn't decide whether to buy kellogg's corn flakes or post bran flakes.

7. she was a member of the liberal party.

8. the north is known for its short days and long nights.

9. the macdonald clan always celebrated new year's together.

10. the boy scouts always met on thursday evening.

11. the presbyterians held their annual bazaar in december.

12. ivan was a world war II veteran.

13. the louvre in paris contains many fine works of art.

14. tova did not know that raheem was so talented.

15. aunt cleo and uncle lucas visited their relatives in new zealand.

16. the house of commons sessions for the year were scheduled to begin in may.

17. it can be said that the chinese people have a rich heritage.

18. the edmonton journal does not print on christmas day

↓ 3

7. As in a two-page letter, the second page of a two-page memo must have a heading which consists of:

    ↓ 2

    a) the name of the person to whom you are sending the memo,
    b) the person's department,
    c) the page number, and
    d) the date.

    ↓ 2

8. There are two different methods of typing the heading:

    ↓ 2

    a) BLOCKED: The four parts of the heading are each typed on a separate line -- all flush with the left margin. With this method the page number must be typed "Page 2", not "-2-", e.g.,

        ↓ 2

        Paul Stevenson
        Personnel Department
        Page 2
        19-- 04 13

        ↓ 3

    b) SPREAD: The three parts of the heading are typed as follows:

        ↓ 2

        Paul Stevenson   -2-   19-- 04 13
        Personnel Department
        ↓ 2
        With this method either "Page 2" or "-2-" may be used.

        ↓ 3

I hope that this answers all your questions on "How to Format Memos."

                              ↓ 2
                              C.G.
                              ↓ 2

Reference Initials
Enclosures (if any)

19. steven read chapter IX of the book and noticed that there was information missing (table 5).

20. holly received her ph.d. in early canadian history.

PERIOD (.) RULES

Use a period . . .

1. at the end of an assertive or imperative sentence

   ```
   I like dancing.
   Look at that sunset.
   ```

2. after most abbreviations and initials

   ```
   74 Queen St.
   Thomas B. Dabrowski
   ```

3. after numbers or letters in an enumeration

   ```
   1., 2., a., b., I., IV.
   ```

COMMA (,) RULES

Use a comma . . .

1. to separate words or phrases used in a series

   ```
   They sell cars, vans, and trucks.
   ```

2. to clarify or to prevent misunderstanding

   ```
   They did it as officers of the company, not
   personally.
   ```

INTEROFFICE MEMOS

ASSIGNMENT

8:66

Key an exact copy of this memo using the spacing indicated.

```
                    INTEROFFICE MEMORANDUM
                              ↓ 3
   TO:      All Staff                DATE:  19-- 09 04
                ↓ 2
   FROM:     Cathy Gibb
                ↓ 2
   SUBJECT:  HOW TO FORMAT MEMOS
                ↓ 3
```

Interoffice memorandums (or memoranda) are used to circulate information to
specific individuals or departments within a company. Memos are usually
60-pica keyed on standard office forms, but they can also be formatted on plain paper.
70-elite A memorandum has no salutation or complimentary closing. There are many formats
for memos. Here is one common form:
↓ 2

1. Use a 60-character pica line or a 70-character elite line. If your memo
    is not a standard size, an alternate method for establishing margins
    would be to space in an equal number of spaces from the left and right
    sides of the page.
    ↓ 2

2. If the memo is keyed on plain paper, centre and key the title MEMO,
    MEMORANDUM, or INTEROFFICE MEMORANDUM in all caps on line seven, followed
    by a triple space. The main words of the heading: TO:, FROM:, SUBJECT:,
    and DATE:, may be placed at the left margin, followed by a colon and two
    spaces. An alternate method is to put TO: and FROM: at the left margin,
    and SUBJECT: and DATE: at the centre of the page.
    ↓ 2

3. Triple space after the headings.
    ↓ 2

4. Single space the text of a memo, and double space between paragraphs.
    The paragraphs are usually blocked. Short memos can be double spaced,
    each paragraph being indented five spaces.
    ↓ 2

5. Key the writer's initials at the centre of the page, a double space below
    the text. If the writer's name does not appear in the FROM: line, place
    it a double space below the text at the centre point.
    ↓ 2

6. Special notations, such as initials, enclosures, etc., are placed at the
    left margin, in the same manner as in a letter.

3. to set off the name of a person being addressed

   ```
   Brian, hurry with that food.
   ```

4. to separate the name of a city from a province

   ```
   Vivian was born in The Pas, Manitoba.
   ```

5. for parenthetical expressions

   ```
   Her size, along with her speed, made her a
   good basketball player.
   ```

6. before short quotations

   ```
   Miguel shouted, "There they are!"
   ```

7. to separate an introductory clause from a main clause

   ```
   When you go to the show, don't forget to
   bring some money.
   ```

8. to set off appositives

   ```
   Jasmin, the lawyer's daughter, lives in that
   house.
   ```

9. after the words "yes" or "no" in a sentence

   ```
   No, it should not be done that way.
   ```

10. to separate items in an address or a date

    ```
    Laurie now lives at 9 Windward Avenue,
    Dartmouth, Nova Scotia.
    Tony was born on Monday, September 5, 1988.
    ```

11. between principal clauses in a compound sentence joined by a conjunction

    ```
    The baseball game was scheduled for Monday,
    but it was delayed by rain until Tuesday.
    ```

12. between co-ordinate adjectives

    ```
    It was a bright, sunny day.
    ```

ASSIGNMENT

8:63

Dear   ¶ Just a note to remind you that the course for which you are registered at the Fine Arts School of Cooking begins on   at   . ¶ If you have any questions, please call us at 489-6513. Your balance due is   . It is payable one week prior to the starting date. Please call to confirm your attendance. Yours truly, George Hopkins, Instructor

ASSIGNMENT

8:64

Dear   ¶ The Harbour Village annual Winter Activity Day will be held on Saturday, January 30, 19--. A complete listing of all the activities offered to club members was sent to you previously. ¶ According to our records, your child   has chosen to partici-pate in   , which will be held at   . Transportation will be by   , and club members depart from the Harbour Village Com-munity Centre at   and return at   . The cost will be $. ¶ Please sign and detach the lower portion of this letter to indi-cate your support for your child's participation in this event. Yours truly, Sandy Vaughan, Club President

---

Club Member: _____

Activity: _____

Parent's Signature: _____

ASSIGNMENT

8:65

Dear   ¶ You are invited to visit your Kindergarten class on   between   and   . Your new friends and teacher will be looking forward to seeing you then. ¶ Please note that you will start school on Thursday, September 4. Children will be met by their teacher in the Kindergarten yard. Junior Kindergarten commences at   each day. Children are dismissed to the Kindergarten yard at   daily. Yours sincerely, Mrs. H. Sutton, Kindergarten Teacher P.S. Please keep this letter for reference in September.

13. between contrasted elements

    `Ginette needed more money, not less.`

14. to show the omission of words that are implied

    `Sandy bought two tickets; Vera, three.`

15. after the complimentary closing in two-point punctuation or closed punctuation in a letter

    `Yours truly,`

16. between a name and a position on the same line of an inside address

    `Mr. Sohan B. Lall, Vice-President.`

COMMA ASSIGNMENT

ASSIGNMENT 5:2

Set a 60-character line.
Key the following sentences, inserting commas where appropriate.
Single space each sentence; double space between sentences.

1. The family picnic was scheduled for July 3 but was cancelled.

2. Avi was surprised although deep down he knew that he had won.

3. Since March Greg has always paid his bill.

4. The merchant charged higher prices not lower.

5. Maria the chemical engineer is taking a sabbatical.

6. Theodore's new address is 532 Hillsborough Road St. John's Newfoundland.

7. The bridge which was broken was being swept away down the stream.

8. No I won't be able to go.

9. Ian Jeanette Beth and Adam went to the market.

APPLYING YOUR SKILLS

FORM LETTERS

Key the following assignments as form letters, leaving blanks in the appropriate places. Make three copies of each letter and then compose the missing information that needs to be filled in.

ASSIGNMENT

8:60

Place a check mark in the appropriate space.

Dear _____ ¶ Enclosed is your invoice for the current year's membership fee and your cheque made payable to us. Unfortunately, we are unable to apply this payment because: ¶ (   ) The written cheque amount and the figures do not agree. (   ) The amount is incorrect. (   ) The cheque is unsigned. ¶ Please return the invoice with a corrected cheque. Yours very truly, B. Sharples, Director of Finance

ASSIGNMENT

8:61

Dear _____ ¶ We are returning your subscription renewal application for the following reason(s): ¶ 1. Amount incorrect -- payment should be _____ . 2. Cheque incorrectly prepared. 3. Seats not available at price indicated; please provide an alternative choice. 4. Seats not available on day indicated; please provide alternative choices. ¶ A postage-paid envelope is enclosed. Please return this form with corrected payment and/or changes indicated. Yours truly, S. Ranschaert, Subscription Office

ASSIGNMENT

8:62

Dear _____ ¶ Thank you for your application for Summer Day Camp for _____ , together with your deposit cheque in the amount of $50.00. ¶ I am happy to accept your child for the period of _____ . Late in May, you will be receiving further details regarding the summer program. ¶ Enclosed please find a Health Card to be filled out and signed by your doctor, along with Medical and Trip Authorization Forms, which should be returned to us prior to June 2, 19--. Yours truly, Muriel Fishman, Director

10. The musician played a long difficult piece.

11. Sylvia wanted to attend the concert but didn't have any money.

12. Why aren't you coming tonight Sebastian?

13. We decided to take the road which led to the forest.

14. Gerda was born on February 12 1980.

15. The doctor moved from Regina Saskatchewan to Calgary Alberta.

16. The day before I keyed an essay in two hours.

17. Sanjay the artist went to Venice for his holidays.

18. Sally won the award for $100; Chris for $50.

19. Why are you going if you don't have the money?

20. Why she came so late no one really knew.

21. Birds cats and of course dogs were for sale at the pet shop.

22. Judy replied "Go if you like."

23. After work Gus used to read the evening newspaper.

24. When you think about it it is really absurd.

COLON (:) RULES

Use a colon . . .

1. to introduce a list of items

> They bought the house for three reasons: the price was right, the location was perfect, and there were good schools in the neighbourhood.

Key an exact copy of this letter, using the spacing indicated.

Key the inside address and the salutation in the appropriate place, depending on the size of the letter.

↓ 15
Supply the current date   1

2
3
4

Dear
    ↓ 2
    A form letter consists of both pre-keyed information and specific   5
insertions. On word processors, electronic equipment, and computers,   6
form letters can be easily printed by using the merge feature. If you   7
have such equipment, check the manual describing how to use this function. 8
If you do not have this type of equipment, each entry must be keyed   9
separately.   10
    ↓ 2
    In form letters, the date, address, salutation, figures, and other   11
information may vary. In order to key a form letter, create an original   12
letter and <u>leave blank lines for the specific information to be inserted</u>   13
<u>later</u>. Here are the parts of a form letter that can be keyed and copied   14
ahead of time: 15
    ↓ 2
1. the "Dear" in the salutation;   16

2. all or most of the body;   17

3. the complimentary closing and the writer's name; and   18

4. other special notations.   19
    ↓ 2
    Parts that may be inserted after the basic information has been   20
keyed and copied include the date; the inside address; the name of the   21
addressee after the "Dear" in the salutation; and any special information   22
in the body that is intended only for the individual addressee.   23
          ↓ 2
          Yours truly,

    ↓ 5 *Mike Bertuzzi*

          Mike Bertuzzi   24

    ↓ 2
MB/yi

SEMI-BLOCK LETTER STYLE
OPEN PUNCTUATION
FORM LETTER

2. to introduce direct quotations of four lines or longer, which are set off from the body of the text.

```
In her speech Kara said:
"I promise to do my best to serve the student
body in the upcoming year.
I know that with your support, we will all
have a memorable time."
```

3. after the salutation in a business letter when two-point punctuation or closed punctuation is used

```
Dear Sir:
Dear Ms. Chronopoulos:
```

4. to separate hours and minutes in expressions of time

```
9:15, 21:30
```

5. between the initials of a letter's dictator and transcriber (the reference initials on a letter)

```
JAM:sc
```

6. after the names of speakers in play scripts

```
Marsha: John, where are you?
John: I'm here in the living room.
```

7. to express ratios

```
6:5, 10:1
```

SEMICOLON (;) RULES

Use a semicolon . . .

1. between clauses in a compound sentence when there is no conjunction

```
The meeting began at eight; Terry arrived at
nine.
```

THE FORM LETTER

Routine office correspondence is often formatted as a **form letter**. A form letter consists of some prekeyed information with some new insertions. On word processors, electronic equipment, and computers, form letters can be easily printed by using the merge feature. If you have such a machine, check the manual describing how to use this function. If you do not have this type of equipment, each entry must be keyed in separately.

In form letters, the date, address, salutation, figures, and other information may vary. In order to key a form letter, create an original letter and leave blank lines for the specific information to be inserted later. Here are the parts of a form letter that can be keyed and copied ahead of time:

1. the "Dear" in the salutation;

2. all or most of the body;

3. the complimentary closing and the writer's name; and

4. other special notations.

Here are the parts of the letter that are inserted after the basic information has been keyed and copied:

1. the date (keyed on line 15);

2. the inside address (of the individual addressee);

3. the name of the addressee (after the "Dear" in the salutation);

4. any information in the body that is intended only for the individual addressee; and

5. any special notation intended only for the individual addressee.

2. between clauses in a long compound sentence that already contains commas

```
Mr. Hunter, who has to use a cane to get
around, will be there; and Mrs. Forkis, who
has just turned eighty, will also attend the
party.
```

3. before conjunctive adverbs such as "therefore," "consequently," "however," etc.

```
The thick cloud cover lifted after supper;
consequently, the brilliantly coloured sunset
was easily visible.
```

4. in a series that already contains commas

```
The following people were elected: Joanne
Chen, president; Dave Zimmerman, vice-
president, and Emma Basmanti, secretary.
```

COLON AND SEMICOLON ASSIGNMENT

**ASSIGNMENT
5:3**

Set a 60-character line.
Key the following sentences, inserting a colon or semicolon where appropriate.
Single space each sentence; double space between sentences.

1. The crowd was very large the food ample.

2. The swimming class had one vacancy consequently, Graham got in.

3. The plane was due at 1530.

4. The rules of the badminton club are no guests on Friday nights, members must pay their dues on time, and only white outfits may be worn on the courts.

5. The following people were successful Julie McWhae, first prize Terri Keggenhoff, second prize and Samantha Game, third prize.

Date Mr. Walter Marsh President Gallery Enterprises 3901 Apache Avenue, NE Albuquerque, NM 87110 Dear Mr. Marsh ¶ This letter confirms our previous conversations concerning the office building located at 3901 Apache Avenue, NE, Albuquerque which you currently occupy. Our firm represents Frank T. Rosenbaum and Johanna M. Rosenbaum, who purchased the properties on April 30, 19-- ¶ As we advised previously, it has been the intent and desire of our clients to take possession of the properties immediately for renovation. However, our clients appreciate the problems this would pose for your company. Accordingly, we shall permit you to remain on the premises throughout July, subject to the condition that our clients receive rental payment in the amount of $1600.00 per month for the months of June and July. ¶ When we met with you on April 25, you agreed to the increased rent for these two months. As we indicated, we see no reason to sign a formal lease for such a short period. My clients are willing to accept an oral representation of your intentions. However, as you will recall, you requested that we put our agreement in writing so that you may submit this document in support of your voucher. ¶ When we settled the purchase of the properties, George T. Black, the realtor with the listing for the properties, signed over to our clients a cheque from your company for $1300.00 for May's rent. The rent for the month of June is due on June 1. Kindly forward to this office a cheque for $1600.00 made payable to Frank T. Rosenbaum and Johanna M. Rosenbaum. We will forward this cheque to our clients. The rent for the month of July should also be forwarded to this office by July 1. ¶ Our clients have indicated that they may wish to begin repairs and maintenance to the exterior of the building while you are still occupying it. We have advised them that we foresee no objections on your part. If, however, any disruption of your business occurs, we will make the necessary adjustments to the work schedule. ¶ It has been a pleasure to work with you during the sale and purchase of these properties. Our clients appreciate your co-operation during this time. Sincerely yours COBB, WEBER, AND BURKE Charles Cobb

6. The boat, which left from Montreal, was delayed by ice and the plane, which departed from Fredericton was rerouted because of fog.

7. Hilary's reasons for quitting were little personal time, little job satisfaction, and no opportunity for advancement.

8. The odds were 5 1 that he would win.

9. His concluding remarks were
   There are gold ships
   And there are silver ships
   But the best ships
   Are friendships

10. There was no record of a reservation Lorne had forgotten to phone the restaurant.

APOSTROPHE (') RULES

Use an apostrophe . . .

1. to denote possession (To show the possessive of singular nouns and plurals not ending in s, add 's. When a word ends in s, place the apostrophe after the s.)

   ```
   All of Jon's toys were in his playpen.
   The police officer's notebook was found on
   the pavement.
   All the children's mittens were missing.
   The students' marks disappointed the teacher.
   ```

2. to indicate a letter or figure has been left out (in contractions)

   ```
   Rebecca graduated in '89.
   It's easy to do.
   Aren't you ready yet?
   ```

Another investment I would recommend is to take the time to make a complete inventory of all your personal effects, in as much detail as possible. Such an inventory, particularly if accompanied by photographs of the interior and contents of your home, would make the adjustment of any loss easier, faster, and more accurate. A word of caution -- when you have taken the time and trouble to make such an inventory, keep it in a safe place. Do not let it become part of the loss.

I hope you are in agreement with the foregoing. I will call you early next week to set up an appointment to discuss your insurance coverage.

Yours truly, DARLENE BROWN INSURANCE AGENCY LTD.
Darlene Brown

ASSIGNMENT
8:57

Mr. Walter B. Rilkofsky of Rilkofsky and O'Neal on 1936 West 14th Avenue, Vancouver, V6J 2K3 is writing to Mr. Andrew Ito, of Ito and Tajiri, Barristers & Solicitors, 1-1-1 Iidabashi, Chiyoda-ku, Tokyo Japan 102

Dear Andrew:

RE: SARAH RUBENSTEIN'S TRIP TO TOKYO, MARCH 11-15, 19--

Sarah has just informed me that she is travelling to Tokyo on the above-noted dates to look into joint business ventures there.

Sarah already has some contacts in Tokyo deriving from work she has done in Canada for some established immigrants. On this trip, she will look into new manufacturing projects in Tokyo (and possible expansion of the work she is doing here).

I have given Sarah your name, address, and telephone number and she will be contacting you upon arriving on March 11, to determine an acceptable time to meet with you. I hope this meeting will be mutually beneficial.

Yours sincerely, Walter Rilkofsky

APOSTROPHE ASSIGNMENT

ASSIGNMENT
5:4

Set a 60-character line.
Key the following sentences, inserting an apostrophe where needed.
Double space between each sentence.

1. Jasons cottage was vandalized.

2. The ladies coats were on sale.

3. The sheeps food was eaten by the cows.

4. Gordons luggage was lost.

5. Wouldnt it be fantastic if you won the lottery?

6. Theres no reason to be angry.

7. The 3s and 4s did not come out clearly on the typewriter.

8. The salesmens convention was held in Saskatoon.

9. The class of 80 held a reunion.

10. How many ss are there in the word Mississippi?

11. He looked like something out of the 1950s.

PARENTHESES ( ) RULES

Use parentheses . . .

1. to enclose figures in legal documents or business papers

   ```
   The appraised value of the property is two
   hundred and twenty-five thousand dollars
   ($225 000.00).
   ```

2. to enclose references

   ```
   Your answer to the question (page 20, number
   4) was incorrect.
   ```

The following unarranged letters are two pages long. Some of them contain postscripts. Format these letters attractively, according to your teacher's instructions for letter and punctuation styles.

ASSIGNMENT 8:56

Mr. and Mrs. J. C. Blackstone, 44 Stone Crescent, Brampton, Ontario LOG 1NO Dear Mr. and Mrs. Blackstone Re: Your Personal Insurance; Homeowner's Policy No. T448811

The above-numbered policy providing coverage for your various personal insurance needs is now due for renewal. I am pleased to confirm that this protection is continued for another year in the amounts and limits shown on the renewal document.

Since inflation continues to make repair and replacement of buildings and contents more expensive, most homeowners' policies contain an inflation protection clause designed to increase the amount of coverage automatically over the policy year at the same rate as the increase in cost of labour and building materials. Your own policy has this added benefit, and your renewal is issued, therefore, at the increased level of protection. However, no one knows your home as well as you do, and I would appreciate your examining your present policy amounts to make sure they are adequate to protect you against a serious loss.

I would like to remind you that the contents and personal effects section of your policy has specific limits with respect to certain items, such as jewellery, watches, furs, and stamp and coin collections. To be fully insured, items of this nature should be professionally appraised and added to the policy on a scheduled all-risk basis. Many clients feel that they have no jewellery of sufficient value to justify special coverage, but price increases have been so dramatic, particularly for items containing gold and diamonds, that these clients could be making a costly mistake. We recently convinced one client to have a ring reevaluated. He had paid $275 for it fourteen years ago. We have now insured it at $3400. As you can see, up-to-date appraisals are a worthwhile investment.

3. to enclose words that do not affect sentence structure

    ```
    In Australia, the winter months (July and
    August) are the coldest months of the years.
    ```

4. to enclose figures in enumerated expressions

    ```
    There are three elements to be considered:
    (1) the rights of the individual; (2) the
    needs of the family; and (3) the good of
    society.
    ```

PARENTHESES ASSIGNMENT

ASSIGNMENT 5:5

Set a 60-character line.
Key the following sentences, inserting parentheses where needed.
Double space between each sentence.

1. Her garden consisted of two vegetables tomatoes and corn.

2. The quote was found in the book of poems page 18, verse 3.

3. The yacht was sold for sixty-five thousand dollars $65 000.

4. The two women president and vice-president attended the meeting.

5. The car was bought for twenty thousand dollars $20 000.

6. The answer was found in the third volume page 96.

7. Look in the Yellow Pages under T for Typewriter Rentals.

8. The two sisters Jane and Jennifer were twins.

9. To qualify Ted must have: 1 proven leadership ability; 2 high marks; and 3 the ability to communicate effectively.

10. The factors in the case were: 1 who had signed the agreement, 2 when the agreement was dated, and 3 the wording of the agreement.

Mrs. Victoria Zimmerman   Today's date

¶ Probably the most important communications from the point of view (the of) business are those ~~that take place~~ between a business (+) its customers. All businesses strive ~~to have~~ for effective communications with their clients. If they are not successful ~~in this~~, lost profits will result ⊙ Yours truly, Colin Amato

QUESTION MARK (?) RULES

Use a question mark . . .

1. after a direct question, but not after an indirect question

   ```
   Where are you going? (Direct question)
   ```
   but
   ```
   Carl wonders why you do that. (Indirect question)
   ```

EXCLAMATION POINT (!) RULES

Use an exclamation point . . .

1. at the end of a sentence expressing strong or sudden emotion

   ```
   You are the joy of my life!
   ```

2. after words or phrases that express strong emotions

   ```
   Wow! We won!
   ```

QUESTION MARK, EXCLAMATION POINT, AND PERIOD ASSIGNMENT

ASSIGNMENT

5:6

Set a 60-character line.
Key the following sentences, inserting the appropriate punctuation marks as required.
Double space between each sentence.

1. Who is going to pick them up at the airport

2. M C Crowder was promoted to the Marketing Dept to succeed J Loney

3. Look out here comes a car

4. Paul and Sabrina expected to go to Peru in May

Format the following assignments as the second of a two-page letter.

Ms Laura Lalonde   −2−   Today's date

In conclusion, I would like to emphasize that desktop publishing is growing rapidly in popularity. More and more companies are relying on this technology to produce items such as newsletters, brochures, catalogues, annual reports, price lists, and much more.

                              Yours truly,

TP:yi   Trevor Parsons
                              President

Mr. Ryan Delacoeur
Page 2
Today's date

Your insurance policy covers accident costs and medical payments in the event of death or bodily injury to drivers, passengers, and pedestrians. Benefits are paid following any car accident, no matter who is injured and regardless of fault. If, as a result of a car accident, you miss time from work, you will receive a specific sum of money on a weekly basis. This amount differs from province to province and is specified in your insurance policy.

Sincerely

Monique Caron
Adjuster

MC:yi

5. The news was absolutely fantastic

6. Won't you have some cheese

7. Sandra moved from 15 High Park Cresc to 5367 Ridge Rd

8. Stop Don't run out in front of parked cars

9. The bicycle was securely locked before he entered the store

10. After hanging up the phone Lana yelled that she had won

HYPHEN (-) RULES

Use a hyphen . . .

1. in some compound expressions (When in doubt, consult your dictionary.)

   ```
   Sengupta invited her brother-in-law and
   sister for dinner.
   ```

2. in some compound adjectives preceding nouns

   ```
   It was a second-rate show.
   ```
   but
   ```
   This show was second rate.
   ```

3. to express fractions that come before a noun

   ```
   a two-thirds share
   ```

4. in spelled out numbers from twenty-one to ninety-nine

   ```
   thirty-two students in the class
   ```

5. to divide a word

   ```
   Your account of your recent adven-
   tures in Honduras was fascinating.
   ```

6. to separate double vowels

   ```
   re-educate, co-operate, co-ordinate
   ```

A bottom margin of six lines, or 2.5 cm, should be left on the first page. The heading for the second page contains the following information: the individual's or company's name, the page number, and the date. This information is keyed on line seven and followed by a triple space.

↓ 7

Mrs. Tina Orchard   -2-   19-- 11 20

↓ 3

The heading is usually keyed at the left margin if full block style is used. If semi-block style is used, then the heading is usually spread. If the spread method is used, the name of the addressee is keyed at the left margin, the page number is centred, and the date is pivoted from the right margin. Leave a triple space after the heading and then continue keying the body.

↓ 2

Postcripts are used to emphasize a particular point already mentioned in the letter, to convey a short message totally unrelated to the main subject of the letter, or to mention material that the letter writer forgot to include in the body.

↓ 2

Postcripts are keyed a double space below the final notation. Single space the postscript at the left margin, unless the paragraphs in the body of the letter are indented, in which case the postcript is also indented.

↓ 2

Yours truly,

↓ 4

Dale Park
Office Manager

↓ 2

DP:yi

↓ 2

PS: This illustrates how to format a postscript in a letter. Notice that the abbreviation PS is followed by a colon and then two spaces are keyed before the postscipt message.

SECOND PAGE OF A TWO-PAGE LETTER
SEMI-BLOCK LETTER STYLE
TWO-POINT PUNCTUATION
POSTSCRIPT NOTATION

7. to avoid confusion in meaning

```
I re-covered my old chair with bright blue
fabric.
but
The police recovered the missing money.
```

HYPHEN ASSIGNMENT

ASSIGNMENT 5:7

Set a 60-character line.
Key the following sentences, inserting hyphens where needed.
Double space between each sentence.

1. Approximately forty seven members attended the workshop.

2. Helena will be twenty one on her next birthday.

3. Jim baked a two layer cake for Margritt's birthday.

4. They purchased a first class ticket to Amsterdam.

5. Jeff was very self controlled.

6. She was considered a left wing radical.

7. Alyson and her daughter in law had lunch together.

8. Tim devoured two thirds of the pie.

9. Over one quarter of the population was over sixty.

10. It is important that everyone cooperate in this crisis.

QUOTATION MARKS (" ") RULES

Use quotation marks . . .

1. to enclose a direct quotation

```
He said, "I did not do it."
```

TWO-PAGE LETTERS

Key an exact copy of this letter, using the spacing indicated.

↓ 15

19-- 12 11

↓ 4

Mrs. Tina Orchard
Parkwood Corporation
1199 Pessis Road   1
Winnipeg, Manitoba
R3X 3L4
   ↓ 2
Dear Mrs. Orchard: 2
     ↓ 2
     The purpose of this letter is to explain how two-page letters are   3
formatted. It will also illustrate how to format a postscript notation.   4
     ↓ 2
     Two-page letters are keyed on a 60-character pica line or a 70-   5
character elite line. The first page is printed on letterhead, while   6
all succeeding pages are placed on plain bond of the same quality as the   7
letterhead. The same spacing, punctuation, and letter styles are used   8
for all pages of a multipage letter.   9
     ↓ 2
     Before continuing on to the second or subsequent pages of a letter,   10
it is important to remember that the last word on the page must not be   11
divided and that two lines of a paragraph should be left at the bottom   12
of the page, carrying at least two lines of a paragraph to the second   13
page. Never use the last page for only the closing lines of a letter,   14
try for a minimum of three lines of the body on the last page.   15
     ↓ 2
     The page heading may be spread or keyed flush with the left   16
margin. See the samples below:
     ↓ 2
Miss Nancy Barkwill   -2-   19-- 11 20   17

                                             or

Miss Nancy Barkwill
Page 2
19-- 11 20   18

2. to enclose titles of songs, articles, poems, or stories (Titles of books, movies, or plays are underscored or keyed in all capital letters, or italicized.)

```
There was a fascinating article in Maclean's
entitled "The New Entrepreneurs."
```

3. to enclose nicknames within full names

```
Allen "Big Al" Grabarkowicz was a very
popular clown.
```

4. to enclose slang expressions

```
Being grounded is "the pits."
```

5. to enclose words or phrases to which attention is directed, in order to make the meaning clear

```
I mistakenly used "and," not "or," as I
intended.
```

PUNCTUATION WITH QUOTATION MARKS

1. Periods and commas are placed *inside* quotation marks.

```
Gerry said, "There is no way that can
happen."
```

2. Semicolons and colons are placed *outside* quotation marks.

```
Sophia said, "I will clean the house today";
however, Chris cleaned it.
```

3. Question marks and exclamation points are placed inside the quotation marks when the statement being quoted is a question or exclamation; otherwise, they are placed outside the quotation marks.

```
Peter queried, "What is going on?"
Did Linda say, "I can be there"?
```

REGISTERED

Ms Tina Chan, 2655 Kent Avenue, Apt. 302, Montreal, Quebec H3S 1A8 Dear Ms Chan ¶ On consulting our admission records, we have noticed that we have not yet received a final, official transcript showing that your degree has been conferred. ¶ Please note that all students registering in the Faculty of Business program are required to submit official proof of graduation. Please submit, before registration on September 7, a transcript from Ryerson Polytechnical Institute showing the courses you took and the marks you received. ¶ Your immediate attention to this matter would be appreciated. Yours truly, Georgette Goodwin, Admissions Office

SPECIAL DELIVERY Ms. Ingrid Papke 2655 Kent Avenue, Apt. 302, Montreal, Quebec H3S 1A8 Dear Ms Papke RE: Second Stage of Application (P) This letter is to confirm that we have received the following items from you: 1. Photostat copy of Canadian citizenship. 2. Photostat copy of Birth Certificate from Yugoslavia. 3. Completed Applicant Address Form. (P) We also understand that the results of your Chest X-Ray, taken last week, will be forwarded directly to us by the Clinic as soon as they are available. (P) The only outstanding item is your deposit of $50.00. This must be sent to us before we can continue to process your application. Please look into this matter as soon as possible. Yours truly, Georgette Goodwin, Admissions Office

If a letter has both a mailing notation and an addressee notation leave a single space between them.

SPECIAL DELIVERY, CONFIDENTIAL, Mrs. Jean Watson, 8600 Fairway Road, Richmond BC V7C 1Y6 Dear Mrs. Watson ¶ Thank you for your interest in my booklet, "It's Your Money." I hope you have found it helpful and informative in setting up your saving and spending plans. ¶ There doesn't seem to be any more that I can add to the plans that you have worked out concerning your long-term investments. I wish you every success in their implementation. ¶ If you think you would like further help, however, I suggest that you talk to the manager of your local bank branch. Yours sincerely, Patricia Burns, Manager, Consumer Education

QUOTATION MARKS ASSIGNMENT

ASSIGNMENT

5:8

Set a 60-character line.
Key the following sentences, inserting quotation marks where necessary.
Single space each sentence; double space between sentences.

1. Hans had just finished reading The Grapes of Wrath by Steinbeck.

2. Victor offered his apology by saying, I didn't realize it meant so much to you.

3. It wasn't until Yvonne discussed Lord of the Flies with her English teacher that she fully understood it.

4. She said the word scene not seem.

5. Fiona decided that the dress was really neat.

6. Luciana asked the class, Is this what you voted for?

7. Patricia said I won't go; consequently, no one went.

8. Myrna took one bite of the food and said it was yucky.

9. Joel responded, I have no option but to proceed.

10. Jim the Hulk Yung was known for his aggressive tackles.

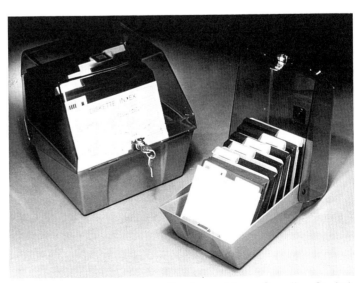

Courtesy of Acco Canadian Co. Ltd.

The following letters contain addressee and mailing notations. Format them attractively, according to your teacher's instructions for letter and punctuation styles.

ASSIGNMENT

8:46

CONFIDENTIAL, Ms Phoebe Johnson, 1900-24 Marquis Ave., Ottawa, Ontario K1J 8J2 Dear Ms Johnson Re: Paul Parish ¶ The above-named individual has applied for registration in our Association and has submitted your name as a reference. ¶ The Association is responsible for maintaining the professional standards of its members and must ensure that applicants have achieved the required qualifications, that they have had satisfactory experience, and that they are of good character. ¶ Your cooperation in providing the information outlined on the attached sheet would be appreciated. No decision in respect of the application can be made until this information is received. ¶ Your reply will be kept confidential. A self-addressed envelope is enclosed for your convenience. Yours very truly, J. R. Gall, Director of Admissions

ASSIGNMENT

8:47

PRIVATE, Bayview Merchants Association, 2901 Bayview Ave., Willowdale, Ontario M2K 1E6 Gentlemen (P) Thank you for your remittance dated June 21, in the amount of $589.93. We hope you were pleased with our service. (P) Upon checking our records, we see that your invoice was for $669.93. Could you please forward the remaining $100.00? Thank you very much. Yours truly, BRIGHT START MARKETING SERVICES, Reg Nighswander, Accounts Director

ASSIGNMENT

8:48

PERSONAL, Mrs. Ruth Henderson, 50 Pipeline Road, Winnipeg, Manitoba R2P J8E Dear Mrs. Henderson ¶ Thank you for your request for the materials on financial planning offered in our television program, "Money — What Every Woman Should Know." ¶ We are very pleased to know that you found the information in the program of value to you in getting your money working. ¶ Setting up a budget and calculating net worth are fundamental to the long-range success of your financial plan. ¶ Please let us know if we can help you at any time in the future. Yours very truly, Patricia Burns, Home Money Management Consultant

NUMBER RULES

Use words for numbers for . . .

1. any number beginning a sentence

   `Forty-three members attended the meeting.`

2. round numbers or approximate numbers

   `More than thirty people applied to go.`

3. names of streets, if they are numbers up to ten

   `First Street`
   but
   `37th Street`

4. the smaller of two numbers placed together in a sentence

   `During the month of May, Sarah did 22 five-minute timed writings.`

5. numbers in legal documents (these are followed by figures in parentheses)

   `The sum of thirteen thousand dollars ($13 000.00) was paid for legal services.`

6. any number up to and including ten in text matter

   `Marek had two parties to go to on the same day.`

7. a number used as an adjective

   `Jorge's grandfather celebrated his seventy-fourth birthday.`

8. centuries (usually)

   `We will soon be entering the twenty-first century.`

SPECIAL MAILING AND HANDLING NOTATIONS

ASSIGNMENT
8:45

Key an exact copy of this letter, spacing the special mailing and handling instructions as indicated.

19-- 04 28

↓ 2 to 4

PERSONAL
REGISTERED

↓ 2 to 4

Ms Lindsey Bohmer   1
2031 West 12th Avenue
Vancouver, British Columbia
V6J 2G2
   ↓ 2
Dear Ms Bohmer: 2
   ↓ 2
    This letter illustrates two additional letter parts; special mailing   3
and handling notations. It is keyed in semi-block style with two-point   4
punctuation.
   ↓ 2
    Mailing notations are included to have a record on file as to how the   5
letter was sent, if a special service was used. Mailing notations are   6
keyed both within the letter and on the envelope. Key the special mailing   7
notation in capitals, two to four lines (variable) below the date, flush   8
with the left margin. Leave two to four lines before the inside address.   9
   ↓ 2
    The handling notation indicates how the item is to be handled after   10
it has been received. Some examples of this type of notation are: 11
PERSONAL, CONFIDENTIAL, and PRIVATE. A handling notation is keyed both   12
in the letter and on the envelope. Like a mailing notation, it is placed   13
at the left margin, in all capitals, two to four lines (variable) below   14
the date. Leave two to four lines before the inside address.   15
   ↓ 2
    If both a special mailing and a handling notation appear in the same   16
letter, the special mailing notation is keyed first, followed by the hand-   17
ling notation on the next line.
      ↓ 2
      yours truly,

↓ 5 *Roberta K. Klein*

Roberta K. Klein

  ↓ 2
RKK/yi

SEMI-BLOCK LETTER STYLE   18
TWO-POINT PUNCTUATION
SPECIAL MAILING AND HANDLING NOTATIONS

Use figures for numbers for . . .

1. numbers over ten

   Nicholas has 39 computer programs.

2. page numbers

   The story starts on page 17.

3. temperature

   The temperature in Montreal was 33°C.

4. weights

   The new baby had a mass of 4 kg.

5. statistics and tables

   26 56 89
   33 34 77

6. invoice and order numbers

   The invoice number for the new computer was
   C347. Our purchase order was #256.

7. dates

   Newfoundland entered Confederation on March 31,
   1949.

8. quantity

   The tube of toothpaste contained 100 mL.

9. dimensions

   The dimensions for Paula's new room are
   7 m x 6 m.

10. distance

    It is approximately 4 km to Ernesto's house.

ASSIGNMENT

8:43

Mrs. Karen Poldvee, 123 Eglinton Ave. E., Toronto, Ontario M4P 1J3 Dear Mrs. Poldvee ¶ Emily Stowe College is pleased to announce a "Women's Place . . . Women's Space" summer seminar series. ¶ Several short, topical seminars of special interest to women will be offered at Emily Stowe College's East York Campus this June. These seminars are:

1. Buying Your Own Home

2. Games Organizations Play

3. Effective Communication and Leadership

4. Women and Money

¶ The first three seminars will be held during the day from 9:30 to 16:00, June 19. "Women and Money" will be offered on two evenings (June 19 and 20). All workshops will cost $50.00 and will take place at the East York Campus, near the Pape subway stop. For more details, please call 469-5981. Yours truly, Marilynn Daye, Information Officer

ASSIGNMENT

8:44

Belmont Plaza, P.O. Box 274, Saint John, NB E2L 3R5 Dear Sir or Madam: SUBJECT: BUSINESS EDUCATION WEEK, APRIL 15–19. During Business Education Week at the Belmont Plaza, students from various high schools will be operating a "Model Office" from 12:00 until 20:00 each day. The following are some of the jobs that the students will undertake: ¶1. Key correspondence and memos from rough draft, or key dictated material using shorthand or dictation equipment. 2. Key items in lists and run off copies. 3. Key labels and other similar tasks. 4. Complete calculations for price lists, invoices, etc. ¶ Please let me know in advance if you have any work that could be done by the students. I can be reached at 530-2678. Yours truly, Lorraine Zylmans, Business Education Director

11. telephone numbers

    `Vangel's new telephone number is 467-9881.`

12. house numbers

    `They live at 158 Cedarbrae Blvd.`

13. room numbers

    `My math class is in room 312.`

14. decimals

    `Doug ran the race in 58.3 s.`

15. sums of money when the sum is more than three words

    ```
    $43.78
    $16 489 157
    ```
    but in text matter
    ```
    ten cents
    sixteen million dollars
    ```

16. expressions of time (usually)

    ```
    I will be there by 17:45.
    ```
    but
    ```
    I arrived at six o'clock.
    ```

17. to be consistent within a sentence

    ```
    Fred has 15 cows, 3 horses, 6 hens, and 17
    goats on his farm.
    ```

18. percentages

    `Fais got 85% in keyboarding.`

The following letters contain enumerations. Format these letters attractively, according to your teacher's instructions for letter and punctuation styles.

ASSIGNMENT

8:41

One-line items in an enumeration are single-spaced. Double spacing is used immediately before and immediately after the entire enumerated list.

Ms Leslie VonDrasek, 5180 Wallace Avenue, Delta, BC V4M 1A1 Dear Ms VonDrasek ¶ Thank you for writing to ask the names of some Olympian gods and goddesses. I have compiled a list of some of the more prominent ones, as shown below.

1. Zeus — King of the Gods
2. Hera — Queen of the Gods
3. Eros — God of Love
4. Aphrodite — Goddess of Love
5. Pluto — King of the Dead
6. Persephone — Queen of the Dead
7. Poseidon — King of the Sea
8. Apollo — God of Music
9. Athena — Goddess of Wisdom
10. Mars — God of War

¶ If you have any other questions that I can research, just drop a line to "Kids Beat," The Osoyoos Times, Box 536, Osoyoos, British Columbia V0H 1V0 Yours truly, Allan Sievert

ASSIGNMENT

8:42

When each item in an enumeration contains more than one line, a double space is left between each item.

Mr. Henry Mulgrew, 729 Wolfe Avenue, Moose Jaw, Saskatchewan S6H 1J6 Dear Mr. Mulgrew ¶ Thank you for writing to me concerning the problems with your 10-speed bike. I have analyzed your problem and think it could be due to one of the following:

1. Your chainwheels may be installed inside-out. This would make the space between the chainwheels slightly too large. Many chainwheels are made with the teeth closer to one edge than to the other. Make sure the two sets of teeth are as close together as possible.

2. Your brand of chain is narrow, making it more likely to slip into the space mentioned above. If this is the problem, try a wider chain.

¶ When you try out these solutions, please drop me a card to let me know how they worked. I was fascinated by the problem you described, but sorry to read that my maintenance articles left a question unanswered. I hope I have helped you. Yours sincerely, THE BICYCLE MAGAZINE Erica McBride, Associate Editor

NUMBER ASSIGNMENT

Set a 60-character line.
Key the following sentences, inserting either a figure or a word as required.
Single space each sentence; double space between sentences.

1. Karen drove at (sixty kilometres per hour, 60 km/hr) through the city.

2. The story "Sleeping Beauty" takes place in the (14th, fourteenth) century.

3. They bought (15, fifteen) shirts, (8, eight) skirts, and (11, eleven) robes.

4. (49, Forty-nine) people were invited to the wedding.

5. The weather report said the temperature would reach (15, fifteen)°C.

6. They placed the accident victim in room (22, twenty-two).

7. Graham could not decide if he should purchase (1 or 2, one or two) cats.

8. Sandy wrote (10 1/2, ten and one-half) pages on the history exam.

9. The caterer prepared a meal for (900, nine hundred) people.

10. The lost invoice was number (42, forty-two).

11. The bus was scheduled to arrive at (10:15, ten fifteen).

12. The record was bought by (99, ninety-nine) students.

13. About (325, three hundred and twenty-five) orders were filled.

14. Sarah moved to a new apartment on (3rd, Third) Avenue.

15. The class average was (60%, sixty per cent).

16. The box had a mass of (16 g, sixteen grams).

17. Her birthday was July (5th, fifth).

ENUMERATIONS

Key an exact copy of this letter, using the spacing indicated.

↓ 15

19-- 04 30

↓ 6

Mr. Uwe Natho
1855 Sargent Avenue
Winnipeg, Manitoba   1
R3H 0E3
↓ 2
Dear Mr. Natho   2
↓ 2
Sometimes you may have to key a letter that contains some form of display. 3
If the display items are numbered, they are called enumerations. If a   4
list is to be enumerated, it is set up in the following manner: 5
↓ 2
1. The items are single spaced, with a double space left between each one. 6
↓ 2
2. Items may begin at the left margin or enumerations may be centred or   7
    indented from the left margin. When indented from the left they are   8
    also indented from the right margin.   9
↓ 2
3. The second line of the enumeration does not begin at the left margin, 10
    but is keyed directly below the beginning of the first word of the   11
    item. It is a good idea to set a tab four spaces in from the margin,   12
    so that you may quickly tab to the appropriate spot after returning   13
    the carriage.
↓ 2
Material that is quoted in the body of a letter is usually indented five   14
to ten spaces from either margin and single spaced. A quote of three or   15
fewer lines may be keyed within the body of the letter.   16
↓ 2
Sincerely yours

↓ 5

Carl Schultz
↓ 2
CS/yi

FULL BLOCK LETTER STYLE   17
OPEN PUNCTUATION
ENUMERATIONS

18. The wholesale price of the book was ($3.25, three dollars and twenty-five cents).

19. The office tower was located on (59th, Fifty-ninth) Street.

20. Chris purchased (three 5-layer, 3 five-layer) cakes.

21. The old stone house was sold for ($100 000, one hundred thousand dollars).

22. The object was (fifty centimetres, 50 cm) long.

23. The party was held at (two hundred and twenty-five, 225) Green Road.

24. The answer was found on page (two hundred and twelve, 212).

25. The couple celebrated their (fifty-first, 51st) anniversary.

SPELL IT CORRECTLY!

In words with *IE* and *EI*, put I before E except . . .

1. in the long *e* sound after *c*

   receive, conceit, ceiling

2. when it is pronounced as the long sound of *ā*

   freight, feign, neighbour

3. when it is pronounced as a long *ī*

   height, sleight

Exceptions

weird	heiress	leisure
neither	protein	foreign
sovereign	either	seize

Send a copy of this letter to Douglas Harding, and a Blind Copy to Sarah French. When the writer does *not* wish the addressee to know that a copy is being sent to someone, the typist prepares a Blind Copy. The notation (BC) appears on the copy only, in the upper left-hand corner above the address, or at the bottom where the regular CC notation is keyed.

Mr. George Huff, 1985-54 Avenue, Langley, BC V3A 3W1 Dear Mr. Huff ¶ Comco Industries is pleased to announce the addition of Sarah French to the Credit Department of our firm. Sarah brings to our department approximately ten years of credit experience, including her responsibilities as Credit Manager for Streb Electronics. ¶ Sarah has been hired by Comco due to the increase in the number of customers we are servicing, as well as our desire to provide a highly competitive service to our customers. Sarah will be Credit Supervisor for the British Columbia Branch, and will also handle several accounts in western Saskatchewan. ¶ Many other changes are occurring within the company, of which you should be aware. We are in the process of strengthening our department in the province of New Brunswick, and Roger Dubois has been appointed Regional Credit Manager for this territory. Michelle Lucas will be reporting to him. Ms Lucas will be responsible primarily for the supervision of the accounts of the Prince Edward Island Branch. ¶ We are confident that these changes will prove advantageous to all of us. Your assistance and cooperation in working with us during this "phase-in" period will be very much appreciated. Yours sincerely, Fran Harwood, Vice-President

Adding a suffix to words ending in Y . . .

1. If *y* is preceded by a vowel, *y* remains.

   ```
   obey----obeyed
   ```

2. If *y* is preceded by a consonant, change *y* to *i*, *unless* the suffix is -ing.

   ```
   enemy----enemies        carry----carrying
   pity-----pities         study----studying
   heavy----heavier
   ```

Exceptions

```
pay-----paid            day----daily
dry-----dryness         shy----shyness
```

SPELLING ASSIGNMENTS

ASSIGNMENT

5:10

Set a 50-character line.
Double space.
Complete the spelling of the following words by inserting *ei or ie* as required.

1. perc__ve
2. profic__nt
3. n__ce
4. conc__t
5. bel__ve
6. r__n
7. sl__gh
8. exper__nce
9. counterf__t
10. y__ld

11. dec__ve
12. retr__ve
13. al__n
14. cash__r
15. ad__u
16. ch__f
17. misch__f
18. l__utenant
19. f__gn
20. fr__ght

The following letters contain copy notations. Format these letters attractively, according to your teacher's instructions for letter and punctuation styles.

ASSIGNMENT

8:37

Mr. Ted Franklin, 2766 West 30th Avenue, Vancouver, British Columbia V6L 1Y9 Dear Mr. Franklin: ¶ I have received your letter of May 14 requesting samples of upholstery fabric from our company. I have passed on your request to our Marketing Department. ¶ You should be hearing from them in the near future. I would like to thank you for your interest in Fraser Upholstery Fabrics. Sincerely, Thomas Nestle, President cc: J. Duckworth, Marketing Department

ASSIGNMENT

8:38

Mr. Charles Greenberg, R.R. #2, P.O. Box 170, Highland Lakes, N.J. 07422, U.S.A., Daer Mr. Greenberg, ¶ We have received your inquiry dated April 7 concerning the Canadian Electrical Code, which is a CSA standard adapted by the provinces into provincial codes e.g., the Ontario Electrical Code. ¶ In some areas, the Canadian Electrical Code is more stringent than its U.S. counterpart, while in other cases they are similar. ¶ The biggest difference between the two documents is in the implementation. The Canadian Electrical Code has been adopted across Canada, while many states and jurisdictions in the United States do not follow the U.S. Code. In addition, there are across Canada certain regulatory authorities, such as Ontario Hydro, that police and enforce the Code. Many states in the United States leave this enforcement up to the manufacturer, and it is the manufacturer's responsibility to follow the code. ¶ I hope the enclosed literature   answer any other questions. Sincerely yours, Constance Killingbeck, Information Officer, CC: American Consumer Association

ASSIGNMENT	Set a 50-character line.
5:11	Double space.
	Centre vertically.
	Key the following words, adding the suffixes indicated.

Example

```
accessory      -s        accessories
boy            -ish      boyish
```

1.	copy	-ing		11.	likely	-hood
2.	industry	-ous		12.	luxury	-es
3.	ratify	-ing		13.	merry	-ly
4.	vacancy	-es		14.	busy	-ing
5.	hasty	-ly		15.	century	-es
6.	dairy	-ing		16.	forgery	-es
7.	discrepancy	-es		17.	forty	-eth
8.	inventory	-es		18.	family	-es
9.	justify	-cation		19.	relay	-s
10.	apply	-ing		20.	voluntary	-ly

In words with a FINAL E. . .

1. drop the *e*, if the suffix begins with a vowel

```
judge----judging advise----advisable
sincere----sincerity
```

2. retain the *e*, if the suffix begins with a consonant

```
manage----management  care----careless
polite----politeness
```

3. retain the *e* to avoid confusion

```
dying----dyeing  singing----singeing
```

Exceptions

```
agreeable  canoeing
argument   truly
```

COPY NOTATIONS

Key an exact copy of this letter.

↓ 15
December 4, 19--

↓ 6

Miss Christine Bilow
1201 rue Sherbrooke, Ouest
Montreal, Quebec   1
H3A 1J1
   ↓ 2
Dear Miss Bilow: 2
   ↓ 2
This letter is keyed in Full Block style with Two-Point punctuation. The   3
special feature it illustrates is the use and format of the Copy or Courtesy 4
Notation.
   ↓ 2
A Copy notation is added to the original letter to indicate to the addressee 5
that a copy or copies have been distributed to the person or persons named   6
at the bottom. Copies can be made by photocopying the original letter. The 7
"cc" notation appears at the bottom of the letter. It is keyed at the left   8
margin, a double space below the reference initials or enclosure notation,   9
whichever appears last. When several copies of a letter are being sent, all 10
names should be keyed in the notation.   11
   ↓ 2
A "Blind Copy" notation is used on all copies except the original. When the 12
"BCC" notation is used, you do not want the addressee to know that a copy is 13
being sent to someone. The "BCC" notation is keyed at the left margin a   14
double space below the reference initials or enclosure notation if there is   15
one.
   ↓ 2
Yours truly,

↓ 5 *Julie Baldwin*

Julie Baldwin
   ↓ 2
JB/yi   16
   ↓ 2
CC: J. Akerfelt
     T. VanStone   17

FULL BLOCK LETTER STYLE
TWO-POINT PUNCTUATION
COPY NOTATION

Form a double final consonant . . .

1. in one-syllable words
   a) that end in a single consonant, for example, hi̱t
   b) where the final consonant is preceded by a si̅ngle vowel, for example, hi̅t
   c) where the s̅uffix to be added begins with a vowel, for example, –i̱ng

       hit————hi̱ṯting

2. Words of more than one syllable follow the preceding rule if the accent falls on the final syllable of the root word.

       begin————begi̱ṉning admit————admi̱ṯting

ASSIGNMENT

5:12

Set a 50-character line.
Double space.
Key the following words, adding the suffixes indicated.
Key the root word at the left margin, tab to the centre, and key the word with the suffix added.
Review the rules before you begin.

Example	
accurate -ly	accurately

1. accommodate	-ing	8. lie	-ing
2. continue	-ous	9. move	-able
3. definite	-ly	10. please	-ure
4. achieve	-ment	11. issue	-ance
5. tie	-ing	12. behave	-ing
6. purpose	-ful	13. impressive	-ness
7. ignore	-ant	14. medicine	-al

ASSIGNMENT 8:33

Mr. Ken Saucier, 14 Oakridge Rd., Winnipeg, Manitoba R5Y 8M3 Dear Mr. Saucier RE: PURCHASE FROM S. CLEAVER OF 358 KING STREET EAST ¶ I understand that we are to act for you in the above matter, and we are pleased to do so. ¶ Would you kindly advise me in whose name you wish to take title; that is, in your name, or in your name and your spouse's name jointly, or in your spouse's name. Kindly provide the names in full. ¶ I hope to hear from you shortly. Yours truly, Elaine Chelsea

ASSIGNMENT 8:34

Mrs. Linda Wong, The House of Wong, 455 Leila Ave., Winnipeg, Manitoba R2P T8E Dear Mrs. Wong Subject: Shallimar Price Increase ¶ Our records indicate that in the past you have purchased from us the Shallimar pattern of china by Bolton. ¶ Bolton has advised us that due to rising production costs, a price increase of 15% will take effect on June 30. ¶ During our spring sale, from May 28 to June 30, we are offering significant reductions on your Bolton pattern. Our sale prices are based on orders that we placed during the past year. This is why we are able to pass the savings on to you. ¶ Our supplies are limited to stock currently on hand, so our deadline for orders is June 30. Please act as soon as possible, because this is the ideal time to make replacements or additions to your set. Yours truly, David T. Murphy, Manager

ASSIGNMENT 8:35

Miss Adrienne Bairstow, P.O. Box 367, Manotick, Ontario K0A 2N0 Dear Adrienne SUBJECT: ALUMNI meeting ¶ The committee has now set a date for the next Alumni Meeting. It is to be held on Thursday, April 15, at in the Civic Auditorium 20:00. ¶ We have many items on the agenda, but the most important ① is the up-coming reunion. Bring your ~~goods~~ creative ideas. Yours truly, Brenda Aronoff, Chairperson

ASSIGNMENT

5:13

Set a 50-character line.
Double space.
Key the following words, adding the suffixes indicated.
Key the root word at the left margin, tab to the centre, and key the word with the suffix added.
Review the rules before you begin.

1.	beg	-ing	11.	admit	-ing
2.	rid	-ance	12.	forget	-ing
3.	knit	-ed	13.	refer	-ed
4.	wrap	-ed	14.	excel	-ing
5.	grant	-ing	15.	seal	-ed
6.	knot	-s	16.	trim	-ing
7.	thin	-ly	17.	fix	-es
8.	sweet	-er	18.	strict	-est
9.	compel	-ing	19.	debt	-or
10.	submit	-ed	20.	control	-ing

Forming plurals . . .

1. for words ending in the *s* sound (*ss*, *sh*, *z*, *ch*, *x*) add *es*

   businesses, taxes, bushes, churches, quizzes

2. for words ending in *y* that are preceded by a consonant, change the *y* to *i* and add *es*

   library----libraries army----armies

3. for words ending in *o*, simply add *s* (Sometimes *es* may be added.)

   hero----heroes

4. for other words, simply add *s*

   boots, trees, buildings

ASSIGNMENT

8:30

The Consumer Club, 1906 Park Place, Halifax, Nova Scotia B3H 4G3 Attention: Mr. Grant Montgomery Gentlemen ¶ This letter is a follow-up to yesterday's telephone conversation. Attached is some literature concerning CSA, including information on our bicycle testing. ¶ We have included your name on our media mailing list so that in future you will receive copies of our press releases. ¶ You are welcome to visit us any time to tour our laboratories in Rexdale. If you or your testing people are aware of any CSA certified products that are potentially hazardous, please inform Ms Alexandra Ferris, Supervisor of CSA's Audits and Investigations Section, (416) 755-2755 as soon as possible, so that immediate action may be taken. ¶ If you have any further questions concerning CSA, please do not hesitate to contact me. Yours sincerely, Constance Killingbeck, Information Officer

ASSIGNMENT

8:31

Gorman Manufacturing Ltd., 5490, rue St.-James ouest, Montréal, Québec H4A 2E9, ATTENTION: MS JEAN HEPBURN, SAFETY COORDINATOR, Gentlemen, We have received your May 16 inquiry concerning defective kettles. (P) Enclosed is our publication "CSA and the Consumer," which contains an article on the kettles. (P) Most of the defective kettles that we checked had had changes to their electrical components, which caused overheating. I hope this answers your questions. Sincerely, Roberta M. Johnson, Information Officer.

The following letters contain subject lines. Format them attractively according to your teacher's instructions for letter and punctuation styles.

ASSIGNMENT

8:32

The subject line is commonly used to refer to a previous letter, a file number, a case number, an invoice number, or some other reference the reader will need to have in hand while reading the correspondence.

Mr. Larry Keech, Clerk-Treasurer, Township of Camden East, Centreville, Ontario K0K 1N0 Dear Mr. Keech Re: Part of Lot 34, Concession 7, Township of Camden East ¶ Please be kind enough to send a Tax Certificate showing all taxes paid to the end of 19-- on the above property. ¶ I would also appreciate it if you would advise me of any outstanding work orders or local improvement taxes levied against this property. I should also be advised as to the zoning designation of this property. Yours very truly, K. Murdock, Barrister

ASSIGNMENT

5:14

Set a 50-character line.
Double space.
At the left margin, key the singular form of the following words, tab to the centre, and key the plural form.

1.	address	11.	child
2.	applicant	12.	foot
3.	brush	13.	box
4.	knife	14.	salesman
5.	arch	15.	remedy
6.	bypass	16.	mass
7.	latch	17.	topaz
8.	hero	18.	discrepancy
9.	radio	19.	casualty
10.	hostess	20.	bookcase

Spelling special cases include . . .

1. **-ARY** and **-ERY** endings
   The -*ary* ending is more common than the -*ery* ending.

   ```
   dictionary, secretary, library, elementary
   stationery, distillery, cemetery
   ```

2. **-ABLE** and **-IBLE** endings
   The -*able* ending *usually* occurs if
   a) the root word is complete

   ```
   noticeable, detectable
   ```

   b) the root word lacks only the final *e*

   ```
   desirable, comparable
   ```

   c) the root word has the *y* changed to *i*

   ```
   reliable, pacifiable
   ```

   The -*ible* ending *usually* occurs if *ion* can be added directly to the root word

   ```
   suggest----suggestion, suggestible,
   access----accession, accessible
   ```

The following letters contain attention lines. Format these letters attractively, according to your teacher's instructions for letter and punctuation styles.

ASSIGNMENT 8:28

Transport Canada, Telecommunications and Electronics Branch, 4900 Yonge St., Willowdale, Ontario M2N 6A5 Attention: Marlon Brunswick Gentlemen ¶ This is in response to your letter requesting a meeting to discuss the plans for a Flight Service Station. ¶ The Board has agreed that they can meet with your committee on Tuesday, May 6, 19-- at 19:00 at the Board office. I hope this time is convenient for you. Yours truly, Mary Preweda, Secretary-Treasurer

ASSIGNMENT 8:29

Fun Time Toys Inc., 131 Sixth Ave. West, Calgary, Alberta T2P 0P8 ATTENTION EMILY HARTZMAN (under score) (:) Gentlemen (P) We received the order you shipped us last week, but it was incomplete. (P) The "Mini-Majic Sets" plus the super sports balls were missing. We ordered 5 dozen of each. (P) Please check your printout and let us know when the balance of the order will be delivered. Yours truly, TERRY'S TOYS, Terry O'Connor, Manager

3. **-ANCE** and **-ENCE** endings

Consult a dictionary for words ending in -*ance* and -*ence*, because there are really no helpful rules that apply to these words.

ASSIGNMENT

5:15

Key the following words, inserting the correct endings, i.e., -*ary* or -*ery*. Use a full sheet of paper.

1. custom__y
2. advers__y
3. annivers__y
4. arch__y
5. auxilli__y
6. benefici__y
7. bin__y
8. bound__y
9. burgl__y
10. commiss__y

11. compliment__y
12. contempor__y
13. diction__y
14. cemet__y
15. element__y
16. extraordin__y
17. heredit__y
18. infirm__y
19. distill__y
20. itiner__y

ASSIGNMENT

5:16

Key the following words, inserting the correct endings, i.e., -*able* or -*ible*.

1. control____
2. adjust____
3. admiss____
4. deplor____
5. inevit____
6. inexhaust____
7. gull____
8. neglig____
9. flex____
10. credit____

11. illeg____
12. change____
13. convert____
14. divis____
15. incap____
16. ed____
17. indestruct____
18. access____
19. vulner____
20. applic____

ATTENTION LINE AND SUBJECT LINE

ASSIGNMENT
8:27

Key an exact copy of this letter, using the spacing indicated.

↓ 15
19-- 11 28

SEMI-BLOCK LETTER STYLE
TWO-POINT PUNCTUATION
ATTENTION LINE
SUBJECT LINE

↓ 6

Segal Motor Supplies
1 Place Ville Marie
Montreal, Quebec   1
H3P 3P7

↓ 2

ATTENTION: JOHN BRENNEN, MANAGER   2

↓ 2

Gentlemen:

↓ 2

SUBJECT: ATTENTION & SUBJECT LINES   3

↓ 2

    This letter is keyed in the semi-block style with two-point   4
punctuation. The special features of this letter are the ATTENTION   5
and SUBJECT LINES.

↓ 2

    An Attention Line is used when a letter is sent to the company,   6
but it is directed to one specific individual or department within   7
the company for action. It is keyed a double space below the inside 8
address. Leave a double space and then key the salutation. Notice   9
that the salutation is Gentlemen, not the name of the person.   10

↓ 2

    The Subject Line is used to tell the reader of the letter   11
immediately what it is about. It is keyed a double space below the   12
salutation. A double space also follows the subject line.   13

↓ 2

    Both the Attention and Subject lines may be centred, indented   14
five spaces, or keyed at the left margin, depending on the letter   15
style used.

↓ 2

Yours sincerely,

↓ 5 *Karen Marques*

Karen Marques

↓ 2

KM/yi   16

FREQUENTLY MISSPELLED WORDS ASSIGNMENTS

ASSIGNMENT

5:17

Lists **A** to **J** below contain 200 frequently misspelled words. Test yourself to see how you rate. Follow these instructions.

Pre-test
Set a 40-character line.
Double space.
Number and key each word as dictated by your teacher.

Homework
For homework, study these words to prepare for another quiz in your next keyboarding class.
Look up meanings of words you do not know.

Post-test
Your teacher may dictate the words to you or ask you to illustrate their meaning by using each one correctly in a sentence.

A	B	C
1. abrupt	1. concede	1. liaison
2. abundance	2. consecutively	2. loose
3. accessible	3. criticism	3. manufacturer
4. accommodate	4. cynical	4. niece
5. acoustics	5. deficit	5. occasion
6. adjournment	6. description	6. pageant
7. affect	7. discrepancy	7. parliamentary
8. amortize	8. encyclopedia	8. perforate
9. apparent	9. exhaust	9. physician
10. architect	10. facsimile	10. absence
11. ascertain	11. fragile	11. accessory
12. assignment	12. grammar	12. accumulate
13. attorneys	13. guidance	13. acquaintance

ASSIGNMENT

8:26

Mr. Henry Montalbetti, 591 Harvey Blvd., Jonquière, Québec G7X 7W1 Dear Mr. Montalbetti ¶ We appreciate your interest in our "Light & Easy" model bicycles. It is always a pleasure to assist an enthusiastic cyclist, such as yourself, who is interested in top quality bicycles. ¶ We are happy to send you the enclosed Collins Bicycles and Accessories catalogue, featuring "Light & Easy" models on pages 3 through 11. Complete specifications are on pages 12 and 13. ¶ Also enclosed is a Collins Accessory and Option Price List, which gives standard frame dimensions, as well as prices. Please note that all Collins products are sold only through authorized Collins dealers. For further details about ordering, we suggest you contact one of these dealers, who will be happy to assist you. ¶ Thank you again for your interest in the "Light & Easy" models. If you should have any further questions, please contact us. Sincerely, COLLINS BICYCLES AND ACCESSORIES, Carl Leung, Consumer Relations

14. bachelor
15. beneficial
16. brilliant
17. bureaus
18. consensus
19. changeable
20. colossal

14. height
15. hosiery
16. idiosyncrasy
17. inflammable
18. jewellery
19. kindergarten
20. ledger

14. admittance
15. alignment
16. altogether
17. analyze
18. appointment
19. asphalt
20. athletics

D

1. audible
2. banana
3. behaviour
4. benefited
5. brochure
6. cancellation
7. ceiling
8. chauffeur
9. commitment
10. condemn
11. conspicuous
12. criticize
13. deceive
14. delegate
15. develop
16. dissatisfied
17. eligible

E

1. fraudulent
2. gorgeous
3. grievance
4. gymnasium
5. hygiene
6. illiterate
7. irrelevant
8. labelling
9. legitimate
10. miscellaneous
11. opponent
12. parallel
13. partial
14. permanent
15. plagiarism
16. accelerate
17. accidentally

F

1. allotment
2. aluminum
3. apostrophe
4. appraisal
5. arrangement
6. assessment
7. attendance
8. auxiliary
9. banquet
10. believable
11. bicycle
12. career
13. cemetery
14. clientele
15. committee
16. confident
17. controlling

ASSIGNMENT
8:24

Mr. and Mrs. John Sorenson, 225 Portage Avenue, Winnipeg, Manitoba R2M 3J9 Dear Mr. and Mrs. Sorenson (P) I am enclosing true copies of your wills dated June 28, 19—. I have placed the original copies in my vault for safekeeping. They are available to you at any time upon written request. (P) I am also enclosing my account in this matter and trust that you will find it satisfactory. Yours very truly, SCOTT AND PARROTT SOLICITORS, Donna Scott

ASSIGNMENT
8:25

Ms. Joanne Daniels, 245 Park Avenue, Truro, Nova Scotia P2V 3M6 Dear Ms Daniels (P) Enclosed is a brochure describing our forthcoming Word Processing seminar to be held in Halifax. I have made the necessary registration arrangements. Office Help Associates is pleased to sponsor your attendance at this seminar. (P) If you have any questions, please do not hesitate to contact me. I look forward to seeing you at the seminar on March 21. Yours sincerely, OFFICE HELP ASSOCIATES, Barbara Ruffeano, Retraining Director

18. enterprise

19. existence

20. feasible

18. achievement

19. acquittal

20. advertisement

18. cylinder

19. deferred

20. delinquent

G

1. dominance
2. eminent
3. exceed
4. facilities
5. fluorescent
6. gauge
7. government
8. guarantee
9. haphazard
10. hindrance
11. hypocrisy
12. irresistible
13. laboratory
14. leisure
15. loneliness
16. maneuver
17. nickel
18. noticeable
19. opposite
20. parliament

H

1. per capita
2. persuade
3. possession
4. preliminary
5. principal
6. procedure
7. prophecy(n)
8. quotient
9. recommend
10. repellent
11. rheumatism
12. ridiculous
13. scissors
14. sovereign
15. surgeon
16. tendency
17. there
18. tragedy
19. unanimous
20. vaccinate

I

1. vice versa
2. waiver
3. weird
4. whose
5. precede
6. presumptuous
7. principle
8. promissory
9. prophesy (v)
10. rapport
11. reconciliation
12. rescind
13. rhyme
14. safety
15. seize
16. simultaneous
17. sufficient
18. surprise
19. synonymous
20. testimonial

ASSIGNMENT

8:22

le 5 janvier 19--, M. Jean Ryan, 180, rue Manor, Ottawa, Ontario K1M 0H2 Monsieur, Comment réagissez-vous lorsque vous constatez que Bell a commis une erreur dans votre compte mensuel de téléphone? C'est le sujet d'un sondage auquel nous demandons à certains de nos abonnés de participer. ¶ Nous sommes conscients du fait qu'il nous arrive de temps en temps de commettre des erreurs dans la facturation de nos abonnés. A l'aide de ce sondage, nous voulons savoir quels sont les erreurs qui vous ennuient le plus. Grace à votre opinion ainsi qu'à celle d'autres abonnés, nous saurons quels aspects de la facturations nous devrions surtout améliorer. ¶ Auriez-vous l'obligeance de remplir le questionnaire ci-joint, au cours des quelques jour qui suivent. C'est un questionnaire court et simple, qui ne prendra plus que dix minutes à remplir. ¶ Après l'avoir rempli, pourriez-vous le mettre dans l'enveloppe affranchie à notre adresse que vous trouverez ci-jointe, et nous le faire renvoyer? ¶ Nous vous remercions d'avance d'avoir collaboré à ce sondage et vous prions d'agréer l'assurance de nos sentiments distingués. Sincèrement, S. Lachenbauer, Directeur, Etudes sur la Facturation téléphonique. Encls.

The following letters contain both a company name and an enclosure notation. Format them attractively, according to your teacher's instructions for letter and punctuation styles.

ASSIGNMENT

8:23

Mrs. Susan Doidge, 4 Oxen Pond Rd., St. John's, Newfoundland A1B 3J1 Dear Mrs. Doidge ¶ I have registered you for the Word Processing Seminar in St. John's, April 25 to 26. We are pleased to have you attend. Attached is a questionnaire which we would appreciate your returning as soon as possible. Your responses will help us determine and respond to the particular needs of the seminar participants. A self-addressed, stamped envelope is enclosed for your convenience. Sincerely, OFFICE HELP ASSOCIATES, Barbara Rufrano, Retraining Director

J

1. triumph
2. unique
3. validate
4. villain
5. warranty
6. whether
7. withdrawal
8. precious
9. prevalent
10. privilege
11. pronunciation
12. publicly
13. relevant
14. rhetoric
15. rhythm
16. susceptible
17. technical
18. their
19. yacht
20. theory

ASSIGNMENT

8:19

Monsieur Yvan Gasse, CP 21, Murdochville, Québec G0E 1W0 Monsieur, ¶ Comme suite à votre lettre du 19 janvier dernier nous sommes obligés de vous faire connaître que nos pratiques consacrées nous mettent dans l'impossibilité de donner suite à votre requête de don d'une voiture GM pour votre "gros lot." ¶ Nous recevons en cours d'années de multiples demandes comme la vôtre et, comme nous ne pourrions matériellement les satisfaire toutes, nous avons pour principe de nous limiter strictement à des projets d'envergure nationale. ¶ Avec nos regrets, nous vous prions d'agréer, cher monsieur, l'assurance de notre plus profond respect. GENERAL MOTORS OF CANADA LIMITED, Ruth I. Milne, Service de relations publiques

The following letters contain enclosure notations. Format them attractively, according to your teacher's instructions for letter and punctuation styles.

ASSIGNMENT

8:20

Mr. Ken Abrossimoff, 331, St-Joseph est., Québec, Québec G1K 3B3 Dear Mr. Abrossimoff ¶ With reference to the duplicate renewal notice you received, we wish to inform you that notices are mailed regularly if our records indicate that membership has not been renewed. ¶ We have examined your account, which indicates that your payment has not yet been received by our office. Although our records are usually accurate, human error is possible. We would appreciate receiving a copy of your payment to resolve this situation. ¶ Kindly use the enclosed envelope, directed to my personal attention. Yours truly, Edward Singh, Membership Secretary

ASSIGNMENT

8:21

Ms Terri Elgar, 10160-101 Street, Edmonton, Alberta T5J 0T1 Dear Ms Elgar ¶ We appreciate your interest in Mountain Grove College and hope the enclosed information will be helpful to you. ¶ Application for prompt admission at all course levels should be submitted by February 23. Applications received later will be considered, depending on places available. ¶ Pretesting for admission to second year courses will be held at Mountain Grove College on Saturday, February 28. This testing will take place in room 321 at 9:00. All examination supplies will be provided. ¶ Upon receipt of your completed application form and fee, interviews will be arranged. Any further inquiries can be forwarded to the Registrar. Yours truly, Ethel McMillan, Admissions Secretary

ASSIGNMENT

5:18

The following words are commonly misspelled. For each word a common misspelling is given as well as the correct spelling.
Using a full sheet of paper, key the correct spelling for each word.

1. truely, truly
2. committment, commitment
3. discrepancy, discrepency
4. questionaire, questionnaire
5. category, catagory
6. perserverance, perseverance
7. occured, occurred
8. embarrass, embarass
9. fulfill, fullfil
10. defendent, defendant
11. lien, lein
12. deductible, deductable
13. temperamental, tempramental
14. ommission, omission
15. descendant, descendent
16. acceptance, acceptence
17. disatisfied, dissatisfied
18. negligible, negligable
19. personnel, personnell
20. secratary, secretary

21. all right, alright
22. mischievious, mischievous
23. precedent, precedant
24. customery, customary
25. collectible, collectable
26. withholding, witholding
27. apoligize, apologize
28. occurence, occurrence
29. fundimental, fundamental
30. exageration, exaggeration
31. jeopardize, jeopardise
32. representative, representitive
33. sergeant, sargeant
34. restaraunt, restaurant
35. complementary, complimentary
36. fued, feud
37. auxilliary, auxiliary
38. bookeepper, bookkeeper
39. facsimile, fascimile
40. maintainence, maintenance

COMPANY NAME AND ENCLOSURE NOTATIONS

The following letters contain a company name. Format the letters attractively, according to your teacher's instructions for letter and punctuation styles.

ASSIGNMENT 8:17

Mr. and Mrs. Pierre Sartre, 4335 Chelsea Crescent, North Vancouver, British Columbia B7R 3J4 Dear Mr. and Mrs. Sartre ¶ With reference to the missed issues of our magazine, *Good Cooking*, please be advised that the magazines were properly addressed and shipped. However, we will be happy to send you under separate cover, two additional copies of these issues. ¶ In the past, we have found that many apartment residents with common mail deliveries, as well as homes with unprotected mailboxes, have a high frequency of missed issues. We suspect that this might be why you have not received all the issues of the magazine. If this is not the case, and if you should experience further problems, please advise your local postal service to investigate. ¶ Should you have any other questions, please contact us again. Thank you for your continued interest in our magazine. Yours sincerely, GOOD COOKING MAGAZINE, Cheryl Kerr, Circulation Department

ASSIGNMENT 8:18

Château Bijou, 1659, rue Sherbrooke ouest, Montréal, Québec, H3H 1E3 Gentlemen (P) Carla Baldwin joined our firm in September 19— as assistant to the vice-president. She fulfilled her responsibilities admirably and conscientiously (P) Our belief in Carla's capabilities was demonstrated by her advancement to assistant to the president and, within one year of employment, to office manager. (P) We recommend Carla without hesitation. Yours very truly, THE KASLAUSKAS COMPANIES, Sharon P. Kaslauskas, President

ASSIGNMENT 5:19

In each of the following pairs of words, one word is spelled incorrectly. Key the correct spelling on a full sheet of paper. Set up your list attractively. Check your spelling in a dictionary if uncertain.

1. supercede, supersede
2. acustom, accustom
3. accross, across
4. acknowledgement, acknowledgment
5. origanal, original
6. accessable, accessible
7. survay, survey
8. occasion, occassion
9. procurment, procurement
10. sufficient, sufficent
11. getting geting
12. ninty, ninety
13. calander, calendar
14. bisiness, business
15. athaletic, athletic
16. convenience, convinience
17. accommodations, accomodations
18. trespass, trespase
19. dispair, despair
20. influence, influance
21. compitent, competent
22. collector, collecter
23. beautiful, beauteful
24. February, Febuary
25. affection, afection
26. definately, definitely
27. sincerly, sincerely
28. imacculate, immaculate
29. skillful, skillfull
30. psychology, phsychology

ASSIGNMENT 5:20

Some of the following words are correctly spelled and some are not. Key the lists, correcting all errors.

A	B
1. already	1. equipped
2. goverment	2. interupt
3. accidant	3. adjust
4. deside	4. hastely
5. accept	5. ledger
6. committe	6. referance

Key an exact copy of this letter, paying special attention to the spacing of the company name and enclosure notations.

↓ 15
19-- 01 30

↓ 6

Mr. Lorne Campbell
10011 Third Avenue South
Lethbridge, Alberta   1
T1J 0J3
  ↓ 2
Dear Mr. Campbell   2
  ↓ 2
This letter illustrates the Full Block style with Open punctuation. You   3
will notice that it also illustrates two additional letter parts, the   4
COMPANY NAME and the ENCLOSURE NOTATION.   5
  ↓ 2
Some companies like to key their name in the closing section of the   6
letter, even though it is already printed on letterhead paper. The   7
Company Name is keyed in all capital letters, a double space below the   8
complimentary closing. Key the name exactly as it appears in the com-   9
pany's letterhead. If it is exceptionally long, it may be centred.   10
  ↓ 2
An Enclosure notation is used to indicate that other papers or documents   11
are attached to the letter. The enclosure notation can be keyed either   12
a single or double space below the reference initials at the left margin.   13
Enc., Encl., or the word Enclosure may be used to indicate that something   14
has been enclosed. If more than one item is enclosed, use the following   15
forms to indicate this: Encs., Enclosures, or Attachments. You may also   16
number and list each enclosure separately: Enclosures: 1. Cheque
2. Invoice No. 346.
  ↓ 2
Yours truly
  ↓ 2
SPECTRUM RECORDS LIMITED   *Company name
                                   in all caps*

↓ 4 *Sonja Evanoff*

Sonja Evanoff   17
Correspondence Director
  ↓ 2
SE/yi
Enclosure   *Enclosure notation*

FULL BLOCK LETTER STYLE
OPEN PUNCTUATION
COMPANY NAME   18
ENCLOSURE NOTATION

7. bussiness

8. minute

9. realy

10. invoise

11. consideration

12. assure

13. foriegn

14. responsability

15. application

16. develope

17. issue

18. receive

19. agreement

20. experiance

21. charactor

22. atheletic

23. practical

24. arrangment

25. organization

7. convenient

8. fourty

9. nuisence

10. beleive

11. guaranteed

12. definitly

13. ninth

14. permenent

15. apologize

16. remittance

17. immediatly

18. morgage

19. bookeeping

20. desireable

21. withhold

22. recomend

23. acknowlege

24. aquainted

25. proceed

ASSIGNMENT 8:14

Ms. Marie Langman, Principal, Charlottetown Public School, 4 Charlottetown Blvd., West Hill, Ontario M1C 2C6. Dear Ms. Langman, (P) On behalf of boys and girls around the world who benefit from the annual CANSAVE Valentine Tree, I would like to extend a special thank you to all students and staff members who participated in this year's program. (P) Schools across Canada have informed us that many special projects have been undertaken during February by youngsters who wish to share their love with others less fortunate. Please express to them and their teachers my sincere appreciation for all their efforts and the hope that they will continue this special Valentine Celebration next year. Yours sincerely, Arthur P. Borowski, President

ASSIGNMENT 8:15

Ms Ginette Leigh Duke, 9 Chipper Crescent, Scarborough, Ontario M1K 4H1. Dear Ms Duke, ¶ Thank you for your inquiry concerning our plant tours. ¶ Tours are conducted on Monday, Tuesday, and Wednesday, at 10:00 and 13:45. The tour lasts just under one hour and finishes at our Thrift Store, where "seconds" (products with small imperfections) are sold. We can accommodate up to, *but no more than*, forty persons on each tour. Smaller groups are also welcome. ¶ You may find it more convenient to telephone to make arrangements for your visit. If not, perhaps you would indicate your preference as soon as possible, so that a firm booking can be made. ¶ Orenda Road is situated off Dixie Road North, one block north of Steeles Avenue. Dixie Road North exits from Highway 401 and the QEW. ¶ We look forward to welcoming you to the Kitchens of Sara Lee. Yours very truly, Joan Yeo, Consumer Relations

SPECIALIZED VOCABULARIES ASSIGNMENTS

The following groups of words will introduce you to some of the specialized vocabularies used in various fields and occupations.
Follow these instructions for Assignments 5:21 to 5:32.

Pre-test
Set a 40-character line.
Double space.
Number and key each word as dictated by your teacher.

Homework
For homework, study these words and prepare for another quiz in your next keyboarding class.
Look up meanings of words you do not know.

Post-test
Your teacher may dictate the words to you, or ask you to illustrate their meaning by using each one correctly in a sentence.

Composition
For each of the following lists of specialized vocabulary, compose a paragraph using at least ten of the words given.

ASSIGNMENT
5:21

1,705,436

NUMBERS

A	B	C
1. one	1. sixth	1. zero
2. two	2. seventh	2. once
3. three	3. eighth	3. double
4. four	4. ninth	4. duplicate
5. five	5. tenth	5. twice
6. six	6. eleventh	6. twin
7. seven	7. twelfth	7. triple
8. eight	8. thirteenth	8. triplicate
9. nine	9. fourteenth	9. quadruple

ASSIGNMENT 8:11	Mr. Douglas Boothroyd, 279 Blake Blvd., Apartment 6, Ottawa, Ontario K1L 6L6 Dear Mr. Boothroyd ¶ The file relating to your application for admission to Administrative Studies has been reviewed by the Administrative Studies Faculty. ¶ We are pleased to inform you that your acceptance into the program has been recommended. A letter of confirmation, together with a statement of standing on admission, will be forwarded to you by the Dean of Administrative Studies. Your admission is, of course, conditional on the satisfactory completion of your undergraduate program. ¶ Professor A. R. Hart has agreed to serve as your program adviser and she would be happy to answer any questions you may have concerning the selection of courses. Yours truly, Ellen Fitzpatrick, Registrar
ASSIGNMENT 8:12	Mr. Frank Marchese, Branch Manager, Catering Operations Ltd., P.O. Box 259, Lester B. Pearson International Airport, Toronto, Ontario M5S 1P5 Dear Mr. Marchese ¶ We are most grateful to you for the catering you provided for our public affairs event on February 12. We received many compliments about the food and the service. Yours truly, Dorothy Ioannou, Public Affairs Manager
ASSIGNMENT 8:13	Madame Marie Leduc, 625, boul. Dorchester, Montréal Québec H3Z 2R3 Madam, ¶ Dans le cadre d'un projet de service régional qui serait établi en 19--, Bell Canada envisage d'abolir les frais d'interurbain entre la circonscription téléphonique de Jonquière et celle de La Baie, incluant Grande Baie, Bagotville, St-Félix d'Otis. ¶ L'avènement de ce nouveau service vous permettrait donc d'appeler sans frais les numéros de téléphone commençant par 542, 547, et 548. Ces indicatifs locaux desservent, en tout ou en partie, les municipalités suivantes: Arvida, Cantin, Chute-à-Caron, Kènogami, Jonquière, Larouche, St-Jean-Vianney, St-Léonard, et Shipshaw. ¶ En vue du fait que la réalisation d'un tel project nécessite l'approbation de la majorité des abonnés concernés et celle du Conseil de la radiodiffusion et des télécommunications canadiennes (CRTC), il nous faut donc savoir ce que vous pensez du projet. ¶ L'abolition des frais d'interurbain entraînerait, dans votre cas, une hausse de tarif de base mensuel, vu qu'à tître d'abonné de La Baie, vous pourrez alors joindre un plus grand nombre de numéros de téléphone sans frais supplémentaires. ¶ En Principe, le tarif de base mensuel est établi en fonction du nombre de numéros de téléphone accessibles sans frais par l'abonné et de la catégorie de votre service, soit résidentielle ou d'affaires. ¶ Le tableau suivant vous indique votre tarif de base actuel, le tarif de base proposé, et la différence imputable à l'implantation d'un service régional. Veuillez agréer, chère madame, mes sentiments distingués.

10. ten	10. fifteenth	10. innumerable
11. eleven	11. sixteenth	11. numerous
12. twelve	12. seventeenth	12. twentieth
13. thirteen	13. eighteenth	13. thirtieth
14. fourteen	14. nineteenth	14. fortieth
15. fifteen	15. thirty	15. fiftieth
16. sixteen	16. forty	16. sixtieth
17. seventeen	17. fifty	17. seventieth
18. eighteen	18. sixty	18. eightieth
19. nineteen	19. seventy	19. hundredth
20. twenty	20. eighty	20. thousandth
21. first	21. ninety	21. millionth
22. second	22. hundred	22. billionth
23. third	23. thousand	23. millionaire
24. fourth	24. million	24. numeric
25. fifth	25. billion	25. decimal

ASSIGNMENT 5:22

OFFICE AUTOMATION

A	B	C
1. automated	1. binary	1. computer
2. conversion	2. facsimile	2. digital
3. electronic	3. feedback	3. integrated
4. mechanization	4. memory	4. monitor
5. processor	5. programming	5. scheduling
6. simulation	6. transceiving	6. verification
7. allocate	7. buffer storage	7. data
8. Fortran	8. hardware	8. malfunction

Mountain Boot Company, 2890 Ashley Road, Victoria, BC V9A 2S8 Dear Sir ¶ In the last two years we have been very happy with the quality and sales of your hiking boots. Unfortunately, however, we have experienced many delays in deliveries. ¶ I would like to suggest the establishment of a warehouse in Eastern Canada. I believe that the volume of goods sold in this part of the country justifies a warehouse operation. Your response to this idea would be appreciated. Yours truly, Bernard Tenenhouse, Shoe Department Manager

ASSIGNMENT 8:10

Mr. J. B. Jeffrey, president, Kiwanis Club of Humber Valley, 9 Hilldowntree Road, Islington, Ontario M9A 2Z4 Dear Mr. Jeffrey, Thank you for your letter of May 15. (P) Unfortunately, we are not in a position to reply positively to all requests of this type. We do try our best to assist in major fund raising events; however, as a result of this we are not in a position to answer the hundreds of requests that fall into your category. (P) We do extend to you our very best wishes and our congratulations for the excellent work being done by the Kiwanis club. Very truly yours, Mr. M. R. Stewart, Public Relations Manager

9. matrix	9. optimum coding	9. parameter
10. redundancy check	10. switch	10. tabulator
11. transfer	11. transmit	11. unconditional
12. flowchart	12. disk	12. input

ASSIGNMENT 5:23

LAW

A	B	C
1. affidavit	1. alias	1. arraign
2. assault	2. attest	2. bribery
3. circumstantial	3. bona fide	3. codicil
4. convict	4. custody	4. decree
5. docket	5. duress	5. embezzlement
6. eviction	6. extradition	6. felony
7. accomplice	7. accused	7. alibi
8. alimony	8. annulment	8. attorney
9. bigamy	9. burglary	9. estate
10. defence	10. condemnation	10. guilty
11. evidence	11. delinquency	11. judgement
12. illegal	12. fugitive	12. negligence
13. malicious	13. imprisonment	13. rebuttal
14. reprieve	14. malpractice	14. slander
15. statutory	15. proxy	15. summons
16. venue	16. rescind	16. trespass
17. homicide	17. subpoena	17. warranty
18. injunction	18. tort	18. indictment
19. litigation	19. incriminate	19. libel
20. misdemeanour	20. larceny	20. manslaughter

Your teacher is your supervisor. Follow his or her instructions for letter and punctuation style as you do each of these assignments. Unless otherwise instructed, use the current date and key an envelope for all letters.

ASSIGNMENT 8:6

Mr. and Mrs. F. Hutchison, 1412 Second Street, Prince George, BC V2L 3B6 Dear Mr. and Mrs. Hutchison ¶ We are pleased that you have chosen us to supply your new kitchen cabinets. ¶ We will be ready to install your Sherwood design cabinets, finished in birch clear varnish, on April 15. As stated in the contract agreement, we will be supplying Sherwood hinges, white porcelain knobs, and molded counters in San Fernando Red. ¶ The final estimate is $4091.85. We look forward to making your "dream kitchen" become a reality. Yours sincerely, Marilyn Craig, Kitchen Co-ordinator

ASSIGNMENT 8:7

Ms Lilian Zieglar, 1909 McDonald Avenue, Prince George, BC V2L 4G3 Dear Miss Zieglar ¶ As promised, I am fowarding to you a copy of the amended Constitution and By-laws of the Canadian Chapter of Secretaries International. These amendments were accepted by the membership and adopted as of May 15, 19--. Mrs. Helen Langdon, our chapter's immediate past president, serves as chairperson of the Nominating Committee. It will be the task of this committee to present to you a slate of board members for election. These members, if elected, will hold office until the annual meeting of the chapter in June 19--. ¶ Please send in your annual membership fee of $55.00 today. Your support is appreciated. Yours sincerely, Marie LeBlanc, Membership Secretary

ASSIGNMENT 8:8

Mrs. Helen LeRiche, 3424-13th Avenue, Regina, Saskatchewan S4T 1P7 Dear Mrs. LeRiche ¶ It will soon be time to plan your summer holidays and I sincerely hope that you will consider Bon Voyage Tours for 19--. ¶ We have much to offer you this year. In addition to our regular favourites, we have some fascinating new holidays planned. ¶ This year, for the first time, we will be organizing trips to Italy. Two weeks will be spent touring this fabulous country. Also planned is our Scottish Highland Tour--ten days of delightful touring. ¶ Closer to home, we are exploring more of Canada's scenic wonders. Featured this year is "Arctic Adventure," a trip through magnificent wilderness along the Dempster Highway. ¶ Space on many of the tours is limited and I would advise you to contact us as soon as you can. We look forward to serving you. Very truly yours, Gerald Maitland, Tour Organizer

21. penitentiary	21. mandatory	21. parole
22. arrest	22. notary public	22. probate
23. chattel	23. perjury	23. bequeath
24. executor	24. bailiff	24. defraud
25. judicial	25. covenant	25. lawsuit
26. loophole	26. juvenile	26. plaintiffs
27. prosecute	27. malice	27. rendered
28. retainer	28. ratification	28. revoke
29. sheriff	29. retroactive	29. testimony
30. trustee	30. statute	30. verdict

ASSIGNMENT 5:24

RETAILING

A	B	C
1. advertisement	1. agent	1. auction
2. bargains	2. brokers	2. competitors
3. consigned	3. consumer	3. counter
4. creditors	4. customer	4. dealers
5. discounts	5. expenses	5. inquiries
6. installed	6. invoicing	6. jobber
7. low-priced	7. packaged	7. markup
8. overstocked	8. prospect	8. purchase
9. profits	9. quota	9. resale
10. retailer	10. seasonable	10. trademark
11. turnover	11. undersell	11. vendor
12. wholesale	12. marketable	12. priced

BUSINESS LETTERS

ASSIGNMENT
8:5

Key an exact copy of this business letter.

↓ 15
19-- 03 09

*Date begins on line 15
(or 2 lines below the letterhead).
Drop approximately 6 lines in a
medium letter.*

↓ 6

Ms Heather Chisholm
5536 Fourth Avenue
Edmonton, Alberta
T6L 1B8
↓ 2
Dear Ms Chishom
↓ 2
This is a sample of a business letter. Business letters are sent from one
company to another, or from a company to an individual. If you obtain a
summer office job, or if you intend to follow a business career, you will
use this kind of letter.
↓ 2
To format a business letter, estimate the number of words contained in the
body, and establish the margins. The most usual line length for letters
is 60-characters, but this can vary according to the length of the letter.
Most letters are printed on good quality bond paper called letterhead.
↓ 2
Begin the date 15 lines from the top of the paper. Single space the inside
address. Double space before and after the salutation, between paragraphs,
and before the complimentary closing. Single space the printed name and
the title (if one is indicated) of the signee. Reference initials tell who
is sending the letter and who keyboarded it. They are placed flush with
the left margin a double space below the name of the position or the sender.
↓ 2
Yours truly

↓ 4 *Carol Gans*

*Drop approximately 4 lines in a
medium letter.*

Carol Gans
Administrative Assistant
↓ 2
CG:yi

1
2
3
4
5
6
7
8
9
10
11
12
13
14
15
16

ASSIGNMENT 5:25

REAL ESTATE

A	B	C
1. easement	1. bungalow	1. covenants
2. acres	2. encumbrance	2. realtor
3. mortgage	3. apartment	3. basement
4. deed	4. carport	4. cottage
5. grading	5. dwelling	5. estate
6. homestead	6. grantor	6. homeowner
7. landlord	7. improvements	7. leaseholder
8. lessee	8. landscaping	8. modernizing
9. occupancy	9. lessor	9. property
10. redecorate	10. premises	10. residence
11. restriction	11. rental	11. suburban
12. tenant	12. tenement	12. zoning

ASSIGNMENT 5:26

MEDICINE

A	B	C
1. anesthetic	1. tuberculosis	1. antihistamine
2. appendectomy	2. antibiotics	2. ulcer
3. hernia	3. electrocardiograph	3. medication
4. insomnia	4. penicillin	4. respiration
5. obesity	5. tetanus	5. abdomen
6. surgery	6. allergy	6. amputate
7. abscess	7. anemia	7. antiseptic
8. anatomy	8. aspirin	8. asthma

l) Mrs. Alison George, Vice-President, Arkell + Associates, 260 St. Mary Ave., Winnipeg, Manitoba R3C 0M6 Personal

m) Canadian Research Foundation, 2nd Floor, Brunswick Bldg., 240 Bank Street, Ottawa, Ontario K2P 1X2

n) Executive Rentals, Room 1801, 18th Floor, 800 Place d'Youville, Quebec, Quebec G1R 3P4 Special Delivery

o) Redford Cosmetics Ltd., 2212 Scarth Street, Suite 2795, Regina, Saskatchewan, S4P 2J9 Registered Mail

Courtesy of Xerox Canada Ltd.

9. arthritis	9. bronchitis	9. calcium
10. bacteria	10. cancer	10. capsule
11. calories	11. cartilage	11. codeine
12. carbohydrate	12. contamination	12. diabetes
13. contagious	13. dentist	13. disease
14. diagnosis	14. diphtheria	14. fracture
15. epidemic	15. headache	15. hygiene
16. hypochondriac	16. hysteria	16. infection
17. influenza	17. laceration	17. laryngitis
18. liniment	18. lozenge	18. massage
19. narcotics	19. nausea	19. nervousness
20. neurosis	20. nourishment	20. perspiration
21. pneumonia	21. prescription	21. psychiatry
22. psychopathic	22. quarantine	22. recuperating
23. respiratory	23. rheumatism	23. transfusion
24. schizophrenia	24. stomach	24. tonsillectomy
25. surgeons	25. symptoms	25. vaccinate

ASSIGNMENT
5:27

INSURANCE

A	B	C
1. actuary	1. annuity	1. assessment
2. beneficiary	2. casualty	2. certificate
3. dividends	3. premium	3. idemnity
4. insurance	4. adjusters	4. public liability
5. underwriter	5. application	5. appraisals
6. arson	6. benefits	6. catastrophe

APPLYING YOUR SKILLS

ENVELOPES

ASSIGNMENT 8:4

Key the following addresses on envelopes, using the correct envelope format. Key the Canadian provinces using the Canada Post abbreviations. Use correct abbreviations for the American states.

a) Pacific Envelope Ltd.
700 W. Georgia St.
Vancouver, British Columbia
V7Y 1C9
Registered

b) Dr. Carolyn Kelly
260 St. Mary Avenue
2nd Floor
Winnipeg, Manitoba
R3C 0M6

c) Mr. Patrick Boccongelle
Vice-President
Pride Packaging Products
P.O. Box 516
St. John's, Newfoundland
A1C 5K4
Confidential

d) Princess Bridal Wear
855 St. Catherine St. E.
12th Floor
Montreal, Quebec
H2L 4N4
Special Delivery

e) Ms Leslie Dragan
Montreal Tower
5151 George Street
Halifax, Nova Scotia
B3J 1M5
Personal

f) Mr. Paul Theroux, President
Theroux Insurance Company
275 Middlefield Road
Menlo Park, California USA
94025

g) Mr. John Anderson
Anderson Jewellers
Suite 1021
1101 S. Winchester Blvd.
San Jose, California USA
95156

h) Williams & Williams Associates
29 Great Tower Street
London, ENGLAND
EC3R 5AQ

i) Rev. Steve Talevski
Ul. Ohridska No. 331
Bitola, Macedonia
YUGOSLAVIA

j) Mr. Harry Chronopoulos
14 Zephyron Street
Agia Paraskevi
Athens, GREECE

k) Prof. J. K. Taylor,
Oliver Building,
10225 - 100th Avenue,
Edmonton, AB
T5J 0A1 Registered

Apartment, floor, or suite numbers should be keyed on a separate line, below the street address. If the street address is very short, however, these numbers may be keyed on the same line. If this method is used, a comma should separate the street address from the apartment number.

7. collision	7. claimant	7. commission
8. comprehensive	8. coverage	8. damage
9. disability	9. duration	9. expiration
10. fatality	10. matures	10. hazardous
11. hospitalized	11. probability	11. lapse
12. licence	12. receipts	12. policy holder
13. preferred risk	13. renewals	13. protection
14. remittance	14. security	14. reimburse
15. risk	15. injured	15. survivor

ASSIGNMENT 5:28

TIME

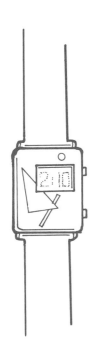

A	B	C
1. afternoon	1. fortnight	1. perpetual
2. ago	2. future	2. postpone
3. always	3. hereafter	3. prematurely
4. anniversary	4. heretofore	4. previously
5. annual	5. hour	5. recent
6. antiquity	6. immediately	6. season
7. before	7. instant	7. second
8. biennial	8. instantaneous	8. semi-annually
9. biannual	9. interim	9. shortly
10. brief	10. intermission	10. sometime
11. century	11. late	11. tardily
12. constantly	12. lifelong	12. term
13. currently	13. lifetime	13. temporary
14. daily	14. meantime	14. thenceforth

INSERTING LETTERS INTO ENVELOPES

Correct methods of folding a letter for insertion into a #8, a #10, and a window envelope are shown below. It is important to use these methods, so that the letter is not cut if fed through an automatic letter opening machine.

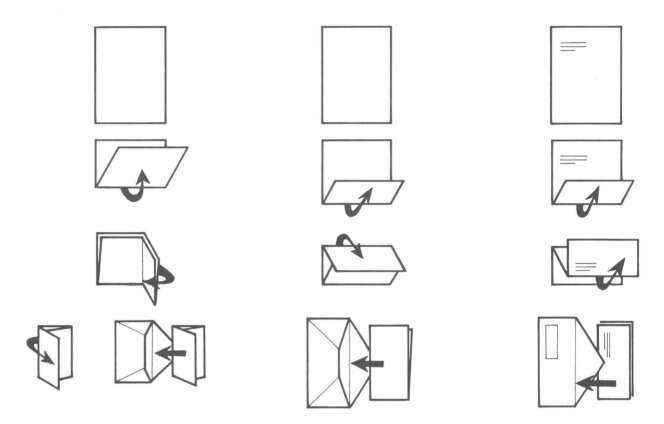

15. date	15. meanwhile	15. thereafter
16. daybreak	16. minute	16. today
17. decade	17. moment	17. tomorrow
18. digital	18. month	18. tonight
19. duration	19. nighttime	19. twilight
20. endlessly	20. noon	20. ultimately
21. early	21. nowadays	21. until
22. eternally	22. occasionally	22. weekly
23. eternity	23. o'clock	23. year
24. forenoon	24. past	24. yesterday
25. formerly	25. permanent	25. young

ASSIGNMENT 5:29

TRANSPORTATION

A	B	C
1. carrier	1. caboose	1. carload
2. cruise	2. collision	2. conductor
3. en route	3. demurrage	3. dispatcher
4. navigation	4. excursion	4. junction
5. voyage	5. purser	5. rebate
6. automobile	6. subway	6. turnpike
7. cargo	7. waybill	7. airport
8. consignment	8. baggage	8. berth
9. crating	9. cartage	9. chauffeur
10. engineer	10. depot	10. conveyor
11. forwarding	11. express	11. diesel
12. highway	12. gauge	12. first class

ABBREVIATIONS FOR CANADA'S PROVINCES AND TERRITORIES

Names may be keyed in full, or with the appropriate abbreviation.

British Columbia	BC	Nova Scotia	NS
Alberta	AB	Prince Edward Island	PE
Saskatchewan	SK	Newfoundland	NF
Manitoba	MB	Labrador	LB
Ontario	ON	Yukon Territory	YT
Quebec	PQ	Northwest Territories	NT
New Brunswick	NB		

ABBREVIATIONS FOR U.S. STATES AND POSSESSIONS

Alabama	AL	Missouri	MO
Alaska	AK	Montana	MT
Arizona	AZ	Nebraska	NE
Arkansas	AR	Nevada	NV
California	CA	New Hampshire	NH
Canal Zone	CZ	New Jersey	NJ
Colorado	CO	New Mexico	NM
Connecticut	CT	New York	NY
Delaware	DE	North Carolina	NC
District of Columbia	DC	North Dakota	ND
Florida	FL	Ohio	OH
Georgia	GA	Oklahoma	OK
Guam	GU	Oregon	OR
Hawaii	HI	Pennsylvania	PA
Idaho	ID	Puerto Rico	PR
Illinois	IL	Rhode Island	RI
Indiana	IN	South Carolina	SC
Iowa	IA	South Dakota	SD
Kansas	KS	Tennessee	TN
Kentucky	KY	Texas	TX
Louisiana	LA	Utah	UT
Maine	ME	Vermont	VT
Maryland	MD	Virginia	VA
Massachusetts	MA	Washington	WA
Michigan	MI	West Virginia	WV
Minnesota	MN	Wisconsin	WI
Mississippi	MS	Wyoming	WY

13. overdue	13. locomotive	13. hauling
14. pedestrian	14. overloaded	14. passenger
15. railroad	15. pier	15. prepay
16. tariff	16. routed	16. salvage
17. tickets	17. taxicab	17. terminal
18. traffic	18. timetable	18. toll
19. warehouse	19. transcontinental	19. tunnel
20. breakage	20. waterfront	20. waterways

ASSIGNMENT *5:30*

FINANCE

A	B	C
1. amortization	1. collateral	1. comptroller
2. contingency	2. currency	2. disbursement
3. prospectus	3. draft	3. expenditure
4. syndicate	4. mortgage	4. subsidiary
5. assets	5. securities	5. accrual
6. deflation	6. bookkeeping	6. broker
7. endorsement	7. depression	7. dividend
8. goodwill	8. financial	8. fiscal
9. insolvent	9. instalment	9. inflation
10. ledger	10. liability	10. interest
11. maturity	11. monetary	11. liquidate
12. reimbursement	12. rebate	12. negotiable
13. repudiation	13. remittance	13. receivable
14. treasurer	14. shareholders	14. repossess
15. promissory note	15. valuation	15. stockbroker

2. Being keying an address of up to five lines, one line below the horizontal centre of the envelope. This is line 12 on a #8 envelope and line 14 on a #10 envelope. Begin the address one line higher if the address consists of six or seven lines. For envelopes of different sizes, such as manila envelopes, use a ruler to find the horizontal centre. Begin keying two lines below this point.

3. Set a tab stop or a left margin five or ten spaces to the left of the centre of the envelope. The number of spaces you leave will depend on the length of the longest line in the address.

4. Single space the address.

5. The city in the address may be keyed in all capital letters.

6. Always include the postal code. Your local post office can supply the code for any address in Canada. Canada Post prefers that the postal code be placed on a separate line at the end of the address.

7. There should be no punctuation at the ends of lines, except following an abbreviation.

8. When addressing an envelope to be sent to a foreign country, key the name of the country in all capital letters.

9. When addressing an envelope to the United States, place the ZIP code three spaces after the name of the state, on the same line (for example, Detroit, MI   25423).

10. Key special handling and mailing instructions in all capitals, a double space below the final line of the return address.

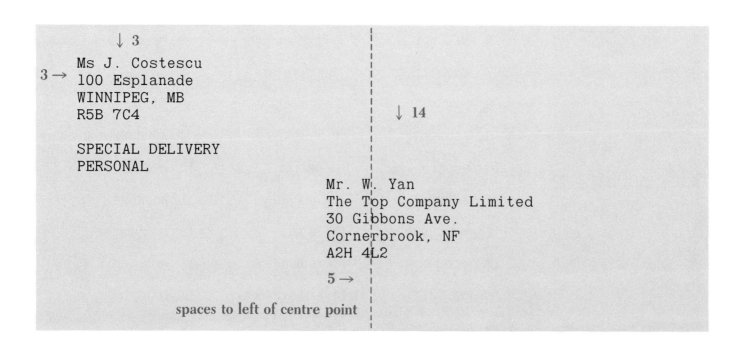

```
        ↓ 3
       Ms J. Costescu
3 →    100 Esplanade
       WINNIPEG, MB
       R5B 7C4                       ↓ 14

       SPECIAL DELIVERY
       PERSONAL

                          Mr. W. Yan
                          The Top Company Limited
                          30 Gibbons Ave.
                          Cornerbrook, NF
                          A2H 4L2

                     5 →

        spaces to left of centre point
```

ASSIGNMENT 5:31

POLITICS AND GOVERNMENT

A	B	C
1. ambassador	1. ballot	1. bureau
2. bureaucrat	2. campaign	2. candidate
3. caucus	3. bi-election	3. conservative
4. convention	4. democracy	4. dictator
5. diplomat	5. electorate	5. federal
6. franchise	6. government	6. impeachment
7. international	7. legislate	7. president
8. liberal	8. lobbying	8. mayor
9. monarchy	9. municipal	9. congress
10. partisan	10. platform	10. senator
11. politician	11. population	11. legislature
12. quorum	12. representative	12. nominate
13. precinct	13. taxes	13. political
14. municipal	14. riding	14. debate
15. alderman	15. vote	15. prime minister

ASSIGNMENT 5:32

ADOPTED FROM OTHER LANGUAGES

A	B	C
1. ad infinitum	1. bona fide	1. caveat emptor
2. habeas corpus	2. in re	2. in toto
3. per annum	3. per capita	3. per diem
4. per se	4. pro rata	4. status quo
5. ultimatum	5. via	5. vice versa

8. At the top of every page but the first, key a heading consisting of

   a) the addressee's name;

   b) the page number;

   c) the date.

   This heading always begins on line seven, and is always followed by a triple space preceding the body of the letter.

9. There are two different styles of formatting the heading:

   a) **Blocked**. Each of the three parts of the heading are keyed on a separate line, flush with the left margin. With this style, the page number must be keyed "Page 2," *not* "-2-."

   b) **Spread**. All three parts of the heading are keyed on one line. With this style, either "-2-" or "Page 2" may be used. In the spread style, the name of the addressee is keyed at the left margin, the page number is centered, and the date is pivoted from the right margin. The blocked style is faster to key and is therefore more commonly used.

BLOCKED:

```
Mr. John Anderson
Page 2
19-- 06 18
```

SPREAD:

```
Mr. John Anderson          -2-                19-- 06 26

                           OR

Mr. John Anderson         Page 2              19-- 06 26
```

ENVELOPES

1. Envelopes come in a variety of sizes. The two most common are called #8 and #10. To format an envelope to accompany a business or a personal business letter, begin by keying the return address three lines from the top and three spaces in from the left edge of the envelope. Single space the return address, including the name of the person sending the letter, the street address, the apartment number if there is one, the city and province, and the postal code.

6. à la mode	6. blasé	6. camouflage
7. coiffure	7. debris	7. début
8. dénouement	8. élite	8. exposé
9. finesse	9. naïve	9. nonchalant
10. passé	10. protégé	10. régime

HOMONYMS

Homonyms are words that are pronounced the same way, but have different spellings and meanings.

```
The heir to the throne inhaled the fresh mountain
air.
```

HOMONYMS ASSIGNMENTS

ASSIGNMENT

5:33

For each of the following homonyms, key a sentence that appropriately conveys the meaning of the word.
Consult a dictionary if you are in doubt about the meaning of a word.

A	B	C	D	E	F
1. add ad	1. feet feat	1. hair hare	1. mail male	1. sail sale	1. tail tale
2. allowed aloud	2. carat carrot	2. heal heel	2. medal meddle	2. scene seen	2. tear tier
3. ate eight	3. cent sent scent	3. hear here	3. miner minor	3. meet meat	3. their there they're
4. band banned	4. cite sight site	4. hole whole	4. oar ore or	4. seas sees seize	4. threw through

DISPLAYED MATERIAL IN LETTERS

Letters often feature information displayed in a numbered list. If the list is not numbered, each item is set off with double spacing. This displayed material is keyed in the following manner:

1. Items are single spaced, with a double space between each item.

2. Items either begin at the left margin, or are centered, or are indented. When enumerations are indented from the left margin, they are also indented from the right margin.

3. The second line of each item does not begin at the left margin, but is keyed directly below the beginning of the first word of the item. Set a tab four spaces in from the margin, so that you may quickly align the items.

Material quoted in the body of a letter is usually indented five to ten spaces from either margin and is single spaced. A quote of one to three lines may be keyed within the body of the letter. In this case, quotation marks are placed at the beginning and the ending of the quote.

TWO-PAGE LETTERS

Follow these guidelines when formatting a two-page letter:

1. Use a 60-character pica line or a 70-character elite line.

2. Use letterhead paper for page 1, and plain bond paper of the same quality for the second and subsequent pages.

3. The spacing, punctuation, and letter style of the second and subsequent pages must match the first page.

4. Leave a margin of approximately six to nine lines at the bottom of the first page.

5. If possible, begin the second page with a new paragraph. If you must divide a paragraph, leave at least two lines on the preceding page and carry over at least two lines of the body to the next page.

6. *Never* divide the last word on a page.

7. *Never* key only the closing lines of a letter on the second page.

5. air heir	5. dear deer	5. hour our	5. one won	5. sew so	5. throne thrown
6. bear bare	6. dew due	6. incite insight	6. pail pale	6. slay sleigh	6. tide tied
7. billed build	7. die dye	7. its it's	7. pain pane	7. soar sore	7. too to
8. blew blue	8. doe dough	8. knead need	8. pair pare	8. sole soul	8. vain vane
9. brake break	9. dyeing dying	9. knew new	9. peace piece	9. some sum	9. wade weighed
10. buy by bye	10. fair fare	10. knot not	10. pole poll	10. son sun	10. waist waste
11. calender calendar	11. flea flee	11. knows noes nose	11. praise prays preys	11. stair stare	11. ware wear
12. capital capitol	12. clause claws	12. leased least	12. rain reign	12. stationary stationery	12. weak week
13. cell sell	13. council counsel	13. lessen lesson	13. right rite wright write	13. straight strait	13. wood would

ASSIGNMENT
5:34

Key the following sentences, selecting the correct word from those given in parentheses.

1. The clerk measured the material carefully because she did not want to (waist, waste) any.

2. Michelle and Susan want to go on holidays for one (weak, week).

3. The (would, wood) did not catch on fire as it was damp from the rain.

4. The farmer put the (yolk, yoke) on the oxen.

5. During the assembly, John is going to (cite, sight, site) a passage from the Bible.

6. Sam had to (peel, peal) the apples for his pie.

```
July 5, 19—
     ↓ 2
REGISTERED MAIL
PERSONAL
     ↓ 2 to 4 (variable)
Miss Cathy Trudeau
307 Kennedy Street
Winnipeg, Manitoba
R3B 2M7
     ↓ 2
Dear Miss Trudeau:
```

THE POSTSCRIPT NOTATION

Postscripts are used:

1. to provide information that the letter writer forgot to include in the body of the letter;

2. to emphasize a particular point already mentioned in the letter; or

3. to convey a short message unrelated to the main topic of the letter.

Here is the standard format for postscript notations:

· Postscripts are keyed a double space below the final notation.

· Single space the postscript flush with the left margin, unless the paragraphs in the body of the letter are indented, in which case the postscript is also indented.

```
SC:yi
Enclosure
     ↓ 2
PS: This is a sample of a postscript
notation.
```

7. The first (scene, seen) of the play was very short.

8. The police will (seas, seize, sees) stolen property as soon as they find it.

9. Ginette's (soar, sore) throat made her lose her voice.

10. Pauline said that (their, they're, there) going home after supper.

11. The wedding cake had four (tears, tiers).

12. The (ore, or, oar) is hauled from the mines.

13. The (pear, pair, pare) tree (boar, bore) much fruit last year.

14. Let us hope that there will be (piece, peace) on earth.

15. The Greek ship was tied up at (pier, peer) number three.

16. John carefully (wrapped, rapt, rapped) Salina's birthday present.

17. There were dozens of (sail, sale) boats in the water yesterday.

18. They took the quickest (root, route) back home from the cottage.

19. Nick had to get a (lone, loan) for his new car.

20. The (sent, scent) of Suzanne's perfume filled the room.

COMMONLY CONFUSED WORDS

ASSIGNMENT

5:35

The words in these pairs are commonly confused with each other. Look up each word in the dictionary, compose a sentence for each word, then key each sentence.

A	B	C	D
1. accede exceed	1. bazaar bizarre	1. consul council counsel	1. elicit illicit
2. accelerate exhilarate	2. breadth breath breathe	2. cooperation corporation	2. emerge immerge
3. accept except	3. choose chose	3. decade decayed	3. emigrant immigrant

```
cc: Noreen Lenihan

CC: Marcel Vanstone

pc Yolanda Coppolino
   Sandy Youngberg
```

BLIND COPY NOTATION

When the writer does *not* wish the addressee to know that a copy of a letter is being sent to someone, a Blind Copy notation (BC) is used. This notation appears on the *copies only*, in the upper left corner above the inside address, or at the bottom of the letter, where the CC notation is usually placed. Here is an example:

```
BC: Chris Antonsen
```

SPECIAL MAILING AND HANDLING NOTATIONS

Mailing notations are keyed both within the letter and on the envelope, so that there is a record on file to show how the letter was sent. Examples of mailing notations are: SPECIAL DELIVERY, REGISTERED MAIL, CERTIFIED MAIL, DELIVERED BY HAND, COURIER, AIR MAIL, etc.

Notations such as PERSONAL, CONFIDENTIAL, PRIVATE, etc., indicate how the letter is to be handled after it is received. These notations should appear on both the letter and the envelope, so that when the letter is received, only the person whose name appears will open it.

Here is the standard format for special mailing and handling notations:

1. Key in all capitals, two to four lines below the date, and flush with the left margin. Leave two to four lines between the notations and the inside address.

2. If both a mailing and a handling notation are to appear, place the handling notation a single space below the mailing notation.

4. access
   excess

4. cloth
   clothe

4. deceased
   diseased

4. expansive
   expensive

5. adapt
   adept
   adopt

5. cleans
   cleanse

5. defer
   differ

5. farther
   further

6. addition
   edition

6. commence
   comments

6. desert
   dessert

6. foreword
   forward

7. advice
   advise

7. compliment
   complement

7. devise
   device

7. formally
   formerly

8. affect
   effect

8. confident
   confidant

8. dew
   do
   due

8. grope
   group

9. angel
   angle

9. confidentially
   confidently

9. discus
   discuss

9. guessed
   guest

10. annual
    annul

10. confirm
    conform

10. dose
    doze

10. higher
    hire

11. holey
    wholly
    holly
    holy

11. poplar
    popular

11. suit
    suite

11. human
    humane

THE ENCLOSURE NOTATION

An enclosure notation serves to signal or remind both the sender and the receiver of a letter that something is enclosed in the same envelope. Sometimes the word "attachment" is used, but the word "enclosure" is more common. This notation is keyed at the left margin, a single or double space below the reference initials. If more than one item is enclosed, this may be indicated by a number, or each specific enclosure may be listed. See samples below.

```
Enclosures

3 Enclosures

Enclosures: 2

Encl.

encl.

Attachment

                     2
Enclosures:  1.  ^   Cheque
             2.      Invoice #4510
             3.      Pamphlet
```

THE COPY OR COURTESY NOTATION

At one time, the abbreviation CC stood for Carbon Copy. Since photo-copiers have replaced carbon paper, the abbreviation CC now means Copy Notation or Courtesy Copy. The term PC for photocopy may also be used.

A CC notation is used when a person other than the addressee is receiving a copy of the same letter. It is keyed flush with the left margin, and two lines below the enclosure or reference initials, whichever comes last.

In the distribution of copies, a check mark is placed beside the name of each person receiving a copy. This eliminates the possibility of sending two copies to one person and none to another. No notation is needed for copies made for files since making a file copy is routine.

Some formats for keying the Courtesy Copy notation are shown below. Notice that multiple recipients are listed in alphabetical order.

HOW WELL DO YOU KNOW CANADA?

ASSIGNMENT 5:36

Key each set of names, and learn how to spell them. They will be dictated to you in your next keyboarding class.

BRITISH COLUMBIA

Victoria	Port Alberni	Chilliwack	Penticton
Alberni	Prince George	Dawson Creek	Port Coquitlam
Cranbrook	Trail	Kelowna	Prince Rupert
Kamloops	White Rock	Vancouver	Vernon
Kimberley	Golden	New Westminster	Nanaimo

ALBERTA

Edmonton	Camrose	Jasper	Beverly
Bowness	Forest Lawn	Lethbridge	Red Deer
Calgary	Grande Prairie	Medicine Hat	Wetaskiwin
Spruce Grove	Calahoo	Carbondaee	Leduc

SASKATCHEWAN

Regina	Estevan	Moose Jaw	Yorkton
Rosetown	La Ronge	Watrous	North Battleford
Saskatoon	Prince Albert	Swift Current	Weyburn
Buffalo Narrows	Wadena	Cree Lake	Uranium City

MANITOBA

Winnipeg	Brandon	Dauphin	Flin Flon
Selkirk	Stony Mountain	St. James	Transcona
Fortier	Brooklands	East Kildonan	Starbuck
Argyle	St. Boniface	The Pas	Portage la Prairie

Other subject line styles are:

```
SUBJECT: POLICY #12345

Subject: Policy Number 12345

Subject: POLICY NO. 12345

RE: JONES VS. SMITH

RE: Claim Number 1943
    Fire Loss Damage
    June 17, 19--
```

THE COMPANY NAME

In a business letter, the name of the writer's firm or organization may be keyed in all capitals, two lines (one double space) below the complimentary closing. The first letter of the company name is aligned with the first letter of the complimentary closing. This style emphasizes the name of the company. This notation does not appear in every letter. Sample placement and set-up are shown below.

```
Yours very truly,
        ↓ 2
SPECTRUM RECORDS LTD.

        ↓ 5


Pauline A. Kralik
President
```

ONTARIO

Toronto	Parry Sound	Belleville	Pembroke
Chatham	Bowmanville	Arnprior	Penetanguishene
Peterborough	Port Colborne	Collingwood	Renfrew
Cobourg	Dryden	Prescott	Dunnville
Riverside	Espanola	St. Catharines	Fort Frances
Simcoe	Sault Ste. Marie	Gananoque	Goderich
Smith's Falls	Guelph	Grimsby	Stoney Creek
Streetsville	Hawkesbury	Sturgeon Falls	Ingersoll
Sudbury	Kapuskasing	Tillsonburg	Lindsay
Timmins	Orillia	Wallaceburg	Ottawa

QUÉBEC

Québec City	Anjou	Beaconsfield	Beauport
Duvernay	Chateauguay	Chomedey	Cap-de-la-Madeleine
Giffard	Grand'Mère	Sherbrooke	Jacques Cartier
Jonquiere	Lafleche	Lauzon	Longueuil
Montmorency	Outremont	Chicoutimi	Plessisville
Point Claire	St. Eustache	Verdun	Trois-Rivières
Baie Comeau	Beauharnois	Boucherville	Charlesbourg
Côte-St.-Luc	Gatineau	Granby	Hull
Joliette	Kenogami	La Tuque	Laval des Rapides
Montmagny	Montréal	Pierrefonds	
Rimouski	Ste.-Foy	Thetford Mines	

Other attention line styles are:

```
ATTENTION: Ms Joan Hendershot

Attention: MS JOAN HENDERSHOT

ATTENTION: MS JOAN HENDERSHOT

Attention: Ms Joan Hendershot

Attention Sales Department

ATTENTION OF THE SALES MANAGER
```

THE SUBJECT LINE

Many writers use a subject line, which is keyed between the salutation and the body. This line draws attention to the main point of the letter. The subject line is most commonly used to identify a previous letter, a file number, a case number, an invoice number, or some other similar reference for the reader's convenience.

The subject line is keyed a double space below the salutation. The same rules apply for keying the subject line as for the attention line. Indent the same number of spaces as for paragraphs, or centre the subject line if you are using a semi-block letter style. If you are using the block or full block style, key the subject line at the left margin. Sample styles and placements are shown below.

```
Dear Ms Peters:
      ↓ 2
SUBJECT: Your Policy Number 12345
      ↓ 2
Enclosed is your revised policy . . .
```

NEW BRUNSWICK

Fredericton	Bathurst	Chatham	Dieppe
Minto	Lancaster	Newcastle	Saint John
Marysville	Campbellton	Dalhousie	Edmundston
Kedgwick	Moncton	Oromocto	Woodstock

NOVA SCOTIA

Halifax	Amherst	Glace Bay	Springhill
Canso	Sydney	Yarmouth	Dartmouth
Bridgewater	New Glasgow	Truro	Digby
Pictou	Sydney	Antigonish	Annapolis Royal

PRINCE EDWARD ISLAND

Charlottetown	Summerside	Kensington	Elmira

NEWFOUNDLAND AND LABRADOR

St. John's	Carbonear	Corner Brook	Wabana
Gander	Stephenville	Windsor	Heart's Content
Grand Falls	Goose Bay	Bonavista	Harbour Grace
Grand Bank	Placentia	Trinity	Twillingate

YUKON

Whitehorse	Dawson	Old Crow

NORTHWEST TERRITORIES

Yellowknife	Teriatuk	Tuktoyaktuk	Fort Simpson
Iqualuit			

ADDITIONAL LETTER PARTS AND NOTATIONS

Business letters must have the essential parts mentioned previously, but there are other parts that may or may not be included. These optional parts of a business letter include:

- Attention Line
- Subject or Reference Line
- Company Name
- Enclosure Notation
- Postscript or Post-Postscript Notation
- Courtesy Copy and Blind Copy Notation
- Addressee Notation and Mailing Notation
- Displayed Material, Quotes, and Enumerations

THE ATTENTION LINE

Especially in legal correspondence, it is sometimes important to address a letter to a company rather than to an individual or department within that company. If the writer knows which individual or department will handle the letter, he or she may speed up handling by indicating the individual or department in an attention line, which is inserted between the inside address and the salutation. (See example below.)

When the semi-block letter style is used, the attention line may be indented the same number of spaces as the paragraphs, or it may be centered horizontally on the page. If the full block or block letter style is used, the attention line is keyed at the left margin. There are various styles for keying the attention line; some are given below.

Note that the salutation in a letter with an attention line is usually Gentlemen, Dear Sir, or Ladies. The name of the person appearing in the attention line is never included in the salutation.

```
Coronation Flowers Limited
21 Commonwealth Avenue
London, Ontario
N6H 3R6
     ↓ 2
ATTENTION: MS JOAN HENDERSHOT
     ↓ 2
Ladies:
```

MODULE
6

CENTERING

Courtesy of Panasonic OA

Key an exact copy of this letter, using the spacing indicated.

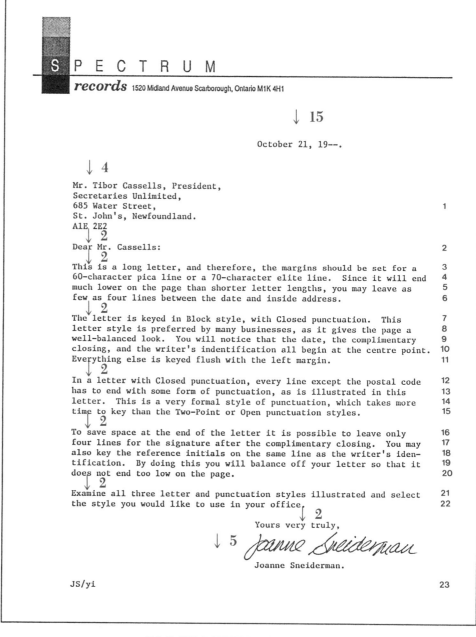

BLOCK LETTER STYLE
CLOSED PUNCTUATION

BLOCK LETTER STYLE
· The date, the complimentary closing, and the writer's identification all begin at the midpoint. Everything else begins at the left margin.

CLOSED PUNCTUATION
· Every line except the postal code ends with some kind of punctuation (except, of course, for run-on lines within the text).

INTRODUCTION

Centering is used to display information in notices, invitations, announcements, advertisements, programs, and menus. A document that is centered well presents the material attractively and emphasizes the most important information so that it catches the eye of the reader.

A variety of display styles, such as vertical and horizontal centering, block centering, pivoting, and the use of leaders will be presented in this module. The accompanying assignments will provide you with many opportunities to format and compose documents using centering techniques.

OBJECTIVES

1. To centre lines horizontally.

2. To determine the starting line for vertical placement on the page.

3. To use a variety of display techniques to highlight important points.

4. To centre vertically and horizontally documents from handwritten and/or unarranged copy.

5. To understand and apply the principles of pivoting and the use of leaders in preparing different documents.

6. To compose and format a variety of documents attractively.

ASSIGNMENT 8:2

Key an exact copy of this letter. Use the spacing indicated.

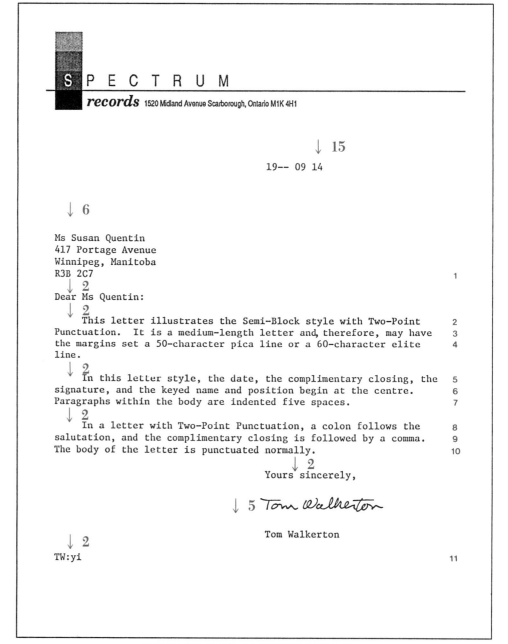

SEMI-BLOCK LETTER STYLE
TWO-POINT PUNCTUATION

SEMI-BLOCK STYLE
· The date, the complimentary closing, the signed name, and the keyed name all begin at the midpoint. Paragraphs are indented five spaces. Everything else begins at the left margin.

TWO-POINT PUNCTUATION
· Two-Point Punctuation is the same as Open Punctuation, except that a colon appears after the salutation, and a comma appears after the complimentary closing.

CONTENTS

Horizontal Centering 202

Reviewing Paper Sizes and Variable Spacing 203

Vertical Centering 204

Display Guidelines and Techniques 205

Centering Assignments 207

    Arranged Material 208

    Partly Arranged Material 210

    Unarranged Material 212

Block Centering 214

Block Centering Assignments 215

    Arranged Material 215

    Partly Arranged Material 217

Pivoting 219

Leaders 219

Pivoting and Leader Assignments 220

    Arranged Material 220

    Partly Arranged Material 222

Two-Page Programs 224

Two-Page Program Assignments 225

    Arranged Material 225

    Partly Arranged Material 228

Centering Composition Assignments 229

ASSIGNMENT

8:1

Key an exact copy of this letter, using the spacing indicated.

NOTE

Students may design appropriate letterheads for their business letters throughout this unit.

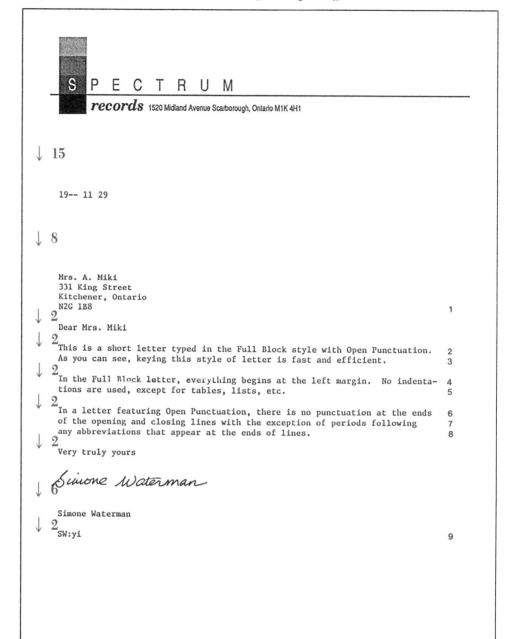

FULL BLOCK LETTER STYLE
OPEN PUNCTUATION

FULL BLOCK STYLE
· All lines begin at the left margin.

OPEN PUNCTUATION
· There is no punctuation at the ends of any lines, except for periods following abbreviations coming at the end of a line (e.g., Rd.) and punctuation within sentences in the body of the letter.

HORIZONTAL CENTERING

Centering is an important formatting skill. Knowing how to centre effectively enables you to present material attractively and to highlight important information in a document. **Horizontal** centering is generally used to set off titles, headings, and other single lines of copy.

HOW TO CENTRE HORIZONTALLY

Horizontal means   < = >

If you are using a typewriter, follow these instructions:

NOTE

An alternate method of finding the centre point of your paper is to determine the width of the sheet by measuring it against the scale on the paper bail. For example, the paper is set in the machine between 0 and 100, the centre point will be 50, and the tab can be set at 50.

1. Clear all margins and tab stops.

2. Check paper guide setting.

3. Insert a piece of paper into the machine.

4. Set a tab stop at the centre of the paper, and tab to the centre point.

5. With your eyes on the line of material to be centered, say each letter to yourself, emphasizing every *second* letter. At the same time, strike the backspace key *once* for every *second* letter, for example, kEyBoArDiNg.

6. If there is one letter left over at the end of a line, ignore it. Do *not* backspace again.

7. Centered lines have no end punctuation, except when a question or an exclamation mark is required, or the line ends with an abbreviation. Punctuation may be used *within* a line.

If you are using an electronic typewriter, a microcomputer, or a word processor, check with your teacher or the operating manual to see which command is used for centering. Centering on one of these machines is relatively easy. You give the centering command, and then key in your copy. You do not have to tab to the midpoint of your paper and then backspace. The machine performs these functions automatically.

ASSIGNMENT

6:1

Centre each of these words.
Double space between each line.

```
Centering                Extended
Horizontal               Spacing
Vertical                 Capitals
Display                  Underscore
```

LETTER AND PUNCTUATION STYLES

Full block
Open punctuation

Block
Two point punctuation

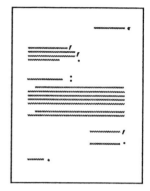

Semi-block
Closed punctuation

REVIEWING PAPER SIZES AND VARIABLE SPACING

In order to centre material vertically, you should know how many lines of text will fit onto different sizes of paper, and how vertical spacing is indicated on rough copy material. Take time to review this information now.

PAPER SIZES

There are 70 lines on a full sheet of letter-size metric paper.
There are 66 lines on a full sheet of letter-size Imperial (P4) paper.

There are 35 lines on a half-sheet of letter-size metric paper.
There are 33 lines on a half-sheet of letter-size Imperial paper.

There are 49 lines on a half-sheet of letter-size metric paper, shorter edge inserted first.
There are 51 lines on a half-sheet of letter-size Imperial paper, shorter edge inserted first.

VARIABLE SPACING

Single spacing (↓ **1**) means leave *no* blank lines between lines of text.
Single spacing (↓ **1**) means leave *no* blank lines between lines of text.

Double spacing (↓ **2**) means leave *one* blank line between lines of text.

Double spacing (↓ **2**) means leave *one* blank line between lines of text.

Triple spacing (↓ **3**) means leave *two* blank lines between lines of text.

Triple spacing (↓ **3**) means leave *two* blank lines between lines of text.

BUSINESS LETTER STYLES

The style of a business letter may be determined by the company, the writer, or the person keying. For the sake of speed and efficiency, offices often choose one standard letter style. Listed below are the three most common letter styles. Your teacher will decide which letter style(s) you will use.

1. **Full block**. The date, inside address, salutation, body, complimentary closing, writer's identification and reference initials, as well as all display lines, such as attention lines and subject lines, begin at the left margin.

2. **Block**. The date, complimentary closing, and writer's identification begin at the centre of the page. The paragraphs are not indented.

3. **Semi-block**. This style is similar to block style, in that the date, complimentary closing, and writer's identification begin at the centre of the page. However, the paragraphs are indented five or ten spaces.

PUNCTUATION STYLES IN BUSINESS LETTERS

There are three basic punctuation styles used in business letters. The two most popular styles are the **open** and the **two-point**. "Standard" and "mixed" punctuation are other names for two-point punctuation.

1. **Open punctuation (0-point)**. In this style, no punctuation marks are used after any display line, except in abbreviations (e.g., St.).

2. **Two-point punctuation**. As the name suggests, there are only two punctuation marks used in this style. A colon is placed after the salutation, and a comma is placed after the complimentary closing.

3. **Closed punctuation (full point)**. In this style, every line has a punctuation mark following it, *except* the postal code in the inside address and the date, if it is keyed in numeric form. This is a very conservative style and requires the most time to key.

These punctuation styles may be used with *any* letter style.

VERTICAL CENTERING

Vertical means $\updownarrow$

Vertical centering is used to position a series of lines in an announcement, program, etc. attractively on the page so that the top margin is the same depth as the bottom margin.

HOW TO CENTRE VERTICALLY

NOTE

Vertical centering means placing the material on the page so that there are the same number of blank lines at the top and at the bottom of the page.

1. Insert a piece of paper into the machine.

2. Count the total number of lines in your assignment, including the blank lines.

3. Subtract this total from the number of lines available on your paper.

4. Divide the result by two, and add one to find your starting line. (Ignore fractions.)

5. Starting from the top edge of the paper, space down the number of lines, and begin keyboarding.

If you are using a word processor or microcomputer, move the cursor down to the calculated line.

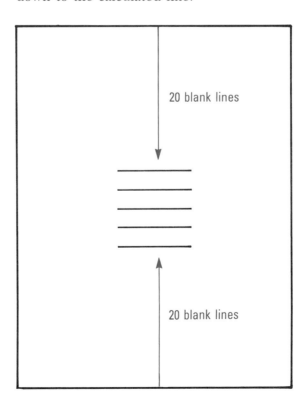

LETTER PLACEMENT CHART

Type of Letter	Length	Line Length Pica Elite	Begin on Line	Number of Lines Between Date and Inside Address	Number of Lines Between Complimentary Closing and Writer's Name
Personal Business	Short	40　50	12	8	6
	Medium	50　60	12	6	5
	Long	60　70	12	4	4
Business	Short	same	date begins on line 15	8	6
	Medium	as	15	6	5
	Long	above	15	4	4

```
                    If you want
                        ↓ 2
                         to
                        ↓ 2
                  vertical centre
                        ↓ 2
                        just
                        ↓ 2
                  follow the rules!
```

Sample Calculations

1. This sample takes 9 lines (5 lines of type plus 4 blank lines used for double spacing).

2. Since the sample is keyed on a half-sheet, wider edge inserted first, subtract 9 lines from 33 lines (33 − 9 = 24).

3. Now, divide 24 by 2 and add 1 (24 ÷ 2 = 12 + 1 = 13).

4. Starting at the top of the page, space down 13 lines. Begin keyboarding.

ASSIGNMENT 6:2

Determine the vertical placement (starting line) for each of the following examples.

PAPER SIZE	NUMBER OF LINES OF TEXT	VARIABLE SPACING	ANSWER
a) Half-sheet	16	SS	?
b) Full sheet	25	DS	?
c) Half-sheet, narrower edge first	11	TS	?

DISPLAY GUIDELINES AND TECHNIQUES

GUIDELINES

When centering material for display, observe the following guidelines:

1. Key important words or ideas on a line by themselves.

2. Key small or insignificant words, such as prepositions or conjunctions, in lower case, and on a line by themselves.

3. Use varied vertical spacing to accentuate key ideas. Leave more space after key ideas.

THE SALUTATION

The title of the addressee appears *without* his or her name and *without* the equivalent of the word Dear.

When addressing a woman whose marital status is not known, always use the term *Madelle*.

In English, the salutation is followed by a colon if two-point or closed punctuation is used. In French, the salutation is followed by a comma, e.g.:

```
Monsieur,
```

THE COMPLIMENTARY CLOSING

The complimentary closing is included as the final sentence in the last paragraph of the letter. The closing is not keyed on a new line as it is in English. There are many different styles of complimentary closings in French. Here is one of the most common:

```
Nous vous prions d'agréer, cher Monsieur/chère
Madame/Madelle, l'assurance de notre plus profond
respect.
```

```
                                    G. Thibodeau
                                    Directeur
```

Five lines usually occur between the complimentary closing and the writer's name and title.

LETTER PLACEMENT

It is now commonplace to use a standard line length for letters, regardless of letter size. This saves time in setting the margins.

A 60-stroke line is the norm. The total amount of space used on the page can be adjusted by increasing or decreasing the space between the date and the inside address (anywhere from 4 to 8 lines) or between the complimentary closing and the writer's (keyed) name (anywhere from 4 to 6 lines).

If you would like to use a more structured method for placing a letter on a page, the following rules apply:

DISPLAY TECHNIQUES

There are various display techniques you can use to give your work a more attractive, professional look. To make the most important parts of your work stand out, use one or several of the following display techniques:

1. Underscoring

2. KEYBOARDING IN ALL CAPITAL LETTERS

3. **Variable spacing**

   Single spacing   Double spacing   Triple spacing
   Single spacing
                     Double spacing
                                       Triple spacing

4. BOLD PRINT
   Make an extra dark copy by keying each character of an important word or words twice. Most electronic typewriters, microcomputers, and word processors can double strike characters automatically.

5. Ornamental keyboarding. This technique may be used to "decorate" special projects; to make title pages; to design borders around headings or entire pages; or to construct large letters. Use your imagination to display your work to best effect.

6. E X T E N D E D   C E N T E R I N G   or
   E X P A N D   P R I N T

   In extended centering, words to be highlighted are spread out. Key *one* space between each letter, and *three* spaces between words:

   T H E   W O R L D   O F   B U S I N E S S

   Expand print is found on electronic typewriters, microcomputers, and word processors. These machines automatically add additional space between characters as you key.

KEYING LETTERS IN FRENCH

Certain parts of letters in French are keyed in a different format compared to that of letters in English. Here are a few points when you are keying in French.

THE DATE LINE

As in English, the date may be keyed in the numeric form, e.g.:

```
19-- 03 12
```

The date may also be keyed in alphanumeric form, but the parts of the date appear in the following order:

definite article: `le`

day of the month: `12`

month: `mars`

year: `19--`

i.e., `le 12 mars, 19--`.

THE INSIDE ADDRESS

The inside address is keyed in exactly the same way in French as in English *except* that

1. the *number* in the *street address* is followed by a comma, and
2. the word *rue, avenue,* or *boulevard* is not capitalized. For example:

```
M. G. Thibodeau
34, rue Duchamp
Trois-Rivières, Québec
G8Z 1K7
```

7. **Reverse print**
   Some electronic typewriters, microcomputers, and word processors offer the ability to print white characters within a solid black background. The machine creates the black background and then lifts off only the character outline. The result is reverse printing.

8. **Justified print (Justify)**
   This feature is also found on some electronic typewriters, microcomputers, and word processors. The machine stretches out the line to fit exactly within the margin. Justified print gives an even right margin. (Unjustified print has a ragged right margin, lines end at different points at the right-hand side of the page.)

CENTERING ASSIGNMENTS

ASSIGNMENT
6:3

Key each of these words using extended centering. Triple space after the title and double space the body.

DAYS OF THE WEEK

MONDAY

TUESDAY

WEDNESDAY

THURSDAY

FRIDAY

SATURDAY

SUNDAY

THE COMPLIMENTARY CLOSING

The complimentary closing is keyboarded a double space below the last line of the body. Only the first word of the complimentary closing is capitalized (for example, Sincerely yours).

If an informal closing such as "Best wishes" is also used, it is keyboarded as a separate paragraph at the end of the letter before the complimentary closing.

THE WRITER'S NAME AND TITLE

The writer's name, title, and sometimes department are placed approximately five lines below the complimentary closing. If this will occupy two or more lines because a position within the company is listed (for example, Jason Symington, President), begin the writer's position one line under the keyboarded name. A business letter always has a handwritten signature and a keyed signature.

THE INITIALS LINE

These letters identify both the writer and the person who keyed the letter. They are placed two lines below the writer's identification.

Usually the writer's initials appear first, followed by the initials of the person who keyed the letter. Here are some common ways of keying reference initials.

```
JPH/ss JPH:SS jph/ss /SS :ss /ss
```

ASSIGNMENT	**ARRANGED MATERIAL**
6:4	

Centre vertically and horizontally on a half-sheet of paper.
Use the spacing illustrated.
Use extended centering for the last line.
Leave three spaces between words in extended centering.

<table>
<tr><td></td><td>PWC*</td></tr>
<tr><td>CASUAL TOUCH</td><td>16</td></tr>
<tr><td>↓ 2</td><td></td></tr>
<tr><td>HAPPY HOLIDAY SALE</td><td>27</td></tr>
<tr><td>↓ 2</td><td></td></tr>
<tr><td>Dressy Blouses for Evening</td><td>43</td></tr>
<tr><td>Now $45.99</td><td>49</td></tr>
<tr><td>↓ 2</td><td></td></tr>
<tr><td>Shetland Sweaters</td><td>61</td></tr>
<tr><td>Now $39.99</td><td>67</td></tr>
<tr><td>↓ 2</td><td></td></tr>
<tr><td>Jersey Dresses</td><td>77</td></tr>
<tr><td>Now $64.99</td><td>83</td></tr>
<tr><td>↓ 3</td><td></td></tr>
<tr><td>O P E N ³∧ 9—9 ³∧ U N T I L ³∧ C H R I S T M A S</td><td>118</td></tr>
</table>

NOTE

When completed, centering assignments have an *uneven* left margin because the words vary in length.

ASSIGNMENT	Centre vertically and horizontally on a half-sheet of paper. Use the spacing illustrated.
6:5	

<table>
<tr><td></td><td>PWC</td></tr>
<tr><td>D I N N E R</td><td>15</td></tr>
<tr><td>↓ 2</td><td></td></tr>
<tr><td>at the</td><td>21</td></tr>
<tr><td>↓ 2</td><td></td></tr>
<tr><td>MANOR HOUSE RESTAURANT</td><td>38</td></tr>
<tr><td>↓ 2</td><td></td></tr>
<tr><td>Cream of Artichoke Soup</td><td>55</td></tr>
<tr><td>or</td><td>57</td></tr>
<tr><td>Iced Watercress Soup</td><td>71</td></tr>
<tr><td>↓ 2</td><td></td></tr>
<tr><td>Fillets of Dover Sole with Cucumber & Tomato</td><td>104</td></tr>
<tr><td>or</td><td>106</td></tr>
<tr><td>Turkey with Chestnut Dressing</td><td>127</td></tr>
<tr><td>↓ 2</td><td></td></tr>
<tr><td>A Salad of Belgian Endive</td><td>146</td></tr>
<tr><td>↓ 2</td><td></td></tr>
<tr><td>Fresh Pumpkin Custard in Ginger Cup</td><td>172</td></tr>
<tr><td>Assorted Fresh Fruit Tarts</td><td>191</td></tr>
<tr><td>↓ 2</td><td></td></tr>
<tr><td>Tea or Coffee</td><td>201</td></tr>
</table>

*PWC = Production Word Count. Your teacher uses the PWC to measure how many words you key per minute on formatted work.

THE DATE LINE

The date is usually entered on line 15, or two lines below the letterhead (if the letterhead takes up more than 5 cm at the top of the page).

Although it is acceptable to key the date using the traditional alphanumeric method (for example, July 1, 1867), it is also common to key the date in numeric form, with year, month, and day keyed in that order. According to this method, July 1, 1867 would appear as 1867 07 01.

THE INSIDE ADDRESS

The inside address in a business letter is the address of the person or company to whom the letter is addressed. It is usually placed five or six lines below the date and single spaced. If the letter is short, the space between the date and the inside address may be increased up to eight lines; if the letter is long, the space may be reduced to only four lines.

In the inside address you must include the name of the person or company to whom the letter is being sent, the street address and the city, province, and postal code. The inside address may also include the person's title or department, if known.

THE SALUTATION

The salutation is always flush with the left margin, a double space below the inside address. Use the addressee's title and surname in the salutation. Some firms use the person's first and last names, e.g., Helen Maura. If you know the person by first name, you may use only the first name in the salutation, along with the greeting.

When addressing a letter to two or more people, use either Gentlemen, Ladies, or Mesdames as the salutation. You can also use Dear Sirs/ Colleagues.

THE BODY (TEXT)

The body begins a double space below the salutation. Single space the body, but leave a double space between paragraphs. Only *extremely short* letters are double spaced. Paragraphs may or may not be indented, depending on the letter style used.

ASSIGNMENT

6:6

Centre vertically and horizontally on a half-sheet of paper.
Follow the proofreader's marks.

BUSINESS Vocabulary

↓ 3

Automated Trans action Machines

↓ 2

Cybernation

↓ 2

Processor Dedicated

↓ 2

Point - of - Sale Terminal stet

↓ 2

Tele processing

ASSIGNMENT

6:7

Key an exact copy of this material on a half-sheet of paper.

RACQUETBALL
↓ 2
MEMBERSHIPS AVAILABLE
Reduced Rates for Balance
of
Membership Year
↓ 2
Six New Courts Playable in January
↓ 2
RED DEER RACQUET CLUB
269-4527

LETTERS

There are three basic kinds of letters: the personal letter, the personal business letter, and the business letter. A personal letter is sent from one friend or relative to another. A personal business letter is sent by an individual to a company or business. A business letter is sent from one company to another, or from a company to an individual.

ESSENTIAL PARTS OF A BUSINESS LETTER

Look carefully at the model business letter on page 291. It contains the following essential parts:

1. Company letterhead.
2. Date line.
3. Inside address.
4. Salutation.
5. Body.
6. Complimentary closing.
7. Writer's name and title.
8. Initials line.

THE LETTERHEAD

A company's letterhead conveys the company's image: modern, conservative, or distinguished. This image is created by the letterhead design and, to some extent, by the quality of paper used. The letterhead also contains basic vital information about the company, such as the correct spelling of the company name, its address, and telephone, FAX, or telex numbers.

ASSIGNMENT 6:8

Key an exact copy of this exercise on a half-sheet of paper, shorter edge inserted first.

> **NOTE**
>
> Small or insignificant words are keyed in lower case.

SARAH G. TAYLOR, D.D.S.
↓ 2
wishes to announce the
↓ 2
RELOCATION
↓ 2
of her office for the
↓ 2
Practice of General Dentistry
↓ 2
to
↓ 2
MEDICAL ARTS BUILDING
170 St. George Road, Suite 619
Winnipeg, Manitoba
R2M 4B4
↓ 2
By Appointment
Phone 753-8800

ASSIGNMENT 6:9

PARTLY ARRANGED MATERIAL

Centre attractively using various display techniques.

SHERRILYN'S/ORIGINAL DESIGNS/alterations/dressmaking/

custom orders/handmade knits and crafts/3288 Queen Street

ASSIGNMENT 6:10

Centre attractively using various display techniques.

THE HONEY BEAR/Natural Foods/a wonderful selection at competitive prices/Dried Fruits and Nuts/Exotic Herbs and Spices/ Imported Honeys Fruit Preserves/Quality Teas and Tea Accessories/Exciting Cook Books/GREAT GIFTS COME NATURALLY

ASSIGNMENT 6:11

Centre attractively using various display techniques.

THE MIRROR SHOP/Mirror Doors/Mirror Walls/ Vanity Mirrors/CUSTOM CUT AND INSTALLED/ free estimates/call collect 742-9651/or/ Visit Our Showroom/6169 Delmar Road

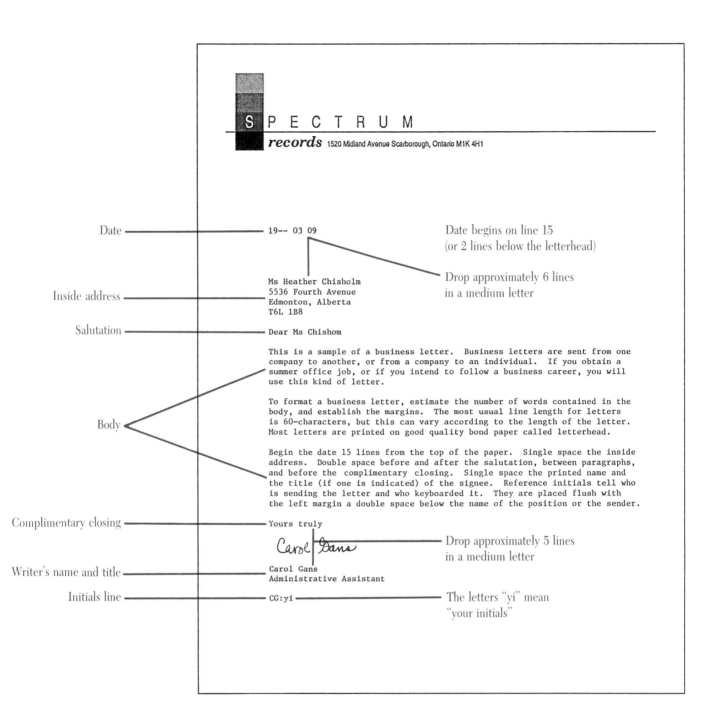

Date —————————— 19-- 03 09   Date begins on line 15
                                     (or 2 lines below the letterhead)

                                     Drop approximately 6 lines
                                     in a medium letter

Inside address ——————— Ms Heather Chisholm
                       5536 Fourth Avenue
                       Edmonton, Alberta
                       T6L 1B8

Salutation ——————————— Dear Ms Chishom

This is a sample of a business letter. Business letters are sent from one
company to another, or from a company to an individual. If you obtain a
summer office job, or if you intend to follow a business career, you will
use this kind of letter.

To format a business letter, estimate the number of words contained in the
body, and establish the margins. The most usual line length for letters
is 60-characters, but this can vary according to the length of the letter.
Most letters are printed on good quality bond paper called letterhead.

Begin the date 15 lines from the top of the paper. Single space the inside
address. Double space before and after the salutation, between paragraphs,
and before the complimentary closing. Single space the printed name and
the title (if one is indicated) of the signee. Reference initials tell who
is sending the letter and who keyboarded it. They are placed flush with
the left margin a double space below the name of the position or the sender.

Complimentary closing ————— Yours truly

                            Carol Gans   Drop approximately 5 lines
                                                in a medium letter

Writer's name and title ——— Carol Gans
                            Administrative Assistant

Initials line ——————————— CG:yi ——————————————— The letters "yi" mean
                                                "your initials"

Full block letter with open punctuation.

SPECTRUM records 1520 Midland Avenue Scarborough, Ontario M1K 4H1

ASSIGNMENT 6:12

Centre attractively using various display techniques.

COME VISIT / HAWAII / Return Flight / via / air Canada / luxurious accommodation / transfers in San Francisco / Rent. a. Car / unlimited mileage / complimentary in-flight meals / fun coupon booklet / ASK YOUR TRAVEL AGENT TODAY !

ASSIGNMENT 6:13

Centre attractively using various display techniques.

NOTICE / HOUSE OF BOOKS / Will NOT be Undersold / All Books 50% off / Original List Price / Open Monday – Saturday / 10:00 – 21:00 / 1238 King Street / halifax , NS

ASSIGNMENT 6:14

Centre attractively using various display techniques.

PRIME OFFICE SPACE FOR LEASE / Bayridge Road and Hillmount Ave. / 10 200 m² / air-conditioned / CENTRAL LOCATION / Occupancy January 1 / FOR MORE INFORMATION CALL / 749-5427

CONTENTS

Letters 292

Essential Parts of a Business Letter 292

Keying Letters in French 295

Letter Placement 296

Business Letter Styles 298

Punctuation Styles in Business Letters 298

Additional Letter Parts and Notations 303

Displayed Material in Letters 309

Two-Page Letters 309

Envelopes 310

Applying Your Skills 314

    Envelopes 314

    Business Letters 316

    Company Name and Enclosure Notations 322

    Attention Line and Subject Line 327

    Copy Notations 331

    Enumerations 334

    Special Mailing and Handling Notations 337

    Two-Page Letters 340

The Form Letter 347

Applying Your Skills 349

    Form Letters 349

Interoffice Memos 351

Applying Your Skills 352

    Memos 352

Composing Letters 362

Composing Memos 363

ASSIGNMENT
6:15

Centre attractively using various display techniques.

Information PROCESSING / Hardware (&) Soft ware / In put / Processing / output / Stadage / Control

ASSIGNMENT
6:16

Centre attractively using various display techniques.

You / are cordially Invited to an /
OPEN HOUSE / Wednesday, January 16 /
14:00 – 16:00 / Learning Resource Centre /
Successful Job Hunting / Career Directions /
Assertiveness Training / Your Self-Image /
Leadership Skills / How to Advance /
Phone 787-7380 For More Information /

CENTERING UNARRANGED MATERIAL

Often you will receive material to be centered attractively with no instructions on how to format it. Use your imagination and judgment to format this material to its best effect.

ASSIGNMENT
6:17

UNARRANGED MATERIAL

Use various display techniques to format this unarranged material.

R E C E P T I O N I S T modern office excellent keying good organizational skills many benefits competitive starting salary apply Box 4932

ASSIGNMENT
6:18

Use various display techniques to format this unarranged material.

The Eyeglass Place featuring fast accurate service with one-year breakage warranty no appointment necessary glasses ready in one hour large selection of frames 984 King St. E. at Princess 460-9183 Open Monday to Saturday.

INTRODUCTION

A company's correspondence is often its most important form of communication with customers and clients. Sometimes a letter is a company's only form of communication.

Each letter reflects not only on the person who dictated it, and the person who keyed it, but also on the company as a whole. So it is important that all letters make a good first impression. Letters that contain errors in keying, spelling, punctuation, and grammar, or that contain poorly made corrections, give the indication that the company's business practices are sloppy and careless.

Interoffice memoranda or memos are used when one employee in the company wishes to communicate, in writing, with another employee or employees in the same company. Memos are often sent to confirm discussions or verbal agreements. Memos are just as important as letters for creating a favourable first impression.

If you can format letters and memos efficiently and accurately, you will be a great asset to any company that hires you.

This module contains numerous assignments to help you become proficient at keying correspondence and memos.

OBJECTIVES

1. To identify and understand the essential parts of a business letter.
2. To know the format for keying letters in French.
3. To identify and key correctly the full block, block, and semi-block letter styles.
4. To know how to key the three punctuation styles used in business letters: open, two-point, closed.
5. To correctly place letters on a page.
6. To identify and key correctly these additional parts of a letter: attention line, subject line, company name, enclosure notation, copy notation, special mailing and handling notations, and postscript.
7. To prepare letters with displayed material.
8. To format a two-page letter.
9. To key addresses on envelopes.
10. To know the format for keying memos.

ASSIGNMENT 6:19

Use various display techniques to format this unarranged material.

The Shade Shop 50% off custom window shades 10% off Roman Shades 15% off woven wood shades 20% off vertical blinds free home service we install over 75 patterns to choose from Factory and Showroom at 100 Bermuda Blvd. Phone 258-9917

ASSIGNMENT 6:20

Use various display techniques to format this unarranged material.

Green Valley Towers 4122 Rosewell Avenue Air-Conditioned Luxury Accommodation Two- and Three- Bedroom Suites featuring coloured appliances full recreation facilities large indoor pool saunas tennis gym squash courts tuck shop Rental Office open Monday - Saturday Phone 459-0011

ASSIGNMENT 6:21

Use various display techniques to format this unarranged material.

Come and see your next car at the International Auto Show February 8-17 at the Exhibition Centre Open Daily from 10:00 Adults $5 Senior Citizens $2.50 Children under 12 $1.50 Free Parking

ASSIGNMENT 6:22

Use various display techniques to format this unarranged material.

Matheson - Paglialunga + Co. Chartered Accountants with offices in Halifax, Montreal, Toronto, London, Winnipeg, Saskatoon, Calgary, Vancouver, Victoria

ASSIGNMENT 6:23

Use various display techniques to format this unarranged material.

Morningstar Secondary School Students' Council Meeting in Room 300 at 8:00 on September 15, 19---.

MODULE

8

Correspondence and Memos

BLOCK CENTERING

When material is to be arranged in an attractive list but not in a decorative format, **block centering** is used. In a list that is block centered, the longest item in the list is centered, and the left margin is set for this item. All other items begin at this left margin.

1. Centre the heading of the column, and key in all caps above the column.

2. Find the longest line in the column.

3. From the centre point, backspace *once* for every *two* strokes in the longest line.

4. Set your left margin at this point.

5. Keyboard the column with each line beginning at this margin.

BUSINESS FORMS COMPOSITION ASSIGNMENTS

ASSIGNMENT

7:77

Design a Purchase Order and fill in the appropriate entries for a company of your choice.

ASSIGNMENT

7:78

Design an Invoice and fill in the appropriate entries for a company of your choice.

ASSIGNMENT

7:79

Design a Statement of Account and fill in the appropriate entries for a company of your choice.

ASSIGNMENT

7:80

Prepare a Balance Sheet for yourself.

BLOCK CENTERING ASSIGNMENTS

ASSIGNMENT

6:24

ARRANGED MATERIAL

Block centre this material on a half-sheet of paper, shorter edge inserted first.
Triple space after the heading.
Single space the body.

	PWC
PARTS OF A BUSINESS LETTER	15
↓ 3	
Letterhead	19
Date	20
Inside Address	23
Attention Line	26
Salutation	28
Body	29
Complimentary Closing —— longest line	33
Signature	35
Typed Name	37
Official Title	40
Reference Initials	44
Enclosure Notation	48
Copy Notation	52
Postscript	54

FILE LABELS ASSIGNMENT

ASSIGNMENT
7:76

Key these names in alphabetical order on separate file labels.

Kinisky, Linda	Fishman, Muriel (Dr.)
Gorman, Whitney	Ince, B.
Pettie, Maggie (Mrs.)	Kukus, Ed.
Deleseluc, Lucielle	Myers, Isabel (Prof.)
Manthie, Renate (Prof.)	Kephardt, Jean
Herzberg, Ruth (Rabbi)	Gauthier, R. J.
Gans, Marvin (Dr.)	Hanna, Ann
Delacourt, Andrew (Prof.)	Saucier, H.

DESIGNING BUSINESS FORMS

Sometimes a company needs a form for a particular job that is unique to that company. It could be as simple as a form letter, or it could be a more advanced and complicated item, such as a stock inventory sheet. Here are some guidelines to follow when you are called upon to design business forms.

1. Make sure the form is easy to understand, and that all instructions are clearly stated.

2. Do not crowd too much information into a small space. Leave enough room for all entries to be made.

3. Make sure the form is simple and convenient to use.

4. Centre the information attractively on the page. Look at the form critically. Are there any improvements that would make it more attractive and easy to understand? If so, include them.

Block centre this exercise on a half-sheet of paper, shorter edge inserted first.
Double space between the main heading and subheading.
Triple space after the subheading.
Double space the body.

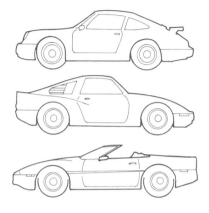

CAR OWNERSHIP
↓ 2
Factors to Consider

↓ 3

Depreciation
↓ 2
Kilometres
↓ 2
Gas
↓ 2
Cost of car
↓ 2
Parking
↓ 2
Oil
↓ 2
Maintenance
↓ 2
Insurance
↓ 2
Licence

Block centre on a half-sheet of paper.
Triple space after the title, and single space the body.

NEW YEAR'S RESOLUTIONS

↓ 3

1. $\overset{2}{\wedge}$ to proofread my work carefully

2. to increase my keyboarding speed

3. to practise keying at least fifteen minutes a day

4. to bring all my supplies to class

5. to drill numbers and special characters

> **NOTE**
>
> When enumerating items, leave two spaces after a period.

FILE LABELS

File labels are either gummed or have an adhesive backing. They come on a roll, which is inserted directly into the machine. The information is keyed and then the labels are separated and attached to file folder tabs. Information on file labels may include names, addresses, subjects, numbers, or geographic areas.

1. Begin keying two or three spaces from the left edge.

2. If gummed labels are used, start keying one line below the centre fold.

3. If adhesive labels are used, begin keying on the second line from the top.

4. Names are keyed in correct filing order, that is, the last name first.

5. Labels may be keyed

   a) in all caps

      BOCONGELLE, MICHAEL

   b) with only the surname capitalized

      BOCONGELLE, Michael

   c) in lower case letters with only the first letter in each name capitalized

      Bocongelle, Michael

6. When keying labels, standard titles (Mr., Mrs., Ms) may be omitted; all other titles are keyed in parentheses.

   BOGONGELLE, MICHAEL (DR.)

ASSIGNMENT

6:27

Block centre on a half-sheet of paper.
Triple space after the title, and single space the body.
Space in *once* for numbers 1 to 9, the "1" in 10 will be at the left margin.

NOTE

When keying numbers or roman numerals, the periods must be aligned.

STUDENT SURVEY QUESTIONNAIRE

↓ 3

1. $\overset{2}{\wedge}$ What subjects are you taking this year?

2. What do you plan to do when you finish school?

3. In which subject did you receive your highest mark?

4. What is your favourite subject this year?

5. What is the highest level of schooling that you have completed?

6. How many words per minute do you keyboard?

7. Do you have a part-time job?

8. What are your leisure time activities?

9. Would you like to work in business?

10. Why are you taking business subjects?

ASSIGNMENT

6:28

PARTLY ARRANGED MATERIAL

Block centre this enumerated list attractively on a half-sheet of paper.

HOW TO COMPLAIN/1. Have your facts straight. Be SPECIFIC!/ 2. Complain to someone in authority./3. Know the date of the purchase./4. Have the name and model number of the product./ 5. Provide your sales slip./6. State a solution acceptable to you.

ASSIGNMENT

6:29

Block centre this list attractively on a half-sheet of paper.

GREEN VALLEY JUNIOR TENNIS CHAMPIONSHIPS/July 31/
· Eligibility--anyone under sixteen years of age/
· Events--Singles, Doubles, and Mixed Doubles/
· Trophies--awarded to winners in each event/
· Dress--whites only/· Entry Fee--$10 per player/
Entry Deadline June 30

3. The **key line**, the line under which the card is filed, is usually followed by a blank line.

4. The rest of the lines may be blocked, or indented three spaces below the key line, using either single or double spacing.

Standard sizes for index cards are 12.5 cm × 7.5 cm and 20 cm × 7.5 cm.

NOTE

The key line may appear in all capital letters.

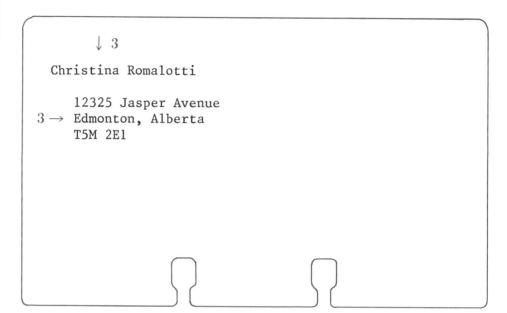

```
          ↓ 3
     Christina Romalotti

          12325 Jasper Avenue
   3 →  Edmonton, Alberta
          T5M 2E1
```

CARD FILES ASSIGNMENT

ASSIGNMENT
7:75

Key these names and addresses on separate index cards.

1. Mr. T. Egizii, 18 Panorama Court, Apartment 1209, Rexdale, Ontario M9W 1P8.

2. Ms Pat Meeson, 3106-212 Fairmont Drive, Saskatoon, Saskatchewan S7M 4P5.

3. Miss Nadine Spagnoli, 45 Rock Manor Dr., Bedford, Nova Scotia B4A 2V5.

4. Mr. James S. Federico, 19 Murphy Street, Trenton, Ontario K8V 4S8.

5. Mrs. Petra Hardt, 1 Norwood Park, Beaksden, Glasgow, Scotland G61 2RF.

ASSIGNMENT

6:30

Block centre this advertisement attractively on a half-sheet of paper, shorter edge inserted first.

SNOW HILLS / Drive Less -- Ski More / in the Heart of Ski Valley /. Sauna /. Entertainment /. Alpine + Cross Country Skiing /. Quality Ski Instruction /. Season's Pass Available

ASSIGNMENT

6:31

Block centre this material attractively on a half-sheet of paper.

Secrets of Italy / September 15 -- October 31 / (Oct.) (Nov.) an unforgettable experience /. Venice /. Florence /. Siena /. Assisi /. Padua /. Capri /. Pompeii /. Rome / First Class Hotels / All Breakfast and Dinners Included .e

PIVOTING

Although printed material is most often aligned with the left margin, there are times when it must be aligned with the right margin. The technique used to align material this way is called **pivoting**.

1. Determine what line-length you need, and set the left margin.

2. Set a tab at the point where the right margin should be. Don't set the right margin.

3. Return to the left margin, and insert a piece of paper into the machine.

4. Tab to the right margin.

5. Look at the first line of your copy, and backspace *once* for *every* character in the line. (This is called "**pivoting the line**.")

6. Keyboard the line and return the carrier.

7. Follow steps 4 to 6 for each line of material to be keyboarded.

CARD FILES

Index cards are sometimes used to record references in conjunction with office files. Often names, addresses, and telephone numbers of clients are listed on separate index cards, or a separate card filing device is used. The cards are then arranged alphabetically by the individual's last name or geographical location.

Courtesy of Apsco Products Ltd.

1. Names are arranged in correct filing order, for example, Mrs. Elizabeth Ann *Cardoso* becomes *Cardoso*, Elizabeth Ann (Mrs.). The titles Mr., Ms, and Miss are usually omitted. All other titles, for example, Dr., Prof., and Rev., are placed in parentheses after the name.

2. Begin keying on the third line, three spaces in from the left edge of the card.

Example

```
                             keyboarding
                               beginning
                                  ending
                                pivoting
```

LEADERS

Periods printed in a row to connect columns are called **leaders**, because the periods "lead" the eye from one column to the next. There are two types of leaders, open and closed. With **open leaders**, there is a space left between each period; with **closed leaders**, there is no space left between the periods. Leaders are most often used with pivoted material.

1. Determine the line-length, and set the left margin stop.

2. Set a tab at the point where the right margin should be.

3. Return to the left margin, and insert a piece of paper into the machine.

4. Keyboard the material that is to appear on the *left* side of the leaders.

5. Tab to the right margin.

6. Pivot the material that is to appear on the right side of the leaders, and keyboard the material.

7. Go back and keyboard the leaders between the two columns, leaving one space before leaders and one space after, as shown in Example 1 on page 219. Leave two spaces before and after open leaders as shown in Example 2.

Example
Closed Leaders

```
Keyboarding¹  ...................¹Karen Steffenson
```

Example 2
Open Leaders

```
Keyboarding ²  . . . . . . . . . . . . . . . . ²Carla Poleto
```

HOW TO KEY A CHEQUE

1. Place the cheque into the typewriter. Use the paper release to adjust the cheque until the line on which you are to key is in the same position as an underscoring line would be. Use the carriage position scale to align cheques.

2. Key the date on the cheque. Do not forget to include the year.

3. The name of the payee (the person to whom the cheque is payable) should be keyed in full without any title such as Mr., Mrs., or Ms. The name should be keyed one space after the heading, "PAY TO THE ORDER OF." Any space left after the name is keyed, should be filled with hyphens.

4. On the same line as the name of the payee, key the amount to be paid in figures. Make sure the amount is keyed *immediately* after the dollar sign. This is a safety precaution to ensure that another digit cannot be keyed after the dollar sign.

5. On the next line, key the amount in words. Start at the left margin. Again, fill in any unused part of the line with hyphens.

6. Do not forget to include the account number.

CHEQUES ASSIGNMENT

ASSIGNMENT 7:74

On the forms provided by your teacher, key the following cheques. Do not forget to key the current year.

Date	Payee	Amount	Account No.	Re:
May 31, 19—	Jordan S. Marks	$125.33	110111	Inv. #890
July 2, 19—	Evana Suter	$891.50	102134	Typewriter
August 4, 19—	S & S Business Forms	$234.25	473988	Stationery
April 21, 19—	Madison Leasing	$ 51.25	879039	Inv. #12358
September 1, 19—	Sheila Cooper	$168.01	980211	Dentist

PIVOTING AND LEADER ASSIGNMENTS

ASSIGNMENT

6:32

ARRANGED MATERIAL

Format attractively on a half-sheet of paper.
Use variable line spacing.

```
            S P R I N G   F E V E R   D A N C E
                 Saturday, March 22, 19--
                           at
                         20:00
                  METROPOLITAN HOTEL
                2371 Lakeshore Road East
                     ADMISSION $5
                   FOR TICKETS CALL
John Sutt[1] .......................................... [1]745-8801
Helen Spasevska ......................................... 728-5008
Sandy Chronos ........................................... 423-7811
Nick Anderson ........................................... 251-5833
```

ASSIGNMENT

6:33

Set a 60-character line.
Double space.
Centre vertically and horizontally on a full sheet of paper.
Use open or closed leaders.

```
                  C O M M O N   D E G R E E S

                            ↓ 3

B.A. ..................................................... Bachelor of Arts
B.A.A. ......................................... Bachelor of Applied Arts
B.Agr. .............................................. Bachelor of Agriculture
B.A.S. ...................................... Bachelor of Applied Science
B.Ch. .............................................. Bachelor of Chemistry
B.Ed. .............................................. Bachelor of Education
B.Lit. .............................................. Bachelor of Literature
B.P.H.E. ................ Bachelor of Physical and Health Education
B.Sc. .............................................. Bachelor of Science
D.D. ..................................................... Doctor of Divinity
```

CHEQUES

There are a number of rules for making out cheques. These rules apply regardless of whether the cheque is keyed or handwritten. These rules exist for the protection of the person issuing the cheque. You must follow these rules exactly, because the writer of the cheque bears the loss if an error is made.

047

April 28 19--

PAY TO
THE ORDER OF Spectrum Records ----------------------------------$145.39

One hundred forty-five ----------------------------------39/100 DOLLARS
100

CANADAV TRUSTCO MORTGAGE COMPANY
9756 WALLACEE AVE. N.,
LISTOWEE, ONT.   N4W LM6

Kathy Preston

⑈047⑈ ⑆1130 2⑈509⑆ ⑈0250 1841⑈8⑈

INTERCHEQUES—Security—Green—881

ASSIGNMENT

6:34

Set a 60-character line.
Double space.
Centre vertically and horizontally on a half-sheet of paper.
Pivot the names from the right margin.
Use closed leaders.
Double space after the main heading.
Triple space after the subheading.

SCHOLARSHIPS AND AWARDS
↓ 2
R.H. King Collegiate
↓ 3

English ....Tom Gabor
Geography ....Tammy Haughton
History .... Esther Gabert
Mathematics .... Meg Chastko
French ....Greg Petroff
Art .... Rick Swartz
Keyboarding .... Kristy Worthner
Family Studies ....Jay Singh

ASSIGNMENT

6:35

Set a 50-character line.
Single space.
Centre vertically on a half-sheet of paper.
Double space after the main title and triple space after the subtitle.
Use closed leaders between columns.

NOTE

Leave one space before the beginning and one space after the end of each leader line.

BARGAIN CITY DEPARTMENT STORES
↓ 2
Phone Orders Accepted
↓ 3

Prince George$^1_\wedge$ ....$^1_\wedge$747-0964
Kelowna 820-5633
Dawson Creek 527-9317
Courtenay 673-0012
Abbotsford 576-0129
Langley 439-0366
Nelson 267-0477
Surrey 744-6655

THE PROFIT AND LOSS STATEMENT

The **profit and loss statement** shows a company's sales, gross profits, expenses, and net profit during a given time period.

ASSIGNMENT

7:72

THE PROFIT AND LOSS STATEMENT

Key the profit and loss statement for the month of June for S & S Business Forms.

THE PROFIT AND LOSS STATEMENT

S & S BUSINESS FORMS

	Month Ending June 30, 19--		Month Ending July 31, 19--
SALES		$23 187	$33 800
DEDUCT COST OF MERCHANDISE SOLD:			
Inventory June 1	$10 300		$11 600
Merchandise Purchases	16 500		12 000
Total Available for Sale	$26 800		$23 600
Inventory June 30	8 200		9 300
Total Cost of Merchandise sold ...		18 600	14 300
GROSS PROFIT		$ 4 587	$19 500
DEDUCT EXPENSES:			
Selling Expense	$ 1 300		$ 2 600
Rent	500		500
Heating & Lighting	255		490
Equipment Depreciation	300		300
Total Expenses		$ 2 355	$ 3 890
NET PROFIT BEFORE TAXES		$ 2 232	$15 610

ASSIGNMENT

7:73

Using the same format and headings given in Assignment 7:72, key the July profit and loss statement for S & S Business Forms.
The July figures are shown in purple.

PARTLY ARRANGED MATERIAL

Set a 60-character line.
Centre vertically on a half-sheet of paper.
Use open leaders.
Centre the last two lines.

The Mendadovi Corporation

Vacation Eligibility Schedule

Six months – one year . . . .   two week/one

year – ten years . . . .   three weeks /ten

years – twenty-five years . . . . four weeks /

twenty-five years plus . . . . five weeks/

Accumulated days may be taken in any year.

Set a 50-character line.
Single space the body.
Centre on a half-sheet of paper.
Use open leaders.
The $ sign appears only at top of column.

FREYA PRODUCT SALES

Sales for 1975 . . . . $5 000 000/
Sales for 1980 . . . . $10 000 000/
Sales for 1985 . . . . $12 000 000/
Sales for 1990 . . . . $ 9 000 000/
Sales for 1995 . . . . $15 000 000/
/

THE BANK RECONCILIATION STATEMENT

The **bank reconciliation statement** shows the financial transactions that have occurred during one month between a company and its bank. It shows deposits and withdrawals as at month-end.

ASSIGNMENT 7:71

THE BANK RECONCILIATION STATEMENT

Format this statement using the guidelines given for keying financial statements.

SPECTRUM RECORDS LTD.

Bank Reconciliation Statement

July 31, 19--

Balance June 30 .... $ 862.44

Cheques cleared
    No. 59 .... $ 24.00
    No. 63 .... 138.66
    No. 64 .... 330.48
    No. 66 .... 100.00
    No. 68 .... 196.00
    TOTAL CHEQUES DRAWN $789.14   73.30

Deposits
    June 4 .... $1 230.00
    June 9 .... 500.00
    TOTAL DEPOSITS $1 730.00   1 803.30

Outstanding Cheques
    No. 62 .... $230.25
    No. 65 .... 10.98
    No. 67 .... 670.50
    TOTAL CHEQUES OUTSTANDING $911.73   891.57

Service charges $6.25

Chequebook Balance July 31 .... $ 885.32

TWO-PAGE PROGRAMS

A two-page program consists of a centered outer cover page, plus a program outline on the inside right-hand page. The program outline usually contains pivoted material with leaders.

1. Take a full sheet of paper and bring the bottom of the page to the top of the page and make a crosswise fold.

2. Insert the shorter edge of the folded paper into the machine with the fold to your *left*. The page now facing you will be the front cover.

3. Key the cover material, centering it vertically and horizontally.

4. Remove the paper from the machine.

5. Fold the paper along the same crosswise fold, but in the opposite direction, so that the *right-hand* page of the inside in on the *outside*, and the cover page is on the inside.

6. Holding the paper so that the keyed material is upside down and the fold is on the *left*, reinsert the paper into the machine.

7. Key the program outline.

8. Remove the paper from the machine, and fold it back so that the cover page is on the outside again.

9. Be careful to insert the same short edge of the paper into the machine both times. Otherwise the program outline will appear upside down.

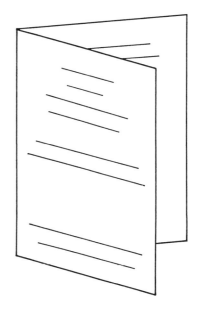

FINANCIAL STATEMENT ASSIGNMENTS

THE BALANCE SHEET

The **balance sheet** shows the financial position (assets and liabilities) of a company at a given time, often at year-end.

ASSIGNMENT 7:70

THE BALANCE SHEET

Key an exact copy of this balance sheet on a full sheet of paper.
Use the spacing illustrated.
Centre vertically.

SPECTRUM RECORDS
↓ 2
BALANCE SHEET
↓ 2
For the Year Ending December 31, 19--

Leave two to three spaces between columns.

Leaders should be preceded and followed by a blank space.

↓ 3

Align all leaders at the right.

Align all $ signs.

Assets
↓ 2

Real Estate Loans		$ 1 250 500
Bonds:		
Government	$1 409 380	
Industrial	2 500 000	
Total Bonds Owned		3 090 380
Stocks		1 200 500
Cash in Banks		5 890 600
↓ 2		
TOTAL ASSETS		$11 992 368

↓ 3

Liabilities
↓ 2

Reserved for Investment Fluctuations	$ 1 000 000
Taxes	990 500
Commission to Agents	180 500
Wages Payable	1 800 000
Accounts Payable	250 000
↓ 2	
TOTAL LIABILITIES	$ 4 221 000

↓2↓2

Use automatic line finders for keying double line.

ASSIGNMENT

6:38

NOTE
Always triple space after a main heading, unless it is followed by a subheading.

Set a 60-character line.
Single space the body.
Centre vertically on a half-sheet of paper.
Use open leaders. Centre the last line.
Allow 32 letters and spaces per line.

THE DAILY PLANET/Advertising Rates

1 insertion ...... $4.20 per agate line per day

2 consecutive insertions ... $4.20 per agate line per day/

3 consecutive insertions ... $3.98 per agate line per day/

4-6 consecutive insertions ... $3.80 per agate line per day/

7-29 consecutive insertions ... $3.53 per agate line per

day/30 consecutive insertions ..... $3.08 per agate

line per day

(Allow 32 letters and spaces per line)

THE FINANCIAL STATEMENT

Financial statement is a general term used to describe balance sheets, bank reconciliation statements, and profit and loss statements. All financial statements have a left-hand column, in which are listed descriptions of the items taken into account, and a right-hand column, which shows amounts saved or owing. Follow these instructions to format financial statements:

1. Centre the statement vertically on a sheet of paper.

2. Use a suitable line length. Statements are usually keyed on a 60-character pica line, or a 70-character elite line.

3. Because the numbers in the right-hand column are aligned along the right margin, you must backspace (pivot) *once* for *each* stroke in the longest item in the right-hand column. Set a tab at that point.

4. To set a tab stop for the next column, backspace once for *each* letter in the longest item in that column, including the spaces between the two columns. (Two to three spaces are usually left between columns in financial statements.)

5. The left-hand column containing descriptions of the items is aligned with the left margin. If there are any subdivisions in this column, they are indented three or four spaces from the left margin.

6. Use leaders to guide the reader's eyes from the "description" column to the "amounts" column(s). You may use open or closed leaders.

7. A dollar sign ($) is keyed to the left of the figure which appears at the top of each column, and to the left of the total. Dollar signs must be aligned.

8. All numbers must be aligned at the right-hand side.

9. Final totals are underscored twice, with the second line keyed close to the first. (Pull the automatic line finder forward and turn the cylinder up slightly. After you have keyed the second line of under-scores, return the automatic line finder to its original position and continue keying.)

TWO-PAGE PROGRAM ASSIGNMENTS

ASSIGNMENT

6:39

ARRANGED MATERIAL

Format this two-page program.
Centre vertically and horizontally.

A) OUTER COVER TEXT

SIR OLIVER MOWAT COLLEGIATE INSTITUTE

↓ 2

presents

↓ 3

C O M M E N C E M E N T 1 9 - -

↓ 2

on

↓ 2

November 15, 19--

↓ 2

at

↓ 2

20:00

Set a 50-character line.
Format this inner page text attractively.
Pivot the second column from the right margin.
Align the enumerations at the left margin, leaving one space before single-digit numbers.

B) INNER PAGE TEXT

SIR OLIVER MOWAT COLLEGIATE INSTITUTE

↓ 2

COMMENCEMENT PROGRAM

↓ 3

1. Processional and O Canada ....Concert Band

↓ 2

2. Invocation .... Elton Springer

↓ 2

3. Principal's Remarks .... Amy Webster

↓ 2

4. Song of Joy .... Concert Band

↓ 2

5. Presentation of Prizes .... Department Heads

↓ 2

NOTE

Leave two spaces after the period in an enumeration.

ASSIGNMENT

7:68

You are working for S & S Business Forms, 36 Provencher Blvd., Winnipeg, Manitoba R2H 3B4.

Key this statement of account on the form provided by your teacher.

TO: Crown Products Incorporated, Suite 152, 80 Hastings Ave., West Palm Beach, Florida U.S.A. 33409. Their billing date is February 4.

Date	Description	Purchases	Credit	Balance
Jan. 6	Invoice #3837	$125.35		$125.35
Jan. 10	Invoice #3921	$ 71.49		196.84
Jan. 15	Invoice #4003	55.98		252.82
Jan. 22	Cheque		$200.00	52.82
Jan. 26	Invoice #4129	198.27		251.09
Jan. 30	Cheque		250.00	1.09
	BALANCE OWING			1.09

ASSIGNMENT

7:69

Key this statement of account, following the instructions given for Assignment 7:68.

TO: Hunt & Harkness Limited, 4919 Twin Branches Way, Atlanta Georgia U.S.A. 30338. Billing date is April 27.

Date	Description	Purchases	Credit	Balance
March 28				$231.85
March 30	Cheque		$231.85	0
April 6	Invoice #22878	55.87		55.87
April 10	Invoice #22993	115.30		171.17
April 18	Invoice #23881	275.88		447.05
	BALANCE OWING			447.05

6. Presentation of Diplomas .... Sandy Gray
↓ 2
7. Presentation of Scholarships .... Holger Engels
↓ 2
8. Valedictory Address ....Lucia Alphonso
↓ 2
9. God Save the Queen ....Concert Band
↓ 2
10. Recessional .... Stage Party

ASSIGNMENT

6:40

Format this two-page program attractively.

A) OUTER COVER TEXT

Application information/for/the Mount Hope Field Naturalists founded in 1920/"To Acquire and Disseminate Knowledge of Natural History"/Information Concerning/Meetings, Study Groups/Outings, Fees

B) INNER PAGE INFORMATION

MEETINGS: Held on the first Monday of the month, the program usually includes an illustrated talk by a leading naturalist or scientist.

STUDY GROUPS: For those who are especially interested in botany, bird study, or the study and conservation of Mount Hope's ravines and waterfront.

OUTINGS: Many outings occur throughout the year, giving members opportunities to study nature at first hand with knowledgeable leaders.

FEES: $16.00 Family
8.50 Senior Family (65+)
12.00 Single
6.00 Student
175.00 Life

THE STATEMENT OF ACCOUNT

At the end of each month, the merchant or supplier sends an individual **statement of account** to each customer. This form lists the purchases and payments made by that customer during the month. The statement lists each invoice, its date, its number, and its total, along with payments made. The balance owing is shown at the bottom of the form. If payment is not made by the purchaser within the time given, for example, thirty days, additional charges may be added to the balance owing on the purchaser's next monthly statement.

STATEMENT OF ACCOUNT ASSIGNMENTS

ASSIGNMENT 7:67

Key an exact copy of this statement of account.

Georgias stationery limited

85 Rockwell Avenue
Toronto, Ontario
M6N 1N9

Statement

TO: Spectrum Records Ltd
     1520 Midland Avenue
     Scarborough, Ontario
     M1K 4H1

BILLING DATE: June 30, 19--

TERMS: Net thirty days

DATE	DESCRIPTION	PURCHASES	CREDITS	BALANCE
May 30				25.30
June 10	Invoice #2487	$253.71		279.01
" 15	Invoice #2581	169.30		448.31
" 22	Invoice #2772	103.50		551.81
" 27	Cheque		$500.00	51.81

BALANCE OWING: $51.81

ASSIGNMENT

6:41

Format this two-page program attractively.
Use triple spacing for the outer cover, and single spacing for the inner page.
Use the display techniques shown.

A) OUTER COVER TEXT

Paula Mercer's Racquet Shop
presents
TIPS FOR TENNIS PLAYERS
a seminar
on
Saturday, April 23, 19 - -
at the
Mayfield Courts
REGISTER TODAY

B) INSIDE PAGE TEXT

1. How to Control the Height of a Flat Serve
2. How to Co-ordinate Your Pass and Serve
3. How to Control the Ball's Direction
4. How to Improve Your Volley
5. How to Improve Your Serve
6. How to Select the PERFECT Racquet
7. Game Strategy

ASSIGNMENT 7:65

You are working for Office & Industrial Supply Company, 2050 Mansfield Street, London, Ontario N7H 3T6.

Key this invoice on the form provided by your teacher. The order, #755-366, has been placed by Spectrum Records.

Use the current date and indicate that the order is to shipped by express. Calculate the sales tax.

The invoice number is 3890.

1 Briefcase #2788	@ $95.00	$ 95.00
6 Pocket calculators #5381	@ 29.98	179.88
6 Adaptors #5382	@ 6.99	41.94
5 Pkgs. telephone message pads	@ 5.95	29.75
Subtotal		$346.57
Sales Tax		
TOTAL		

ASSIGNMENT 7:66

You are now working for S & S Business Forms, 36 Provencher Blvd., Winnipeg, Manitoba R2H 3B4.

You have to prepare an invoice to send to Spectrum Records for their order #9135.

The goods are to be sent by air express. Use today's date for the invoice. Spectrum Records Ltd. is located at 1520 Midland Avenue, Scarborough, Ontario M1K 4H1.

1000 Letterhead (as per sample)	@ $ 25.00/500	$ 50.00
5000 Window envelopes #B2351L	@ 162.00/5000	162.00
1000 Interoffice memos #B3011C	@ 89.20/1000	89.20
Subtotal		$301.20
Sales Tax		
TOTAL		

Format this two-page program attractively.
Use the display techniques shown.

A) OUTER COVER TEXT

ANNOUNCING THE OPENING

of COMPUTER WORLD

224 Bagot Drive

featuring

A COMPLETE LINE OF

COMPUTERS

Come Visit Our Showroom Today

B) INSIDE PAGE TEXT

FEATURES OF COMPUTER WORLD

1. A Wide Computer Selection

2. Software Specialists

3. Diskettes

4. Colour Monitors

5. A Variety of Printers

THE INVOICE

An **invoice** is a written record of goods shipped by the merchant or supplier to the purchaser. It is set up in a fashion similar to the purchase order. The invoice describes the goods sent, the quantity, the unit price of each item, and the total cost of the shipment. It may show other useful information, such as the method of shipment and the charges, and any discounts, where applicable. When preparing an invoice, be sure to make at least *three* copies.

1. The original goes to the customer. (The original is mailed separately from the shipment.)

2. The second copy is sent directly with the goods.

3. The third copy is kept by the seller for accounting purposes.

INVOICE ASSIGNMENTS

ASSIGNMENT 7:64

Key an exact copy of this invoice on the form provided by your teacher.

Georgias stationery limited

85 Rockwell Avenue
Toronto, Ontario
M6N 1N9

Invoice

TO: Spectrum Records Ltd.
1520 Midland Avenue
Scarborough, Ontario
M1K 4H1

DATE: June 7, 19--
PURCHASE ORDER #: 2387
INVOICE #: 7611
VIA: Truck

QUANTITY	DESCRIPTION	PRICE	
3	5 cm Binders #842116 (black)	$ 7.00	$21.00
1 box	1000 #10 Envelopes	19.80	19.80
2 pkgs.	Paper (letter size) #258	8.95	17.90
50	Presentation covers #X5916	.20	10.00
	Subtotal		$68.70
	Ontario Sales Tax @ 8%		5.50
	TOTAL		74.20

ASSIGNMENT

6:43

PARTLY ARRANGED MATERIAL

Format this material attractively as a two-page program.

Y O U/are cordially invited to attend/SECRETARIAL CAREERS/at/ Progress College/419 Centennial Court/on/Tuesday, November 17, 19--/16:00 to 19:00/R.S.V.P./Secondary School Liaison Office/630- 5681, Ext. 300

Session I--The Current Market for Secretarial Personnel

Session II--Basic Skills Required by Business

Session III--Problems Encountered by Secretarial Personnel

Session IV--Word Processing Programs

ASSIGNMENT

6:44

Format this material attractively as a two-page program. Use your own display techniques.

ROBERT WISEMAN/in/THE HAUNTED HOUSE/a comedy thriller/ with/Denise Forbes/Penny Hart/Marc Amyot/Stage Manager/William O'Hagan/Lighting/Jenny Thomas/Lighting Director/Andrew De LaCoure/

CAST OF CHARACTERS/(in order of appearance)/Jeffery Worrell . . . Robert Wiseman/Myra Worrell . . . Denise Forbes/Helga Korineck . . . Penny Hart/Porter Mitchum . . . Marc Amyot/

SYNOPSIS OF SCENES/Scene I: a summer afternoon/Scene II: that evening/Scene III: the next morning/there will be one fifteen-minute intermission.

ASSIGNMENT 7:62

Spectrum Records needs the goods listed below.
Key a purchase order for these items.
Your teacher will provide you with a purchase order form.

TO: Office & Industrial Supply Company, 2050 Mansfield Street, London, Ontario N7H 3T6. Use today's date. The order number is 755-366. The goods are to be shipped by express. Calculate the tax applicable to your order at the current rate. Do not forget to sign your order.

1 Briefcase #2788	@	$95.00	$ 95.00
6 Pocket calculators #5381	@	29.98	179.88
6 Adaptors #5382	@	6.99	41.94
5 Pkgs. telephone message pads	@	5.95	29.75
Subtotal			$346.57
Sales Tax			_____
TOTAL			

ASSIGNMENT 7:63

Key a purchase order for these items needed by Spectrum Records.

TO: S & S Business Forms, 36 Provencher Blvd., Winnipeg, Manitoba R2H 3B4. Use today's date. The order number is 9135. The goods are to be shipped Air Express, C.O.D. Calculate the tax to be included. Remember that the order has to be signed.

1000 Letterhead as per sample attached @ $25.00 per 500 sheets

= $50.00

5000 Window envelopes #B2351L @ $162.00 per 5000

1000 Interoffice memos #B3011C @ $89.20 per 1000

Subtotal $301.20   Sales Tax _____ TOTAL _____

CENTERING COMPOSITION ASSIGNMENTS

ASSIGNMENT
6:45
Compose and key a centered announcement of an after-school keyboarding-club meeting.

ASSIGNMENT
6:46
Compose and key a centered announcement of a sale at a computer store, listing examples of items for sale.

ASSIGNMENT
6:47
Compose and key a centered invitation to a seminar on business careers.

ASSIGNMENT
6:48
Compose and key a centered invitation to a gala opening of a business you would like to own.

ASSIGNMENT
6:49
Compose and key a centered notice about a "Key-A-Thon" to raise money for a specific charity.

ASSIGNMENT
6:50
Compose and key a centered advertisement listing details of your services as a keyboarding tutor.

ASSIGNMENT
6:51
Compose and key a centered advertisement stating that you are offering to key reports and other materials for a fee.

ASSIGNMENT
6:52
Compose and key a centered announcement of an upcoming keyboarding contest for schools in your area.

ASSIGNMENT
6:53
Compose and key a two-page program for a computer conference.

PURCHASE ORDER ASSIGNMENTS

ASSIGNMENT
7:61

Key an exact copy of this purchase order on the form provided by your teacher.

NOTE

All entries must be aligned.

Purchase order

SPECTRUM

records 1520 Midland Avenue Scarborough, Ontario M1K 4H1

TO: 2 Georgias Stationery Ltd.
∧ 85 Rockwell Avenue
Toronto, Ontario
M6N 1N9

DATE: 2 May 31, 19--
∧
PURCHASE ORDER #: 2387

REQUESITION #: 4912

VIA: Truck

QUANTITY	DESCRIPTION	PRICE	
3 2 →	→ 5 cm Binders #842116 (Black) ↓2	$ 7.00	$21.00 ← 2
1 box	1000 #10 Envelopes	19.80 ← 2	19.80
2 pkgs ← 2	Paper (letter size) #258	8.95	17.90
50	Presentation Covers #X5916	.20	10.00
	Subtotal		$68.70
	Ontario Sales Tax @ 8%		5.50
	TOTAL		$74.20

Signature _____

MODULE

7

TABLES AND BUSINESS FORMS

Courtesy of Xerox Canada Inc.

THE PURCHASE ORDER

NOTE

Prices are not always shown, as prices of some items could vary and because special discounts could be applied after the purchase order has been filled out.

A **purchase order** is used for ordering supplies or goods from a manufacturer, wholesaler, or supplier. When keying a purchase order, you should include the following information:

1. The name and address of the company from which the goods are being purchased. (The address of the purchasing firm [your firm] is already printed on the form.)

2. The date on which the goods are being ordered.

3. The order number (most purchase orders are prenumbered).

4. The method of shipment.

5. Quantities, descriptions, and prices of goods being ordered. Each of these items should be typed in its appropriate column. Make sure that you set tab stops to make keying faster. Double space the body, unless there are many items being ordered. Capitalize the first word of each item in the description.

6. A minimum of two copies of the purchase order are made: the original and at least one copy for your files.
   Most manufactured purchase orders come with at least two copies and carbons attached.

INTRODUCTION

Tables are used to format material in columns or tabular form. Information displayed in this way is easy to read.

Business forms, such as invoices and purchase orders, are used extensively by both large and small companies. Business forms are prepared by keying information on preprinted forms. Forms can also be created on a computer system.

More and more businesses are turning to computer-generated forms because this method saves time. Once the form document has been created, it remains the same, and only the data varies, such as names, addresses, dates, purchase invoice numbers and account numbers. Many companies also order their business forms from other companies that specialize in manufacturing these forms. Special attention must be paid when aligning and formatting data on documents.

In this module, you will format and key tables ranging in difficulty from simple one-column lists to ruled and boxed tables. You will also design and produce your own business forms and use the tabulator for efficient keying on business forms. If you are using a microcomputer or word processor, refer to the manual for information on setting tabs and automatic alignment.

OBJECTIVES

1. To format tables so that the information is both attractive and easy to read.

2. To format and key tables ranging from simple one-column lists, to tables with short and long column headings, to ruled and boxed tables.

3. To format and key tables from unarranged and handwritten copy.

4. To compose and format tables directly on the machine.

5. To understand the use of business forms.

6. To learn how to key purchase orders, invoices, statements of account, financial statements, cheques, and index cards.

7. To use the machine for efficient keying on business forms.

8. To prepare file labels for general jobs.

9. To design and produce your own business forms.

GUIDELINES FOR KEYING ON PREPRINTED BUSINESS FORMS

Follow these guidelines for keying on preprinted forms:

1. Start keying two or three spaces after the printed guide word:

   TO: ²⁄∧ M. Sutton

2. Align keyed material with bottom of printed guide word:

   TO: M. Sutton

3. Align columns of numbers using the decimal point:

   ```
   1234
    345.5
     45.2
   ```

4. Leave two or three spaces between keyed material and vertical lines:

   ```
   Quantity   |   Description
              |        ↓ 2
       12     |      Notebooks
        3  ²∧ | ²∧   Binders
       50     |      Pencils
   ```

5. "Description" columns like the one above are aligned at the left.

6. For faster keying, set tab stops where needed.

7. Start the list of items a double space below the horizontal line.

8. Use single spacing. (Double spacing may be used if there are only a few items.)

CONTENTS

Formatting Tables 235

Formatting Tables Assignments 236

    Arranged Material 236

    Partly Arranged Material 239

    Unarranged Material 240

Tables with Long Column Headings 240

Long Column Headings Assignments 242

    Arranged Material 242

    Partly Arranged Material 244

Tables with Short Column Headings 246

Short Column Headings Assignments 247

    Arranged Material 247

    Partly Arranged Material 250

Tables with Mixed Column Headings 251

Mixed Column Headings Assignments 252

    Arranged Material 252

    Unarranged Material 255

Tables with Two-Line Column Headings 257

Two-Line Column Headings Assignments 257

    Arranged Material 257

Ruled Tables 259

Ruled Tables Assignments 260

    Arranged Material 260

    Partly Arranged Material 261

Formatting Boxed Tables 262

Boxed Tables Assignments 263

    Arranged Material 263

Technique

1. When you are keying on lines, the letters should be *slightly above* the actual line.

2. To test your line placement, set your ribbon selector on *stencil* (white), so that the ink will not show, or use the correcting key.

3. Insert your paper, and adjust it so that when you key the underscore, it rests on the line. (This procedure ensures that the letters will be positioned slightly above the line.)

4. Return your ribbon selector back to "ribbon" and key the letters.

```
too high above the line

too low on the line

just right!
```

ASSIGNMENT
7:60

Key these names on a sheet of *lined* paper.

1. Col. Paolo G. Toscani
2. Bernard Silverberg
3. Richard Robichaud
4. John S. Ma
5. Gorman Knitting Mills Ltd.
6. Henry Charles Gresmanis
7. Dr. Collin Pelpola
8. Samuel Topcusglu
9. George Czarnecki
10. Sandy Strachan

Tables Composition Assignments 266

Using Business Forms 266

Keying on Lines 267

Guidelines for Keying on Preprinted
Business Forms 269

The Purchase Order 270

Purchase Order Assignments 271

The Invoice 273

Invoice Assignments 273

The Statement of Account 275

Statement of Account Assignments 275

The Financial Statement 277

Financial Statement Assignments 278

Cheques 281

Cheques Assignment 282

Card Files 283

Card Files Assignment 284

File Labels 285

File Labels Assignment 286

Designing Business Forms 286

Business Form Composition Assignments 287

KEYING ON LINES

From time to time you may be required to key on a printed form, such as an employment application. In the sample below, notice how the letters are *slightly* above the line, and the "tails" or descenders of certain letters just touch the line.

JOHN WILEY & SONS CANADA LIMITED

APPLICATION FOR EMPLOYMENT
(PLEASE PRINT)

Position being applied for	Date available to begin work	Minimum Salary Required
Office Receptionist	Immediately	$25 000/year

PERSONAL

Last Name	First Name	Middle Name(s)
ODYNSKY,	Nadia	Christine

Present Address	No. Street	Apt.	City	Province	Postal Code
55 Stansbury Crescent,			Scarborough ,	Ontario	M1K 4R7

Telephone Number
Home   (416) 555-2010
Business (416) 555-7999

Have You Worked For Wiley Previously?
☐ Yes   If Yes Dates
☒ No   Position

Are you legally eligible to work in Canada?
☒ Yes ☐ No

Are you between 18 and 65 years of age?
☒ Yes ☐ No

Are you willing to re-locate?
☐ Yes ☒ No.

Preferred location
Toronto area

Do you have a valid driver's licence?
☒ Yes ☐ No.

EDUCATION

SECONDARY SCHOOL

Highest grade or level completed   Sir Oliver Mowat C.I.   Grade 12

Type of certificate or diploma received   O.S.S.G.D.

BUSINESS, TRADE OR TECHNICAL SCHOOL

Name of Program	Length of Program
N/A	

Licence, certificate or diploma awarded?
☐ Yes   ☐ No

COMMUNITY COLLEGE

Name of Program	Length of Program
N/A	

Diploma received?   ☐ Yes   ☐ No

Other courses, workshops, seminars

UNIVERSITY

Length of Program	Degree awarded	
N/A	☐ Yes ☐ No	☐ U/Grad. ☐ Grad.

Major subject(s)

Licences, Certificates, Degrees

"APPROVED BY THE ONTARIO HUMAN RIGHTS COMMISSION"

FORMATTING TABLES

Most tables have a main heading, plus headings for each column. A column heading may be longer or shorter than the longest item in the column. The main heading and the subheading (if there is one) are centered over the table. Each column heading is centered over the appropriate column.

Follow these guidelines when formatting a table:

1. Clear all previously set tabs and margins.

2. Determine the vertical placement of the table.

3. Insert the paper into the machine, and place the print point indicator on the first line of the text.

4. Centre and key the heading or title in all capital letters. Triple space after it.

5. Find the longest item in each column.

6. Determine how many spaces will be left between columns. When there are three or more columns, leave three to eight spaces between columns. When there are two columns, you may leave up to ten spaces.

7. Position the paper so that its centre point aligns with the print point indicator.

8. Backspace *once* for every *two* characters in the longest entry in each column, and *once* for every *two* spaces between the columns.

9. Set the left margin at this point.

10. Strike the space bar *once* for *each* character in the longest item in the first column, and *once* for *each* of the spaces that follow it.

11. Set a tab stop at this point.

12. From this tab stop, strike the space bar *once* for *each* character in the longest item in the second column, and *once* for *each* of the spaces that follow the second column.

13. Set the rest of the tab stops in the same manner.

If you are using a microcomputer or word processor, check with your teacher or consult your operating manual for information on setting tabs and automatic alignment.

TABLES COMPOSITION ASSIGNMENTS

ASSIGNMENT
7:54

Under the heading, SUPPLIES FOR MY OFFICE, compose and key a two-column table, with a minimum of ten entries.

ASSIGNMENT
7:55

Under the main heading, IMPORTANT DATES, compose and key a two-column table with the subheadings Event and Date. List a minimum of seven important days and dates, for example, Valentine's Day, your birthday, etc.

ASSIGNMENT
7:56

Using the main heading, DIRECTORY, compose and key a three-column table with the subheadings, Name, Address, and Phone. Enter a minimum of five entries for the people you call most frequently.

ASSIGNMENT
7:57

Using the main heading, MY TIMETABLE, compose and key a three-column table with the subheadings, Subject, Teacher, and Room. List the appropriate information in each column.

ASSIGNMENT
7:58

Using the main heading, CAREERS IN THE BUSINESS WORLD, compose and key a four-column ruled table. Key a minimum of four careers in each column. Use the subheadings, Professional, Service, Communications, and Office.

ASSIGNMENT
7:59

Using the main heading, A BUSINESS WARDROBE, compose and key a three-column ruled table. The subheadings are, Item, Colour, Approximate Cost. Place a minimum of five entries in each column.

USING BUSINESS FORMS

Using business forms for keying work that is performed as part of the regular office routine saves time and prevents a lot of unnecessary keyboarding. Although some companies produce their own business forms, most forms are now manufactured by specialized firms. Business forms are printed and sold to many companies across Canada. There may be times, however, when you must design and produce your own business forms for general jobs.

FORMATTING TABLES ASSIGNMENTS

ASSIGNMENT

7:1

ARRANGED MATERIAL

Set up this table on a half-sheet of paper.
Use the horizontal spacing indicated.

TABULATION

When	keying	work	in
tabulated	form,	tab	across
the	page	from	one
column	to	the	next.
	6	6	6
tabulated	keying	work	across
left margin	Tab 1	Tab 2	Tab 3

ASSIGNMENT

7:2

Format and key the following two-column table on a half-sheet of paper.
Double space between the lines of the title, and triple space between the
title and the body.
Single space the body, and leave ten spaces between columns.

POSTAL ABBREVIATIONS
for
CANADA

British Columbia	BC
Alberta	AB
Saskatchewan	SK
Manitoba	MB
Ontario	ON
Quebec	PQ
New Brunswick	NB
Nova Scotia	NS
Prince Edward Island	PE
Newfoundland	NF
Labrador	LB
Yukon Territory	YT
Northwest Territories	NT

Format this boxed table attractively.
Use a full sheet of paper, longer edge inserted first.
Align all numbers.

OPERATING EXPENSES

Month	Fixed Portion Less Depreciation	Variable Portion %	Amount	Total
January	$16 000	3	$11 520	$27 520
February	16 000	5	19 200	35 200
March	16 000	6	23 040	39 040
April	16 000	7	26 880	42 880
May	16 000	6	23 040	39 040
June	16 000	8	30 720	46 720
July	16 000	9	34 560	50 560
August	16 000	10	38 400	54 400
September	16 000	12	46 080	62 080
October	16 000	9	34 560	50 560
November	16 000	10	38 400	54 400
December	16 000	5	57 600	73 600
Totals	$192 000	100%	$384 000	$576 000

ASSIGNMENT

7:3

Centre vertically on a half-sheet of paper.
Single space the body.
Leave six spaces between columns.

NOTE

If there are no accents on your machine, put them in with pen.

ENDROITS INTERESSANTS

↓ 3

Aquarium de Montréal	Christ Church Cathedral
Maison de Radio-Canada	Musée McCord
Place des Arts	McGill University
Voyageur Bus Terminal	Place Bonaventure
Place Ville-Marie	Central Station
Eglise Notre-Dame	Planétarium Dow
St. Patrick's Church	Windsor Station
Université du Québec	Concordia University
Forum	Musée des Beaux-Arts

ASSIGNMENT

7:52

Format this boxed table attractively.
Leave five spaces between columns.
Use a full sheet of paper.

A CHART SHOWING

THE LAW OF SUPPLY AND DEMAND

Season	Summer	Fall	Winter	Spring
Situation	many people barbecue; but the young cattle born in late winter are not ready for market	barbecues end; cattle are ready for market	farmers must kill cattle; can't afford to feed them all winter	beef herds have been cut back; out come the barbecues again
Supply	LOW	RISING	STILL RISING	FALLING
Demand	HIGH	FALLING	STEADY	RISING
Price	HIGH	FALLING	STILL FALLING	RISING

Centre vertically on a half-sheet of paper.
Double space the body.
Leave eight spaces between columns.

HOTELS CENTRE-VILLE

↓ 3

Maritimes	Richelieu-Howard Johnson
Ramada Inn	Queen Elizabeth
Ritz-Carlton	Bonaventure
Constellation	Holiday Inn
Les Quatre Saisons	Quality Inn
Sheraton-Mount Royal	Loews LaCité
Royal Roussilion	Holiday Inn-Place Dupuis
Méridien-Montréal	Le Régence-Hyatt
Le Sherbourg	Windsor

Centre vertically on a half-sheet of paper.
Centre the heading, and triple space.
Single space the body.
Leave five spaces between columns.

COMMONLY MISSPELLED WORDS

acceptt	believe	Dimunution	familiar
acquire	benign	dispel	fascinate
accidentally	bussiness	dis appearence	foriegn
acquaintance	cheif	effect	goverment
address	conscience	emabarrass	harass
all right	correspondent	enviornment	hindrance
already	devise	exaggerate	height

BOXED TABLES ASSIGNMENTS

ARRANGED MATERIAL

Format this boxed table attractively.
Use a full sheet of paper, longer edge inserted first.

NOTE

Boxed tables may sometimes have vertical lines at both the left and right margins, forming a complete box for the table.

NOTE

Leave one full space between the digit and the metric symbol each time.

METRIC UNITS FOR EVERYDAY USE ↓ 1			
2 → Physical Quantity	↓ 2 Unit ↓ 1	Symbol	Relationship
Length	↓ 2 kilometre	km	1 km = 1000 m
	metre	m	1 m = 100 cm ← 2
	centimetre	cm	1 cm = 10 mm
	millimetre ↓ 1	mm	10 mm = 1 cm
Volume	↓ 2 cubic metre	m³	1 m³ = 1000 L
	litre	L	
	millilitre ↓ 1	mL	1 L = 1000 mL
Mass	↓ 2 tonne	t	1 t = 1000 kg
	kilogram	kg	1 kg = 1000 g
	gram	g	1 g = 1000 mg
	milligram ↓ 1	mg	1 mg = 0.001 g

PARTLY ARRANGED MATERIAL

Centre vertically on a half-sheet of paper.
Triple space after the heading.
Double space the body.
Leave eight spaces between columns.
Slash mark (/) means new column.

LOCAL TELEVISION STATIONS/ CKGN   Bancroft/

CKVR   Barrie/ CBLT   Toronto/ CKGN   Paris/

CJOH   Ottawa/ CKNX   Wingham/ CFPL   London/

CHCH   Hamilton/ CKWS   Kingston/ CHEX   Peterborough/

CKCO   Kitchener/ CKGN   Uxbridge

Centre vertically on a half-sheet of paper.
Triple space after the heading.
Double space the body.
Leave eight spaces between columns.

STANDARD PAPER SIZES/P1   56 cm x 86 cm/P2

43 cm x 56 cm/P3   28 cm x 43 cm/P4   21.5 cm x

28 cm/P5   14 cm x 21.5 cm/P6   10.7 cm x 14 cm

Centre vertically on a half-sheet of paper.
Triple space after the heading.
Double space the body.
Leave eight spaces between columns.

ABBREVIATED NAMES/Charles   Chas./Edward   Edw./

George   Geo./James   Jas./Joseph   Jos./Robert

Robt./Thomas   Thos./William   Wm.

ASSIGNMENT

7:50

Format this ruled table attractively.
Use a full sheet of paper, longer edge inserted first.

Main Heading: PAUL YANG'S MONTHLY BALANCE

Subheading: March 31, 19—

Column Headings:	Account	Amount Due on Bill	Amount Paid	Monthly Balance

Body: VISA, $526, $100, $426/Fairview Dept. Store, $235, $150,

$85/Goldman's Repair Shop, $56, $560/Pancake Place, $45,

$25, $20/Bank Loan, $5000, $180, $4820

FORMATTING BOXED TABLES

Boxed tables are simply ruled tables (with solid lines of underscoring), to which vertical lines have been added in order to separate the columns.

1. Vertical lines are keyed after the contents of the table and the horizontal lines have been keyed.

2. Remove the paper from the machine. Then reinsert it so that the horizontal lines appear vertical.

3. Find the centre point between each column and line it up with the carriage position scale on the card holder. Do this alignment by eye.

4. Key a solid line of underscores between the top and bottom lines of underscoring already keyed on the page. (These lines of underscoring will now be at the extreme left and extreme right of the page, respectively.)

5. Vertical lines may also be drawn by hand. Insert a pen or pencil in the notch or hole in the card holder, and turn the cylinder knob. (You must first position the paper so that the hole in the card holder is aligned with the centre point between the columns.)

ASSIGNMENT 7:9

UNARRANGED MATERIAL

Centre vertically on a half-sheet of paper.
Arrange the items into three columns.

BASIC OFFICE SUPPLIES

pens, pencils, erasers, stapler, staple remover, note pad, paper, stationery, envelopes, elastics, ruler, reference books, telephone, telephone book, diskettes, paper clips, calendar, date stamp, scissors, file labels, file folders

ASSIGNMENT 7:10

Centre vertically on a half-sheet of paper.
Arrange the items into two columns.

career vocabulary

data sheet, job application form, job application letter, job interview, references, Trade journals, fringe benefits, conditions of work, aptitude, skills

TABLES WITH LONG COLUMN HEADINGS

Column headings make reading a table easier. Some column headings may be longer than any of the material listed in the column. These headings are centered over the respective columns.

1. Clear all previously set tabs and margins.
2. Determine the vertical placement of the table.
3. Insert the paper into the machine.

Centre vertically on a half-sheet of paper.
Use the spacing illustrated.
Centre column headings over columns.

AROUND THE WORLD TRAVEL
↓ 2
HOLIDAY CRUISE DATES
↓ 1

| ↓ 3 | ↓ 2 | |
Destination	Place of Departure ↓ 1 ↓ 2	Date of Departure
Kobe	Hong Kong	May 3
San Francisco 6	Kobe 6	May 10
Tokyo	Vancouver	May 17
Honolulu	Hong Kong	May 24

↓ 1

PARTLY ARRANGED MATERIAL

Format this ruled table attractively.
Use a full sheet of paper, longer edge inserted first.

Main Heading: DORVAL'S HARDWARE STORE

Subheading: Expense Breakdown Statement

19— (key current year)

Column Headings: Operating   January-   July-
                   Expenses   June   December   Total

Body: Rent, $25 000, $25 000, $50 000/Advertising, $10 000, $14 000, $24 000/Salaries, $40 500, $45 000, $85 500/

Storage, $5000, $6500, $11 500/

Freight Charges, $5300, $7200, $13 500/Miscellaneous, $5000, $6000, $11 000/Total, $90 300, $103 700, $195 500

4. Centre and key the main heading or title in all capital letters. Triple space after it.

5. Position the paper so that its centre point aligns with the print point indicator.

6. Backspace *once* for every *two* characters in each column heading, and once for every *two* spaces *between* columns. (The column headings this time are the longest entries.)

7. Set a left margin at this point.

8. Strike the space bar *once* for *each* character in the first column heading, and *once* for *each* space that follows.

9. Set a tab stop at this point.

10. From this tab stop, strike the space bar *once* for *each* character in the second column heading, and *once* for *each* of the spaces that follows the second column heading.

11. Set a tab stop at this point.

12. Key the first column heading at the left margin, and the rest of the headings at the tab stops.

13. To centre a column under its heading, move the print point indicator to the space under the first character in the heading. Strike the space bar *once* for every *two* characters in the heading. Then backspace *once* for every *two* characters in the longest entry in the column.

14. This is the starting point for every entry in the column. It is a good idea to reset your margin at this point. (Since all the headings have now been keyed, clear their tab stops.) Follow this procedure for the other columns in the table, setting new tab stops for the items in each column.

15. Align numbers so that digits appear under digits and decimal points under decimal points.

RULED TABLES ASSIGNMENTS

ASSIGNMENT

7:47

ARRANGED MATERIAL

Centre vertically on a half-sheet of paper.
Use the spacing illustrated.
Centre column headings over columns.

EASY LISTENING STEREOS
↓ 2
Authorized Dealers
↓ 1
↓ 2

Dealer ↓ 1	City	Phone
↓ 2		
Parsons Electronics	Victoria, BC	(604) 368-2177
Royal Radio & Stereo	Edmonton, AB	(403) 425-3510
Enright's Stereo Company 4	Saskatoon, SK 4	(306) 665-4595
House of Music	Winnipeg, MB	(204) 943-2165
Terrific Sounds Co.	London, ON	(519) 679-4211
Quality Electronics	Montreal, PQ	(514) 282-6704
Atlantic Electronics	Halifax, NS	(902) 345-7899
Sounds of Tomorrow ↓ 1	Toronto, ON	(416) 366-1711

LONG COLUMN HEADINGS ASSIGNMENTS

ASSIGNMENT 7:11

ARRANGED MATERIAL

Centre vertically on a half-sheet of paper.
Single space the body, and follow the spacing indicated for the rest.
Leave five spaces between columns.

NOTE

Triple space before column headings, and double space after them. Column headings are typed in lower case and underscored.

ROLLS OF COINS

↓ 3

Denomination	5	Number of Coins	5	Value of Roll
		↓ 2		
Quarters		40		$10.00
Dimes		50		5.00
Nickels		40		2.00
Pennies		50		.50

ASSIGNMENT 7:12

Centre vertically on a half-sheet of paper.
Single space the body, and follow the spacing indicated for the rest.
Leave five spaces between columns.

GOLDEN WHEAT BAKERY

↓ 2

Selection and Price List

↓ 3

Types of Bread	Price	Buns and Rolls	Price per Dozen
		↓ 2	
Home Style	$ .75	Kaiser	$4.10
Whole Wheat	1.15	Dinner Rolls	2.28
Granola	1.50	Cheese	3.60
Bran	1.39	Crusty	2.28
Raisin	1.99	Hamburger	2.16
Sesame	.99	Bagels	2.38
Sour Dough	1.89	Subs	1.99
Dark Rye	1.59	Hot Dog	1.75
Cheese & Onion	2.10	Raisin	3.36

Centre vertically on a half-sheet of paper.
Triple space after the main heading and the column headings.
Double space the body.
Leave eight spaces between columns.

RENSEIGNEMENTS UTILES

3 ↓

En Cas d'Urgence	Numéro de téléphone
2 ↓	
Police	934-3132
Pompier	872-1212
L'hôpital Ste-Justine	731-4931
Hôtel Dieu	935-0971
Clinique dentaire	872-9973
Tel-Aide	874-0917
Ambulance	738-8822
Clinique psychiatrique	939-3329

RULED TABLES

A ruled table is set off by a solid line of underscores above and below the headings. A solid line of underscores is also inserted at the bottom of the table, for balance.

1. To leave one blank line between the line of type and the underscore, return the carrier *once*. Then key the line of underscores. To leave a blank line after the underscore, return the carrier *twice*.

2. Key the underscore, beginning at the left margin and ending at the last stroke of the longest line in the last column. Setting a right margin stop at the last stroke of the longest line will ensure that the underscores rule the table correctly.

Centre vertically on a half-sheet of paper.
Single space the body, and follow the spacing indicated for the rest.
Leave six spaces between columns.

ANYTIME GIFT SUGGESTIONS

from

THE HOBBY HORSE

Aunt Lela	Grandfather	My Friends
mugs	ties	plants
soap dish	books	cards
trivet	chess set	trays
scarf	planter	miniatures
pottery	puzzles	candles

Centre vertically on a half-sheet of paper.
Double space the body.
Correct text according to the proofreader's marks.
Leave five spaces between columns.

WORD PROCESSING TASKS

↓ 3

Automatic Functions	Editing Functions
Alignment	Ading
C entering	Deleting
Indenting	merging
Justyfing	Movingtext
Page Endings	Replacing
Spacing	Merging Letters
Underscoring	Mergin Addresses

ASSIGNMENT 7:44

Centre vertically on a half-sheet of paper.
Double space the body.
Leave eight spaces between columns.

MIGHTY FEAST BREAKFAST CEREAL

3 ↓

Nutrient value per serving	number of grams
2 ↓	
Protein	5.7 g
Fat	0.2 g
Total carbohydrates	20.6 g
Sucrose and other sugars	3.3 g
Starch	17.0 g
Dietary fibre	0.3 g

ASSIGNMENT 7:45

Centre vertically on a half-sheet of paper.
Double space the body.
Leave five spaces between columns.
Calculate and fill in the "Total" column.

EMPLOYEE SALARIES

2 ↓

for the week of

2 ↓

January 7–13

3 ↓

Employee	Hours Worked	Rate per Hour	Total
2 ↓			
Flamenco	34	$8.40
Killison	34	7.20
Janssen	42	6.0
Kampitan	48	5.80
Linkovich	40 42	6.50
Nekhis	48	7.20
Rhea	44	8.00

ASSIGNMENT

7:15

Centre vertically on a half-sheet of paper.
Single space the body, and follow the spacing indicated for the rest.
Leave five spaces between columns.

BRYANT & MONTADOR, INC.
↓ 2
Sales Growth
↓ 2
1986-1989

↓ 3

Previous Year's Sales	Sales Increase	Growth
↓ 2		
$750 000	− 150 000	− 20%
600 000	+ 225 000	+ 35%
825 000	+ 75 000	+ 9%
900 000	+ 30 000	+ 3%

ASSIGNMENT

7:16

PARTLY ARRANGED MATERIAL

Format this material attractively.
Use various display techniques to set off important information.

SANDY BEACH -- AVALON / The Family Cottage Resort / Rate Schedule / Cottage Accommodation, Weekly Rates, Daily Rates / 2-Bedroom, $180, $34 / 3-Bedroom, $210, $45 / 4-Bedroom, $280, $56 / 3-Bedroom Deluxe $300, $68 / 4 Bedroom Deluxe, $390, $75

ASSIGNMENT

7:17

Format this material attractively.

ENERGY VALUE OF SOME FOODS / Food Item, Calories, Kilojoules / Apple, 70, 293 / Egg Roll, 240, 1004 / Ice cream, 255, 1066 / Milk, 160, 669 / Pizza, 315, 1318 / Raisins, 480, 2008 / Orange, 65, 272

TABLES WITH TWO-LINE COLUMN HEADINGS

When a column heading is too long to be keyed on one line, use two or more lines.

1. Centre *each* line of the column heading separately above the column.
2. Underscore the *last* line of the heading.
3. Always single space between lines of a heading.

TWO-LINE COLUMN HEADINGS ASSIGNMENTS

ASSIGNMENT

7:43

ARRANGED MATERIAL

Format this table on a full sheet of paper.
Use the spacing indicated.

C O N F I D E N T I A L
↓ 2
Proposed Salary Increases for
↓ 2
Branch Managers

↓ 3

Branch Office	Name of Manager	Present Salary	Proposed Salary
	↓ 2		
Arnprior, ON	J. Adamson	$46 300	$47 800
Brandon, MB	M. Korinet	46 530	48 000
Chilliwack, BC	K. Mercer	46 800	48 200
Calgary, AB	J. Duke	48 500	50 100
Dauphin, MB	A. Babliani	45 750	48 200
Edmonton, AB	J. Odynsky	47 600	48 550
Gander, NF 4	H. Ratcliff 4	47 000 4	48 500
Gananoque, ON	A. Tan	46 900	48 750
Kingston, ON	E. Barber	47 600	48 500
Montreal, PQ	P. Lambert	46 900	48 250

ASSIGNMENT

7:18

Format this material attractively.

CONCERT TICKET BOOKINGS/Paid Customers, Ticket Number, Price/R. Jonkes, 436, $6.00/B. Simpson, 513, $7.50/J. Thompson, 512, $5.50/Y. Pak, 246, $6.00/S. Bochek, 840, $5.50/D. Massey, 723, $6.00/W. Smolska, 779, $7.50/V. Cruickshank, 337, $6.00/A. Poirer, 582, $5.50/L. Roehrs, 720, $7.50

> **NOTE**
>
> Place the $ sign at the beginning of each column only.

ASSIGNMENT

7:19

Format this material attractively.

WEST HILL ANIMAL CLINIC/Animal-Owner List/Owner's Surname, Animal, Animal's Name, Age/Kaufman, Poodle, Fluffy, 1/ Inkster, Cat, Morris, 1/Lamrock, Snake, Slinky, 2/O'Neil, Dog, Bridey, 4/Difebo, Cat, Muffin, 3/Coe, Canary, Inky, 2/Sengupta, Dog, Chimo, 5

ASSIGNMENT

7:20

Format this material attractively.
Use various display techniques to set off important information.

THE FRIDAY NIGHT HOCKEY CLUB/Total Points List/PLAYER'S NAME, GOALS, ASSISTS, TOTAL/Buddy Marks, 36, 29, 65/Erin Ferreira, 01, 39, 40/Rob Piitz, 02, 19, 21,/Rae Hull, 07, 25, 32/ Terry Yore, 05, 17, 22/Steve Bix, 08, 15, 23

ASSIGNMENT

7:21

Format this material attractively.

MONTHLY INTEREST CALCULATIONS
12% Interest Rate
Monthly Date, Payments, Interest, Balance on $100 at 12%

January 1, $8.33, $1.00, $91.67/February 1, 8.33, .92, 83.34/March 1, 8.33, .83, 75.01/April 1, 8.33, .75, 66.68/May 1, 8.33, .67, 58.35/ June 1, 8.33, .58, 50.02/July 1, 8.33, .50, 41.69/August 1, 8.33, .42, 33.36/September 1, 8.33, .33, 25.00/October 1, 8.33, .25, 16.70/ November 1, 8.33, .17, 8.37/December 1, 8.33, .08

ASSIGNMENT

7:40

Format this material attractively.

ABBREVIATIONS / <u>Abbreviation</u>, <u>Meaning</u> / amt., amount / Ave., Avenue / bal., balance / chap., chapter / Co., Company / c/o, care of / doz., dozen / Dr., Doctor / fig., figure / fwd., forward / jr., junior / Ltd., Limited / p., page / pp., pages / pkg., package / St., Street

ASSIGNMENT

7:41

Format this material attractively.

FIELD'S DEPARTMENT STORE / <u>Outstanding Accounts</u> / <u>Customer</u>, <u>Address</u>, <u>Amount Owing</u> / L. Hamamoto, 32 Fanshawe Court, $500.25 / D. Legault, 1062 Kingsway Cres., $227.73 / D. St. Martin, 632 Spruce Rd., $206.55 / T. Bernhardt, 6 Bellsize Rd., $195.45 / J. Sahota, 491 Highridge Sq., $1100.00 / L. Kavanaugh, 4519 Delray Blvd., $75.29 / J. Dhaliwal, 9 Old Quarry Rd., $52.96 / L. Olijnyk, 329 Glengarry Ave. $49.52

ASSIGNMENT

7:42

Format this material attractively.

NOTE

If a word cannot be divided, key it in full in the second column.

WORD DIVISION / Word, <u>Best Division</u> / neither / nineteen / oblige / occurred / opportunity / parallel / perhaps / perseverance / pleasant / privilege / questionnaire / realize / recognize / rhyme / safety / shining / similar / strength / tragedy / triumphant

TABLES WITH SHORT COLUMN HEADINGS

In some tables, column headings may be shorter than any of the material in the column. These headings are centered over the longest entry in the column.

1. Clear all previously set tabs and margins.

2. Determine the vertical placement of the table.

3. Insert the paper into the machine.

4. Centre and key the main heading or title in all capital letters. Triple space after it.

5. Find the longest item in each column.

6. Determine how many spaces will be left between columns.

7. Position the paper so that its centre point aligns with the print point indicator.

8. Backspace *once* for every *two* characters in the longest entry in each column, and *once* for every *two* spaces between the columns.

9. Set the left margin at this point.

10. Strike the space bar *once* for *each* character in the longest item in the first column, and *once* for *each* of the spaces that follow it.

11. Set a tab stop at this point.

12. Set the remaining tab stops using this method.

13. To centre the first column heading, start at the left margin, and strike the space bar *once* for every *two* characters in the longest entry in the column. Do *not* space for odd characters at the end.

14. Now backspace *once* for every *two* characters in the column heading.

15. Key the heading. (It will be centered over the longest entry in the column.)

16. To centre the second column heading, follow steps 13 to 15, starting at the second tab stop instead of the left margin.

ASSIGNMENT	UNARRANGED MATERIAL
7:37	Format this material attractively.

ABBREVIATIONS FOR THE PROVINCES AND TERRITORIES/ Province, Abbreviation /British Columbia, BC / Alberta, AB/ Saskatchewan, SK/ Manitoba, MB/ Ontario, ON/ Quebec, PQ/ New Brunswick, NB/ Nova Scotia, NS/ Prince Edward Island, PE/ Newfoundland, NF/ Labrador, LB/ Yukon Territory, YT / Northwest Territories, NT

ASSIGNMENT	Format this material attractively.
7:38	EXECUTIVE FLIGHTS/From Toronto to Halifax/Depart, Arrive, Routing, Frequency, Aircraft/8:10, 11:05, NONSTOP, Daily, B-727/ 12:00, 14:55, NONSTOP, Daily, B-727/14:05, 17:00, NONSTOP, Daily, DC-9/17:25, 20:20, NONSTOP, Daily, B-727/20:05, 23:00, NONSTOP, Daily, DC-9

ASSIGNMENT	Format this material attractively.
7:39	Armand Holdings Ltd./Employee Evaluation Chart/for the period of/ July 1 - October 1/Employee, Attitude, Productivity, Appearance/ D. Masalis, good, average, poor/J. Ling, excellent, good, excellent/ Y. Ritz, poor, poor, poor/H. Hehner, excellent, good, good/L. Gingras, excellent, excellent, excellent/L. Bouma, good, excellent, good

SHORT COLUMN HEADINGS ASSIGNMENTS

ASSIGNMENT

7:22

ARRANGED MATERIAL

Format this table on a half-sheet of paper.
Use the spacing indicated.
Single space the body.

NOTE

Triple space before a column heading and double space after.

BIRTHSTONES

↓ 3

Months	Stones
↓ 2	
January	Garnet
February	Amethyst
March	Bloodstone ← longest
April	Diamond item
May	Emerald
June 8	Pearl
July	Ruby
August	Onyx
longest → September	Sapphire
item October	Opal
November	Topaz
December	Turquoise

ASSIGNMENT

7:23

Centre vertically on a half-sheet of paper.
Single space the body.
Leave six spaces between columns.

STAFF DIRECTORY

↓ 3

Name	Address	Phone
	↓ 2	
Browne, Chella	351 Orange Cres.	358-5142
Burgess, Janis	1462 Listowell Cres.	649-3315
Cemi, Amalia	43 Leuty Ave.	237-1082
Costescu, Marg	4 Chine Dr.	359-4221
Foulkes, Helena	46 Thornbeck Dr.	642-0055
Milovanovic, Pavel	33 Emmeline Cres.	239-5516
Neissen, Frank	4612 Tuscarora Dr.	350-1524
Nighswander, Reg	1 Massey Square	649-1629
Smolska, Eva	505 Newgate St.	640-1455

Centre vertically on a half-sheet of paper.
Single space the body.
Leave eight spaces between columns.

HOTEL DIEU HOSPITAL
↓ 2
ANNUAL
↓ 2
Lucky Jackpot Draw
↓ 3

Prize Value	Winner
↓ 2	
$100 000	Ms Ethel Rosenthal
10 000	Mr. Robert Theroux
5 000	Ms Jill Mo
1 000	Dr. Hilary Stubich

Centre vertically on a half-sheet of paper.
Triple space after the main heading.
Double space after the column headings.
Double space the body.
Under the "Mark" column, insert the proofreader's marks in pen.
Leave six spaces between columns.

SOME PROOFREADER'S MARKS

Mark	Meaning	Sample
∧	insert a word	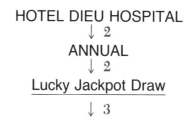 the ∧(red) pen
#	insert a space	the jaggededge #
⊙	insert a period	I stayed ⊙
⋏	insert a comma	pears⋏ plums, and grapes
≡	capitalize	≡olga
lc	lower case	be Happy (lc)
͜	close up	Feb͡ruary
5	indent 5 spaces to the right	5 Food prices
∿	transpose	the (boy sad)

ASSIGNMENT

7:24

Centre vertically on a half-sheet of paper.
Triple space after the main heading.
Double space after the column heading.
Double space the body.
Leave five spaces between the columns.

CLEAR WRITING TERMS

Vague	Clear
having opted for these rules	having accepted these rules
speak directly to the problem	discuss
this is to say that	this means
a good case can be made that	for instance
does not lend itself well to	is not appropriate
talk in terms of	describe
serve to suggest	suggest
less than sympathetic	unsympathetic

ASSIGNMENT

7:25

Centre vertically on a half-sheet of paper.
Triple space after the main heading.
Double space after the column headings.
Single space the body.
Leave eight spaces between columns.

		PWC
SOME PLURALS OF SINGULAR WORDS		18
↓ 3		
Singular	Plural	39
↓ 2		
memorandum	memoranda or memorandums	48
crisis	crises	51
analysis	analyses	55
formula	formulae or formulas	61
parenthesis	parentheses	66
datum	data	69
appendix	appendixes or appendices	76
criterion	criteria	80

ASSIGNMENT

7:34

Format this table on a half-sheet of paper.
Use the spacing illustrated.

NON-ENGLISH ABBREVIATIONS

↓ 3

Abbreviation		Meaning
↓ 2		
e.g.		for example
et al.		and other people
etc.		and so forth
ibid.		in the same place
ss i.e.	5	that is
N.B.		note well
op. cit.		in the work cited
P.S.		postscript
R.S.V.P.		please reply
re		in the matter of
viz.		namely
vs.		versus

ASSIGNMENT 7:26

Centre vertically on a half-sheet of paper.
Single space the body.
Leave four spaces between columns.

TRAVEL ITINERARY
↓2
for
↓2
W. J. Goldman
^
↓3

Date	Flitght	Departure	Arrival
		↓2	
May 23	AC 2A(2)	9:35 Montreal	10:45 Toronto
May 25	AC 237	8:00 Toronto	9:15 Windsor
May 27	AC 205	10:00 Windsor	12:00 Ottawa
May 29 stet	AC 301	8:30 Ottawa	9:30 Windsor

ASSIGNMENT 7:27

Centre vertically on a half-sheet of paper.
Single space the body.
Leave six spaces between columns.

TYPES OF RETAILING OUTLETS
↓3

Type	Example
	↓2
Convenience Store	Becker's
Department Store	Eaton's
Discount Store	K-Mart
Door-to-Door Sales	Fuller Brush
General Store	Tom's General Store (independent)
Mail-Order House	Sears
Selling Services	H. & R. Block Tax Services
Single-Line Outlets	Midas Muffler
Single-Line Products	Classics Bookstores
Supermarket	Safeway
Vending Machines	Canteen of Canada

9. Set the left margin at this point.

10. Strike the space bar *once* for each character in the longest entry in the first column, and *once* for *each* space following it. The longest entry may be either a column heading or an entry in the column.

11. Set a tab stop at this point.

12. Follow this procedure for all other columns in the table.

13. Where column headings are the longest item, re-set the margin or tab stop so that the column is centered under it.

MIXED COLUMN HEADINGS ASSIGNMENTS

ASSIGNMENT
7:33

ARRANGED MATERIAL

Centre vertically on a half-sheet of paper.
Use extended centering for the main heading.
Double space the body.
Leave six spaces between columns.

S Y M B O L S

↓ 3

Symbol		Meaning		Sample
		↓ 2		
&		ampersand		Salmon & White
*		asterisk		Cooking*
°		degree		15°C
/	6	diagonal	6	their/there
%		per cent		100%
:		ratio		5 : 9
#		number		#899
( )		parentheses		(Look at it.)
@		at		5 @ 15¢ each

ASSIGNMENT

7:28

PARTLY ARRANGED MATERIAL

Format attractively on a half-sheet of paper.

METHODS OF ENUMERATION

Method	Sample
Arabic Numbers	1, 2, 3, 4, 5
Capital Letters	A, B, C, D, E
Small Letters	(a) (b) (c) (d) (e)
Capital Roman Numerals	I, II, III, IV, V
Small Roman Numerals	(i) (ii) (iii) (iv) (v)

ASSIGNMENT

7:29

Format attractively on a half-sheet of paper.

LONG DISTANCE CALLS/COMMUNICATIONS INTERUR-BAINES/English, French/Collect, Frais virés/Bill to third number, Troisième numéro/Credit card, carte de crédit/Person-to-person, De personne à personne/Overseas, Service outre-mer

ASSIGNMENT

7:30

Format attractively on a half-sheet of paper.

PIERRES ET FLEURS DU MOIS/Mois, Pierres, Fleurs/janvier, grenat, oeillet/février, améthyste, violette/mars, sanguine, jonquille/ avril, diamant, pois de senteur/mai, emeraude, mugnet/juin, perle, rose/juillet, rubis, pied-d'alouette/août, sardoine, glaïeul/sep-tembre, saphir, aster/octobre, opale, calendule/novembre, topaze, chrysanthème/décembre, turquoise, narcisse

ASSIGNMENT

7:31

Format attractively on a half-sheet of paper.

SNAIDERO & ASSOCIATES/list of office responsibilities/Secretary, Duty/M. Brouillard, mail handling, incoming calls, outgoing calls, making appointments, purchasing supplies/K. Zendal, transcribing, reproducing material, general organization and planning/filing, taking minutes/R. McCowan, greeting visitors, special projects, making travel arrangements, miscellaneous, word processing

ASSIGNMENT

7:32

Format attractively on a half-sheet of paper.

INGLEWOOD BUSINESS ASSOCIATION/A N N U A L/Activity Day/January 30/Organizers, Activity, Cost/Preston & Korinke, Downhill Skiing, $20.00/Fleming & Saunders, Cross-Country Skiing, $16.00/Neissen & Cameron, Ice Skating, $6.00/Le Riche & Sharples, Roller Skating, $5.50/Bradley & Shenory, Snowshoeing, $7.50/Thomaidis & Phair, Horseback Riding, $10.50

TABLES WITH MIXED COLUMN HEADINGS

Sometimes a table will contain both short and long column headings. If the column heading is *long*, centre the *column* under it. If the column heading is *short*, centre the *heading* over the *column*.

1. Clear all previously set tabs and margins.
2. Determine the vertical placement of the table.
3. Insert the paper into the machine.
4. Centre and key the main heading in all capital letters. Triple space after it.
5. Find the longest item in each column.
6. Determine how many spaces will be left between columns.
7. Position the paper so that its centre point aligns with the print point indicator.
8. Backspace *once* for every *two* characters in the longest item in each column, and *once* for every *two* spaces between columns. The longest entry may be either a column heading or an entry in the column.

APPLYING YOUR SKILLS—ITINERARIES

ASSIGNMENT

10:38

Format this itinerary using the spacing indicated.

↓ 7
ITINERARY
↓ 2
Ginette Whiteside's Western Trip
↓ 2
Monday, July 2, 19-- to Wednesday, July 4, 19--

↓ 3

Monday, July 2, 19--
↓ 2

NOTE

There are several ways to set up an itinerary; select one that suits your needs.

16:00 (EST)	Depart Toronto, via Air Canada Flight 161 One stopover Dinner served

↓ 2

21:15 (MST)	Arrive Calgary Reservations confirmed at Palliser Hotel (receipt attached)

↓ 3

Tuesday, July 3, 19--
↓ 2

09:00 (MST)	Appointment with Samantha Logan, President of Anderson and Logan Electric, 138 Second Street.

↓ 2

12:00 (MST)	Luncheon meeting with Bill Mundale, Canadian Manufacturers' Association, at Calgary Inn.

↓ 2

15:00 (MST)	Meet Mr. Eric Princeton for a tour of the Princeton Manufacturing plant, 487 Queen Street.

↓ 3

Wednesday, July 4, 19--
↓ 2

08:00 (MST)	Depart Calgary, via Air Canada 747, Flight No. 233, No stopovers, breakfast.

↓ 2

09:20 (PST)	Arrive Vancouver, meeting room confirmed at Hotel Vancouver.

↓ 2

11:00 (PST)	Meeting with Mr. John Difebo, Manager of R.T.K. Manufacturing at Hotel Vancouver.

↓ 2

14:00 (PST)	Depart Vancouver via Air Canada Flight 277, one stopover, lunch served.

↓ 2

20:30 (EST)	Arrive Toronto.

THE NUMBER KEYPAD

If your keyboard has a number keypad, learn how to use it so that you may key numbers more efficiently. Accurate and speedy keying of numbers is an important part of keyboarding skill development.

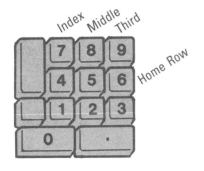

USING THE KEYPAD

1. Put the middle finger of your right hand over the 5 key of the number keypad.

2. Put your index finger over the 4 key, and your third finger over the 6 key.

3. Use your fourth finger to tap the "enter" or ± key.

4. Drop your middle finger down to strike the 2 key.

5. Drop your index finger down to strike the 1 key.

6. Drop your third finger down to strike the 3 key.

7. Move your middle finger up to strike the 8 key.

8. Move your index finger up to strike the 7 key.

9. Move your third finger up to strike the 9 key.

10. Use your thumb to strike 0.

11. Space after each group of three digits, using your right thumb to tap the space bar.

12. Say the numbers as you strike the keys, that is, *555 enter, 656 enter*, etc.

ASSIGNMENT	Plan the itinerary of a trip you would like to take.
10:39	

COMPOSING OUTLINES, NOTES, AND REPORTS

Compose and key a rough draft of each of the following assignments. Proofread your rough draft, using the appropriate proofreader's marks, and then key the report again, making all the corrections and changes you have indicated.

ASSIGNMENT	Prepare an outline of good work habits required in a business environment.
10:40	

ASSIGNMENT	Prepare an outline of the interpersonal skills required to get along with co-workers.
10:41	

ASSIGNMENT	Prepare an outline and a description of the Business Studies courses offered at your school.
10:42	

ASSIGNMENT	Bring a set of notes from another subject to class and format them attractively.
10:43	

ASSIGNMENT

2:28

Set a 60-character line.
Double space.
Key each paragraph once.

5 → How much money do you have to work with? Look at your past earnings and spending patterns. List as well as you can an outline showing where the money went. If you do not know where your money goes, then you have very little chance of getting it to go where you want it to. It may be hard for you to remember what you spent, since you probably did not keep a record of your cash flow. Once you keep a list, you may find that a lot of cash, no doubt, just slips through your fingers. You can't do anything about the past, but you can change what you will do in the future.

ASSIGNMENT

2:29

Key according to the instructions for Assignment 2:28.

5 → The first point in managing your money is to decide what you want and need. You know there is not enough money for everything, because your money supply is limited. You know that when you use money for one item, you lose the chance of using it for another item you might want. You know yourself, and you know what you want, and what is of value to you. This means planning your choices.

The second point is acting on your decisions. Once you have decided how you will use your money, you want to be sure you use it in the best way. An informed buyer gets better value for her money. There are a number of ways to increase the value you buy with every purchase.

ASSIGNMENT
10:44

Prepare reports on the following topics:

Applying For a Job

Stress in the Workplace

Getting Ahead in Your Job

The Computerized Office

Time Management Skills

The Successful Image

The Importance of Communication

Ergonomics

Business Careers

ASSIGNMENT
10:45

Prepare an article reviewing a book or a movie for your school newspaper.

ASSIGNMENT
10:46

Prepare the minutes of a club's or organization's meeting.

ASSIGNMENT
10:47

Have your teacher arrange a field trip to a modern office or make an appointment to tour one on your own. Based on the information you gather on your field trip, prepare a report that includes the following:

    a) changing trends in office procedures;

    b) employer expectations;

    c) the expanding role of office workers, including administrative skills;

    d) opportunities for advancement;

    e) salary ranges;

    f) automation in the office;

    g) unusual career choices.

10. The students of the school were leaving.

11. The delivery truck dropped off the book.

12. He chose a great birthday gift for them.

ASSIGNMENT 2:27

MORE PARAGRAPH DRILLS

Set a 50-character line.
Double space.
Key each paragraph once.
Indent 5 spaces for the first line.

1. 5 → Choosing the location of a house wisely may mean a saving of thousands of dollars. Shopping around for a name-brand product may save a worthwhile amount. Buying summer clothes after July 1, when the summer sales begin, may mean getting large discounts. How are you going to manage your money so that you match it with your needs and wants? How are you going to get started with a money management plan that allows you to reach your goals?

2. 5 → After our needs have been satisfied, we all have many things we would like to have. These wants vary from person to person. Ryan wants a bike and Emily would like a stereo. Mira would like to go to the baseball game, but Dave wants to see a new movie. Our wants are endless. Even if you could make a list of all the things you would like to have and were able to get everything on the list, you would soon find many other wants to take their place.

3. 5 → We all share the need for food, shelter, and clothing. These are called basic needs. We need them to survive. Some families call a car or a television set a basic need, because they cannot imagine life without them. The average Canadian household has two radios and one television set. Most have telephone and electrical services. These things are not necessary for our survival, but we have come to take them for granted.

MODULE
11

CAREER
SEARCH

Courtesy of Biltrite Nightingale Inc.

Pages 432–434 in Module 11 have been adapted from *The World of Business*, Second Edition, by Terry G. Murphy et al., © 1987 by John Wiley & Sons Canada Limited. Adapted by permission of the publisher.

15. Oscar and Olivia ordered the oranges on October 1.

16. Patricia and Percival plucked the perfect peaches.

17. Quinta and Quincy are quite quiet when they quilt.

18. Ralph and Rosalyn reacted strongly to the reports.

19. Stephanie and Stanford skied the slippery slopes.

20. Thomasina and Timothy were terrific touch typists.

21. Uriah and Ursula were urged to undo the umbrellas.

22. Val and Vaughen vaulted over the vase with vigour.

23. Warren and Walt washed the white woolens in water.

24. Xenos and Xavier were excited by the oxen exhibit.

25. Yoland and Yves yanked the young yak from the bay.

26. Zachary and Zelda were dazzled by the zany zebras.

ASSIGNMENT
2:26

Set a 50-character line.
Double space.
Key each line once.

1. The baseball team won three games today.

2. One hot day we all went for a long walk.

3. A little child fell off her orange bike.

4. Four cows quickly jumped over the fence.

5. They ran into a sidewalk with the bikes.

6. She found keyboarding an interesting subject.

7. We all went shopping to buy green shoes.

8. After one day of work he was very tired.

9. Fire destroyed your brand new buildings.

INTRODUCTION

Statistics show that the "average" Canadian holds four or more jobs throughout adulthood. Your first job will reveal whether your interests and aptitudes are compatible with your career choice, and it will give you a chance to prove your abilities. Work that suits your interests and talents and allows you to exercise some initiative is most likely to lead to job satisfaction and success.

A determined, confident, and well-trained individual can always find employment. Finding a good job requires planning, preparation, and persistence. Your objective should be to match your capabilities with the requirements of a specific job—a job that you will be pleased to accept, one that will give you a sense of being needed, an opportunity for growth, and reasonable financial rewards.

OBJECTIVES

1. To consider your interests, aptitudes, and goals when choosing a career.

2. To learn the main sources of information about jobs.

3. To prepare a letter of application.

4. To prepare a resumé.

5. To complete a job application form.

6. To prepare for a job interview.

7. To undergo a successful job interview.

8. To appropriately follow up a job interview.

11. rocks throw prowl gowns whale usual world

12. their vogue digit signs rigid robot corps

13. forms shame civic aught amble focus widow

14. flake chair blame bland audit amend fight

15. *proxy bugle malts snake camel widow paint*

ASSIGNMENT 2:25

MORE SENTENCE DRILLS

Set a 50-character line.
Double space.
Key each line once.

1. *Annabel and Allan attended the audition in August.*

2. *Barbara and Brian bought the bananas in Brantford.*

3. *Carley and Clwis caught the catfish in California.*

4. *Donald and Dawn donated a dozen dishes to Delores.*

5. *Eve and Ed ate ten eggs in the egg-eating contest.*

6. Fran and Fred fought off a frantic fox with force.

7. Grant and Gina gave great green grapes to the gnu.

8. Henry and Hanna helped the hunter with his hammer.

9. Irene and Irvin ate ice cream until they were ill.

10. Jan and Jay were judged the winners of the jingle.

11. *Kenneth and Katherine bought the kite in Kamloops.*

12. *Lorne and Lou-Anne liked the look of the lanterns.*

13. *Mindy and Marvin were mezmerized by the magicians.*

14. *Neil and Nan knew not to gnaw on nuts before noon.*

CONTENTS

Assessing Yourself: The Personal Inventory 432

Job Information Resources 433

Applying For a Job 435

The Covering Letter 436

The Resumé 438

Formatting a Resumé 438

The Job Application Form 441

Preparing For Job Interviews 444

The Successful Interview 444

Following Up an Interview 446

Career Search Assignment 448

Career Report Assignment 449

Formatting Your Career Report 450

ASSIGNMENT 2:23

Set a 60-character line.
Double space.
Key each line once.

1. ex express explain exclude extra expand

2. im impossible immediate improve imposed

3. in intent include increase insight into

4. out outcome outlawed outlooks outlining

5. pro provide proceed protein progressive

6. re retain remit review regards receipts

7. un uncertain undo unwise uncover unload

8. fore foresee forefront forearm forebode

ASSIGNMENT 2:24

Set a 60-character line.
Double space.
Key each line once.

1. do so is an am he of or us by if ox me to do so

2. sow pen cod oak for man may nap dug bug tie nap

3. ham sit pan lap bus rod toe fix dog six hay rug

4. dig rye tub pan map six and the fir eye did die

5. Six men own pay she sir cut box bit rob sob wow

6. fuel melt wish kept soap worm fowl bowl sigh

7. roam turn held half they coal sock goal tidy

8. then hair girl them fork disk rush pale such

9. down city busy body than sick work make both

10. duty with land also busy city from half held

ASSESSING YOURSELF: THE PERSONAL INVENTORY

What special skills and qualities do you have that would be of value to an employer? Completing a personal inventory is one way of answering this question. This is not for your employer, but for you. It will help you to assess what your capabilities are, and will assist you in the preparation of your resumé.

ASSIGNMENT 11:1

1. Answer the following questions to complete a personal inventory. Be honest in answering the questions and take the time to respond carefully. Format your answers attractively and place them in a binder.

   a) What things have I done successfully?

   b) What things have I done for which people have congratulated me?

   c) What things do I really like to do?

   d) What things do I dislike doing?

   e) What school subjects do I like best? Why?

   f) What subjects do I dislike? Why?

   g) What extra-curricular activities have I participated in at school? Have I enjoyed them? Why? Why not?

   h) What are my hobbies and recreational activities? Why do I like or dislike them? [If you don't have any specific hobbies, list some that you would like to do and give reasons why these activities appeal to you.]

   i) What paid work experience have I had? What did I like or dislike about each job? What volunteer jobs have I done? What did I like or dislike about each one?

   j) What skills do I have—keyboarding, shorthand (number of words per minute), machine transcription ability, filing, word processing, etc.?

   k) What specialized knowledge do I have—bookkeeping, law, data processing, etc.?

   l) In which three fields could I make a career? What would I like/dislike about working in each of these fields?

   m) What are my personal ambitions? Why do I want to attain these goals?

12. robot corps forms shame civic aught amble focus

13. blame bland audit amend fight proxy bugle banks

14. cares types dance sixty brats penny funny money

15. dress guess messy cause right wrong clown frown

ASSIGNMENT 2:22

Set a 60-character line.
Double space.
Key each line once.

PHRASES

1. if they, by us, it is, if it, of me, to do, to go

2. to the, of the, do the, she did, he did, he may

3. by me, by him, by them, by us, by her, she can

4. did she, can he, may the, with the, if they, go by

5. they got, they make, they show, they did, sign for

6. if it does, to do that, to do so, if it is

7. it is work, for the man, she did the, if they do

8. and they did, to do the, to do this, if they come

9. he shall be, to do so, if it is, can we go

10. will you arrive, come in please, thank you for

n) What are my abilities, talents, and strong points?

o) What are my weak points? What am I doing to improve them?

2. Review your inventory. Look through the classified section of the newspaper to see if you can find a job for which you are qualified.

3. Flip through magazines and cut out pictures that answer the question "Who am I?" Prepare a collage with the same title.

JOB INFORMATION RESOURCES

Many job information resources can help you in your job search. These include:

STUDENT SERVICES/ STUDENT PLACEMENT OFFICE

Your counsellors and teachers can help you identify your interests and evaluate your special talents and abilities. They also sometimes receive notices of job opportunities from employers, and forward these to graduates or post them on bulletin boards.

NEWSPAPERS

Most classified ads in newspapers contain a Help Wanted section listing a variety of jobs. Most employers ask applicants to respond by letter or to phone for an appointment, although occasionally an ad requests a personal visit.

CANADA EMPLOYMENT CENTRE

The Canada Employment Centre is a federal government agency that files information on individuals available for work, as well as information on job vacancies. CEC branches help match applicants with employers, both locally and across Canada. The agency also has special offices to help students find summer employment. Branches are often set up on college and university campuses.

ASSIGNMENT 2:20

Set a 60-character line.
Double space.
Key once.

5 → Some of you when you enter the working world will be involved in the production of goods and services necessary in a modern business. Examples of jobs in production are machine operators, welders, technicians, farmers, and forestry workers. Many of you will be involved in marketing jobs. All of the activities involved in getting goods and services from the producer to the consumer are part of marketing. These include many jobs in stores, advertising, transportation, and sales. Still others will work in the area of business communications. Modern businesses need many trained office workers—secretaries, stenographers, and clerical workers. In addition, one of the fastest growing job markets is for people trained in computer-related skills.

ASSIGNMENT 2:21

MORE WORDS AND PHRASES DRILLS

Set a 60-character line.
Double space.
Key each line once.

WORDS

1. sow pen cod oak for man may nap dug brg by tie nap

2. cow run go oat bus rod toe fix dog six hay rug dig

3. six and the do so is an aun he of or us by fir eye

4. pay she her sir ait boo bit us by go for rob sob

5. hat cat sat net set at bat ran hay day mod fun fig

6. fuel melt wish kept soap worm fowl bowl sigh roam

7. done come half they coal sock goal tidy then hair

8. dish rush pale such down city busy body than sick

9. duty with land also busy city from half held roam

10. book desk type pain love hate risk flat high down

11. throw prowl gowns whale usual world their vogue

PRIVATE AND TEMPORARY EMPLOYMENT AGENCIES

These agencies offer many services similar to those provided by the Canada Employment Centre. They are usually private businesses that charge a fee for their services, which is usually paid by the employer.

FRIENDS AND RELATIVES

Employed friends and relatives are often a good informal source of job information. They may have the "inside story" concerning job openings, work conditions, and opportunities for advancement at their work sites. Employers often prefer to hire someone recommended by one of their employees, so spread the word that you are looking for work.

PERSONNEL DEPARTMENTS

Finally, you can telephone the personnel departments of selected businesses in a particular area, and complete a job application form at each company. This form asks for details regarding your education, employment, and personal background. If there is no position available immediately, the personnel manager will usually keep your application on file for review when a job vacancy does arise. You may need to repeat this procedure at a later date, if you do not find a job on the first attempt. Although you are searching without leads, this strategy can be effective because the employer might be impressed by your determination.

TRADE JOURNALS

Check your library for specialized magazines that publish information about particular businesses, industries, or professions. These "trade journals" often feature advertisements for job opportunities in specialized fields. Many employers advertise job vacancies in the classified sections of trade journals.

Remember that finding a job often depends on the overall unemployment in an area. If there is high unemployment in your area, it may be difficult to find a job because of competition. Be realistic when looking for a job—you may not find the "perfect" job the first time around. However, any job will help you find out more about yourself and about how to be a good employee. Also, actual work experience will give you credibility, as well as references, as you continue to search for your "ideal" job.

ASSIGNMENT

2:18

Set a 60-character line.
Double space.
Key once.

5 → When destroying paper records, care should be taken with respect to the nature of the record and the information it contains. While material may appear to be useless or of little value, records such as invoices, research reports, and marketing studies are of definite value to competitors or disgruntled employees. Payroll records are also extremely sensitive. Every organization creates information which, in the wrong hands, is a potential threat. Thus, a controlled method of destruction is necessary. Documents can be destroyed by burial, disintegration, incineration, or shredding.

ASSIGNMENT

2:19

Set a 60-character line.
Double space.
Key once.

5 → The business world revolves around information. Information recorded on paper, microfilms and magnetic media. Information in the form of correspondence, contracts, invoices, orders, and reports. Today, the volume of records - a fair share generated by computers, copiers, and other advanced forms of office technology - shows no signs of decreasing. Quite the contrary. The average company usually doubles its entire volume of records every ten years. To keep pace with this "information explosion," it is essential that business records be handled efficiently.

ASSIGNMENT

11:2

1. Format attractively the information in "Job Information Resources" above and place it in your binder under the title "Job Search."

2. Bring some classified sections of newspapers to class. Study the jobs available, and select those for which you feel you are qualified now, and one that you would like to have five years from now. Cut these out and place them in your binder under the title "Job Opportunities."

APPLYING FOR A JOB

When you have learned of an opening for a job that appeals to you, your next step is to apply for that position. This usually involves submitting a covering letter, accompanied by your resumé (and any letters of reference you can supply); filling in an application form; and being interviewed personally for the job.

ASSIGNMENT 2:16

PARAGRAPH DRILLS

Set a 50-character line.
Double space.
Indent five spaces for the first line of a paragraph.
Key once.

5→ Regardless of their type, retained records, once created, pass through three stages. Understanding this "life process" is important. The Active Use and Storage Stage is the "birth" stage whereby records are referenced frequently. Because immediate access is important, records remain in the office or close to the users. The Semi-active Use and Storage Stage is the period when a record is retained for occasional reference and/or legal reasons. It includes those records that are scheduled for permanent retention. Except for certain vital records which require permanent retention, all others can be assigned a pre-determined period of retention, after which they may be destroyed. This is the Destruction Stage and it completes the life cycle of all records. Whether a company is big or small, its records will pass through this cycle.

ASSIGNMENT 2:17

Set a 60-character line.
Double space.
Key once.

5→ An old saying goes: "Build a better mousetrap and the world will beat a path to your door." Businesses are always looking for new and better products to sell to consumers. Successful businesses change as the wants and needs of consumers change. Many products that are available today were not even invented thirty-five years ago. Colour televisions, electronic calculators, and touch-tone telephones are examples.

THE COVERING LETTER

The covering letter you submit gives a prospective employer a first impression of you and your capabilities. Make your letter interesting but to the point. Prepare it carefully. Errors in keyboarding, composition, or grammar can cause an employer to reject your application. Always submit an original letter, and file a copy for your records. Never submit a form letter.

FIRST PARAGRAPH

Introduce yourself and state the reason for your letter. If you are replying to an advertisement, refer to it explicitly.

SECOND AND THIRD PARAGRAPHS

Outline your qualifications—education, academic achievements, and most importantly, related work experience. Mention that a resumé is enclosed. Highlight your most important qualifications and describe these in detail.

FOURTH PARAGRAPH

Ask for a personal interview. Make it convenient for the prospective employer to get in touch with you by providing your telephone number, and, if you like, indicate when you can most easily be reached. Thank the employer for taking the time to consider your application.

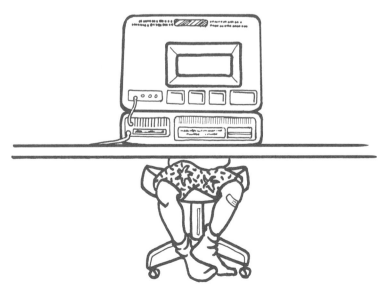

10. resistible responsible reversible sensible susceptible

11. acceptable adjustable repairable capable payable movable

12. fashionable employable debatable charitable accountable

13. inevitable incapable imaginable excusable durable available

14. conceivable disable enforceable exchangeable improbable

15. deliverable detachable endurable inexcusable memorable

ASSIGNMENT 2:15

Set a 50-character line.
Double space.
Key each line once.

1. Je veux manger un sandwich.

2. Je ne veux pas manger de sandwich.

3. Vous allez chercher des fraises?

4. Vous allez faire des exercises?

5. Vous n'allez pas fermer la porte?

6. Quand est-ce que vous commencerez?

7. Il veut toujours demander de l'argent.

8. Qu'est-ce que tu fais le samedi en hiver?

9. Qui est-ce qu'elle veut voir?

10. Nous n'avons pas de devoirs.

Key this sample letter of application using the spacing indicated, then prepare your own.

↓ 12

83 Peppertree Drive
West Hill, Ontario
M3B 2C6
June 30, 19--

↓ 5

Ms Michelle Wagner
Personnel Manager
New Era Office Systems Ltd.
555 Yonge Street
Toronto, Ontario
M4Y 1Y7
↓ 2
Dear Ms Wagner:
↓ 2
I wish to apply for the secretarial position advertised by your company in the June 29, 19— edition of The Toronto Star.
↓ 2
I recently graduated from Sir Oliver Mowat Collegiate Institute with a major in Business Studies. My keyboarding speed is 60–65 words per minute, and I also have excellent word processing and accounting skills. A copy of my resumé is enclosed.
↓ 2
Through the school's co-op program I have been employed by S & S Data Systems this past year. My duties as a secretary included transcription, word processing, and records management. I enjoyed this work and found it very challenging.
↓ 2
I would appreciate an opportunity to discuss the advertised position with you. I am available for an interview at your convenience. My telephone number is 284-0285.

↓ 2
Sincerely yours,

↓ 5 *Nadia Odynsky*

Nadia Odynsky

Encl.

9. community mommy immaterial dummy jimmy rummy mummy

10. winner funnier funny sunny annum inner penny running runner

11. book took look rooster school zoom wood too broom blood

12. poppy sloppy shopping snappy happy apple upper shopper

13. erroneous arrange burrs hurry worry furry borrow sorrow

14. stress recess compressing aggressive essential assured

15. hitting putty quitting cutting bottles bottom matter

16. The cabby was robbed on the street.

17. Bill dropped his book on the floor at school.

18. Sally was happy to go shopping for books.

19. Tell Betty to sell her deed to meet all bills.

20. Jimmy struggled to pull Buddy off the muddy street.

ASSIGNMENT 2:14

Set a 60-character line.
Double space.
Key each line once.

1. abundance acceptance accordance acquaintance admittance

2. allowance ambulance annoyance arrogance clearance

3. countenance distance disturbance endurance enhance entrance

4. grievance guidance ignorance importance instance insurance

5. performance reliance reluctance remembrance romance

6. accessible admissible collapsible collectible convertible

7. digestible divisible eligible feasible flexible gullible

8. incredible intangible intelligible invincible invisible

9. irrepressible negligible permissible plausible possible

THE RESUME

Your resumé is a means of selling yourself to an employer. Employers use resumés as a screening device for selecting prospective employees for interviews, so it is important that your resumé is clear and concise, both in format and content.

A resumé should include information of interest to the potential employer. Obviously, it should list your name, address, and telephone number. When you apply for your first permanent job, your potential employer will be most curious about your educational achievements. Details regarding your education should include grades, special awards, skill levels (such as keyboarding speed), and specific courses that would be useful in the job you're applying for.

You should list your participation in any extra-curricular activities, such as sports, clubs, Student Council, etc. Your potential employer also needs to know what work experience you have had, whether full-time or part-time, as well as volunteer work (if it involved business skills).

Your resumé may also list the names, addresses, and telephone numbers of three references who are prepared to recommend you to your potential employer. Be sure to ask the people you cite for permission to use them as references. Another common option is to state, "References available upon request."

LETTERS OF REFERENCE

Letters of reference benefit any job applicant, and should contain information about you that is relevant to the job for which you are applying. For example, if you are applying for a secretarial job, a letter from your keyboarding or data processing teacher would be appropriate. It is also useful to have a letter from someone respected in the community who can testify to your good character.

FORMATTING A RESUME

There are several ways to format a resumé. Here are some general guidelines:

1. Be conservative in your choice of paper; white or off-white is advised.

2. Use a 60-character pica, or a 70-character elite line. Begin on line 7. Single space, but triple space between sections.

$\dfrac{1}{2}$

46. ;.$\frac{1}{2}$; ;.$\frac{1}{2}$; ;.$\frac{1}{2}$; ;.$\frac{1}{2}$; $\frac{1}{2}\frac{1}{2}\frac{1}{2}$ $\frac{1}{2}\frac{1}{2}\frac{1}{2}$ $\frac{1}{2}\frac{1}{2}\frac{1}{2}$;.$\frac{1}{2}$; ;.$\frac{1}{2}$;

47. $45\frac{1}{2}$ $67\frac{1}{2}$ $35\frac{1}{2}$ $11\frac{1}{2}$ $80\frac{1}{2}$ $90\frac{1}{2}$ $76\frac{1}{2}$ $42\frac{1}{2}$ $14\frac{1}{2}$

48. *when I was 23½ I saw the job I liked.*

$\dfrac{1}{4}$

49. ;.$\frac{1}{4}$; ;.$\frac{1}{4}$; ;.$\frac{1}{4}$; ;.$\frac{1}{4}$; $\frac{1}{4}\frac{1}{4}\frac{1}{4}$ $\frac{1}{4}\frac{1}{4}\frac{1}{4}$ $\frac{1}{4}\frac{1}{4}\frac{1}{4}$;.$\frac{1}{4}$; ;.$\frac{1}{4}$;

50. $67\frac{1}{4}$ $90\frac{1}{4}$ $76\frac{1}{4}$ $32\frac{1}{4}$ $17\frac{1}{4}$ $89\frac{1}{4}$ $50\frac{1}{4}$ $44\frac{1}{4}$ $99\frac{1}{4}$

51. *He had 24¼ laps to go in the event.*

52. ;.$\frac{1}{2}$=; ;.$\frac{1}{2}$=; ;.$\frac{1}{2}$=; ;=; ;=; ;=; = = = = = =

$=$

53. 2 - 1 = 1 4 - 2 = 2 7 - 4 = 3 7 - 6 = 1

54. *He found that the numbers 5 − 3 = 2.*

55. ;.$\frac{1}{2}$+; ;.$\frac{1}{2}$+; ;.$\frac{1}{2}$+; ;+; ;+; ;+; + + + + + +

$+$

56. 3 + 5 = 8 4 + 7 = 11 2 + 1 = 3 4 + 5 = 9

57. *I added 23 + 67, 56 + 78, and 61 + 7*

ASSIGNMENT 2:13

WORDS AND SENTENCES DRILLS

Set a 60-character line.
Double space.
Key each line once.

What is your goal: speed or accuracy?

1. bobbin stabbed cabby robbed babble hobby bubble cabbage

2. succeed success accord accordingly accordance accessible

3. daddy huddle buddy middle cuddle riddle addition adding

4. meet been feed street freezer deer seen keeping deed succeed

5. fluffy stuff sniffing daffy ruffle coffee fluff muffle off

6. giggle doggie wiggle struggle smuggle digging bigger biggest

7. withheld withholding withhold withheld witholding withheld

8. sell fall hall well pull wall bill kill holly gull tell fill

3. Use a high-quality copying process; the appearance of your resumé is vital.

4. There is no need to include personal data such as height, weight, marital status, etc.

5. *Proofread* your resumé *several times* and then have someone else proofread it.

22. ;'; ;'; ;'; '''' '''' '''' ;'; ;'; ;';

Do not leave a space after an apostrophe (').

' 23. Jill's book, Sue's purse, Bill's comb

24. *Nancy's uncle visited from Calgary.*

25. ;"; ;"; ;"; """" """" """" ;"; ;"; ;";

" 26. "The Tomorrow-Tamer" "Ballad of Me"

27. *Tommy said, "Of course I can't go."*

28. ;/; ;/; ;/; /// /// /// ;/; ;/; ;/;

/ 29. 3/5 7/8 5/6 2/3 7/0 8/0 2/4 3/6 4/8

30. *Edward had eaten 5 5/8 chocolates.*

31. ;?; ;?; ;?; ??? ??? ??? ;?; ;?;

Leave two spaces after a question mark (?).

? 32. Yes? No? Maybe? Perhaps? No?

33. *Can you come? Yes, I can come.*

34. lo(l lo(l lo(l ;p); ;p); ;p); ( ) ( )

( ) 35. (Jim) (Sandy) (Kevin) (Dave) (Ryan)

36. *Marshall's story (see page 49) won.*

37. aq!a aq!a aq!a a!a a!a a!a !!! !!!

Leave two spaces after an exclamation mark (!).

! 38. Look out! Watch Out! Don't Race!

39. *The sign at the top read "Look Out!"*

40. ;p-; ;p-; ;p-; ;-; ;-; ;-; --- ---

— 41. self-control, vice-presidents, co-op

42. *Rhoda was vice-president of Jim's.*

— 43. ;p_; ;p_; ;p_; ;_; ;_; ;_; __ __

44. Jane Mary Tom Edna Kelly Cam David

45. *Leona will have to come at once!*

ASSIGNMENT
11:4   Key this sample resumé using the spacing indicated, then prepare your own.

RESUME
↓ 3

NADIA S. ODYNSKY
↓ 2
83 Peppertree Drive
West Hill, Ontario
M3B 2C6
↓ 2
(416) 284-0285
↓ 3

EDUCATION
 ↓ 2
<u>19-- to 19--: Sir Oliver Mowat Collegiate Institute</u>. Graduated in June with
the majority of my options in Business Studies (Information Processing,
Marketing, Law, Keyboarding, Introduction to Business, and Shorthand)
 ↓ 2
<u>19-- to 19--: Emily Stowe Public School</u>.

 ↓ 3

WORK EXPERIENCE
 ↓ 2
September 15, 19-- to June 15, 19-- participated in Sir Oliver Mowat C.I.'s
Co-op Program; worked for S & S Data Systems as a secretary. Duties
included transcription, word processing, and records management.
 ↓ 2
June 30, 19-- to August 30, 19--: Receptionist for Foxbar Real Estate.
Duties included keyboarding, telephone answering, assisting clients, and
handling mail.
 ↓ 2
September 19-- to June 19--: Treasurer for Sir Oliver Mowat C.I.'s
Student Council.

 ↓ 3

ASSIGNMENT 2:12

SPECIAL CHARACTER DRILLS

Set a 40-character line.
Double space.
Key each line once.

1. fr$f fr$f fr$f f$f f$f f$f $$$ $$$

$

2. $1.00 $15.00 $64.61 $15.99 $89.76

3. *He paid $62.47 for the 11 baskets.*

4. ju&j ju&j ju&j j&j j&j j&j &&& &&&

&

5. Tye & Hav Pye & Sloane King & Tsai

6. *The firm of Lowe & West was famous.*

7. de#d de#d de#d d#d d#d d#d ### ###

#

8. #59 #93 #153 #8434 #513 #5398 #153

9. *Order #415 was missing from box 5.*

10. ki*k ki*k ki*k k*k k*k k*k *** ***

*

11. Smith* Yellow* Water* Books* Read*

12. *The asterisk * signals a footnote.*

13. fr%f fr%f fr%f f%f f%f f%f %%% %%%

%

14. 55% 69% 10% 67% 23% 75% 66% 78% 20%

15. *Paul got a mark of 75% on the test.*

16. jy¢j jy¢j jy¢j j¢j j¢j j¢j ¢¢¢ ¢¢¢

¢

17. 80¢ 75¢ 33¢ 99¢ 56¢ 72¢ 11¢ 10¢ 45¢

18. *Jocelyn paid 89¢ for the big cakes.*

19. sw@s sw@s sw@s s@s s@s s@s @@@ @@@

@

20. 3 apples @ 20¢ each 18 plums @ 25¢

21. *I saw 3 m of rope @ 9¢ per metre.*

SPECIAL SKILLS AND ABILITIES
  ↓ 2
Keyboarding speed: 60-65 words per minute
Word Processing and computer skills (Wang, IBM, WordPerfect)
  ↓ 3

REFERENCES
  ↓ 2

Mrs. Sheila Culliford, Teacher   Ms Susan MacLennan, President
Business Studies   S & S Data Systems
Sir Oliver Mowat C.I.   1286 Midland Avenue
5400 Lawrence Ave. E.   Scarborough, Ontario
West Hill, Ontario   M1K 4R7
M1C 2C6   ↓ 2
  ↓ 2   (416) 555-9811
(416) 555-9384

THE JOB APPLICATION FORM

You can obtain a job application form from the personnel department of a prospective employer. Fill in the required information neatly and accurately, using the data in your resumé as a guide. Generally, the following information is asked for on a job application form:

- Name, address, telephone number
- Citizenship
- Social Insurance Number
- Position applied for
- Education
- Work experience
- Personal interests
- Business and personal references (names, addresses, and telephone numbers)

Be sure to have all the necessary information on hand as you complete the application form.

ASSIGNMENT 2:10

TABULATION DRILLS

Clear your machine of all tab stops.
Set the left margin 20 spaces in from the edge of the paper.
Set tab stops at 20 space intervals from the left margin.
Single space.
Press the tab bar without looking at it to key the next word on the line.

stop	raid	blue	sore
apple	rattle	desk	type
risk	new	chair	door
handle	care	room	broom
pen	paper	read	mark
cake	green	picture	pencil
cook	bake	hot	cold
feet	hands	eyes	mouth

ASSIGNMENT 2:11

Key according to the instructions for Assignment 2:10.

and	234	the	387
for	387	did	463
who	890	may	376
not	378	got	735
rug	876	top	489
man	365	rat	393
cap	263	yet	376
put	583	hit	860

GUIDELINES FOR KEYING AN APPLICATION FORM

1. Horizontal rules for responses are provided on most application forms. You must align your paper in the machine so that the typescript will be slightly above the rules. If you are using a word processor, you may wish to align your form in the same manner.

2. Leave two spaces to the right of an item before you key your response.

3. Begin responses two spaces to the right of a vertical line.

When you have completed the form, submit it to the personnel manager or to the person cited in the job advertisement. Include your letter of application, a copy of your resumé, and any letters of reference. If the employer is impressed with your application, you will be contacted for a personal interview.

21. page 100 page 214 page 921 page 746 page 890

22. 1389 King St. 482 Bay St. 6 Queen Rd. 5831 Elm Rd.

23. 5839 Nelson St. 81 Norris St. 29 Roy St. 1 Jay Rd.

24. 493 Chaplin Ave. 950 Green Cres. 9213 Indian Blvd.

25. Invoice 852 Invoice 7810 Invoice 9451 Invoice 85133

26. Order 4168 Order 5671 Order 2316 Order 3416 Order 1

27. Account 6833 Account 9341 Account 9008 Account 2655

28. M4R 1R3 P9J 6Y3 K1J 6L6 H2T 5D9 S2M 5W4 V6J P9A

29. M5J 8E2 X6H 6Y5 V5G 9S2 T8M 1R2 S8B 6T9 R9W 5X0

30. H5P 6Y3 B3P 9E9 K3F 5N8 J8M 3E2 G7P 3X2 S5Y 6M2

31. For homework read pages 234-240, 635-715, and 718-732.

32. I worked 42 3/4 weeks one year and then 40 3/4 weeks.

33. There were 1563 Halifax passengers on the 747 planes.

34. Mary bought 3 pencils; 4 pens; 5 books; and 6 binders.

35. Mike called 583-4815 to clear up the $38 on invoice 4.

36. Did Nora and Christian catch 44 or 55 fish on July 15?

37. They will need 14 buses for the 300 students involved.

38. The proposed dates for the trip are May 15, 16 and 17.

39. Correct the invoices 4315, 53164, 8142, 1463 and 1900.

40. In October, mail orders for item 1538 were 2 345 543.

ASSIGNMENT

11:5

Key an application form provided by your teacher.

SAMPLE JOB APPLICATION FORM

> **NOTE**
>
> Read newspaper ads to get an idea of current salary levels.

JOHN WILEY & SONS CANADA LIMITED

APPLICATION FOR EMPLOYMENT
(PLEASE PRINT)

Position being applied for	Date available to begin work	Minimum Salary Required

PERSONAL

Last Name	First Name	Middle Name(s)

Present Address	No. Street	Apt.	City	Province	Postal Code

Telephone Number
Home ( )
Business ( )

Have You Worked For Wiley Previously?
☐ Yes   If Yes Dates
☐ No   Position

Are you legally eligible to work in Canada?
☐ Yes ☐ No

Are you between 18 and 65 years of age?
☐ Yes ☐ No

Are you willing to re-locate?
☐ Yes ☐ No.

Preferred location

Do you have a valid driver's licence?
☐ Yes ☐ No.

EDUCATION

SECONDARY SCHOOL	BUSINESS, TRADE OR TECHNICAL SCHOOL	
Highest grade or level completed	Name of Program	Length of Program
Type of certificate or diploma received	Licence, certificate or diploma awarded? ☐ Yes ☐ No	

COMMUNITY COLLEGE		UNIVERSITY		
Name of Program	Length of Program	Length of Program	Degree awarded ☐ Yes ☐ No	☐ U/Grad. ☐ Grad.
Diploma received? ☐ Yes ☐ No		Major subject(s)		
Other courses, workshops, seminars		Licences, Certificates, Degrees		

"APPROVED BY THE ONTARIO HUMAN RIGHTS COMMISSION"

LETTER-NUMBER COMBINATION DRILLS

Set a 60-character line.
Double space.
Key each line once.

1. we 23 up 70 do 39 or 94 if 84 to 59 me 63 so 29

2. wee 233 you 679 row 492 wet 235 top 590 rot 495

3. rye 463 woe 293 tie 583 owe 923 pie 083 ire 843

4. 10 cats 20 children 30 cows 40 candies 50 cases

5. 5 apples 15 plums 25 peaches 35 pears 45 grapes

6. 11 papers 21 pens 31 pencils 41 rulers 51 clips

7. phone 385-6784 phone 346-6792 phone 593-3477

8. phone 134-7649 phone 260-6745 phone 987-4531

9. phone 349-7695 phone 516-7118 phone 546-7892

10. January 1 February 3 March 7 April 8 May 3 June 9

11. October 31 December 25 February 14 September 30

12. April 25 March 15 February 25 July 5 September 29

13. Apt. 4 Apt. 8 Apt. 1 Apt. 7 Apt. 2 Apt. 9

14. Apt. 19 Apt. 59 Apt. 23 Apt. 60 Apt. 14

15. Apt. 1007 Apt. 1115 Apt. 3409 Apt. 6497

16. Box 83 Box 64 Box 39 Box 99 Box 23 Box 67

17. Box 100 Box 295 Box 948 Box 931 Box 214

18. Box 135 Box 863 Box 909 Box 348 Box 789

19. page 8 page 2 page 1 page 8 page 7 page 4

20. page 39 page 92 page 12 page 62 page 92

PREPARING FOR JOB INTERVIEWS

While searching for a job, it is wise to try to set up several interviews for the sake of experience, even if you are not absolutely certain you would accept a definite job offer in each case. Before undergoing an interview, you should be prepared to complete the following statements:

1. I can best describe myself as . . .
2. I would like to have this job because . . .
3. I was successful in school because . . .
4. I feel I was successful at my last job because . . .
5. I have become familiar with this type of work by . . .
6. My long-term career plans include . . .
7. I left my last job because . . .
8. In my spare time, I . . .

THE SUCCESSFUL INTERVIEW

A personal interview gives you a chance to demonstrate to a prospective employer that you are the right person for the job. To do this effectively, you must know which of your professional and personal attributes are worth mentioning, and you must feel comfortable and confident when presenting yourself in the interview. Here are some guidelines for a successful interview:

1. Prepare for each interview. Find out as much as possible about the company beforehand (its products and services; branch locations; how long it has been in business, etc.).
2. The evening before the interview, organize what you will wear. Select appropriate, "business-like" clothing.
3. Do not stay up late the night before the interview.
4. Write down the exact time and place of the interview and the interviewer's name. Don't rely on your memory.
5. Make sure you have precise directions to the company, and find out how much travel time to allow, so that you won't arrive late for the interview.

8. 3 dogs 33 doors 333 dolls 33 ducks 333

9. Did the 13 logs go 3 ways in 13 boats?

10. fr4f fr4f fr4f f4f f4f f4f 444 444 444

11. 4 furs 44 flies 444 fields 4 fleas 444

12. Fay lost 14 of her 141 pages 4 times.

13. ft5f ft5f ft5f f5f f5f f5f 555 555 555

14. 5 friends 55 flowers 555 fines 5 foxes

15. In 15 weeks 5 fit women flew 5 flags.

16. jy6j jy6j jy6j j6j j6j j6j 666 666 666

17. 6 jobs 66 jams 666 jars 6 jeans 6 jobs

18. John saw 16 pens, 6 pies, and 66 pigs.

19. ju7j ju7j ju7j j7j j7j j7j 777 777 777

20. 7 jogs 77 jigs 777 jets 7 jars 77 jobs

21. Jana had 7 jars, 17 jeeps and 77 jets.

22. ki8k ki8k ki8k k8k k8k k8k 888 888 888

23. 8 kits 88 kilts 888 keys 8 kids 8 kits

24. Katherine left at 18:18 from gate 818.

25. lo9l lo9l lo9l l9l l9l l9l 999 999 999

26. 9 lies 99 lips 999 lids 9 laws 99 legs

27. Lee stayed at chalet 99 with 9 others.

28. ;p0; ;p0; ;p0; ;0; ;0; ;0; 000 000 000

29. 0 pegs 10 pins 30 pies 40 pits 50 pots

30. Paula phoned at 10:00 and 10:30 today.

6. Arrive a few minutes early so that you can relax and prepare yourself mentally.

7. Take a pen and notepad with you in case you want to jot down information or are asked to complete an application form.

8. Shake hands and greet the interviewer, by name, if possible, and introduce yourself.

9. Do not chew gum or smoke, even if you are invited to do so. If you are nervous, handling a cigarette or chewing gum will exaggerate your anxiety.

10. Avoid nervous movements such as playing with a ring on your finger or twisting a lock of hair.

11. Look directly at the person to whom you are speaking. Eye contact is important. Be relaxed, polite, and self-controlled.

12. Do not feel intimidated because you are being "sized up." Remember, you are also sizing up the job and the company.

13. Answer questions in a straightforward manner.

14. Do not exaggerate your skills and abilities. If you accept a job on false pretences, you will be exposed later on.

15. Be co-operative: if you are asked to take a test or provide references, do so.

16. Let the interviewer know your career goals and objectives.

17. Ask relevant questions about the company:

   - Does the interviewer have an annual report or some brochures you could take away with you?

   - How many people does the company employ?

   - What employee benefits are offered?

   - Is there a probationary period?

   - What is the company's vacation policy?

18. When the interview concludes, leave promptly and express your thanks. In parting, reinforce your genuine interest in accepting the job and your willingness to begin work at the employer's convenience.

ASSIGNMENT

11:6

Role play some imaginary interviews. Choose a partner and create a skit highlighting appropriate behaviour during an interview. Then create a skit that portrays inappropriate behaviour. Use video equipment if it is available. Present your skits to the class for discussion.

ASSIGNMENT 2:7

COMMON PHRASES DRILLS

Set a 60-character line.
Double space.
Key each line once.

1. you were, you are, they are, you are only, are you free

2. as we look, looking forward to, in my case, in any way

3. in fact, we were, as you are, as you can see, if it was

4. on my desk, before you start, are you going, when is a

5. in any case, in these cases, in that case, in our case

6. agree with the, agree with you, all manner, all over a

7. almost always, almost over, already been, also stating

8. as a general rule, as a matter of fact, as a possible

9. as early as possible, as far as, as fast as, as before

10. is it so, as far as, any other, all right, can you come

ASSIGNMENT 2:8

NUMBER DRILLS

Set a 40-character line.
Double space.
Key each line once.

1. aq1a aq1a aq1a a1a a1a a1a 111 111 111

2. 1 ant 11 apes 111 actors 1 axe 11 aims

3. *Arty bought 11 pairs of size 11 socks.*

4. sw2s sw2s sw2s s2s s2s s2s 222 222 222

5. 2 suits 22 socks 222 snakes 2 seals 22

6. *Sue saw 22 ships, 12 snails and 2 subs.*

7. de3d de3d de3d d3d d3d d3d 333 333 333

FOLLOWING UP AN INTERVIEW

Following each interview, write down a list of the things you did well and the things you should improve upon in your next interview. Although it is not impossible, few applicants get a job after their first interview. It is important to learn from your interviews, so that you will do better in succeeding ones. Here are some guidelines for following up an interview:

1. After each interview, write a brief letter thanking the interviewer for taking the time to see you. State that you are still interested in the position.

2. Do not use a thank-you letter to convey information you forgot to provide during the interview.

3. Note when the prospective employer said that he or she would contact you. If you were told that you would be notified in two or three days, don't phone the day after the interview to see if a decision has been made! Be patient. If you are not contacted within a week, phone or write a brief letter stating that you are still interested in the job.

4. If a job is offered to you, notify the employer of your acceptance as soon as possible. Say that you will report for work at the time and place designated.

5. After accepting a job, extend your thanks, by phone or in writing, to those who agreed to act as references for you.

6. When you accept a job, you should immediately notify any other employers to whom you applied, as well as the people who referred you to them.

7. Don't be discouraged if you don't get the first job you apply for. Persevere until you get the job you want.

W

1. who cow how why war sew wit bow wax tow way

2. wear show wish sway wait slow wall wink wash

3. sweet sword waste swing woven sweat watch

4. winter rework weaver switch willow anyway wobble

5. *wedding rainbow western shallow whisper swallow*

X

1. axe tax fix mix fox box axe tax fix mix fox box

2. axis taxi maxi text axes exam oxen jinx exit

3. boxes relax exact sexes maxim telex proxy mixer

4. expert excite exempt oxides taxing exiled exotic

5. *exhaust exactly exhibit express complex excerpt*

Y

1. you sly yet fly yen sky yam try fry cry mayl lay

2. yard rays yarn yawn year jelly yell yoga yolk

3. young rainy syrup rayon yield relay moody muddy

4. yonder injury highly styles yachts martyr yogurt

5. *younger jointly happily symbols systems yelling*

Z

1. zany zest zeal zero zeta zinc zing zone zoom jazz

2. zygote zombie zebra amaze dozen prize fuzzy dizzy

3. quartz dazzle puzzle zigzag gazebo gazette breeze

4. zipper zephyr zircon quartz snazzy sizzle zenith

5. *realize quizzed seizure analyze squeeze bazaars*

ASSIGNMENT 11:7

Key an exact copy of this follow-up letter, using the spacing indicated.

↓ 12

83 Peppertree Drive
West Hill, Ontario
M3B 2C6
July 8, 19--

↓ 6

Ms Michelle Wagner
Personnel Manager
New Era Office Systems Ltd.
555 Yonge Street
Toronto, Ontario
M4Y 1Y7
↓ 2
Dear Ms Wagner:
↓ 2
Thank you very much for taking the time on July 6
to discuss my suitability for the position of
secretary with your company.
↓ 2
Although you will, no doubt, interview many
applicants, I hope that my school record and my co-
op program experience will keep my name on the
"preferred" list of candidates.
↓ 2
Working for a company as dynamic as New Era Office
Systems would be a challenging and rewarding
experience. I would appreciate the opportunity to
offer you my services.

↓ 2
Yours truly,

↓ 5 *Nadia Odynsky*

Nadia Odynsky

ASSIGNMENT 11:8

1. Compose a follow-up letter to a company to which you have applied, thanking the interviewer for taking the time to interview you.

2. Not having heard from your interviewer for a week or so, write a short letter reemphasizing your desire to work for the firm. Refer clearly to the date of the interview and the position you applied for.

S

1. sad ask sat his sum gas sow was sap has sun

2. sack pass saga risk sale last slip wish slim

3. sleep prose salad grass sauce paste sense carts

4. saddle impass salary rascal saucer recess series

5. *salvage consist shields deserve signals process*

T

1. tea act two oat tap ate top art ten rat tow

2. team stop true gate tour colt toad stem tile

3. trust putty about trump tight hints trace import

4. travel typist rating talcum repeat taught habits

5. *tourist quality tremble quartet thought thistle*

U

1. upon push unit quay user quit used quiz undo

2. upper punch uncle query ulcer quiet ultra quite

3. utmost quartz useful quotes unwrap result urgent

4. ukulele sunken undergo grounds upright uranium

5. *ultimate produce universe quibble umbrella*

V

1. view rave vase cave lava veal save void envy

2. voice shave vowel envoy vocal every vivid devil

3. volley starve violet govern vulgar proven volume

4. vinegar quiver voltage review vulture heaven

5. *volatile private visitors unravel violence reserve*

CAREER SEARCH ASSIGNMENT

Interview a friend, a relative or someone whose work is closely related to your choice of career. Try to choose someone with more than two years' business experience. The following questions are suggestions only. Ask your own questions relevant to the type of job that interests you.

1. How long have you been in your present job?

2. What are your specific duties and responsibilities?

3. What responsibilities do you enjoy most in your job?

4. What are some disagreeable aspects of your job?

5. How would you rate the following characteristics in order of importance in your job?

    a) attitude   b) attire   c) cooperation

    d) skill   e) promptness   f) dependability

6. What personal attributes do you feel are necessary or desirable in your line of work?

7. What is your education?

8. Do you feel this education has been adequate for your present job? If not, what additional training do you think you need?

9. What additional training, if any, did you have for this position?

10. What was your starting salary in your first job?

11. Since beginning work in this field, by what percentage has your pay increased?

12. To what do you attribute your on-the-job success?

13. What other careers could you branch into with the work experience you now have?

14. What advice could you offer about finding employment in this field?

CAREER REPORT ASSIGNMENT

Write a report on a career that interests you. Use the headings below to structure your report, and write complete sentences for each topic. Consult your library, the student services division of your school, someone you know in that career, and any other resources you can think of.

O

1. oat who oil toe old tow odd low one foe out

2. oven book oval look oboe only once onto omit

3. oasis proof other ratio ocean gooey order ounce

4. object propel occupy gossip orphan govern orange

5. obscure purpose obvious towards oppress opinion

P

1. pay ape pit tap pew top pot tip pep pig pie

2. pour pulp pray pass upon soup reap pawn pica

3. peace rapid photo apron piano apple pouch press

4. person prompt phrase recipe pillar employ polite

5. persist reports prosper rephie poultry precise

Q

1. quit quaf quad quag quay quid quip quiz quell

2. quack equal qualm quiet quill queen query quays

3. quaint equals quartz equate quaver quilts quotes

4. quadric quacker qualify quandary quality quantum

5. quadrant request quantity require acquire quarrels

R

1. rat ark rip arm ran bar rye tar ram her rim

2. rink purr rate rare rift care rage bearing

3. right purse rebel recur round cover rusty horse

4. rabbit quarry racket record raffle reform recipe

5. radiate quarrel records regrets release reserve

WHY I CHOSE TO RESEARCH THIS PARTICULAR CAREER

- State the career you have chosen.
- In paragraph form, explain why this career interests you.

PERSONAL GOALS

- Who am I? (Write three statements to answer this question.)
- Specify one important aptitude (e.g., organizational skills) that you would like to develop in your chosen career.
- State one aspect of a job that, on the basis of past work experience, you would like to avoid in your chosen career.
- What are your specific, long-term goals concerning:
  a) education?
  b) career?
  c) income?

EDUCATIONAL REQUIREMENTS

- Research the educational attainments you will need to gain entry into your career. Include:
  a) high school courses;
  b) universities or colleges that offer training in your field;
  c) major courses you should study at the post-secondary level (e.g., Commerce).

JOB DEFINITION AND DESCRIPTION

- Write a definition of the career you have selected.
- Write a job description detailing tasks and responsibilities.
- Discover the salary range for this career (from entry level up).
- Find out about advancement requirements and opportunities in this career.
- If possible, find a visual or an ad depicting the career.

K

1. kit sky key yak kin kea ken koa kit kid keg

2. kite skin kale hike keen bike kelp like neck

3. okay kayak slick kiosk trick kitty skill skunk

4. kaiser nickel kernel fickle kidney sicken kitten

5. *kitchen quicken kinship pickles knuckles kettles*

L

1. low owl lie all lap oil lad ill lab nil lot lily

2. lake pill load call link bell lack flew lead

3. ledge pulse ladle qualm legal rally level relic

4. labour miller ledger legend fields legion fling

5. *lacquer profile leisure railing leopard recital*

M

1. met tam mat him mom ram mud sum men dim mop

2. myth whim moss skim meal memo trim mink most

3. music might motor magic motto moult mourn moral

4. mystic remote muzzle impact impair impend muscle

5. *mystery promise monarch remind miracle meeting*

N

1. not ton nil pan nor bin nut won new ten nap

2. nice rain skin next sent near zone norm cone

3. night tense north rainy nylon nurse numb rayon

4. nutmeg ransom number ration noodle brains nibble

5. *nurture connect nostril prolong notices pronoun*

ADVANTAGES AND DISADVANTAGES

In paragraph form, state several positive aspects of this career.

In paragraph form, state several negative aspects of this career.

TEN YEARS FROM TODAY . . .

Write a paragraph describing what you see yourself doing ten years from today.

FORMATTING YOUR CAREER REPORT

1. Key your report using double spacing and a 70-character elite line.

2. With the exception of page 1, number all the pages of the report. Begin page 1 on line 13. Centre the page numbers for the other pages on line 7, and triple space.

3. Indent five spaces for paragraphs.

4. Leave 2.5 cm at the bottom of each page.

5. Key an appropriate heading for each of the sections. Key these section headings in capitals, flush left. Triple space before a section heading and double space after it.

6. Prepare a creative, attractive title page.

7. Prepare a Contents page to follow the title page.

8. Prepare a Bibliography.

9. Organize your report into the following sequence:

    a) Title Page

    b) Contents Page

    c) Body of Report

    d) Bibliography

G

1. got ago gab ego gas sag gum rag got tag gap nag

2. gall sign gear flag gain slag gash toga goes snug

3. green magic great agree ghost tiger gypsy gully

4. gossip magnet ginger rugger regain ground bright

5. *general magnate grammar regress gravity against*

H

1. hit the hat who has shy his why hay hut hip

2. hill rash hall echo heel show hint what home

3. heart wheel hitch hello shown haven shell house

4. hazard rather hotels sought hooves wishes honour

5. *hostess refresh helmet shovels horrors fishing*

I

1. ice kin ink tin ivy sit its pin irk pie inn

2. isle side itch ripe idol bird into quit iris

3. icing night idiom image idiot built imply guide

4. icicle ignite raisin junior filing immune impass

5. *illegal merrily imagery dialing imitate confirm*

J

1. jam jot jet jut jay jar jaw jig joy jog jam

2. jump just jeer jive jest jade jail jazz ajar

3. jabber major jelly jewel judge joker juice jolly

4. jackal jacket jangle jargon jersey jester jiggle

5. *janitor project journal majesty jubilee jugular*

MODULE

12

ON THE JOB

Courtesy of Xerox Canada Ltd.

C

1. cue ace cat car can cap cup cob caw cab cad

2. call ache can arch cone pace chin race cake

3. civic dance cause catch focus choke place quick

4. cavity jacket cherry shacks choose common commit

5. classic perfect climate machine compass luckier

D

1. dew and doe did dot aid die odd dip old dog dad

2. deep idea draw idle drop idol dear yard dust edge

3. drill board drive flood delay digit dodge radio

4. desire madden driver fridge digest duplex divide

5. diamond product durable radiant disturb scandal

E

1. egg let ego get eat bet elm hen elf wee end men

2. edge race evil reel even peal exam seen earn been

3. enter raise exalt sleep eight eager erode depot

4. eleven magpie employ reduce entire reflex engage

5. emotion proceed errand quarter element referee

F

1. foe oaf fad elf far fit fun fig fog for fir fur

2. fear gift fill golf from safe flag flee full half

3. frill refer faint after fancy offer final safer

4. friend profit facial raffle favour refuge fizzle

5. factory magnify fashion qualify fitting refrain

INTRODUCTION

Module 12 consolidates the various skills you have mastered throughout this course. In this module, you will be assigned a hypothetical summer job. You have been hired by Rainbow Foods Limited to work in their head office. The job entails "floating" from one department to another, filling in for staff on vacation. You will perform a variety of office tasks, some routine, some more complex. In formatting correspondence for each department you are assigned to, use the letter and punctuation style specified by your supervisor (teacher).

Courtesy of Acco Canadian Co. Ltd.

OBJECTIVES

1. To complete a variety of simulated office assignments.
2. To review and apply the skills and concepts you have learned in this text.

Courtesy of Acco Canadian Co. Ltd.

ASSIGNMENT
2:6

LETTER DRILLS

Set a 50-character line.
Double space.
Key each line once.

Strike the keys quickly.

A

1. ape sad ask tap all sat ate ran age tan ant way

2. arch rake able talk airy slap axle boat avid claw

3. abate break about blank argue track agree treat

4. appeal salads annual weasel awaken launch asthma

5. *another darling average maintain anybody railway*

B

1. bee cab bat cob bar rob boy sob bye ebb bib dab

2. beat knob brow able boat grab ball back bean balk

3. brain bribe badge scrub brake abuse boast bring

4. baffle rubber ballot dabble banter bubble shabby

5. *banquet macabre biology bubbles boycott problem*

CONTENTS

Public Relations Department 454

Office of the Vice-President 459

Marketing Division 464

Accounting Department 468

5. The seats are marked A, B, C, D, E, F, G, H, and I.

6. or so if an us am ox do is ah of to me go ma pa

7. the yam sod jam ape pay row hap cow man bow via

8. girl held wish nape work pelt fight make both

9. blame panels firms ivory title usual gowns laugh

10. eighty profit turkey handle bushel mantle chapel

11. It is the duty of the clan to pay for fuel used.

Do not rest your wrists on the machine.

12. dew sad caw age rat was vat add few bat get fez

13. cat axe sag awe ace gas fad cad bad webs sew saw

14. Stew deaf case rage vase rest base west dear frees

15. sagas wards water zebra eager feast tease badge

Keep your elbows dropped comfortably at your sides.

16. freeze drawer verses trader cadets extras sagged

17. dear dials beets wears cad reads after cabarets

18. lip nip nil oil joy pom mop hop hip you ilk imp

19. pin him you mom nun kin pop ink lip nip nil mum

20. pink pill moon kill mill link look nook only

21. jump upon join limp lily kink lion yolk pool

22. onion imply nylon plump pylon phony poppy onion

23. mop oil pool jolly up only oh kinky pun nylon

PUBLIC RELATIONS DEPARTMENT

rainbow foods limited

22 Worcester Road, Rexdale, Ontario M9W 1L1

In your first posting at Rainbow Foods, you will replace a vacationing secretary in the Public Relations Department. You will work for Ms Joanna Kendall, Director of Public Relations. Letter style used is full block with open punctuation.

ASSIGNMENT

12:1

Key the following letter from Joanna Kendall, Director of Public Relations, to Sarah Rashid, Media Communications Representative, 388 Montroyal Blvd., North Vancouver, British Columbia V7N 1P3. The topic is the Vancouver exhibit of Rainbow Foods' antique soup tureen collection.

```
Dear Sarah
(P) I would like to bring you up-to-date regarding
the latest developments in Rainbow Foods' antique
soup tureen exhibit, to be displayed this fall at
the Vancouver Centennial Museum. Here is an
overview of the program of events:(P) 1. On Friday,
October 24, business colleagues, museum and
government officials, and company executives will
preview the display. Invitations to the preview
will be mailed out in mid-August. 2. A buffet will
be held prior to the preview. Executives from
Montreal and Toronto will attend, along with
Vancouver sales management personnel. 3. The
display will open to the public on Sunday, October
26, and will run for one month. Please see the
enclosed press release for details. A mailing list
has been compiled, and invitations will be sent
well in advance of the exhibit. I shall arrive in
Vancouver in early September to finalize all
arrangements. (P) Similar exhibits in Toronto and
Montreal have been successful. We are confident
that public response to the exhibit will be
enthusiastic in Vancouver as well. Sincerely yours,
```

4. May was amazed by Bo. Check the coat racks please.

5. Violet quickly examined the three broken zippers.

6. Zack was very excited about the expensive bicycle.

ASSIGNMENT 2:4

SHIFTING DRILLS

Set a 50-character line.
Double space.
Key each line once.

This accuracy drill is good for shifting problems.

1. aAa bBb cCc dDd eEe fFf gGg hHh ili jJj kKk

2. lLl mMm nNn oOo pPp qQq rRr sSs tTt uUu vVv

3. wWw xXx yYy zZz a A b B c C d D e E f F g G

4. Abigail Barbara Candace Darlene Edwina Fran

5. Geoffrey Harold Irving Jeremy Kenneth Lucas

6. Meredith Nancy Orville Peter Quentin Robert

7. Stephen Terence Ursula Vivien Xanthe Yvonne

8. Zelda Adam Bonnie Caroline Deidre Elizabeth

9. Canada Africa Russia England Norway Finland

10. Paris Oslo Winnipeg Kingston Detroit London

11. Laurie, Sandra, and Michelle went to Italy.

ASSIGNMENT 2:5

SPACE BAR DRILLS

Set a 50-character line.
Double space.
Key each line once.

This accuracy drill is good for spacing problems.

1. a b c d e f g h i j k l m n o p q r s t u v w x y z

2. z y x w v u t s r q p o n m l k j i h g f e d c b a

3. I thought. You bought. She fought. She squawked.

4. Go to the show with 1, 2, 3, 4, 5, 6, or 7 friends.

ASSIGNMENT

12:2

Format an attractive invitation for the Rainbow Foods antique soup tureen exhibit. Include the following information: The exhibit will take place from October 26 to November 26, 19—; it will be held in the Main Hall of the Vancouver Centennial Museum; the exhibit hours are 10 a.m. to 6 p.m., daily; admission is free.

ASSIGNMENT

12:3

Key a final version of this rough-draft form letter for copying. It will be sent to the special guests who will attend the preview of the Rainbow Foods soup tureen exhibit. The letter will be signed by Joanna Kendall, Director of Public Relations.

August 15, 19--

Dear

¶This fall, from October 26 until Nov*ember* 26, a unique exhibit will be displayed in the main Hall of the Vancouver Centennial Museum. This exhibit will feature antique soup tureens from the Rainbow Foods Collection. (P)Over ⑤0 years ago, Rainbow Foods began a collection of fascinating soup tureens from many countries, ~~and~~ dating from the 1700s to the mid-1800s. The exhibit has travelled to leading museums, including the Victoria and albert Museum in London, the Smithsonian Institutions in Washington, the Royal Ontario Museum in Toronto, and the Museum of Fine Arts in Montreal. (P) A private showing of this display has been arranged for

∧We would like October 24, from 4 p.m. until 7 p.m. ~~for~~ you to join us and our British Columbia management team for this event and for a buffet, beginning at 7 p.m. Yours sincerely,

SKILL DEVELOPMENT ASSIGNMENTS

ASSIGNMENT 2:1

Set a 50-character line.
Double space.
Key each line once.

Set either a speed or accuracy goal.

1. a;sldkfjghghfjdksla; a;sldkfjghfjdksla; a;sldkfjgh

2. lad sad ask add all has gas lads dad lag sags fads

3. hall fall gash flag lass half glad adds slag glass

4. salad halls falls glass flash shall flasks slash

5. half a glass; a glad lad; ask a glad lass; a dash

6. Dad has half a glass. Hal has a gash. Dad adds.

ASSIGNMENT 2:2

Set a 50-character line.
Double space.
Key each line once.

If you are working on speed, don't worry about errors.

1. two ore row pot you pew wet try out try fat rot or

2. if is up to of so at as do if up is to at is we in

3. tow row fat try you ore row rid doe ate hat pot we

4. wore trip tree pour arms wept does tell worry quit

5. two of us; up the sky; if it is; yes it is; up the

6. He did his work well. He ate it all up. Yes, sir.

ASSIGNMENT 2:3

Set a 50-character line.
Double space.
Key each line once.

If you are building speed, key at a slightly uncomfortable rate.

1. may sum jam one can man van ban nib bin dab van on

2. back comb buzz fuzz oxen dizzy amazed next very it

3. next year; not now; me home; by the; yes come in

Key this letter and an envelope to Janice Langley, Rainbow Foods' British Columbia sales representative. The letter outlines details of the buffet following the preview of the display, to which executives from Toronto, Montreal, and Vancouver have been invited. The letter is from Joanna Kendall, Director of Public Relations. Determine the paragraphing and correct any errors.

Janice Langley, Rainbow Foods Limited, 1100
Chestnut Street, Vancouver, BC V6J 3J9
Dear Janice, I am looking forwarde to the varius
activities we have planned for the display opening
and would like to go voer some of the details with
you. An invitation to the buffet is being sent to
20 guests. A list of their names and addresses
attached. The buffet is scheduled for 7 p.m.
Rainbow Foods will pay for this event on Friday
evening. It conection with the coast of the dinner,
please let me know whom we should pay--the museum
or the caterer. I will arrive ta the museum at 3
p.m. on October 24. Please have a portable PA
system availeable so that we can welcome our guests
and outline the plans for the evening. I think I
have covered all the main topics. Phone me if there
are any problems. Yours Truley,

DEVELOPING SPEED AND ACCURACY

The initial step in improving keyboarding speed and accuracy is to decide which area to work on first. You can't work on *both* speed and accuracy improvement at the same time. Which area will you tackle first? Speed or accuracy?

The following guidelines will help you achieve your goals, regardless of the area you choose:

1. Set short-term goals for yourself. If you are keyboarding to improve accuracy, try to reduce your errors by 1 or 2. For example, if you previously keyed a timing with 6 errors, aim for 4 or 5 the next time. If you are trying to improve your speed, aim at an increase of 1 or 2 wpm. For example, if you are keying 30 wpm now, aim for 31 or 32 wpm.

2. Spend 10 to 20 minutes building your stroking skills as soon as you come to class.

3. Keep a record of your individual speed and accuracy performance. As soon as you reach a goal, set yourself a new one.

IMPROVING ACCURACY

1. Always key at a *comfortable* rate.

2. If you have an individual problem with shifting, key words and sentences that are filled with lots of capitals.

3. If you have difficulty with spacing and punctuation, key short lines with lots of punctuation.

4. If you make many misstrokes, try saying the letters to yourself as you key them.

IMPROVING SPEED

Key at a rate that is *slightly uncomfortable*, and don't worry about errors. Remember, you are working on speed, *not* accuracy, at this point.

Key the following names and addresses in an attractive list to be enclosed with the letter of invitation. Then key each name and address on a separate index card for Joanna Kendall's secretary.

```
Mr. and Mrs. W. Beach, 1520 West 35th Avenue,
Vancouver, BC V6M 1H2
Mr. and Mrs. John Hepburn, 105 East Durham Street,
New Westminster, BC V3L 4H8
Mr. and Mrs. R. Rajamani, 6370 Portland St. South,
Burnaby, BC V5J 2R9
Mr. K. Byron, 6670 Gainsborough Drive, Richmond, BC
V7E 3Z8
Mrs. G. Wannamaker, 9679 Townline Division, Surrey,
BC V3V 2T1
Mr. and Mrs. Pierre Vanier, 12268-214 Street, Maple
Ridge, BC V2X 5E2
Mr. and Mrs. William Ying, 6150 Southland Place,
Vancouver, BC V6N 1N1
Mr. C. Dixon, 4636 Hoskins Street, North Vancouver,
BC V7K 2R1
Ms J. McIntyre, 566 Braeman East, North Vancouver,
BC V7N 1R3
Mr. and Mrs. Henry Fong, 1157 Lytton Place, North
Vancouver, BC V7H 2A9
Mr. and Mrs. H. Van Clef, 6330 MacDonald St.,
Vancouver, BC V6N 1E6
Mr. and Mrs. P. Misra, 2687 West 49th Ave.,
Vancouver, BC V6N 3S5
```

Key the following letter from Joanna Kendall, Director of Public Relations, to Mr. Tony Cousins, Retail Sales Manager, Holiday Inn Hotel, Vancouver, British Columbia V6B 1Y4. Send a copy of this letter to Janice Langley, Rainbow Foods' British Columbia representative. Correct any errors.

```
Dear Mr. Cousins, Please reserve double-room
accommodation at your hotel for the following
people: Mr. and Mrs. J.B. Gage, Arriving November
1; Mr. Paola Visconti, Arriving November 2; Mrs.
Jean Pritchard, Arriving November 3; and Mr. and
Mrs. J. Rubinsky, arriving November 4. These guests
will be visiting Vancouver in connection with the
Rainbow Foods soup tureen display at the Vancouver
Centennial Museum. Checkout times are undetermined
at this point, but these guests will probably
depart on November 6 or 7. Our British Columbia
representative will contact you to confirm all
dates. Yours sincerely,
```

CONTENTS

Developing Speed and Accuracy 45

Skill Development Assignments 46

    Shifting Drills 47

    Space Bar Drills 48

    Letter Drills 49

    Common Phrases Drills 56

    Number Drills 56

    Letter-Number Combination Drills 58

    Tabulation Drills 60

    Special Characters Drills 61

    Words and Sentences Drills 63

    Paragraph Drills 66

    More Words and Phrases Drills 68

    More Sentence Drills 71

    More Paragraph Drills 73

The Number Keypad 75

Number Keypad Assignments 76

Rainbow Foods is preparing a promotional recipe booklet entitled *Souper Soups & Sandwiches*, to be distributed free to consumers. Joanna Kendall has asked you to key the information needed for a request form to be designed by the Marketing Division's art director. This form will be printed on labels and posted in supermarkets. The form must feature the mailing address of Rainbow Foods Limited (22 Worcester Road, Rexdale, Ontario M9W 1L1), and spaces for the consumer's name, address, apartment or townhouse number, city or town, province, postal code, and whether a French or English version is preferred.

Souper Soups & Sandwiches

rainbow foods limited

22 Worcester Road, Rexdale, Ontario M9W 1L1

INTRODUCTION

Keyboarding drills help you to develop the good stroking skills that are essential for effective production keyboarding. Speed and accuracy are the keys to successful production keyboarding. The drills in this module are designed to assist you and improve your skills in these areas.

Skill improvement in keyboarding, or any other activity, begins with personal goal-setting. Guidelines to help you establish your own goals for improving your keyboarding skill and accuracy are also included in this module.

OBJECTIVES

1. To improve keyboard manipulation.

2. To increase keying speed.

3. To improve accuracy.

4. To increase proficiency at keying numbers, letters, special characters, words, phrases, sentences, and paragraphs.

OFFICE OF THE VICE-PRESIDENT

You are now sent to the office of the Vice-President of Rainbow Foods, Olga Werner. Ms Werner prefers her letters to be keyed in block style with two-point punctuation.

ASSIGNMENT

12:8

Key a letter and an envelope from Olga Werner, Vice-President, to Rorke Associates, Office Design Consultants, 236 Besserer St., Ottawa, Ontario K1N 6B1; Attention: Mr. Ken Desjardins. Correct all errors.

I regret to inform you that the proposed lay out for the new Personnel department is not satisfactory for 2 reasons: 1. It does not provide sufficient privacy for Personnel Department employees, and, In my opinion, there is a wasted space in the central area. 2. the positioning of the Director's desk dees not provide enough privacy. I have made some suggestions regarding the floor plan in an attempt to over come these problems. A copy of the altered floor plan wille be sent under separate cover. I hope this floor plan will provide the privacy required and make much better use of the available space. I would like to point out that the personnel department requires a large storage area for files. In the floor plan, it is not clear whether the storage area adjacent to the washroom would be available to the Marketing Division or to the Personnel Department. Please clarify this before the plans are finalized, and then contact me as soon as these problems have been resolved. yours truly,

MODULE

2

SKILL
DEVELOPMENT

Courtesy of Xerox Canada Inc.

ASSIGNMENT 12:9

Key this memo to all department managers concerning the new office addition for the Personnel Department. The memo is from Olga Werner, Vice-President. Determine appropriate paragraphing.

During the past few weeks, I have received many comments about the layout of the new office addition. One major comment concerns privacy and the feasibility of creating private offices with ceiling-high partitions for all managers. Unfortunately, space limitations in the new department will prohibit the construction of private, enclosed offices for all managerial staff. Also, a private, ceiling-high office costs approximately $6000 to $8000 to construct, and ceiling-high partitions create air circulation problems. A limited number of private offices, therefore, will be ascribed on a seniority basis. I hope I have clearly explained the company's position on this matter, and assure you that the new space has been designed to ensure as much privacy as possible for all staff.

ASSIGNMENT 12:10

Key the following letter from Olga Werner, Vice-President, to the attention of Helen Khademi, Price & Innis, 102 University Ave., Toronto, ON M5J 1V5. Place an attention notation on both the letter and the envelope.

Gentlemen:
    Upon your request, I have contacted our Production Planning Department to determine the production schedule of Rainbow soup for the next fiscal year.
    As it turns out, 79% of all tomato soup scheduled for production during this fiscal year will be produced during the growing season. The remaining 21% will be produced out of season. This out-of-season production is necessary because in-season capacity cannot meet total consumer demand.
Yours sincerely,

6. **Equals sign:** (5 + 6 = 11)
   - Keyboard a hyphen.

   - Backspace once, move the paper up slightly, and strike another hyphen.

   - Leave a space before and after this sign.

7. **Multiplication sign** (2 x 3)
   - Keyboard a small *x*.

   - Leave a space before and after this sign.

8. **Division sign:** (10 ÷ 2)
   - Keyboard a colon.

   - Backspace once, and strike a hyphen.

   - Leave a space before and after this sign.

ASSIGNMENT 12:11

Olga Werner is launching an employee fitness campaign at Rainbow Foods. To publicize this campaign, she wants you to set up an attractive bulletin board announcement containing the following information:

```
Fitness in the workplace. Fitness benefits
everyone, so come to the lunchtime fitness classes
held daily from noon until 1 p.m. A YMCA fitness
expert will lead the classes in the employee
lounge. Fitness--you owe it to yourself; sign up
today.
```

ASSIGNMENT 12:12

Send the following memo from Olga Werner to the Marketing Division, concerning travel arrangements.

```
(P) It is my responsibility to authorize requests
for travel arrangements. In most cases, these
requests are arriving in my office after the travel
arrangements have been made. In future, please
arrange to have these requests forwarded for
approval before your trips. (P) I also ask that you
supply Ann Morozuk with information regarding where
you can be located when you are out of town. I
would appreciate your following this procedure on
every occasion when you plan to be away from the
office.
```

ASSIGNMENT 12:13

Send this letter to Rorke Associates, Office Design Consultants, 236 Besserer St., Ottawa, Ontario K1N 6B1; Attention: Ms Katie Rorke. Determine appropriate paragraphing.

```
Gentlemen Subject: Office Chairs The re-upholstered
office chair that you sent to us for approval is
now on display in our office. I believe everyone
has had the opportunity to try out this chair and
responses have been favourable. It is certainly an
improvement over the previous chairs we had in the
office. I would like you to proceed with the re-
upholstering of all our other chairs. These chairs
will fit in beautifully with our new office decor
and they will definitely enhance the work
environment. I look forward to collaborating with
you on future office furnishing projects. Yours
sincerely,
```

CONSTRUCTING SPECIAL CHARACTERS

Some special characters not found on all keyboards can be constructed by using combinations of other characters. Here are some of these characters. Try constructing them now.

1. **Exclamation mark:** `(Look at that!)`
   - Keyboard an apostrophe.
   - Backspace once.
   - Strike a period under the apostrophe.
   - Leave two spaces after an exclamation mark.

2. **Degree sign:** `(20°)`
   - Pull the automatic line finder forward and move the paper down slightly, or turn the cylinder knob down slightly.
   - Strike a small *o*.
   - Do *not* leave a space after the last digit.

3. **Superscript and Subscript:** `(3² or H₂0)`
   - To keyboard a **superscript**, or raised number, turn the cylinder knob down slightly, and strike the number.
   - To keyboard a **subscript**, or lowered number, turn the cylinder knob up slightly, and strike the number.
   - Do *not* leave a space between the raised or lowered character and the character immediately before it.

4. **Addition sign:** `(2 + 2)`
   - Strike a hyphen.
   - Backspace once, and keyboard an apostrophe.
   - Backspace once, use the cylinder knob to raise the paper slightly, and strike another apostrophe.
   - Leave a space before and after this sign.

5. **Minus sign:** `(4 − 2)`
   - Strike a hyphen.
   - Leave a space before and after this sign.

ASSIGNMENT

12:14

Centre this agenda vertically and horizontally on a full sheet of paper.

rainbow foods limited

22 Worcester Road, Rexdale, Ontario M9W 1L1

```
Rainbow Foods Limited
Agenda for Vice-President's Staff Committee Meeting
July 20, 19--
Staff Conference Room
10:00 a.m.
1. Review of Minutes of Previous Meeting (July 2)
2. Tomato Growing Operations
3. Antique Soup Tureen Display in Vancouver
4. Food Services
5. Office Addition (for Personnel Department)
6. New Business
```

	D		E		F
1.	studio	1.	medium	1.	loveliness
2.	wooden	2.	accommodations	2.	knocking
3.	compelling	3.	reconciliation	3.	courteous
4.	orientation	4.	proprietor	4.	succeed
5.	adept	5.	preface	5.	January
6.	self-made	6.	melody	6.	previous
7.	sitting	7.	practical	7.	polling
8.	agree	8.	ex-president	8.	highly
9.	eclipsed	9.	echo	9.	explosion
10.	separate	10.	oblige	10.	manifesto
11.	father	11.	shouldn't	11.	achieve
12.	chapter 8	12.	15 200 985	12.	continually
13.	missing	13.	various	13.	Alexander
14.	crucial	14.	Amsterdam	14.	Section III
15.	30 strokes	15.	ancient	15.	though
16.	Herminio	16.	shipper	16.	$23 000
17.	wouldn't	17.	recreation	17.	mid-Pacific
18.	change	18.	selling	18.	filling
19.	abbreviate	19.	page 10	19.	don't
20.	carrying	20.	serious	20.	getting

ASSIGNMENT 1:3

Key the following assignments using a 60-character line. Make the appropriate line-end decisions so that the lines stop at, or as close as possible to, the right margin.
If you are using a typewriter, remember to listen for the bell.
Begin on line 7.
Double space the text.

NOTE

1. Lines must end as close to the right margin as possible.

2. Do *not* divide words at the ends of more than two consecutive lines.

3. Avoid keyboarding beyond the right margin.

NOTE

The number of strokes from the bell to the right margin varies from typewriter to typewriter.

1. 5 → What is money? A dime is only a piece of metal, a dollar is only a piece of paper, and neither has much practical value--although you could use a dime as a screwdriver in an emergency, and you might use a dollar bill to light a fire. Money, in fact, is worth something only because society accepts it as a way to measure the value of goods and services by a common standard.

2. 5 → Ask a fellow student how rich he is and he will probably count the cash in his pocket and maybe add to that his bank balance if he's lucky enough to have one. One thing is certain, he will use money terms to tell you how rich he is. Does it follow, then, that riches can be defined as money? Possessions can be converted into money, and we all know that money can be converted into possessions or into the services we buy from others.

Prepare the minutes of the Vice-President's Staff Committee meeting.

rainbow foods limited

22 Worcester Road, Rexdale, Ontario M9W 1L1

Rainbow Foods Limited, Minutes of Meeting of Vice-President's Staff Committee, July 20, 19—, 10 a.m.

PRESENT: J. Harkness, K. Ballentine, L. Robichaud, D. Neilson, J. Funamoto

1. MINUTES: The minutes of the last meeting on July 2 were read and approved.
2. TOMATO GROWING OPERATIONS: Jon Harkness announced that the quality of tomatoes has been irregular compared to that in previous years.
3. SOUP TUREEN DISPLAY: Karen Ballentine announced that details regarding the Rainbow Foods soup tureen display at the Vancouver Centennial Museum are being finalized and that the exhibit will open on October 26.
4. FOOD SERVICES: Nutrition demonstrations featuring Rainbow Foods products are being featured at several supermarkets across Canada. Lise Robichaud reported that these workshops are going very well and are expected to continue into August.
5. OFFICE ADDITION: Doug Neilson read a report from the contractor assuring us that the time lost because of problems with underground services has been made up, and construction is once again on schedule. In about two weeks, it will be necessary to bar access to the main entrance for approximately three weeks while renovations are underway.
6. NEW BUSINESS: Joyce Funamoto announced that according to the latest computer data, inventories are low and production is high. Barring weather problems, maximum production is expected at both Rainbow food processing plants this summer.
7. ADJOURNMENT: The meeting adjourned at 11:50 a.m.

WORD DIVISION ASSIGNMENTS

ASSIGNMENT

1:2

Set a 40-character line.
Begin on line 7.
Set a tab stop at the midpoint (see "Clearing and Setting Tabs," page 19).
Set the line space regulator for 2 (double space).
Key each word in the column at the left margin.
Tab to the midpoint and keyboard the word again, showing it divided at the *best possible place*. Use the hyphen key to indicate the division.

A	B	C
1. Johnson	1. thrilled	1. specified
2. bargain	2. friends	2. saucer
3. there's	3. emerged	3. strength
4. background	4. experiencing	4. manufacture
5. UNICEF	5. instalment	5. Saskatchewan
6. following	6. schooling	6. Angela
7. transfer	7. barred	7. well-known
8. prefix	8. vice-president	8. brother-in-law
9. planting	9. exceed	9. CNE
10. alter	10. permitted	10. issue
11. self-addressed	11. likely	11. knead
12. extraordinary	12. guilty	12. killing
13. knotting	13. chased	13. tongue
14. amazed	14. truly	14. justification
15. announcement	15. obeying	15. surely
16. alien	16. Sebastian	16. sunflower
17. rowed	17. continually	17. arouse
18. business	18. branches	18. go-between
19. quizzed	19. piano	19. perseverance
20. latches	20. axis	20. aroma

MARKETING DIVISION

You are now working in the Marketing Division for Mr. Jeff Solomon, Marketing Manager. Use the block letter style and two-point punctuation in the following assignments.

ASSIGNMENT

12:16

Key this letter and an envelope.

```
Price & Innis, 102 University Ave., Toronto,
Ontario M5J 1V5 Attention: Mr. Tom Stubin Dear Tom,
(P) Senior management has given us approval to
proceed with the development of the new line of
frozen foods, to be launched next February, which
you and I discussed by phone last week. (P) Rainbow
Foods will require an intensive advertising
campaign for this new product line. I look forward
to your initial thoughts on this subject. Please
let me know when it would be convenient for you to
meet with us, either in Toronto or Vancouver. Yours
truly, copy to Olga Werner, Vice-President
```

ASSIGNMENT

12:17

The following memo contains many errors. Key it correctly. The memo, from Jeff Solomon, Marketing Manager, to Dianne Zeller, pertains to evaluation of sales promotions. Send a copy to the Sales Department. Determine the paragraphing.

```
A copc of the Promotion Evaluation Report prepared
by bruce Abramsky will bee circulated within the
next week This Evaluation covers the key points
that we should assess in the area of oru trade
advertising and promotions. I would like to
implement this report immediataly. This is a
Marketng Department responsiblty however much of
the information will be supplied by our Sales
Department. I would like the individual who set up
the Evaluation to report directly too me as the
results come in.
```

6. Divide hyphenated words only after the hyphen.

   `self-addressed, vice-president`

7. Do *not* divide a word unless there are at least three letters before and after the division.

   `key-board, per-son`

8. Do *not* divide a word of less than six letters. Use the margin release key and finish the word.

   `gypsy, oily, telex`

9. Do *not* divide proper names or abbreviations.

   `Canada, Denys, C.N.I.B.`

10. Do *not* divide words that are pronounced as one syllable.

    `stopped, thought, jumped`

11. Do *not* divide figures.

    `286 741 632,  813 650`

12. Do *not* divide contractions.

    `can't, won't, doesn't`

13. Do *not* divide the last word in more than two consecutive lines, i.e., don't leave a row of hyphens at the edge of a page.

14. Do *not* divide the last word in a paragraph or on a page.

ASSIGNMENT 12:18

Key a final version of this rough-draft memo from Jeff Solomon, Marketing Manager, to the Marketing Division. The memo concerns interdepartmental communications.

¶In our efforts to get things done quickly and
efficiently, there are still occassions when
members of the Marketing division are not
communicating adequately with key personnel in
other departments.

¶It is very difficult (write to) a memo covering our
many communication needs so let's deal specifically
with ② very important areas Production and pricing.
When communicating with other departments in these
two important areas, please be certain that all
correspondence pertaining to Production includes a
copy for Juan Mendes, and that Pricing
Correspondence includes a copy for Evelyn Duval.

ASSIGNMENT 12:19

Using an appropriate format, key the following report to Mr. Jeff Soloman, Marketing Manager. It is from Sylvia Lee and concerns her field trip to Eastern Canada. Prepare an appropriate title page.

Purpose
This report summarizes observations made during a
field trip undertaken on July 21, 22 and 23 to
St. John's, Halifax, and Charlottetown
respectively.
Objectives
This field trip was undertaken to observe the
retail situation of our canned soups throughout the
Eastern Region. At the same time, I wanted to
discuss any possible improvements to our marketing
programs with the respective district sales
managers.
St. John's--Monday, July 21, 19--
Generally speaking, the outlets appear to be
responding positively to the "Souper Soup"
promotion currently in progress. Often our soups
receive price reduction and prominent displays in
supermarket chains. When not reduced, prices are
at least competitive with the other major brands.
These prices are usually within two cents of each
other.

LINE ENDINGS—WORD DIVISION

Making line-ending decisions on computers and word processors is simple. Most word processing systems have some sort of hyphenation capability. For example, a system may simply highlight words that require end-of-line hyphens; the operator then determines the proper location for the hyphen in these highlighted words. Other systems not only flag the words that require hyphens, but also determine the correct position for the hyphens.

If you are using a typewriter, a bell will sound to indicate that you have a limited number of spaces left on the line. When you hear the bell, you will have to make a line-end decision. To make the right decision, ask yourself these questions:

1. Can I complete the word I am entering?

2. Should I divide the word? If so, where?

3. Should I use the margin release key and complete the word?

Regardless of the type of equipment you are using, you should ensure that text material is well balanced on the page. End each line as close to the right margin as possible.

The following guidelines for correct word division apply in all keyboarding situations. If you are uncertain where to divide a word, consult a dictionary.

WORD DIVISION GUIDELINES

1. Divide a word at the end of a line only when it is absolutely necessary.

2. Divide a word only between syllables, and as close to the middle of the word as possible.

    `detri-mental, claustro-phobia, benevo-lent`

3. Divide words that consist of a root and a prefix between the prefix and the root.

    `inter-state, pro-found`

4. a) Divide words that consist of a root and a suffix between the root and the suffix.

    `sing-ing, stand-ard`

   b) If the root ends in a double consonant, divide the word after the double consonant.

    `spell-ing, puff-ing`

5. When two vowels that appear together are clearly pronounced, divide the word between the vowels.

    `experi-ence, gladi-ator`

While in good distribution, our tomato soup, in particular, suffers from a can-crushing problem. In a number of stores I visited, crushed cans and unstuck labels had damaged sales.

Halifax--Tuesday, July 22, 19--

Our "Souper Soup" display was featured prominently in many of the Halifax chains. Where end-of-aisle displays were used, market growth was 20 percent higher than in areas where such displays were not used.

As was the case in St. John's, pricing is very favourable compared to that of major brands. There is good support from retailers in terms of shelf positioning and exposure.

Charlottetown--Wednesday, July 23, 19--

In this city, private-label soups seem to be more popular than brand names. The price difference between private-label soups and brand-name soups is sustantial, ranging from 25 to 30 percent higher for the latter. This is reflected in the large amount of shelf space that private-label soups occupy. Inroads can be made with our products in this area if we can convert consumers to our products, by means of a massive sales campaign and more competitive pricing.

Conclusions

This field trip was extremely worthwhile. It provided the opportunity to observe, first-hand, the problems that we are encountering with our marketing promotions. It also allowed me to discuss some other more subtle problems with the district managers, and to obtain their viewpoints on possible solutions. I feel that this type of field trip should be undertaken at least once a year in each sales region by a marketing representative.

6. The doctor was well liked. He had many patients.

7. What do you think of this? Did you ever hear of anything like it?

8. Look out! A car is coming.

9. The members included: Sherri, Jeff, Mark, and Tova.

10. 5→ Caveat Emptor means Let the Buyer Beware!Today's consumers must make more choices than ever before. Think about some of your more recent purchases and consider your answers to the following questions: Was the item available for sale last year? Have you ever purchased the item before?Where did you get the information to help you make your decision?

11. Ana ate 1 1/2 oranges.

12. Rovet&Clarke were famous lawyers.

13. 69 m @ 60¢/m.

14. 5→ J&D Variety Stores were well known for their bargains.They had over 6000 items in stock. Bananas were sold for $1.20/kg.Their profit at the end of the year was $80 000.Other prices included: 1 doz.eggs@$1.30,12 oranges@ $1.75,and cucumbers @3 for $1.00.More than 2/3 of their customers came from other parts of town.

15. He paid 60¢ for the candy.

16. Josie's average was 85%.

17. 5→ Scott paid 99 ¢ for the ballpoint pen,which was advertised as containing 33% more ink.Its regular price was 95¢, so he felt he had made a wise decision. This meant he still had 61 ¢ left from his allowance.Over 50% of his allowance was spent on bus fare.

Courtesy of Olivetti Canada Ltd.

ASSIGNMENT 12:20

Jeff Solomon has asked you to set up the following nutritional information for Rainbow Foods' "Good Morning Natural Cereal" label. The information is to be sent to an advertising agency.

Nutrient value per Serving (28 g)

Food Energy	104 calories
Protein	6.2 g
Fat	0.3 g
Total Carbohydrates, Sucrose, and Other Sugars	2.3 g
Starch	16.0 g
Dietary Fibre	0.4 g

Vitamins and Minerals per Serving

Vitamin B₁, Thiamine	0.5 mg
Vitamin B₂, Riboflavin	1.5 mg
Vitamin B₃, Niacinamide	7.0 mg
Iron	5.0 mg

ASSIGNMENT 12:21

Format a merchandise order form for consumers to fill out if they wish to order Rainbow-designed promotional products (for example, T-shirts, coffee mugs, jogging suits, etc.). The information on the form must include:

1. Merchandise Order Form (heading)
2. Ship to/Address/City/Province/Postal Code
3. Item No., Quantity, Description, Price per Item, Payment (cheque, postal money order or credit card), Total (column headings)

Do *not* leave any space between:

1. quotation marks and the words enclosed

   ```
   Julius said, "We should all go on holidays."
   ```

2. parentheses and the words enclosed

   ```
   The exercise (see page 91) was the most
   difficult I have ever done.
   ```

3. the number symbol and the number it refers to

   ```
   Jessi ordered #4567 from the book list.
   ```

4. a whole number and a fraction key

   ```
   There are only 13½ pies left on the shelf.
   ```

SPACE BAR ASSIGNMENTS

ASSIGNMENT

1:1

Set a 50-character line.
Double space.
Key each sentence and paragraph once, leaving the appropriate number of spaces before and after punctuation marks.

NOTE

Strike the space bar *once* after
1. a comma;

2. a semicolon;

3. a period following an abbreviation (if two initials appear together, either *one* or *no* space may be left between them).

1. I saw zebras, elephants, and snakes at the zoo.

2. Jonathan bought the painting. Cecilia bought nothing.

3. Mrs. Hill and J. Bradshaw attended the meeting.

4. Miss K. R. Chong is production supervisor.

5. 5→ Mr.J.R.Singh and Mrs.R.B. Caldwell led a discussion on the topic of computers. He assembled the information;she presented it.Their talk covered Parts of the Computer,Hardware,Software,and How Computers Started.Dr.Smula thanked them for giving the presentation.

ASSIGNMENT

12:22

Compose and key a letter of congratulations to Mr. Tom Stubin of the advertising firm of Price & Innis, 102 University Ave., Toronto, Ontario M5J 1V5, for winning the Canadian Marketing Award for the year's best magazine ad. The letter will be signed by Jeff Solomon, Marketing Manager.

rainbow foods *limited*

22 Worcester Road, Rexdale, Ontario M9W 1L1

ACCOUNTING DEPARTMENT

By the end of the summer, you are working for Maxine Schultz, an executive in the Accounting Department. She has no preference as to letter style, so use any style you like.

ASSIGNMENT

12:23

Key a final version of this rough-draft memo from Maxine Schultz, Senior Accountant, to all staff in the Accounting Department concerning objectives for the current fiscal year. Determine the paragraphing.

(2) months of our present fiscal year have already passed. I know that you have all set some objectives to be acheived within the next (10) months. I am asking you to prepare, by the end of this week, a list of the major objectives that you aim to accomplish during the year. (1) of my objectives will bee to consult with each of you after each quarter to review the objectives you have set, discuss their status and, if neccessary, work together to remove any obstacles preventing your from achieving your goals.

2. the & sign (ampersand sign means "and")

```
The firm of Watson & Margles was just formed.
```

3. the @ sign (means "at")

```
One dozen eggs @ $1.50/dozen.
```

4. groups of three digits in large numbers

```
The price of the apartment building was
$10 900 500.00.
```

Do *not* leave any space before:

1. the ¢ sign

```
The chocolate bar cost 69¢.
```

2. The % sign

```
They paid 14% interest on their loan for
their house.
```

Do *not* leave any space before or after:

1. a hyphen

```
Laurie placed the letter in a self-addressed
envelope.
```

2. a dash

```
Can you--will you--help me now?
```

3. a colon in expressions of time

```
My favourite television program starts at
17:30 every Monday.
```

4. a decimal

```
He ran the race in 38.5 s.
```

ASSIGNMENT 12:24

Maxine Schultz has asked you to prepare an attractively centred advertisement for the following position in the Accounting Department. Key the ad according to the information below:

```
Wanted an Executive Assistant who must know how to
delegate tasks, communicate effectively, and work
well with others, and who has an aptitude for
working with numbers. If interested, please send
resumé to Rainbow Foods Limited, 22 Worcester Road,
Rexdale, Ontario M9W 1L1: Attention: Ms Maxine
Schultz, Accounting Department.
```

ASSIGNMENT 12:25

Key labels for the following files in the Accounting Department. Begin five spaces in from the edge of the label on the second line.

Agendas, Minutes of Meetings, Departmental Memos, Accounting Department Objectives, Budget Recommendations, Committee Reports, Annual Reports, Vacation Schedule, Form Letters, Pension Fund, Annual Statements

ASSIGNMENT 12:26

Key the following agenda for an Accounting Department meeting.

```
Date: July 30, 19--; Place: Conference Room--
Accounting Department; Time 9:30 a.m., AGENDA
1. Treasurer's Report
2. Auditor's Report
3. Financial Statements
4. Notes to Financial Statements
5. Proposed Budget
6. Staff Reports
7. Committee Reports
8. New Business
9. Adjournment
```

SPACE BAR RULES

Leave *two* letter spaces after:

1. a period at the end of a sentence

   ```
   Michael was born on April 28.^^It was a
   Tuesday.
   ```

2. a question mark at the end of a sentence

   ```
   Where did you buy your computer?^^How much
   did you pay for it?
   ```

3. an exclamation mark at the end of a sentence

   ```
   Wow!^^What a great movie!
   ```

4. a colon separating parts of a sentence

   ```
   Alexander's wallet contained the following:^^
   money, credit cards, and driver's licence.
   ```

Leave *one* letter space after:

1. a comma

   ```
   For my holiday,^I packed my swimsuit,^evening
   clothes,^casual wear,^and toiletry items.
   ```

2. a period following an abbreviation

   ```
   Mr.^Gupta and Dr.^Angelov went to the
   conference.
   ```

3. a semicolon

   ```
   Sarah arrived at noon;^the others came later.
   ```

Leave *one* letter space before and after:

1. a constructed fraction

   ```
   Ginette was able to buy the shares at 10 7/8.
   ```

ASSIGNMENT 12:27

Format the following evaluation form attractively for the Accounting Department workshops to be held on August 3, 19—. Key the following instruction: Please rate the following workshops by circling the number you believe most accurately reflects the success of each seminar you attended. Don't forget to include an appropriate title for the evaluation form.

Workshop Topics	Excellent	Worthwhile	Good	Fair	Poor
Keynote Address: Phyllis Collins	5	4	3	2	1
Current Software Concepts	5	4	3	2	1
Desktop Publishing	5	4	3	2	1
Stress in the Workplace	5	4	3	2	1
Time Management	5	4	3	2	1
Creative Thinking	5	4	3	2	1

ASSIGNMENT 12:28

Key the following vacation schedule

ACCOUNTING DEPARTMENT HOLIDAY SCHEDULE, Name, Date, Maria Collacello, July 5 - July 26; John Cooper, February 3 - February 17; Linda Elgar, March 17 - March 24; Mary Beth MacDonald, July 26 - August 3; Eva Martin, August 10 - August 24; Carlos Diaz, August 15 - August 22; Fritz Grau, October 3 - October 24.

4. As soon as a key is struck, return your finger quickly to its position on the home row.

5. Keep your wrists off the keyboard frame.

6. Keep your elbows fairly close to your body. Slant your forearms upward to the keyboard. Keep hand, wrist, and arm movements to a minimum.

Striking the keys

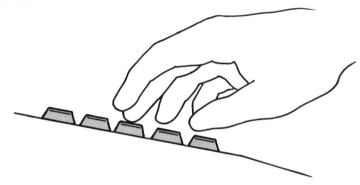

THE SPACE BAR AND CARRIER RETURN

1. Strike the space bar with the thumb of the right hand, using a sharp, quick stroke.

2. To return the carrier, press the return key with your *right* little finger while keeping the right index finger anchored on the *j* key. After you have struck the return key, return your little finger to the *;* key.

3. Microcomputers and word processors can return automatically at the end of a line. This function is called **word wraparound**. If you want to return *before* the end of a line, simply strike the return or enter key.

ASSIGNMENT

12:29

The Accounting Department is expanding into new offices and you have been asked to help set up your new work area.

This will involve purchasing basic office supplies, including a desk, a chair, a filing cabinet and file folders, correspondence trays, card files, stationery, a stapler, and any other items you can think of (exclude computers and typewriters). You have been given a budget of $2000.

1. In groups assigned by your teacher, prepare an inventory of the office equipment items you will need. Try to create as complete a list as possible (don't forget essential items such as paper clips, etc.).

2. Consult an office supply store catalogue and look up the prices of the equipment you have listed. Try to stay under or within the budget, as much as possible.

3. In a table, prepare a list of your equipment and the price of each item. Total the amount you spent.

FINGER PLACEMENT ON THE HOME ROW

The middle row of letters on any QWERTY keyboard is referred to as the home row.

1. Place your *left* little finger on the letter *a*, the outside key of the home row.

2. The other three fingers of your left hand will naturally fall into place; the third finger on the letter *s*, the middle finger on *d*, and the index finger on *f*.

3. Place your *right* little finger on the semicolon key, on the right-hand side of the home row.

4. The other three fingers of your right hand will now fall into place; the third finger on *l*, the middle finger on *k*, and the right index finger on *j*. There will be two uncovered keys, *g* and *h*, between your two index fingers.

Keep your fingers curved.

STRIKING THE KEYS

1. *Curve* your fingers over the home row keys at all times.

2. Strike the middle of the key with the pad of your finger, using a short, snappy stroke.

3. Apply medium pressure to all keys and maintain a steady rhythm.

MODULE

13

INTRODUCTION TO DESKTOP PUBLISHING

CORRECT KEYBOARDING TECHNIQUE

If you are comfortable at your work station, you will be more productive. Correct keyboarding technique results in less tension and greater accuracy. Technique is one of the most important factors affecting your keyboarding performance.

1. Sit up straight, with your body one hand-span from the keyboard.

2. Keep your shoulders straight, not hunched. Lean your body forward slightly.

3. Your feet should be flat on the floor, with one foot slightly ahead of the other.

4. Curve your fingers slightly, resting them lightly on the home row keys (see page 30).

5. With your elbows loosely at your sides, slant your wrists and forearms slightly upward to the keyboard. The palms of your hands and your wrists should *not* be touching the keyboard.

6. Keep your eyes on the copy.

PREPARING TO KEYBOARD

NOTE

If you are using a microcomputer or word processor, insert the diskette(s), load your program, and set the margins according to the instructions in your operating manual.

1. Place the copy to be keyed to the *right* of your machine, either on an angle or on a stand.

2. Insert the paper. Begin on line 6 from the top of the page. (If you are sharing a printer for a microcomputer or word processor, this step may be done when you are ready to print your document.)

3. Set the line space regulator for single spacing.

4. Place your fingers correctly on the home row (see page 30).

*Courtesy of
Acco Canadian Co. Ltd.*

INTRODUCTION

ASSIGNMENT

3:1

Key this report using a 60-character line with double spacing, and a 5-character tab.

                    INTRODUCTION TO DESKTOP PUBLISHING

     What is desktop publishing or DTP? This is a general term used for
computer programs that help an editor prepare publications. There are four
levels of DTP. The one you will use is called "personal publishing," in
which text and graphics are put together on a stand-alone microcomputer. For
our purposes, a publication is anything that is printed in large amounts,
such as a notice about a parent-teacher meeting, or your school newspaper.

     In this module, you will learn how to prepare simple publications. You
will learn new vocabulary and procedures by keying reports that provide the
information you need to produce your own publications. All of the
assignments can be completed on a microcomputer or a typewriter.

     The format shown in the instructions above (60-character line, double
spacing, with a 5-character tab) should be used for all the reports in this
module. This report will be the first page of handbook that you will prepare
by keying the assignments and placing them into a binder.

     After you finish keying all the reports, you will practise some of the
tasks necessary to produce a school newspaper. The layout of these pages
provides examples, but not rigid guidelines, for page composition. The
quality and the appearance of any publication depends on the knowledge and
artistic creativity of its editor, who could well be you.

OBJECTIVES

1. To learn some basic procedures in preparing a publication.

2. To prepare a handbook on desktop publishing.

3. To learn some rules of graphic design and page composition.

4. To prepare some text materials and captions.

10. CAREER SEARCH
   a) Title Page
   b) Assignments

11. ON THE JOB—OFFICE SIMULATION
   a) Title Page
   b) Assignments

WORK STATION ROUTINE

Working at a desk that is cluttered with extra books, personal belongings, and unnecessary supplies is both distracting and inefficient. When you come into the classroom, you should:

1. clear everything except paper, pen or pencil, copy stand, and your text from your work station;

2. begin warm-up drills as soon as you are settled at your work station, using either your text or drills supplied by your teacher.

At the end of class, you should:

1. throw out all garbage;

2. turn off your machine and cover it;

3. push in your chair;

4. make sure you have removed all of your belongings from inside the desk.

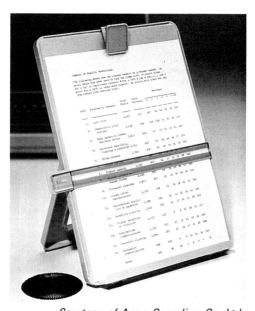

Courtesy of Acco Canadian Co. Ltd.